Images of a Queen

IMAGES
OF A QUEEN

Mary Stuart
in Sixteenth-Century Literature

BY JAMES EMERSON PHILLIPS

University of California Press
Berkeley and Los Angeles   1964

TO GENEVA

UNIVERSITY OF CALIFORNIA PRESS

BERKELEY AND LOS ANGELES, CALIFORNIA

CAMBRIDGE UNIVERSITY PRESS

LONDON, ENGLAND

PREFACE

The present survey of sixteenth-century literature dealing with Mary Queen of Scots has two objectives. The first, developed in the text, is to relate the history of this literature, the circumstances that shaped it, and something of its character. The second, developed mainly in the notes, is to provide a bibliographical record of the individual works that comprise the Marian literature. Neither objective, of course, can be completely independent of the other. But, broadly speaking, for the sake of the general reader I have sought to unburden the text of those technical details that will be of interest principally to the specialist. Since the specialist, however, can perhaps best evaluate the bibliographical and documentary data in the context of the literary history, I have thought it desirable to give the significant technical information about each work in a note at that point where the item is principally discussed in the text, rather than in a separate bibliography. Accordingly, the notes constitute a roughly chronological catalogue of literature dealing with Mary Stuart between 1554 and 1603, and the Index provides an alphabetical short-title guide by author, or by title for anonymous works, to all items mentioned in the text and notes.

Items recorded in John Scott's classic guide to Marian literature, *A Bibliography of Works Relating to Mary Queen of Scots, 1544-1700,* which is organized on a chronological basis, are identified by his entry numbers. I have not thought it necessary to indicate item numbers for the helpful but less complete bibliographies in A. C. Southern, *Elizabethan Recusant Prose, 1559-1582,* and A. F. Allison and D. M. Rogers, *A Catalogue of Catholic Books in English Printed Abroad or Secretly in England,* nor have I attempted to sort out and correct the duplication and multiplication of entries in S. A. Tannenbaum, *Mary Stuart: A Bibliography.* To the items recorded in these earlier listings I have added as many more items for the period to 1603; they are assembled here for the first time.

A fellowship from the John Simon Guggenheim Memorial Foundation made possible the basic research for this study. My tentative finds were first presented in a seminar at the Huntington Library in San Marino, California. The response of this group of scholars encouraged me to expand and develop the study considerably beyond its original limits, and generous support from the Faculty Research Committee of the University of California, Los Angeles, enabled me to do so. Friendly and knowledgeable help came from librarians at numerous institutions in addition to my own, including the Huntington Library, the Folger Shakespeare Library in Washington, D. C., the Morgan Library in New York City, the New York Public Library, the British Museum, the National Library of Scotland, and the Bibliothèque Nationale. As might be expected with so controversial a subject as the Queen of Scots, the reactions of friends good enough to read the manuscript have been varied. All, however, have been helpful. I am especially grateful for the comments of my mentor and colleague, Lily B. Campbell, for the advice of Helen Gardner, for the assistance of Franklin M. Dickey, for the suggestions of Hugh G. Dick, John Espey, and Lowry Nelson, Jr., for the editorial labors of M. V. Kahl, and—beyond all—for the aid and comfort of my wife, to whom this book is dedicated.

J. E. P.

CONTENTS

Images of a Queen

PROLOGUE

On an evening in Paris in 1554, Mary Stuart, Queen of Scots, then twelve years old, appeared with five other young ladies in a pageant produced to welcome Henri II, King of France, upon his return to court from a trip through his realm. At the time of the pageant, Mary had been living in France for seven years. Born in Scotland in 1542, she had become Queen of Scots at the age of one week upon the death of her father, James V. Five years later her mother, Mary of Lorraine, a sister of the King of France and regent of Scotland during her daughter's minority, had sent the girl to Paris to be reared in the Catholic court there and to become betrothed to the young Queen's own first cousin, the Dauphin Francis, son of Henri II and heir to the throne of France. By 1554, when Mary participated in the pageant welcoming Henri, the youthful Queen of Scots was destined to become Queen of France as well.

On the night of the pageant Mary was presented in the role of a Delphic oracle to speak two lines of Latin verse that the distinguished poet, Melin de Saint-Gelais, had written for her to address to her royal betrothed. Thus the twelve-year-old Queen of Scots greeted her fiancé, the twelve-year-old Dauphin, who bore the title, among others, of Duc de Bretagne, with these words:

> Delphica Delphini si mentem oracula tangunt,
> Britanibus junges regna Britana tuis.
> (If Delphic oracles move the mind of the Dauphin,
> You will join Britain's realms with your Bretons.)[1]

Few in the Parisian audience that night would have missed the full import of these lines. Not only did they give Mary the idealized role of a demigoddess, but they gave pointed expression to a prevailing French hope that by his marriage to the Queen of Scots the Dauphin would, when he became king, wear not only the crowns of France and Scotland, but that of England as well—for as a great-granddaughter of the Tudor Henry VII, Mary could claim a legitimate place in the line of succession to the English throne.[2]

Brief as was her appearance on this occasion, the lines she spoke are worth special note on two scores. They constitute what is probably the earliest literary treatment of the Queen of Scots, and as such they mark the beginning of a flood of literature that continued with increasing momentum through the remainder of the sixteenth century.[3] What is perhaps even more significant, Saint-Gelais' lines, in their use of literary hyperbole to make a political point, foreshadow the method and the motive alike of this body of Marian literature. On both scores the Delphic verses spoken by Mary serve, therefore, to indicate the scope and nature of the present study.

Primarily, the following pages attempt to survey, for the first time, the literature dealing with the Queen of Scots and produced in Britain and on the Continent from the pageant of 1554 until 1603, at which time the death of Elizabeth and the accession of Mary's son James as King of England brought at least a temporary decrease in the output. It is a body of literature impressive in quantity, if not always in quality, embracing over four hundred separately published titles. The authors range from unidentified hacks through competent journalistic poets like Robert Sempill and skillful neo-Latinists like Pope Urban VIII to such major literary figures as Ronsard, who addressed some of his more felicitous lyrics to the Queen of Scots, and Edmund Spenser, who, from a quite different point of view, dealt with her story in Book V of *The Faerie Queene*. The forms include most of the literary types recognized in the period—lyric, narrative, and expository poetry; dramas; epistles in prose and in verse; biographies and martyrologies—as well as tracts and pamphlets which might more properly be regarded as journalism. Among the works, this survey identifies Jean de Bordes' *Maria Stuarta Tragoedia*, produced in 1589, two years after her death, as the first in a long line of Marian dramas that stretches down through Schiller and Maxwell Anderson, and will probably stretch beyond. Perhaps a more influential work that the survey reveals is the official account and justification of the execution of Mary at Fotheringay Castle, prepared by Elizabeth's chief minister, Lord Burghley, and widely published abroad, most likely with the approval of Queen Elizabeth herself.

Although some of the literary works dealing with Mary Stuart have hitherto been considered individually, and many have been described collectively in the magnificent *Bibliography of Works Relating to Mary Queen of Scotts, 1544-1700* published by John Scott in 1896, there has been no attempt to present an account of the contemporary Marian literature as a whole. In the following pages I have been mainly concerned with providing such an account by describing in generally chronological order the nature and circumstances of this literature.

The justification for such a survey, apart from what seems to be a perennial interest inherent in the central figure herself, grows out of the second implication noted in the oracular lines by Saint-Gelais. In endowing Mary with the attributes of a semideified prophetess while giving her lines that proclaimed France's aspirations to control both Scotland and England, the poet was creating an image designed to enhance a political argument. Practical politics in France at the time probably inspired him to do so. The betrothal of Mary and Francis was ardently supported at the French court by the party headed by Mary's uncles, the Duc du Guise and the Cardinal of Lorraine, the celebrated "brothers Guise" of Henri II. It was just as ardently opposed by the parties, Catholic as well as Huguenot, that probably had nothing personally against Mary but still resisted any development that might increase the power and prestige of the rival Guise faction.[4] Hence Saint-Gelais, as a protégé of the brothers Guise, apparently felt obligated not only to state the main political argument in favor of the match, but also to emphasize the point by presenting the bride-to-be in the most flattering terms possible for the occasion.

In this respect, his Delphic lines are truly oracular, for without significant exception the same impulse to create an image of Mary that would enhance the political purpose at hand was to characterize all the literature dealing with the Queen of Scots produced in Britain and on the Continent in the sixteenth century. Of course, as often as not the impulse was directed to create a very unflattering image in support of an opposite political argument. In either case, the resultant literature must be regarded as essentially a literature of propaganda, always implicitly and frequently explicitly intended by the writer to sway his readers on larger political and religious issues by first swaying their judgment of Mary.

The larger issues were those of the titanic struggle in the sixteenth century between the forces of Catholicism and Protestantism for the control of Europe. In relation to this struggle, the Queen of Scots was destined to be an evident symbol. She was born and reared a loyal Roman Catholic, and died one; she was the rightful queen of Presbyterian Scotland; and because of her descent from Henry VII she could claim to be in the line of succession to the throne of Protestant England—although at what precise point in the line was to prove a matter of controversy. These, basically, were the qualifications that made her a cause for hope among Catholics and of fear among Protestants, and—more broadly—a symbol for both. Readers familiar mainly with efforts by later writers to explain the woman herself in romantic, biographical, or psychological terms need to be reminded, perhaps, that Mary's contemporaries—who, incidentally, produced many of the documents upon which these subsequent interpretations have been based—regularly shaped their own portraits of the Queen of Scots in terms of their larger political and religious hopes or fears.

As a result of this combination of historical forces and literary motives, two quite different, even contradictory, images of the Queen of Scots evolved in the literature of the period, one of a Circe and the other of a saint. Neither corresponds very closely with what the best and most recent historical scholarship tells us of the woman herself, but neither, I venture to say, has ever since been entirely out of the imaginations—and sometimes the minds— of men. One is the image of a sinister and adulterous murderess constantly plotting with every Machiavellian trick to destroy England and Protestantism. The other is that of a supremely beautiful woman, a devoted wife and mother, and an innocent martyr for the faith in which she died. Both images, in nature and technique, are closer to allegory than to historical or psychological truth, but this, perhaps, is to be expected in an age when allegory and symbol remained powerful intellectual and artistic inheritances from the middle ages.

How these two portraits of Mary came to be created is the story to be told in the following pages. It involves not only a descriptive account of the literary works themselves, but also an examination of the political and religious affiliations of the writers, the circumstances of publication, and the often ingenious devices of censorship and bibliographical deception employed by both sides to build one image and suppress the other. To borrow a useful if opprobrious term from the twentieth century, it is a study in image building. As such, it is less another history of Mary, Queen of Scots than it is the history of an idea.

I PRAISE BY ALL PARTIES:

1554-1564

Although Saint-Gelais' lines for the pageant of 1554 can be said generally to have foreshadowed the body of literature on Mary Stuart, they anticipate much more specifically the poetry and prose that appeared in the decade immediately following them. Like the Delphic pronouncement, the Marian literature that was produced not only in France but also in Scotland and England during this period was extravagant in praising her virtues and attractions. But also like the Delphic pronouncement, it was consistently inspired and molded by larger political purposes. To understand the dynastic and religious interests that shaped the resulting idealized image of Mary, it will be necessary at the outset to review briefly the circumstances of her marriage to the Dauphin of France and the events that followed.

When Francis I, King of France, died in 1547, his government passed nominally into the hands of his son and successor, Henri II, but it actually rested in the hands of Henri's powerful brothers, Francis of Lorraine, Duc du Guise, and Charles, Cardinal of Lorraine, both of whom were to figure prominently in the history of Mary, Queen of Scots. Through their sister, Mary of Lorraine, the mother of Mary and regent of Scotland in her daughter's absence, the brothers Guise already exercised influential control in Scottish affairs. By marrying their nephew, the Dauphin Francis, to their niece, the Queen of Scots, they hoped not only to consolidate their control of Scotland, but eventually to extend their power to England as well,[1] for from the time of her birth Mary had claimed, or had had claimed for her, at least a place in the succession to the English throne, and perhaps a right to the throne itself. Her father, James V of Scotland, was the son of Margaret Tudor, who in turn was a daughter of the first of the Tudors, Henry VII. Needless to say, Mary's claim was disputed by the English Tudors, and subsequently with particular heat by her cousin once removed, Elizabeth of England. But to the brothers Guise in 1554, Mary's claim to England seemed as valid, and as attractive, as her actual possession of Scotland. Ignoring English protests against the claims and the obvious intention of the French scheme, they proceeded to arrange for the wedding.

The political ambitions involved in the marriage are clearly revealed by the deceptive nature and circumstances of the formal agreement the Guises drew up for their niece and nephew. On the one hand, the open and published terms of the marriage contract, to which representatives from Scotland had agreed only after prolonged opposition and bargaining, left Scotland an independent realm under the temporary joint sovereignty of Mary Stuart and her young husband-to-be. But according to a secret premarriage agreement, which her uncles had persuaded the youthful Queen to sign without the knowledge of the Scottish emissaries, Scotland and all rights that Mary might have to the kingdom of England were made over in free gift to the crown of France in the event of her death without issue.[2] Such an agreement left little doubt that the Guise policies aimed at nothing less than the complete absorption of Scotland—and presumably of England—by France. When, a year after their marriage, Mary and Francis were proclaimed King and Queen of England and Ireland as well as of France and Scotland, the full scope of the Guise ambitions in negotiating the match became clear to all the world.

Needless to say, the Guise policies and plans met with intense and active opposition, not only in England and in Scotland, where it might have been expected, but also in France itself, where Catholic factions in rivalry with the house of Guise, as well as Protestant Huguenots, sought any means of breaking the hold of the two brothers on French affairs.[3] From such quarters came strenuous and open objection to a marriage so designed to strengthen Guise power and Catholic influence. To answer such objections, the Guises, among other measures, inspired a sizable body of literature written to defend the betrothal and marriage by portraying Mary as a "good catch" from the French point of view.

Even before the marriage took place, French poets were at work on this theme. Besides his sibylline pageant, Saint-Gelais wrote a poem eulogizing Mary's physical and intellectual attractions as political assets to the Dauphin.[4] Similarly, a French sonnet on the approaching marriage, written by Jacques Tahureau and published by him in 1554 in a volume of verse dedicated to one of the Guise brothers, the Cardinal of Lorraine, congratulated Francis on acquiring a goddess of "telle beauté" and "celeste courage," and Mary in turn on acquiring a name that would make her immortal.[5] Shortly before the marriage a more famous poet expressed the same theme more explicitly. Joachim Du Bellay emphasized the political values of Mary's personal charms both in a sonnet licensed for publication in Paris in 1557 and in a Latin poem celebrating the impending union.[6] Addressing the Queen of Scots, he wrote in the former that not without purpose had heaven given her such beauty of spirit and of face, together with royal grace and honor. By her marriage with the Dauphin, he continued, the Fates decreed that she would crush Spanish pride and bring France and England together in a league of peace and friendship heralding a new golden age. Since a Spanish marriage for the Dauphin was a principal aim of those French Catholics who opposed the plans of the brothers Guise, Du Bellay's reference to "Spanish pride" is an unmistakable example of the political impulse behind his portrait of Mary. Even more striking, perhaps, is the implication that Mary's claim to England was the real basis of her charm for Frenchmen.

Such was the political atmosphere in which Pierre de Ronsard published the first of the many poems he was to address to the

Queen of Scots. Entitled "A La Royne d'Escosse," the poem appeared with others in a collection published in 1556.[7] As Ronsard reminds the Queen in these lines, he had as a youth lived in Scotland at the court of her father, James V; since her arrival in France, he had served her as tutor in poetry.[8] Under these circumstances, his eulogies of Mary probably had as much personal as political incentive. In the present piece, after hailing her as "O belle & plus que belle & agréable Aurore," he simply offers his humble services "À vous, à vostre race, et à vostre couronne." Subsequently, however, on the occasion of her marriage to Francis, Ronsard was to make the political theme far more explicit.

The wedding of the Queen of Scots and the Dauphin of France took place at Notre Dame Cathedral on April 24, 1558. A handsomely printed description of the ceremony itself was immediately published in Paris, Lyon, and Rouen.[9] But more revealing of the political motives that determined much of the literary praise of Mary at this time were the wedding hymns produced in quantity by major and minor poets alike, both in France and abroad. All these take the form, more or less, of the classical epithalamium, and much of their extravagant praise of Mary in terms of mythological perfections must be regarded, accordingly, as conventional features of the traditional form. Nevertheless, whether the virtues celebrated were real or conventional, or a mixture, the poets never failed to make clear their political purposes in extolling the youthful Scottish bride.

The outright propaganda purpose of these marriage songs is nowhere made more apparent than in the Latin epithalamium written by Michel L'Hôpital, or Hospitalius, and published in Paris on the occasion of the wedding in 1558.[10] L'Hôpital, who became chancellor of the realm when Francis and Mary ascended the throne of France, subsequently turned against Mary, after her return to Scotland, and wrote rather sternly in condemnation of her. In 1558, however, he was strongly in favor of the marriage and of the underlying Guise policies favoring a union with Britain. In fact, he was probably the author of a prose discourse, published in 1558, defending the claim of the Dauphin Francis to be King of Scotland upon his marriage to Mary Stuart.[11]

At the very outset of his epithalamic *Carmen*, L'Hôpital makes clear that he is writing for political persuasion. Not being qualified, he says, to write of the royal couple's "unripen'd joys" and "precocious love," he maintains that he is better fitted by his position as a councilor to "quell the scoffers with a statesman's verse." [12] His epithalamium, in other words, was directed to those elements, Protestant and Catholic alike, who objected to the match proposed in the interests of the brothers Guise. He then proceeds in his verses to give a résumé of all the advantages, political and personal, that would accrue to France as a result of this union. Moreover, he warns "scoffers" of the consequences should France, by rejecting Mary Stuart, alienate Scotland and turn that country to an alliance with England or Spain against France. But although directing the whole of his argument to "scoffers" at the marriage, L'Hôpital nevertheless insists that they represent only a dissident minority. The majority of the French people, he says, rejoice at the union; only a few "of Factions host" think a better match could be made for the Dauphin with the Infanta of Spain. Posterity, he concludes, will approve the Scottish match, "Though many a scoffer mock'd the heaven-predicted doom." [13] L'Hôpital was perhaps more candid in acknowledging the opposition to the Guise policy, and in explicitly writing his marriage hymn to answer the opposition, than were the other poets who wrote epithalamia, but they no less than he seem to have been politically motivated in celebrating the royal wedding in 1558.

The principal argument advanced by L'Hôpital and other epithalamists was the political gain for France in acquiring new territory and revenues. The Dauphin was regularly addressed as "King of Scotland," and Scotland itself was described as henceforth subservient to France—a position most of the French poets seemed to find quite right and proper. Thus L'Hôpital remarked somewhat patronizingly that Mary's dowry was "a kingly crown, a subject land. / Light is its weight, in truth, with ours compared," but, he added, nonetheless useful to France.[14] In a *Hymne* addressed to one of the brothers Guise—Charles, Cardinal of Lorraine—Ronsard went so far as to offer the Queen of Scots and her dowry of a realm as a tribute to the influential prelate; elsewhere he congratulated

Henri II on having a son like Francis who, by marrying the most beautiful queen alive, had joined not only Scotland but England as well to the crown of France.[15] Adrianus Turnebus, in an *Epithalamium* that invokes a multitude of mythological figures to bestow their particular blessings on the pair, concludes that the union of the two realms will be as strong and indivisible as the connubial bonds of the royal couple—an ironically accurate prediction.[16] Réné (or Renatus) Guillon, in a nuptial song devoted far more to extolling members of the Guise family than the Scottish bride, voiced a similar assumption regarding the union of the realms in an involved horticultural figure that crosses the white lily of France with the white rose of Mary's Yorkist ancestors.[17] Here again, perhaps, was a not-too-subtle hint at Mary's claim, and hence her French husband's claim, to the throne of England as well as to that of Scotland.

A second argument that runs through the epithalamia is the inevitable belief of French poets that the Scots themselves would recognize and welcome the blessings of French control. L'Hôpital, for example, was quite sure that Mary's father, the late James V of Scotland, would rejoice in heaven at the union, "Nor would he shrink his ancient realm to see / Rank'd second in the regal blazonry." [18] Similarly, the anonymous author of another marriage hymn published at this time, having observed that Nostradamus had long since predicted this happy union, called on the Scots to rejoice and give thanks to God for their new king; "Should you not be comforted?" he asks the Scottish people.[19] Another poet, having endowed the bride with all the qualities of the nine muses and the groom with the qualities of Adonis and Ganymede, concluded that the Scots should consider themselves fortunate to find themselves under the rule of such a king.[20]

The culminating argument of the marriage hymns is the picture of a glorious dynasty—French, of course—that would dominate not only the British Isles, but eventually the whole of Europe. L'Hôpital, for example, concluded his wedding song with a vision of the future consequences of the happy union of Mary and Francis:

> The hour will come, when a refulgent race
> Of gallant boys our royal halls shall grace:

To each a separate throne assign'd shall be—
Gaul to the first, the second Lombardy

. . . .

And this shall Scotland, that Britannia guide:
While other scepters other sons shall bear—
So shall one house the world's vast empire share.[21]

Jean de Baïf, one of the principal poets of the Pléiade, incorporated
the same vision into the song he published on the occasion of the
wedding; "without murder and war," he wrote, "France and Scotland will with England be united." [22] Joannes Mercerius predicted
not only a union of Scotland and England under the crown of
France, but, further, the subjugation of the Low Countries, Spain,
Flanders, and Italy.[23] An Italian could scarcely be expected to
concede French domination of Italy as a happy consequence of the
marriage, but Gabriel Symeoni, a Florentine poet who spent some
time in France in the service of the Duc du Guise, otherwise shared
the imperialistic dream of the epithalamists. In a three-part
epithalamium published in Paris in 1559 in honor of the weddings
of the Duke of Savoy, Philip of Spain, and Francis, the Italian poet
admits that, by the union of the Dauphin and the Queen of Scots,
France will control at least the lands that surround "Mar Britanno." [24] Allowing full poetic license to the epithalamists, their
vision of a world dominated by France as a result of the marriage
of Francis and Mary probably does not go greatly beyond the hopes
and ambitions entertained by the brothers Guise themselves.

Meanwhile, two Scots poets, in marriage hymns produced in
1558, took a somewhat different view of the political implications
of the union. George Buchanan, in his "Epithalamium," and Sir
Richard Maitland, in "Off the Quenis Maryage with the Dolphin
of France," hailed the bride and groom with the conventional
lavishness of rhetoric and imagery characteristic of epithalamia.
But neither was willing to concede the subordination of Scotland
to anybody. Buchanan, the brilliant Scots humanist who was subsequently to become Mary's archfoe in the battle of the books about
her, was still one of her admirers when he wrote his "Epithalamium." He congratulated Francis on his marriage with a beauty
rivaling Helen of Troy, and—in the rather startling language of

Buchanan's nineteenth-century translator—"With a wife so well explored." [25] Buchanan devoted most of his poem, however, to an account of the glory and the independence of Scotland. He describes the rich intellectual history of Mary's country, noting that no less a person than France's own Charlemagne sought out the learned of Scotland for his profit.[26] He observes that the Scots have long enjoyed freedom from any foreign yoke, and to support his argument he recites the history of Scotland's repulsing of all invaders, including, rather pointedly, the Norman French.[27] There is no question that Buchanan at this time approved of the alliance, but, as his principal biographer says, he "stoutly maintained that France was quite as much a gainer as Scotland, and that the understanding between the two countries must be as between two perfectly equal Powers." [28]

Exactly the same point of the equality of the two realms is made in Sir Richard Maitland's wedding poem.[29] Maitland, father of the far more celebrated William Maitland of Lethington who was Mary's principal secretary after her subsequent return to Scotland, was, like Buchanan, Protestant in his sympathies but a faithful follower of the Queen in the years preceding her later marriage to Lord Darnley. His poem is flattering in its praise of Mary as a bride, but emphatic in its insistence on the continuing equality and independence of Scotland. The point of his epithalamium appears when he writes in conclusion:

> Scots and French now live in unity,
> As you were brothers born in one country
> Without all manner of suspicion.
> Each one to other keep true fraternity
> Defending other both by land and sea.[30]

Whether Buchanan and Maitland were aware of the secret agreement between Mary and the brothers Guise by which Scotland was made anything but a power equal to France is uncertain. In any event, the effect of their marriage hymns, insofar as the political themes are concerned, is to deny the main contention of the French poets, and to assert the continued independence and glory of Scotland.

If the Scottish and French poets failed to see eye to eye on the political consequences of the marriage, they were unanimous in their opinion of the personal character and attributes of the bride herself. As portrayed in the epithalamia from both sides of the channel, Mary comes to embody, for one political reason or another, a whole mythology of classical deities and muses. She is Helen in beauty, Lucrece in chastity, Pallas in wisdom, Ceres in riches, and Juno in power.[31] She is the recipient of all the talents that the muses have to bestow.[32] Even L'Hôpital, while disclaiming, as a staid statesman, any ability to describe "precocious love," "unripen'd joys," and similar matters, nonetheless made a creditable effort when he wrote that Mary

> In form and face out-beaming all her train
> Still with such grace, such majesty combines,
> You'd think her frame a deity enshrines.
> Nor lacks she the high gifts of Pallas sage,
> Discretion passing far her sex, her age . . .[33]

George Buchanan agreed that in beauty Mary outshone Helen of Troy, but as a Calvinist reformer in the making he insisted that her real attractions were her wisdom, intellectual accomplishments, and moral grandeur.[34] Perhaps the best summary of the attitude of Scottish and French poets alike towards Mary is found in an "Inscription" written for her on the occasion of her marriage by Jacques de la Taille, a promising poet who died in 1562 at the age of twenty. Here Mary herself, somewhat immodestly, is made to sum up both the spirit and content of the epithalamic catalogues of her classical virtues and attractions when she exclaims that Zeus, who drew from all the beauties of Greece to create a Juno, would today need only Mary's beauty to create such a goddess.[35]

Much of this lavish praise springs, of course, from the conventional rhetoric of the classical epithalamium, but in the majority of the wedding hymns written for Mary and Francis the rhetoric seems to have been employed as much to meet the need for political persuasion as to satisfy the requirements of the literary form. L'Hôpital, for example, made his panegyric on Mary one of the arguments he used against those scoffers who felt that the Scottish marriage was unworthy of France. After warning them of the political consequences that would follow rejection of Mary he asks:

> In face, form, beauty, dowry, virtue rare,
> Where shall they find a brighter lovelier fair? [36]

Joannes Mercerius similarly described Mary's personal qualities in terms of what they would add to the greater glory of France.[37] George Buchanan adapted his own account of Mary's personal qualities to his central theme of Scotland's independent prestige and glory. He praised not only her beauty, her wisdom, and her "moral grandeur," but also her descent from a long line of fiercely independent kings—all by way of reminding Francis and the French that this was a marriage of equals.[38]

The immediate political purpose in celebrating Mary's personal qualities is suggested, finally, by the notable absence of one quality that was to be the keynote in later literature written about her. That was her Roman Catholic faith. She is consistently portrayed in the wedding hymns as chaste and pure, beautiful to a fault, potentially as faithful in marriage as Penelope, endowed with awe-inspiring regal authority, gifted in all the arts, and possessed of an intellect and wisdom unsurpassed—all remarkable qualities indeed in an adolescent girl. But her religious piety and faith are barely mentioned in the literature of 1558. Her virtues as now sung are uniformly secular when not, in fact, pagan, and there is little or nothing to foreshadow the saint and martyr of the literature of 1587, when she died on the block in England. Yet Mary was undoubtedly as devout a Catholic in 1558 as she was in 1587. However, the religious question was not now the major issue in the political situation involving Mary either in France or in Scotland. Rather, the right to Scotland and England which she brought with her, and the brilliant personal qualities which could be attributed to her as bride of the French Dauphin became the sum and substance of Mary's character and personality.

The same treatment of Mary, determined by similar political circumstances, marks the literature on the accession of Francis and Mary as King and Queen of France on July 10, 1559. Now the Guises' fondest hopes seemed to have been realized. Not only did the young couple claim to unite France and Scotland, but they openly proclaimed their right to the throne of England as well. They quartered the arms of England with their own, and designated themselves "King and Queen of France, Scotland, England, and Ireland"—moves destined to be a basic cause of Mary's troubles with England for the rest of her life.[39] For the moment, however, such claims provided French poets with their principal theme in singing Mary's praises. Du Bellay and L'Hôpital celebrated the accession with poems on the union of the three realms, which was also the theme of Latin verses inscribed on a triumphal arch erected to welcome the new king and queen to Chatelleraut in November, 1559.[40] Ronsard, as always where Mary was concerned, rose to the occasion with an ingenious sonnet, characteristically Gallic in attitude, in which he imagined that Jupiter had decreed that Mary should govern England for three months, Scotland for three, and France for six in each year.[41] Elizabeth of England through her ambassadors sharply protested the publication of such claims to the throne which she herself had ascended in the year just preceding. Otherwise, insofar as literary treatment of the subject was concerned, England as well as Scotland greeted the accession of Mary with cold silence.

The imperial dreams of the poets and the brothers Guise were short-lived. In December, 1560, the frail and sickly Francis died, thus ending the hope for a dynasty of "gallant boys," in L'Hôpital's phrase, that would rule the world. In Scotland, George Buchanan wrote a Latin poem on the sad event. Of course, he did not express regret at the end of the dynastic dream, but he sorrowfully predicted, with some accuracy, the civil strife that would now begin to plague France.[42] Meanwhile, Mary Stuart, a dowager queen at the age of eighteen and not too popular with her mother-in-law, Catherine de' Medici, left France in August, 1561, to return to Scotland as queen.

Romantic historians are fond of describing the dismal fog that greeted Mary on her arrival in Scotland as an omen of the troubles that were about to begin for her. And in truth, the forces that were to work her ultimate destruction were already operating there. During Mary's residence in France, John Knox had accomplished the reformation of the Scottish church. Although an active Catholic group continued the struggle to regain power, the Protestant Lords of the Congregation, as Knox termed his theocratic governing body, had established both civil and ecclesiastical control of the country in 1559. Such was the situation when Mary, a devout Catholic who had given no sign that she intended to alter her faith, arrived to assume supreme authority in her homeland. In England, meanwhile, Elizabeth had made clear two fundamental points, in her own policy concerning Scotland, which were bound to complicate Mary's problem. The Protestant Queen of England, anxious for the security that a friendly Scotland responsive to her control would bring to her northern border, had indicated that she would throw her influence behind the dominant Presbyterian party.[43] She had made it equally clear that she would actively oppose any effort on Mary's part to force the Scottish claim to the English throne.[44] On both these counts, the Queen of Scots, a firm Catholic whose assumption of the right and title to the succession in England had been widely publicized, could expect trouble sooner or later.

But until Mary herself forced these issues by choosing Henry, Lord Darnley, as her husband in 1565, the dangers and troubles were more potential than actual. They are not reflected at all in the sizable body of French, Scottish, and English literature about Mary that appeared in the four years after her arrival in Scotland. Whatever the rumblings beneath, the surface itself remained tranquil, and until 1565 the literature is for the most part a continuation of the eulogistic traditions and conventions that first appeared in the epithalamia of 1558.

These patterns of praise are first evident, not surprisingly, in the numerous French poems written on the occasion of Mary's departure from France. Ronsard addressed several poems of regretful farewell to the Scottish Queen at this time, in which Mary appears as a paragon of beauty, majesty, grace, chastity, and fortitude not differing greatly from the paragon portrayed in the epithalamia.[45] Her physical attractions are dazzling, if conventionalized—skin of alabaster and hair of gold, mouth a treasury of ruby and pearls, radiant eyes that turn night into day. Her moral qualities—"la vertú, la bonté, la pitie," for example—are no less splendid. She is, in fact, the epitome of all that convention attributed to the ideal lady of the courtly-love tradition, quite indistinguishable from Petrarch's Laura, and with her departure Ronsard feels as hopeless and despairing as any traditional courtly lover, from Petrarch to Sidney.

Obviously, no political or propaganda purpose can be assigned to verses of this sort. Although Ronsard repeated some of the political themes from his earlier lyrics celebrating the French marriage, for the most part his poems addressed to the Queen in Scotland are more personal in inspiration. An even more intimate and celebrated personal association accounts for another piece of eulogistic poetry purportedly addressed to the Queen of Scots at this time. This was the verse written in 1562 or 1563 by Pierre de Chastellard, the accomplished young courtier who had followed Mary from France and who apparently tried to carry his admiration for her beyond the purely literary bounds of the courtly-love convention. He was discovered hiding beneath her bed one night, and, consequently, a few days later his head was cut off. It has been suggested that this episode, the delight of romantically inclined historians of Mary, must be explained in terms of unromantic political maneuverings, for Chastellard was a Protestant Huguenot, and it is possible that his approach to the Catholic Queen of Scots was part of a scheme to compromise her honor and blackmail her into submitting to the Protestant control she had steadfastly resisted.[46]

In any event, Chastellard's one surviving poem addressed to Mary, whether personally or politically inspired, is perhaps even more ardent than anything Ronsard produced. Still, the idealization of the Queen's attractions and the courtly response of the two poets to these beauties is basically the same. Like most poets in the courtly-love tradition, Chastellard is far more concerned with his own wretchedness than with the person who presumably causes it. For him, the Queen of Scots is "an immortal goddess" whose cruelty and beauty, he says with unsuspecting irony, will cause his death.[47] It may be said of Chastellard that he at least had the courage of his conventions; according to Brantôme, a contemporary chronicler particularly sensitive to romance, Chastellard, as he stood on the scaffold, addressed his Queen as "la plus belle et la plus cruelle princesse du monde." [48] John Knox, a far less romantic historian who might not have understood the full courtly significance of the remark, reported that Chastellard simply exclaimed, "O cruelle dame!" [49]

Mary's arrival in Scotland also called forth poems by Scotsmen that, although celebrating the beauties and virtues of the Queen in similar conventional fashion, are more obviously designed to serve political ends. Sir Richard Maitland, for example, who earlier had found the Queen's French marriage an occasion for some political propagandizing, used her arrival in Scotland for the same purpose. At the outset of the poem he wrote for this event, he hailed Mary's return in eulogistic terms, but he plainly insinuates that she will have to earn the loyalty and love of her subjects.[50] He then proceeds in the main part of his piece to tell her how this can be done—principally by choosing men of conscience, justice, learning, and experience for her council, and by marrying a suitable husband as soon as possible, for "thy honour and our utilitie / Who will and may mantein our libertie." In view of Maitland's Protestant sympathies, the implication in his lines was probably clear enough to Mary. In a rather touching conclusion promising unswerving fidelity, he observes that although he had served her mother loyally, he may not serve the new queen so well, "because I may nocht see." His blindness had taken him out of the field of active politics almost altogether by this time.

A similar pattern of personal eulogy and political advice appears in "Ane New Yeir Gift to the Quene Mary when sche come first Hame," presented by Alexander Scott in 1562. Scott, a resident of Edinburgh who holds a distinguished place in the history of Scottish vernacular poetry, was Protestant in sympathy without being an extremist.[51] However, beneath its surface of genial personal greeting, Scott's New Year's gift to the Queen clearly reflects the anti-Catholic feeling prevalent in Scotland under the Presbyterian regime. He begins with a catalogue of Mary's royal qualities, hailing her, for example, as "our lion with the fleur-de-lis" and "our gem and joyful genetrice." [52] But he proceeds at once to a frank account of what the people of Scotland expect and deserve from her. He urges her to exercise clemency and considerate treatment of all, yet he implores her to reform the corrupt manners and morals of the clergy, to put an end to appropriation of church lands by the nobility, and to punish the "papists." He concludes, as did Maitland, with an expression of hope for her early and happy marriage—to a Protestant, one infers.

The chorus of welcome was joined by George Buchanan himself, her future archenemy and now already linked with the Protestant Kirk. He composed a number of Latin poems in her honor during these first years of her reign, including three laudatory epigrams and the dedication of his Latin paraphrase of the Psalms.[53] The last, hailing Mary as a "nymph" who has graced Scotland with her beauty and virtue, is characteristic of Buchanan's conciliatory tone and attitude in this season of calm before the storm. On the other side, Ninian Winzet, in appealing to her to maintain the Catholic faith in Scotland, addressed her as a "mirour of al godliness, constance, and continence, integritie, wisdum, and of al haeroical vertewis." [54] It seems clear that at this stage of the conflict between Protestantism and Catholicism in Scotland, both sides were still hopeful of winning over the Queen herself. At any rate, she was as yet enough outside the struggle to permit a Protestant and a Catholic to address her in the same eulogistic terms of welcome.

In England, meanwhile, there were no poems of welcome to the returning Queen of Scots. The claim to the English throne which the brothers Guise had originally inspired Mary to make when she married Francis still rankled in Elizabeth. Particularly infuriating to the Queen of England was the Scottish Queen's persistent refusal to ratify the Treaty of Edinburgh, by the terms of which Mary, among other concessions, would have renounced her English claims.[55] The history of a French work asserting these claims, published in 1561 by one Gabriel de Saconay, is indicative both of Elizabeth's attitude and of how political propaganda concerning Mary Stuart was controlled in the sixteenth century.[56] Saconay, an ecclesiastical censor in Lyons and a zealous foe of Protestantism, defended Mary's right to the throne of England by defaming the characters of Henry VIII and Anne Boleyn and by denying the legitimacy of their daughter Elizabeth. No less a person than John Calvin called the attention of Nicholas Throckmorton, Elizabeth's ambassador in Paris, to the book by Saconay so damaging to her title and her reputation. Just a week before Mary's arrival in Scotland, Throckmorton sent a copy of the book to William Cecil, Elizabeth's chief councilor, apparently fearing to send so libelous a work to the Queen herself. But the book fell into Elizabeth's hands at once. During the next two months she wrote on the average of once a week demanding that this "lewd book" be suppressed, and that a reply to its charges be published at once. Throckmorton did his best to accomplish her wishes, although he confided privately to Cecil, sensibly enough, that an answer such as the Queen demanded would simply give further publicity to the whole unsavory business. Finally, through the offices of Catherine de' Medici, whose voice was still powerful in France, the brothers Guise, fearful of going too far in antagonizing the English Queen, agreed to withdraw the first edition of Saconay's work and to have the offending passages rewritten. Apparently this satisfied Elizabeth, although there is no indication that the parsimonious Queen of England ever sent Catherine the "three or four hackneys" that Throckmorton thought would be a suitable token of thanks and appreciation for the suppression of the book.

Angry as Elizabeth was in this affair, it is significant of her attitude toward Mary at this time that she did not once complain about the Scottish Queen herself. Elizabeth chose now, as on so many occasions later, to attack the political and religious parties that stood behind Mary, meanwhile playing the role of friendly sister and helper to her royal rival. To this end, for example, shortly after the arrival of Mary in Scotland, Elizabeth went through the motions of arranging a meeting with her in England. The conference never took place, but Elizabeth's announced intentions of making a friendly approach to differences between herself and Mary are revealed in, among other places, an elaborate entertainment prepared for the proposed occasion. Entitled "Devices to be shewed before the Queenes Majestie, by way of masking," the spectacle was designed to continue through three successive evenings, and had it been produced it would surely have been one of the most extravagant courtly entertainments ever authorized by the usually thrifty Queen of England.[57]

According to the surviving scenario, the masque was to have amity and concord as its principal themes. On the first night, allegorical figures representing Prudence and Temperance were to enter on lions and imprison Discord and False Rumor, whereupon the English ladies in the audience would dance with the Scottish gentlemen. On the second night, Peace was to enter in a chariot drawn by an elephant, to dwell in the world forever, and the English gentlemen were to dance with the visiting Scottish ladies. On the last night, Disdain on a wild boar and Evil Inclination on an enormous serpent were to attempt to free Discord and False Rumor from the prison where they had been placed two nights before. Valiant Courage, in the person of Hercules, was then to defeat them, although Disdain would escape. As a finale, all the ladies in the audience were to adjourn to the gardens "pour entonner une chanson pleine d'harmonie sur tous ces événements."

The point of all this would certainly not have been lost on Mary, had she come to England to witness it and to receive, probably less entertainingly but more directly, the same political argument from Elizabeth herself. According to the climax of the masque, the two queens were to suppress their "Evil Inclinations"; in an allegory produced in Protestant Elizabethan England this could only mean that Mary was to renounce her claims to the English throne and her apparent subservience to her French uncles, the brothers Guise. Disdain, which the scenario glosses as "Impious Persons," such as these Catholic uncles might be construed in England to be, would probably scorn the resulting peace and continue to be troublemakers in the world of Elizabeth and Mary. But if Mary expected to live in "Amity" with her sister queen, here were clearly the terms.

Insofar as Elizabeth's attitude is reflected in literary treatments of the Queen of Scots, she continued to maintain the friendly and conciliatory approach represented by the masque. As late as 1564, for example, she won Mary's expressed gratitude by imprisoning "some . . . for making a book" in England against the Queen of Scots.[58] In this instance, Elizabeth's action was so effective that no trace of the offending book remains. As a result of gestures such as this, some outside observers were convinced that an era of sisterly love between the two queens had begun. In 1565, Pietro Bizarri, an Italian Protestant refugee who was living in England at the time, felt free to dedicate one of his works to Elizabeth in flattering terms, and another to Mary, claiming for the latter the wisdom of Jove, the learning of Clio, and the chastity of Diana.[59] With unintended irony he predicted, moreover, that neither because of religious nor political controversy would Mary give her subjects cause to be disturbed. Even more striking, perhaps, is the fact that Ronsard, within a single poem written about this time, and apparently overcome by the outward signs of amicability between the two queens, could write of Elizabeth as "belle Royne honneste & vertueuse," of Mary as "la Royne sage & belle," and of both as "ces deux Roynes, fameuses / En beauté . . . / Deux Venus qui voudroient au rivage aborder." [60]

Although Elizabeth, like the Presbyterians in Scotland, may have had misgivings about Mary's political and religious ideas, these feelings were not expressed openly or with hostility in the literary treatments of the Queen of Scots that appeared before the Darnley marriage, nor did they affect the adulatory representation of her virtues in these works. In wedding hymns, farewell poems, songs of welcome, dedications, and the masque of amity and concord, all remains cordial and even flattering. The literary portrait of Mary during the first decade of her career, then, is consistent if highly conventionalized. In both respects it is like the painted portraits of the Renaissance: stylized rather than realistic, stiff and formal in line, rich in mythological decorative detail, and generally fulsome. To the casual reader of the literature in which this picture is painted, there are few indications of any other possible conception of her character, for political circumstances were such that no other conception was necessary or desirable. A reader might, of course, catch the ominous undertones in the eulogies by Maitland and Scott, or in Elizabeth's masque. But even then it is doubtful that he would have forecast the violence of the literary battle that began when Mary chose Darnley as her second husband.

II EMERGENCE OF THE ISSUES:

1565-1568

After the death of her first husband, Francis II, Mary considered—and others considered for her—a number of matrimonial prospects, including the half-witted son of Philip II, Don Carlos of Spain, and Robert Dudley, Earl of Leicester, the favorite of Queen Elizabeth. Mary apparently decided for herself and finally chose Henry Stuart, Lord Darnley. Whatever his personal attractions may have been, Darnley had two political qualifications that must have appealed to Mary. In the first place, through his mother, Margaret Douglas, Countess of Lennox, a daughter of Henry VIII's sister Margaret, Darnley had a claim to the English throne almost as strong as that of Mary herself, who was his second cousin. In the second place—and probably as important in Mary's eyes—Darnley was a Roman Catholic.

Whether or not Mary regarded Darnley with the passion often attributed to her, it seems clear that her political motive in choosing him was a part of her plan to free herself from domination by the Protestant-English party then in power in Scotland. Since 1559 this party, whose center was the group of aristocratic followers of John Knox known as the Lords of the Congregation, had had as its principal leader James Stuart, Earl of Murray, a natural son of James V and, accordingly, a half-brother of the Queen of Scots. Murray, originally a supporter of Mary's Catholic mother during the latter's regency, had accompanied the young Queen to France when she first went there in 1548, and had returned there to witness her marriage to Francis in 1558. In 1559, however, he had shifted his support to the Protestant Kirk and the pro-English party in Scotland. By the time of Mary's return, he was probably the most influential political figure in the country, and, as such, one of the young Queen's principal advisers.

In line with her ambition to break away from the control of men who opposed both her political and her religious ideas, Mary, soon after her return, supplanted Murray and the Protestant lords with Scottish Catholic leaders and the Earl of Bothwell as her immediate advisers. For aid and comfort she turned increasingly away from England and toward the Pope and her Guisian relatives in France. Finally, she took as her most trusted confidant her secretary, David Rizzio, a devout Catholic who had come to her from Italy.[1] When Murray and the Protestant nobles rebelled against such obvious designs on their own power, Mary crushed the military uprising they inspired and Murray fled to exile in England. Then, on July 29, 1565, she married Darnley, hoping to find in him, a Catholic of the English blood royal, a consort strong enough to help her establish her own power and eventually restore her own religion in Scotland—and subsequently, perhaps, even in England.[2]

Aside from the fact that Darnley proved a feeble instrument for this or any other purpose, such a marriage inevitably brought to the surface those issues that had been hidden since Mary's return from France. By marrying a Catholic, she aroused the open hostility of her half brother Murray and the Protestant faction he headed in Scotland. And by marrying a man whose claim to the succession in England was almost as good as her own, she aroused increased apprehension and hostility in Elizabeth. In terms of these two basic issues, the literary warfare over Mary Stuart now began in earnest.[3]

The immediate reaction to the Darnley marriage was concentrated on Mary's claim, now reinforced by her husband's, to the English succession. This issue was inevitably raised in the poems written to celebrate both the marriage itself, in 1565, and the birth of James to Mary and Darnley in the following year. Among the first to renew Mary's English claim was Sir Thomas Craig, the distinguished Scottish advocate who, decades later, was to write the most comprehensive legal argument supporting that claim, and who was destined to see his prediction come true in the accession of Mary's son to the English throne.[4] In an *Epithalamium* published in Edinburgh in 1565 Craig, despite some expressed misgivings about Darnley's activities as a playboy, foretold a union of the realms of Scotland and England under the offspring of this marriage, and explicitly indicated that there were now no doubts about Elizabeth's successor.[5]

The birth of James provided tangible grounds for such hope, as a number of birthday odes published in honor of the event were quick to suggest. Craig celebrated the occasion with a *Genethliacum* in which he predicted a wealth of blessings for James, and his eventual succession, through his parents' right, to the English throne.[6] George Buchanan, who was later to become tutor to the young prince, began his own birthday ode on the same note, although he devoted most of the poem—possibly with an eye to his own future—to outlining the proper education for a destined king of Scotland and England.[7] Catholic writers for once agreed with Protestants on the significance of the event, probably because Catholics and Protestants alike realized that control of James meant eventually control of the religious and political destinies of both Scotland and England. Such was surely the foresight of Patrick Adamson, who in 1566 published a *Genethliacum* in Paris upon the occasion of the royal birth. Adamson, a consistent foe of Protestantism in Scotland who was to employ his pen in behalf of Mary on numerous later occasions, was far more blunt than either of his Protestant counterparts, for he asserted not only the right of the infant James to the succession in England, but also the same right of his mother before him. In line with Saconay's controversial book on the English succession, the Scottish poet hailed James as the rightful heir to the kingdoms of Scotland, England, and Ireland in place of the illegitimate usurper, Elizabeth. Adamson then proceeded to describe the newborn prince as a potential warrior of outstanding leadership and strength who would relieve England of the tyranny under which she suffered, and who would extirpate the heresy that was leading that nation to eternal ruin.[8]

Although these marriage and birthday poems concentrate on the heir and his prospects, they also pay their compliments, at least in passing, to the wife and mother. The portrait of Mary that emerges, though dim in outline because secondary in interest, is little changed from that in the earlier literature. Craig, in his *Epithalamium*, praises her beauty, her wit, and (despite her previous marriage) her "royal virginity." Adamson celebrates her imperial character and her imperial claims. Buchanan congratulates James on having drunk, together with his milk, a love of sacred justice and virtue from his mother's breast. By poets still hopeful that Mary would fulfill their political and religious dreams, the Scottish Queen's attributes continued to be idealized.

The bold pronouncement of Mary's and James's claims promptly stirred a violent reaction in England. Adamson's *Genethliacum* in particular aroused Elizabeth's wrath. She demanded of her ambassadors in Scotland and France, and of Mary Stuart herself, that this "slanderous libel," this "lewd and evil writing of Adamson, the Scot," be suppressed at once and the author punished.[9] The Spanish ambassador, hearing of the furor, was of the understandable opinion that "these [English] people have made more of the matter than it deserves," [10] and he would probably have agreed with Throckmorton's view, in connection with the Saconay affair, that protest simply created publicity. But again, Elizabeth's pressure could not be resisted. The Queen of Scots proclaimed publicly that the poem was not written or published with her consent, and the King of France, in whose country the work was printed, had the book suppressed there and the author imprisoned.[11]

It might be remarked in passing that Elizabeth's whole behavior on this occasion, as on many similar occasions in the future, could have struck a contemporary observer as somewhat contradictory. While demanding the imprisonment of Adamson for asserting the right of Mary and James to the English throne, the English Queen was at the same time holding one John Hales in prison for writing a tract in defense of the title of Lady Katherine Grey, a niece of

Henry VIII, against the claim of Mary Stuart.[12] The fact seems that Elizabeth, now as later, simply did not want the succession question discussed by anyone from any point of view. "I know," she said at the time, "the inconstancy of the people of England, how they ever mislike the present government and have their eyes fixed upon that person that is next to succeed," and from this position, as one of the ablest of modern historians of her reign has pointed out, she "never deviated up to the very moment of her death." [13]

Her attitude is further exemplified at the time of the Adamson affair by two other efforts on her part to suppress all speculation about the succession. When Mary's ambassador complained to Elizabeth that an Englishman had written a book against Mary's right to the succession, the English Queen exclaimed that she "knew nothing of it, but would order steps to be taken." [14] On another occasion, when the Scottish Queen protested an attack on her claims made by the law students at Lincoln's Inn in London in November, 1566, the English Queen must have acted with prompt severity against the alleged offenders, for Mary herself wrote to thank William Cecil, Elizabeth's principal minister, for "the reparation of the offense committed." [15]

Despite Elizabeth's apparent distaste for any discussion of the succession question, however, in England the published advertisements of Mary's claim provoked at least one published effort to refute the claim and to introduce, probably for the first time in print, a suggestion that Mary was regarded in certain quarters as something less than a goddess. The book that Elizabeth had assured Mary she "knew nothing of" was probably a work published on December 7, 1565, with the title *Allegations against the Surmisid Title of the Quine of Scotts and the favorers of the same.*[16] Her assurances to Mary to the contrary notwithstanding, Elizabeth may in fact have been fully aware of this tract. On more than one later occasion she was to pretend ignorance and indignation about an anti-Marian propaganda work, the publication of which she or her Council had unofficially permitted if not instigated. In any event, the *Allegations* was clearly inspired by the arguments advanced in Mary's favor as a result of the Darnley marriage. There are frequent references in the tract to "the marriage now" and to the "sondrie dealyngs & suspicyouse practisis abroade." [17] After thus indicating the occasion, the anonymous author proceeds to argue the case against Mary's English claim, introducing for the first time in print the points that, for the next twenty years, were to be emphasized again and again in the controversial literature on the succession question.

First, the author expressed dismay at the prospect of England's coming under the subjection of Scotland, which, he believed, the succession of Mary and her heirs would surely mean. England, he wrote, would become thereby "as bond & subjecte unto A foraine nation . . . a people by custom & almost nature our ennymies, thursty of our blud, poore & myserable by ther contre, & envyouse of our welfare." [18] Second, he argued at length to prove that the succession in England was subject to the laws of England, and that these laws specifically excluded from the throne a foreigner such as he construed the Scottish Queen to be. Third, he argued against the assertion of Mary's supporters that by her marriage to Darnley her claim to the English throne was doubly strengthened. To their argument the anonymous author replied with the unsubstantiated charge that, since Darnley's mother was illegitimate, he actually weakened Mary's claims "with the more spotte & gretter inconveniences." [19] Last, and most emphatically, the writer of the *Allegations* reveals the religious basis of the whole controversy over the succession. He admonished the "blind, stubborn, and disobedient" advocates of Mary's right to the English throne to drop these claims by which, he charged, they were simply seeking to effect a change in the church that Elizabeth had established in England to the great comfort and satisfaction of all her subjects.[20] Here, at last, was a statement of the religious issue that probably accounted as much for Mary's hopes as it did for Elizabeth's fears in the matter of the succession.

The conception of Mary's character that emerges from the *Allegations* is necessarily dim, since the work is concerned more with legal arguments than with personalities. But, although deferentially asserting that if Mary were legally entitled to the succession in England he would never presume to argue against her right, the author nonetheless insinuates that she is disqualified because she is a foreigner, a representative of a cruel, barbaric, and bloodthirsty race, and the pawn of alien forces (i.e., the Guises) seeking to saddle England with a corrupt religion. Thus, to enhance his politico-religious argument he suggests a conception of Mary's personality somewhat darker in tone than the radiant image portrayed in the epithalamic literature inspired by different political motives.

Meanwhile, the Darnley marriage had also brought into the open field of the battle of the books, as an issue quite independent of the succession arguments, the fundamental religious conflict between Mary and her predominantly Protestant subjects and neighbors. Anyone familiar with the celebrated interviews between John Knox and the Queen of Scots shortly after her return from France will realize that the issue of religion had been a principal cause of contention between Catholic Mary and the Protestant leaders who controlled her country.[21] There is no evidence prior to the time of the Darnley marriage, however, that this problem had been the cause of an open break or of a propaganda assault on either side. It is true, of course, that Mary had taken Knox's pamphlet entitled *The First Blast of the Trumpet against the Monstruous Regiment of Women,* published in 1558 before her return to Scotland, as an attack on herself because of her religion. In Knox's own words, she labored earnestly to have the book "confuted by the censure of the learned in divers realms; and farther, that she lauboreth to inflambe the hartes of princes against the writer." [22] In this instance, at least, Mary was being somewhat hypersensitive. Knox's work had been directed mainly against Mary Tudor and Mary Stuart's mother, the Queen Regent of Scotland. Moreover, Elizabeth of England was even more incensed than Mary Stuart by this blast against women rulers, and labored even more effectively than the Scottish Queen to have it answered.[23] Insofar as literature specifically directed at, or by, the Queen of Scots on the religious issue is concerned, both sides held their fire until the Darnley marriage.

Then, in 1565, the armed truce that existed between Mary and her Protestant lords and ministers ended. In choosing the Catholic Lord Darnley for a husband over the expressed opposition of

Elizabeth, the Earl of Murray, and their Protestant supporters in Scotland, Mary clearly threw in her lot with the Catholic nobles in Scotland and with her Guisian relatives abroad.[24] In the hopelessly complex and controversial events that followed, the basic struggle between Protestantism and Catholicism for control of Scotland and eventually of England is one of the few things that remain clear and certain, even if we admit that parties on both sides were using the pretext of religion to gain their own personal and political ends. The story of this conflict in terms of the accompanying political maneuvers and physical violence, the stabbings and dynamitings, is too well known and too easily available to require detail here, but the conflict in terms of the propaganda literature circulated by both sides remains to be told.

From the beginning, the Protestant attack on Mary was directed not against her religion per se, but rather against what was portrayed as the weakness and immorality of her character. Such an attack, viewed from the advantageous point of historical perspective, was clearly designed to justify the ultimate removal of the Queen on personal rather than religious grounds. This line was to be steadfastly maintained not only up to the moment her head fell at Fotheringay, but for decades, even centuries, beyond. The attack was launched in 1565, the year of the Darnley marriage, with a poem by one Thomas Jeney entitled "Maister Randolphes Phantasey: a breffe calgulacion of the procedinges in Scotlande from the first of Julie to the Last of Decembre." [25] The poem purports to be an account by Thomas Randolph, Elizabeth's ambassador in Scotland, of a dream in which the true circumstances and consequences of the Darnley marriage were revealed to him by the Queen of Scots herself. The theme of the poem is the tragic mistake that Mary made in choosing a husband in accordance with the dictates not of her reason and wisdom, but of her lustful passions.

In a long introduction, composed in awkward poulter's measure, Jeney makes his spokesman, Randolph, describe the civil turmoil rife in Scotland at the close of 1565, following the marriage. Randolph attributes the situation to the willful Queen who, to gratify her lust, spurned the wise counsel of such honest advisers as the Earl of Murray and others of the Protestant party:

I saw them chased away, the Queen would not abide
Their grave advice that counselled her to watch a better tide.
Her will had wound her so to wrestle in this wrong
That no restraint might rest her rage, her extremes to suborn.[26]

After a tedious rehearsal of the parallel lives of tyrants in history, whose passions had similarly led them to commit bloody crimes, the poet makes Randolph—to no surprise of the reader—fall asleep, and in a vision be approached and addressed by the Scottish Queen herself. She restates in her own words most of what Jeney said in the prologue. She confesses that her beauty and her courtly graces (those same qualities that were the subject of all but universal eulogy a few short years before) are the cause of her undoing and of Scotland's; for, "without the restraint of a sensual bit" she married "such one as I deemed would serve my Lust" and infected her court with "wanton slight of effeminate force." Any who opposed her passion she drove out of Scotland with the sword, she admits, adding, "so much was enflamed my Rigour and hate." Now she laments the ruin her lust and her willfulness have brought to the realm:

> I enjoyed my will and all was mine;
> Then I resolved to reform mine unrest
> With such delights as I like best,
>
> The miserable state his misorder wrought
> With woefull wreck in this my commonweal
> I saw, where oft resorted to my thought
> The sour mishaps that discord doth reveal
> Where divided minds may nothing conceal;
> But outbreathing Envy, debate, and strife
> Intends nothing else but civil mischief.[27]

It is characteristic of the literature dealing with Mary at this time that, although there is no direct reference to her religion at any point in the poem, Jeney indirectly reveals the religious conflict behind the whole diatribe against Mary's personal character. He reiterates the charge that she has forsaken the sage and honest counsel of Murray and his group—all supporters of Protestantism—to follow the lusts and ambitions of the Catholic Lord Darnley.

He also makes frequent reference to the influence of the brothers Guise on Mary's conduct; she is made to announce, in fact, that she is Guisian on her mother's side, "rather given wholly to wield with the sword, / than work that [which] wisdom have firmly affied." [28] In view of the fact that Mary looked to Catholics abroad, and to her Guise relatives in particular, for support for her Catholic marriage, the anti-Catholic propaganda in these references is unmistakable. The religious and political purpose of the poem is clear enough, but the method employed it just as clearly that of effective, if somewhat irrelevant, personal abuse. Jeney's propagandistic technique was soon to be perfected far beyond his very dull dream, but the method of attack itself was to remain that of the anti-Marian propaganda for some years to come. The portrait of the Queen of Scots as a sinister creature driven by voluptuous desires began to emerge at this time, and at this stage it was largely the product of the political forces at work in Scotland and England.

Although "Maister Randolphes Phantasey" was apparently never printed in the sixteenth century, it had a manuscript circulation wide enough to arouse a storm of wrathful protest from the Scottish Queen and her supporters. Mary was at first persuaded that Randolph himself had written the libel; her complaints to Elizabeth on this score, demanding that the work be suppressed and the author punished, were as frequent and violent as were Elizabeth's own protests about Saconay and Adamson on the succession issue.[29] As a matter of fact, although Randolph was probably innocent of the authorship, Elizabeth's government may have indeed instigated the poem, for Jeney was in Scotland at the time in the employ of Sir William Cecil, Elizabeth's principal councilor. Moreover, in a dedicatory epistle to Randolph, Jeney admits that he "compiled this tragedy" because "some of my countrymen entreated me to write what I saw which chiefly by their procurement I have done."[30] Mary's efforts to pin down responsibility for the poem were fruitless, however. In reply to her protests, Elizabeth personally assured her that the English government would search out the truth of the authorship, and that "the punishment shall be worthy of the crime." [31] There is no indication that she ever did so, but, shrewd bargainer that she always was, Elizabeth may well have had the "Phantasey" and Mary's objections to it in mind when she offered, a few months later, to suppress "a certain book" if Mary in turn would suppress the work that had so offended Elizabeth, Adamson's *Genethliacum*.[32] Mary met her end of the bargain, as we have seen, by denying responsibility for Adamson's poem and by causing it to be suppressed in France. Elizabeth apparently lived up to her end by refusing to permit Jeney's poem to get beyond manuscript circulation. In any event, neither piece of propaganda was further referred to by either of the rival queens.

Before sharper pens could carry Jeney's propaganda method to new extremes in the attack on Mary, the Catholic supporters of the Queen of Scots were afforded occasion to develop a counterattack. The occasion was the murder of David Rizzio, the Queen's Italian secretary, in Mary's apartment at Holyrood palace on the night of March 9, 1566. The Protestant lords, now led by the Earl of Morton and Patrick Ruthven while Murray was in exile in England, hoped that by removing Rizzio, the symbol of Continental and Catholic influence in Scotland, they might restore control of Mary and her realm to the Scottish Protestant party.[33] Playing on the vanity and perhaps the jealousy of Darnley, they persuaded him to join the venture and promised to reward him with the crown matrimonial if and when the Protestant lords were restored to power. The plan succeeded insofar as disposing of Rizzio was concerned, but, under pressure from Mary, Darnley revealed to her the ultimate aims of the lords. Thereupon, Mary persuaded her half brother Murray to return to her side, thus splitting the Protestant faction, and Morton and Ruthven took Murray's place in exile.

In essence, this episode represents an abortive attempt on the part of the Protestant lords to reëstablish their control of the church and state in Scotland. If the Protestants accompanied their move against Rizzio and the Catholic party with published propaganda of any sort, no trace of it survives. However, there are indications that a whispering campaign was carried on, mainly for Darnley's benefit, to the effect that Mary's relations with her Italian secretary were something more than official.[34]

The Rizzio episode was chiefly significant, so far as literature dealing with the Queen of Scots is concerned, as the occasion for a Catholic defense of her character and conduct against the kind of charges brought in "Maister Randolphes Phantasey." The counterattack took the form of reports widely published under Catholic auspices that purported to give a true version of what happened in the Rizzio affair, and why. The first of these was an account printed on the Continent in 1566, the year of the murder itself, and frequently reprinted in pro-Marian literature thereafter. Now extant in two Latin editions and one German, the work bears titles the sense of which might be expressed thus: "A brief and plain account of the treason not long since perpetrated by some Scottish rebels against their most serene queen, faithfully reported from the letters of a distinguished nobleman." [35] The identity of this nobleman who supplied the basic data, or of the author of the account itself, is not known. But whatever its origins, the published work was a carefully calculated effort to turn the Rizzio affair to service in the cause of Mary in particular and Catholicism in general.

According to this version, the Earl of Murray was the archconspirator behind the murder. The fact that he happened to be in England at the time, in exile, is explained away by the contention that, after setting the plot in motion, he went across the border to seek aid and support from the heretical Queen of England. In the affair as Murray purportedly planned it, not only Rizzio, but Mary herself and the unborn prince whom she was carrying, as well as all the Catholics in Scotland, were to be killed in a general uprising. Thereupon, says the account, Murray would ascend the throne and establish false religion throughout the land. But fortunately, the narrative continues, the scheme did not work out as planned. Only a "secretary named Rizzio, a man about fifty years old," was killed, and the Queen managed to escape with her remorseful husband. Shortly thereafter, the account concludes, Mary returned to suppress the rebels and to drive their leaders into England. Nothing is said in the report about the temporary restoration, at Mary's request, of the Protestant Earl of Murray to his half sister's favor.

Murray is the unmitigated villain of this piece, and Mary Stuart emerges as the innocent, long-suffering, but fearless heroine. She is pictured as laboring sincerely for the happiness and security of her realm, and for its salvation through the restoration of the ancient and true faith. Rizzio's only crime was to assist her in these efforts. But in the end, the author of the account observes, the courageous Queen outwitted the conspirators and the rebellion collapsed, as must all rebellions against the anointed lieutenants of God. Thus this serene Queen escaped the bloody death the heretic rebels had intended for her.

The author does not hesitate to select and alter facts to create this impression of Mary. He ignores the inconvenient fact of her reconciliation with the purported chief villain, Murray. Although Protestant insinuations of her adultery with Rizzio may be distortion in one direction, the assertion in reply that he was fifty years old and the inference that he was thus scarcely attractive to a young woman of Mary's tastes and experience is distortion in another, for Rizzio was in his thirties at the time of his death. As a result of such changes and manipulations, the account becomes as much of a propaganda piece as "Maister Randolphes Phantasey."

A similar interpretation of the Rizzio murder is introduced briefly into a document that received even wider circulation than the anonymous account just described. This was the printed and somewhat amplified version of an address delivered by Peter Frarin at the great Catholic stronghold of Louvain. Entitled *An Oration against the Unlawfull Insurrections of the Protestantes of our time, under pretence to Refourme Religion,* the address itself was delivered in 1565, before the murder of Rizzio.[36] But the published versions of the oration which appeared in 1566 seem to have taken advantage of events in Scotland to add illustrative examples in support of Frarin's thesis that heretic rebels constitute a threat to established authority everywhere. With reference to the Rizzio episode, the contemporary English translation of Frarin's printed oration observes:

It were too long to rehearse, how the noble Queen of Scotland was driven a great while to live like a poor private woman in her own realm, to obey her own subjects, & to do no more than they gave her leave: yea, and in mean time was every day and every hour in great peril & danger of her life among them.[37]

In these accounts of the Rizzio affair the main outlines of the Catholic campaign for Mary that were to prevail for the rest of the century can be detected for the first time. Now she is portrayed as the innocent Catholic victim of Protestants in general and of the Earl of Murray in particular. Although she is not yet depicted as a martyr, her purity, strength, and serenity of religious faith come to occupy a place not found in the earlier marriage portraits. Flaws in the picture, such as the subsequent reconciliation with her Protestant half brother, are brushed out. In addition, the Queen of Scots is made an example to Catholic princes everywhere, with the warning that they should stamp out the Protestant heresy in their realms if they wish to preserve their authority. Protestants, so the argument ran, by their proclaimed political theories and by their evident political practices, believe in the right of subjects to resist and overthrow their divinely ordained rulers. The threat to Mary's authority in Scotland, accordingly, was to be regarded as a threat to royal authority wherever heretics are tolerated. If using Mary in this fashion as an example to arouse Catholic princes against Protestantism may seem to be capitalizing on her misadventures for the greater glory of the church, subsequent events were to prove the effectiveness of the device as propaganda on her behalf and on behalf of her faith.

Insofar as literature on the Queen of Scots is concerned, then, the main lines both of attack and defense had been firmly established before fresh events gave new vigor and impetus to the literary warfare. Under circumstances that, to put the matter calmly, are still a subject of dispute, Mary's second husband, Lord Darnley, was strangled and/or blown up in Edinburgh in the early morning hours of February 9, 1567. On the following May 15, Mary acquired a third husband, the Catholic Earl of Bothwell. By August of the same year, after the battle of Carberry Hill, the Queen of Scots had been imprisoned in Lochleven Castle by the Protestant lords, forced to abdicate in favor of her infant son, and persuaded, by one means or another, to relinquish control of Scotland to the regency of her half brother, the Earl of Murray. Bothwell meanwhile fled to Denmark, where, after a divorce from Mary approved by the Pope in 1570, he died insane in 1578.

Fortunately, the nature of the present survey does not demand a detailed consideration of all the disputed points in this most controversial episode. It is enough to say that Mary's foes charged she had committed adultery with Bothwell and had conspired with him in the murder of Darnley, while her friends claimed that her late husband had been murdered by Protestant rebels who then tricked her into a marriage with Bothwell. The relatively simple and uncontested fact of importance for our purpose is that a Catholic queen had been forced from the throne and her Catholic supporters driven from power, while a Protestant party assumed control of the church, the state, and the new king himself. The flood of literature accompanying these sensational events of 1567 had as its ultimate aim either the justification and preservation, or the denunciation and alteration, of this basic situation. But the methods of justification and denunciation were in no way essentially different from those introduced on both sides in 1565. To win popular support for their move, and to silence opposition both at home and abroad, the Protestant party sought to discredit the Queen and to justify her removal not in terms of her religion, which was the real issue, but in terms of her private character and conduct. On the other side, Mary's advocates sought to arouse Catholics everywhere to her defense by exonerating her character and by attributing all her difficulties to the scheming political ambitions of Murray and to the subversive and rebellious practices asserted to be characteristic of the Protestant heresy.

The Protestant campaign in support of the deposition of Mary opened with a flood of ephemeral handbills and placards that appeared all over Edinburgh within hours after the murder of Darnley. These were mainly concerned with charging Bothwell with the crime, but they also suggested that the Queen of Scots was implicated, and that she was involved in an adulterous relationship with the murderer. A placard posted on a cross in Edinburgh, for example, proclaimed that Bothwell was "an abominable adulterer and worse, and that by reason that he has murdered the husband of her that he intends to marry, whose promise he had long before the murder was done." [38] Even more lurid was a poster decorated with Latin mottoes and a colored drawing of the Queen as a mermaid and Bothwell as a hare, both surrounded by swords. Since "mermaid" was synonymous with "prostitute" in sixteenth-century usage, the purport of the placard was obvious, and it is not surprising to find Mary herself making strenuous but futile efforts to bring the deviser of the cartoon to task.[39]

The burden of the Protestant campaign against Mary was carried, however, not by ephemera such as placards and handbills, but by a series of broadside ballads published in Edinburgh during and immediately after the events culminating in the abdication of Mary in July, 1567. The circumstances under which these ballads were produced make it clear that they were, in effect, the official propaganda of the Protestant party headed by the Earl of Murray. Most of the broadsides were written by Robert Sempill, a Protestant of the extreme Knoxian type whose tireless and skillful pen was regularly employed in the service of the Kirk, and all of them were printed by Robert Lekprevik, the major publisher of Protestant works after the Reformation in Scotland.[40]

Throughout the ballads, the purposes and methods of the Protestant campaign launched at the time of the Darnley marriage are consistently if somewhat more violently developed. The ultimate aim of the broadside attack becomes explicit in Sempill's ballad entitled *Ane Declaratioun of the Lordis iust Quarrell,* printed by Lekprevik in Edinburgh in 1567.[41] Sempill, who probably was familiar with the Rizzio accounts, anticipated the Catholic charge —against Murray in particular and Protestants in general as violators of royal authority—that was sure to follow the deposition of Mary. He was probably aware, too, that the charge had to be answered, since Elizabeth of England, always jealous of her own royal authority, was at the same time upbraiding the Scots with the same charge of violating sovereignty.

In his *Declaratioun* Sempill seeks to answer the expected attack and to justify the enforced abdication of Mary. His ballad is written in the form of a dialogue between Erideilus, who questions the right of a subject people to punish, imprison, or depose a sovereign ruler, and Philandrius, who explains the circumstances under which such things may be done. Philandrius, obviously speaking for the Scottish Presbyterians, bases his argument on the political philosophy of popular sovereignty which George Buchanan, some years later, was to develop more fully for the same purpose in the same cause. Kings, says Philandrius, were originally elected by the will of the people, and thus the final authority in a state rests with the people themselves. When a king abuses his authority, which is only delegated to him by the sovereign will of the people, then the people may take back their authority, remove the king, and put another in his place. As Philandrius asks rhetorically:

> May they not put an order to the head,
> Who in beginning did the head up make?
> May they not set one better in the stead,
> If it from vice cannot be called back?
> Lest this be done, Realms will go to wrack,
> Namely, when that the crime is so patent,
> That neither requires judge nor argument.[42]

The occasion for this exercising of the sovereign right of the people, Philandrius continues, is any action on the part of the ruler that endangers the good reputation of the realm or interferes with the administration of justice. Since murder and adultery are actions that have such effects, the people of Scotland have no alternative but to withdraw their authority from Mary, who is guilty of such crimes, and give it to her son. And so they have done. By the end of this discourse, Erideilus, who had protested the action against Mary, is so overwhelmed by the reasonableness of the argument that "he waxit reid for schame" and walks away.

To justify their moves against Mary, then, the Protestants had simply to develop the theme introduced in their literature of 1565 and show, as Sempill put it, that her "crime is so patent, / That neither requires judge nor argument." The scurrilous, lashing invective of Sempill was well suited to this purpose of degrading the character and conduct of the Queen. There is no reference to her religious faith or to the underlying political issues in any of these numerous ballads; rather, the themes are those of lust, adultery, murder, abnormal sexual practices, promiscuity, and the like.[43] In one ballad, for example, Sempill identifies Mary with

the vicious and perverted women of classical and Biblical history—
most regularly with Clytemnestra, Delilah, and Jezebel. At another
point he expresses the hope that her "doleful death" will be even
worse than that of Jezebel, who, he says, was thrown from a window
to the ground where "cruel hounds" lapped up her blood and
gnawed "her wicked bones." [44] The murder of Darnley, in which
he implicates Mary, he finds appalling enough, of course, but he
reserves the heavy fire of his broadsides for the relations between
the Queen and Bothwell. Here he finds the principal justification
for the rising against her. He accuses the two of turning the royal
palace into a "bordel," and again and again he denounces "her
lecherous life," her "whoredom and harlotry," and the "filthy lust"
over which she tried to throw the "color of wedding." Of Bothwell
he writes:

> Such filthy lust in Sardanapalus,
> Such cruelty in Nero did not reign;
> Such brutish life in Heliogabalus,
> Such traitor mind to slay his Lord and King
> In false Phocas breast did never spring;
> Such beastly buggery Sodom has not seen,
> As ruled in him who ruled Realm and Queen.[45]

If Mary in this last passage seems to be an innocent seduced by
Bothwell, she is more often portrayed in Sempill's broadsides as
the archseducer herself. In this respect the argument echoes Jeney's
poem on the Darnley marriage. After describing the lecherous
desires that led her to persuade Bothwell to murder the King,
Sempill concludes that we may perceive the malice and the mischance that ensue when Venus "gettis in hir gouernance" her
blinded subjects and entangles them in her snare.[46] He further
concludes that although it is bad to murder a king, it is worse to
supplant him in bed with the murderer himself. To achieve her
lustful ends, says Sempill, Mary exercised every device of deceit,
cruel cunning, and scheming treachery, so that the poet has lost
his faith in the entire sex; a woman's wiles, he concludes, "Are
Medea's halters to bring us to your net." [47] If it was necessary to
defame Mary's character completely, in order to discredit her

religion and to justify deposing her under a theory of government that placed supreme authority in the people, Sempill was a good man for the job. Judged both by the virulence of his attack and the resultant storm of public feeling that enabled Murray's faction to depose the Queen, Sempill was eminently successful as a propagandist.

Meanwhile, the same line of attack was developed, though somewhat more moderately, in Latin poems by Michel L'Hôpital, who so short a time before had been full of praise for Mary as a chaste Penelope, and by Thomas Maitland, whose blind father had been one of her ardent supporters in Scotland.[48] With the murder of Darnley, the literary battle against Mary was launched with full force.

In Protestant England the need for finding grounds to justify the deposition of a sovereign queen was no less pressing than it was in Scotland. Elizabeth's contradictory public and private feelings were governing factors in English reactions to the murder of Darnley and the enforced abdication of the Queen of Scots. On the one hand, Elizabeth the political realist and defender of the Protestant faith could not help but be satisfied with the turn of events north of the border which put the Protestant party in control of the country. But on the other hand, as a political theorist, she could not help but be shocked by the treatment accorded a sister queen by rebellious subjects. Conyers Read sums up Elizabeth's ambivalent attitude when he writes:

On principle she disapproved of the course which Mary's subjects had taken. It was contrary to her whole notion of sovereignty, to recognize any right in subjects to resist lawfully constituted authority. But Elizabeth never allowed her principles to stand in the way of practical expediency. In point of fact events in Scotland had gone very much to her taste. The policy which Mary had been attempting to carry out had been subversive of Elizabeth's interests, and the Protestant lords, rebels though they were, had rendered her a great service in preventing its success.[49]

Accordingly, an official attitude that emphasized—perhaps more in sorrow than in anger—a legal and philosophical justification of events in Scotland was in order. The arguments developed by the

Scottish Protestant propagandists were, with some modifications, well suited to this purpose.

It is not surprising, then, to find in an English work produced at this time a development of the contention that when murder and adultery are involved, there is justification in the laws of God and man for deposing a sovereign queen. The work was John Pikeryng's *Horestes,* a play presented at the English court late in 1567, only a few months after Mary's enforced abdication, and apparently printed at the same time.[50] The piece, which historians of drama call one of the principal bridges between the medieval morality play and Elizabethan tragedy, is a dramatization of William Caxton's version of the classical legend of Orestes and Clytemnestra in *The Recuyell of the Historyes of Troye.* Freely intermixing with Greek myth such personified abstractions from the medieval morality plays as Vice, Truth, and Fame, and such realistic low-comedy characters as Haltersycke and Hempstryng, Pikeryng tells the story of Orestes's revenge on his mother Clytemnestra, who had persuaded her lover Egisthus to murder her husband Agamemnon, to marry her, and to share with her the rule of the kingdom of Mycenae. "Horestes," as Pikeryng spells the son's name, receives the sanction of the gods and the support of the subjects of Mycenae to depose and slay his mother and her paramour.

As most of the commentators on English drama have observed, Pikeryng was clearly attempting to reflect in his adaptation of the Greek legend the events that had taken place in Scotland only a few months before the play was presented. The fact that in the Scottish propaganda literature produced by Sempill Mary was frequently equated with Clytemnestra suggests in itself that Pikeryng regarded the classical material in the same light.[51] The remarkable parallels between the charges of immorality brought against Clytemnestra in the play and those brought against Mary Stuart in contemporary propaganda literature leave little doubt as to Pikeryng's ultimate purpose. Moreover, the alterations he made in adapting his source material reveal a deliberate effort to cut the classical cloth to the pattern of Scottish political problems. In general, he transforms Caxton's rather simple account of a son who is ordained by the gods to avenge his father's death into a drama in which the central characters spend an undramatic amount of time discussing all phases of the problem of deposing and punishing a sovereign queen.

Horestes himself states the critical issue in the problem of dealing with Clytemnestra—and with Mary Stuart—when at the outset of the play he ponders the conflicting demands of loyalty and justice, of pity and vengeance. He is torn between the appeal of Nature to "Forgive the fault and to pity," and the requirement of justice to punish "th'adultrous dame" who "on whoredom murder vile / Hath heaped up, not contented her spousal bed to fill." [52] His words against Clytemnestra bear a remarkable resemblance to those directed by Sempill against Mary when the balladist wrote: "Hard it was to see your Prince with murder pressed; / Harder, I say, him, in his place possessed, / The deed that did . . . now Bridegroom." [53]

Faced with this dilemma, Horestes sets out to resolve his doubts. First, he receives assurance that punishment of Clytemnestra for her sins is the will of the gods, very much as the Scottish rebel lords were assured by Sempill that "God has to you the power lent" to "Take God's quarrell also in hand, / And purge us from hypocrisy." [54] Horestes then consults Idumeus (an elder statesman in Pikeryng's play) and the Council about the legality of proceeding against the Queen. He is assured at length by both, in language marked more by legal learning than by dramatic inspiration, that such punishment is required by the laws of God, of Nature, and of Man.[55] Armed with these arguments and justifications, Horestes is able to reply to Nature, who appeals to him to spare his mother in the name of pity and to avoid the charge of tyranny, and finally to confront Clytemnestra herself in the climactic scene of the play. She implores his forgiveness, but he denies it in a long lecture summarizing the legalistic charges against her and concluding:

> Wherefore, the poet Juvenal doth think it for the best,
> That those that live licentiously should bridled be with pain
> And so others that else would sin, thereby they might restrain.
> For thus he saith, that Cities are well governed indeed,
> Where punishment for wicked ones by law is so decreed.[56]

Having thus sent her off to execution, Horestes soon receives assurance that he has acted justly; when Menelaus arrives on the scene to avenge, in turn, the death of his sister Clytemnestra, he is so overwhelmed by the force of Horestes's justifications that he gives his daughter Hermione in marriage to the hero. Final confirmation of the rightness of Horestes's reason comes from the Nobles and Commons of the realm when they hail him as their rightful king.

In only one significant respect does Pikeryng's treatment of the Clytemnestra-Mary Stuart parallel differ from that of the Scottish Protestants. The latter, it will be recalled, justified the deposing of a queen charged with murder and adultery on the grounds that the people confer sovereignty and the people have the right to withdraw sovereignty; as Sempill put it, "May they not put an order to the head, / Who in beginning did the head up make?" Elizabeth's antipathy to Presbyterian doctrines of popular sovereignty of this sort was, and is, common knowledge. Probably in deference to her feelings on the subject Pikeryng shifted the legalistic justification of deposing a queen away from both the divine fatalism of Caxton and the popular sovereignty of Scottish propagandists to a doctrine more acceptable to the English Queen. Like all the Tudors, Elizabeth was willing to concede that God will sometimes call up special instruments to inflict His judgment on erring kings; the calling-up of her grandfather Henry VII to remove Richard III was an inescapable case in point. It is not surprising, then, to find that Pikeryng departs from his sources to give particular emphasis to the decree of the gods that made Horestes a special instrument of divine vengeance on Clytemnestra.

By presenting the justification for deposing Mary under the guise of a considerably altered version of the classical legend of Horestes and Clytemnestra, Pikeryng succeeded in finding a way out of the Elizabethan dilemma concerning the treatment of the Queen of Scots. Rebellion in general, and the rebellion of the Scottish subjects in particular, was not condoned, and this must have been gratifying to Elizabeth. But the fruits of the rebels' efforts, which were equally pleasing to the English Queen, receive both divine and legal sanction as a sign of God's extraordinary intervention. Moreover, should Mary have complained, as she often did, against the publication of a scurrilous attack upon her in England, Elizabeth could always have replied that Pikeryng's *Horestes*, after all, dealt with events remote in time and place. *Honi soit qui mal y pense.*

Thus in England and Scotland alike, the Protestant effort to justify deposing a Catholic queen by attacking her personal character proved effective. Meanwhile, Mary's attempts to stem the flood of propaganda against her were of little avail even during the few short months she remained in power after the murder of Darnley. Following her abdication, of course, her supporters had little opportunity to circulate literature in her defense in Scotland. Apparently a few placards and libels attacking the new order and defending the Queen were posted surreptitiously around Edinburgh by Mary's party. These were at least effective enough to call for a reply by Sempill, circulated in manuscript under the title, "Ane Answer maid to ye Sklanderaris that blasphemis ye Regent and ye rest of ye Lordis." [57] But the Regency now established under Murray rigorously suppressed all efforts to present Mary's side of the story. For example, an anonymous "Rhime in defence of the Queen of Scots against the Earl of Murray" survives only in a manuscript copy to afford some idea of the direction taken by pro-Marian propaganda in these crucial days. [58]

Fragmentary as these remains are, they make it clear that during the hectic final months of 1567 the defense of Mary followed exactly those lines established in 1565. That is, Murray more than ever is depicted as the archvillain of the piece, conspiring to secure the throne for himself; and the Protestants in general are held up, also more than ever, as the factious disturbers of civil order that all heretics must inevitably be. Sempill's "Answer . . . to ye Sklanderaris," which he addresses "to all the papistis of this toun," indicates that the pro-Marian bills attacked Murray on personal grounds, making much of the fact that he was illegitimate to account for his villainous behavior toward Mary. To this charge, incidentally, Sempill makes the curious reply in defense of Murray that some of history's best people, including William the Conqueror, were bastards.

The theme of Murray's villainy receives its fullest development in the anonymous "Rhime in defence of the Queen of Scots," which bears the subtitle, "The double Dealinge of the Rebells, in Scotland." In conspiring for the throne and secretly plotting to kill not only Queen Mary but the young prince entrusted to his care after her abdication, Murray is likened to Richard III, although he "doth surpass his [Richard's] wilie wit / A thousand fold and more." [59] Mary herself is depicted as a "good and vertuous Queen" who is the innocent victim of all these machinations. If the author has any fault to find with her, it is only that she was too simple, trusting, and honest for her own good. She allowed herself to be persuaded by her worst enemies that she should marry her husband's murderer:

> And thus this simple Queen each way
> Was wrapt in woe and care,
> For they that have not skill of craft
> Are soonest caught in snare.[60]

At the end, the poet introduces the familiar theme of the lesson to all sovereign princes contained in the treatment accorded Mary by rebellious heretics. There is also a prediction—possibly wishful but partly accurate—that Mary's supporters would rise to rescue her from Lochleven Castle, where she was being held under guard at the time, and restore her to her throne.

Thanks to the effective censorship of the Regent Murray's government, defenses of Mary like this anonymous "Rhime" were apparently few and far between. They are, however, sufficient to indicate that, just as the anti-Marian literature of 1567 developed in force the attack launched two years earlier, so also the pro-Marian literature continued to develop themes already established. After Mary's subsequent flight to England, of course, the propaganda purposes and problems on both sides were to be radically altered, giving rise to new types of attack and defense. But even then many of the elements introduced in the literature of these last hectic years of Mary's rule in Scotland were to remain regular features in the writing about her well beyond the day of her death.

Meanwhile, after eleven months of imprisonment in Lochleven

Castle, Mary escaped under circumstances that were to be a boon to romance writers ever after. Her Catholic supporters, as the author of the "Rhime" had predicted, rallied to her cause and at the battle of Langside made a last effort to overthrow the Presbyterian regency and restore Mary to her throne. The effort failed, and on May 16, 1568, the Queen of Scots crossed Solway Firth in a small rowboat to enter England. She took with her a hope for aid and comfort from Elizabeth which, indeed, her sister queen had persistently led her to expect she might receive.[61] Far more important in determining her future fate, she took with her into Protestant England those two issues that made her a primary cause of contention wherever she was—her Catholic faith, and her claims to the English succession.

III ELIZABETHAN "SEMI-PUBLICITY" AGAINST MARY: 1568-1586

When Mary of Scotland arrived in England as a refugee on May 16, 1568, she was immediately placed in what today would be called "protective custody" at Carlisle Castle, in the far north of Elizabeth's realm. There she was carefully watched, but shown the deference due her sovereign rank. From the very first she demanded that, in accordance with promises she believed had been given her, Elizabeth should aid her in regaining her throne in Scotland.[1]

Elizabeth responded by calling a conference of commissioners, representing Mary, the Scottish Protestants, and the English government, who were directed to investigate the whole situation and make a recommendation to the English Queen. The commission first met at York in October, 1568, but came to no conclusion. Then, at Elizabeth's order, it moved its hearings to Westminster where, in November, the celebrated Casket Letters, purportedly written by Mary to Bothwell and implicating her in the murder of Darnley, were officially introduced by the Scottish Protestants in evidence against their deposed Queen. Even before the letters were presented, however, Mary's commissioners walked out of the conference on the grounds that Elizabeth had refused—as indeed she had—to hear the Scottish Queen defend herself in person. Thereupon, Elizabeth declined to come to a decision in the matter, arguing that Mary's case had not been fully presented by the Scottish Queen's representatives, and the conferences came to nothing. The charges of murder and adultery brought against Mary by the Scots, and the charges of unlawful rebellion brought against the Scots by Mary remained officially unclarified in the eyes of Elizabeth's government. On this basis the Queen of Scots continued to be kept in England in a custody that became increasingly restrictive.

From the moment she crossed the border, Mary plunged herself —or was herself plunged by others—into ceaseless activity in behalf of her claims to the English succession and her loyalty to her Catholic faith. Only five months after her arrival, for example, she wrote to the Queen of Spain, with an irony that may not have been completely unconscious, that she would suppress the Protestant heresy in England even though she died in the attempt.[2] In this cause she immediately proceeded to receive the homage and support of the leading Catholic nobility who dominated the north of England where she now resided.[3]

Chief among these was the first peer of the realm himself, the Catholic Duke of Norfolk, who had, at the time of the York-Westminster conferences, been suggested as a husband for Mary not only by her Catholic advisors, but also by such members of Elizabeth's council as the Earls of Leicester and of Pembroke, and even, in a qualified fashion, by Mr. Secretary Cecil himself. Elizabeth, once she got wind of the proposal, would have none of it, and she severely rebuked her councilors who had entertained such an idea. But her opposition by no means deterred Norfolk or Mary's Catholic supporters from continuing to press for the match, with results that were subsequently fatal to Norfolk.[4]

Meanwhile, Mary had become the center around which an open revolt of the northern English Catholic lords was organizing itself. In November, 1569, the so-called Northern Rebellion broke under the leadership of the Earls of Northumberland and Westmoreland. With the release of Mary and the restoration of the "old faith" as their proclaimed cause, the rebels marched against Elizabeth's strongholds in the north of England. Mary herself announced at the time that with Philip of Spain's help "she would be Queen of England in three months, and Mass would be said all over the country," [5] but Elizabeth's intelligence service and her loyal aristocrats promptly crushed the rebellion before it was even well under way.

Mary, however, was undaunted. A Papal Bull issued in January, 1570, and released in England the following May, aided and abetted her in her persistent efforts to free herself, to claim Elizabeth's throne, and to reëstablish Catholicism in England, for the Bull excommunicated Elizabeth and relieved all faithful Englishmen from obedience to their heretical Queen. Mary resumed her practice of revealing her hopes and aspirations in letters written to France and to Spain and to the Pope—letters all carefully intercepted and interpreted by Elizabeth's alert counterespionage agencies.[6] In 1571, through an Italian merchant resident in London, one Roberto di Ridolfi, the Scottish Queen allowed herself to become involved in a vast and hopeless scheme whereby six thousand Spanish soldiers were to land in England to join English Catholics in a revolt that would remove Elizabeth, restore the old faith, release the Queen of Scots, marry her to the Duke of Norfolk, and place her on the English throne. The Duke let himself be dragged into the plot, but, again, the conspiracy was disclosed; Norfolk was tried and executed for his complicity, and Mary, for her involvement, was placed in a custody that amounted to imprisonment.

As these events of the first four years of Mary's sojourn in England show, the arrival of the Scottish Queen in her sister monarch's domain brought Elizabeth face to face with a problem that events in Scotland had already made familiar to her: what was a sovereign Protestant queen to do with a sovereign Catholic queen who was related by blood and whose position was theoretically inviolate, but whose activities were patently inimical to Protestantism and to the Protestant queen's own sovereignty? As Matthew Parker, the Archbishop of Canterbury, remarked upon hearing that Mary had crossed over into England, "Our good Queen has the wolf by the ears." [7]

On the one hand, Elizabeth had reasons both private and public for wishing to make it clear to England and the world that Mary was not a prisoner and a deposed queen, but was rather a sovereign temporarily accepting the hospitality of a sister monarch. Elizabeth's deepest personal feelings ran counter to any act that might seem to compromise the principle of absolute royal sovereignty. Moreover, political reality supported her in this attitude. The very appearance of conniving with the Scottish rebels, as she continued to call them, would not only provide France, Spain, and the Pope with an excuse for uniting against her in the name of Mary and of royal sovereignty everywhere, but would also set a bad example to Elizabeth's own subjects, as Catholic propaganda was constantly reminding her.[8] For such reasons, it was essential that Elizabeth appear to the world to be treating Mary as an equal and independent sovereign. On the other hand, Mary's reiterated claim to the English succession and promise to restore Catholicism in Britain, together with her schemes to rally Catholic Europe about her in these causes, forced Elizabeth to make the Scottish Queen as ineffective an agent toward these ends as possible. To the English Queen this meant not only holding Mary under strict observation and control in England, but also, as Mary's principal biographer puts it, "to get her rival rendered as innocuous as possible"; accordingly, Elizabeth was anxious that Mary's "reputation might be so damaged that she would cease to be regarded, even by the keenest of Catholics, as a religious champion." [9] How to do this damage and at the same time preserve the principle of inviolate royal sovereignty was the dilemma that Elizabeth faced.

The solution, which is the key to English propaganda concerning Mary for the ensuing twenty years, was probably suggested by William Cecil, Elizabeth's closest advisor, who argued that the danger Mary presented because of her claims and her religion would be greatly diminished if Elizabeth "could secure a kind of semi-publicity to an authentic history of [Mary's] mis-doings." [10] This was exactly what Elizabeth proceeded to do. Officially, she permitted no word of derogation against Mary to be published in England and publicly she committed herself to the defense of Mary as a sister queen and anointed sovereign. But unofficially, she—or more likely her ministers—permitted and sometimes probably even instigated published attacks on Mary's character and conduct that were the kind of "semi-publicity" that would damage Mary's effectiveness as a cause for Catholic Europe. When the attacks were called to her attention, as they usually were by Mary's defenders, Elizabeth could quite truly disclaim them as "unauthorized" and point to the licensed English publications, often endorsed "Seen and Allowed," in which the Queen of Scots was treated with deference and respect. Despite pressure and provocation to do otherwise, Elizabeth rigidly adhered to this policy until the eve of Mary's death. The political realities of the situation at home and abroad left the English Queen with no alternative.[11]

The policy of officially and ostensibly protecting Mary from published attacks was implemented on March 1, 1569—scarcely two months after the conferences at York and Westminster—with a Proclamation "against importing unlawful books." [12] It was occasioned by the appearance in England of a group of pamphlets, presumably published "abroad" but actually produced in England with the knowledge of Elizabeth's government, that violently attacked the character and activities of the Scottish Queen.[13] Proclamations against such attacks on Mary were published fairly frequently during the ensuing twenty-year period, as if to reassert the government's official attitude. As George Whetstone, a writer looking back on these events from later in the reign, put it, Elizabeth was so careful of Mary's honor "that she forbad the bookes of her faultes, to be conversant among her English subjects which almost in every other nation were made vulgar." [14]

Meanwhile, Elizabeth's policy was further demonstrated in the books allowed to be published in England and dealing with matters involving the Queen of Scots. Under Elizabethan regulation of the press, all books printed in the realm, regardless of subject, were required to be licensed or authorized by some designated representative of the crown, most frequently the Archbishop of Canterbury, the Bishop of London, or members of the Privy

Council.[15] Books properly licensed clearly indicated the name of the publisher and the place and date of publication; very often, too, they included the familiar "Seen and Allowed" or similar endorsement indicating official clearance. An author or printer who issued a book without approval was subject not only to the suppression and confiscation of his work, but also to fine, imprisonment, and even corporal punishment himself. As the principal modern authority on Elizabethan publishing has observed, "The conditions of publication in England were largely determined by Tudor . . . policy in relation to the various phases of the religious conflict, for no matter what party was in power, its principal concern as regards printing was to suppress what it stigmatized as heretical and seditious writing." [16] Conversely, it could authorize for publication only what current policy deemed orthodox and loyal. Hence, by permitting only those books to be licensed that dealt deferentially, if at all, with Mary, even though she might actually have been deeply and dangerously involved in the events described, Elizabeth was further able to maintain her attitude of protective benevolence.

A striking aspect of this Elizabethan propaganda control regarding the Queen of Scots is found in the extensive body of ballads and tracts dealing with the Northern Rebellion of 1569.[17] Some dozen of these, designed to arouse the feelings of loyal Protestant Englishmen against the Catholic rebels, were published in 1569 and 1570, apparently with official allowance if not, indeed, by official instigation. They bore titles such as: *To the Queenes Majesties poore deceived Subjects of the North; or, A warning agaynst the dangerous practises of Papistes; or, Joyfull Newes for true Subjects, to God and the Crowne, The Rebelles are cooled, their Bragges be put down.* Even though this rebellion had as its stated aim the liberation of Mary, her enthronement in England, and the restoration of Catholicism, the Elizabethan balladists and pamphleteers do not once mention her name in their tracts, let alone attack her. One of them, Thomas Norton, perhaps hinted at the Protestant charges of immorality that had been brought against her, in his pamphlet entitled *A disclosing of the great Bull.* Here, in adapting the legend of Pasiphae, Queen of Crete, who became enamored of a bull, he allegorically identifies this "bull" with the ecclesiastical edict directed by the Pope against Elizabeth, and adds, in what is possibly a reference to Mary, that "lecherous Pasiphae may well be applyed to treason in hye estates, addicted to papistrie, forsaking Gods ordinaunce of humane royall government." [18] Norton must have felt that even this oblique reference was going too far beyond what royal policy might allow, for in his next pamphlet on the rebellion he says at the outset that "the Author protesteth, that as he meaneth not herein to hurt the fame of any singular person unnamed whose doinges importe no perill to her Majestie, so can there be no personage any worse advise be geven, than to applie that to themselves which they need not." [19] So effective was the government's licensing policy as a propaganda control that a contemporary reader whose sole information came from authorized accounts of the Northern Rebellion would probably never have been aware of the Queen of Scots's implication in the plot.

A similar manifestation of Elizabeth's official attitude is found in the licensed publications that accompanied the decline and fall of the Duke of Norfolk. Norfolk, who had been involved with Mary and the northern earls in the early stages of the Rebellion of 1569, but had withdrawn, was even more deeply involved in the Ridolfi conspiracy of 1571, again as a proposed husband for Mary should she gain her release. This time he did not withdraw. The conspiracy broken, he was attainted in January, 1572, and executed in June of that year. The trial and execution of so eminent and popular a peer as Norfolk obviously called for some kind of justification, and licensed publications to this end were immediately forthcoming. But the Queen of Scots, closely connected as she was with the Duke's fate, was never mentioned in them. In such diverse works as a formal address on Norfolk's fall made by the Recorder of London to the London Companies; a ballad account by William Elderton entitled *The Dekaye of the Duke;* and the historical account of these events in Richard Grafton's *Chronicles,* published in 1572, the Duke's fate is explained simply in terms of papal, Catholic, and other vaguely defined forces inimical to Elizabeth.[20] Mary herself is not directly attacked as a coconspirator in any of these popular works. All implicitly adopt the attitude of Elderton in his ballad when he wrote, with reference to Norfolk, that it would make too long a story to tell in detail of "How manie devices to do her grace wrong, / By Pope holie practice were pact in his brains."

Meanwhile, however, the fact that Mary was regularly the center around which these Catholic plots against Elizabeth developed made increasingly clear the need to devote some of the "semi-publicity" to the authentic history of her misdoings that Cecil recommended in order to render the Queen of Scots less attractive both at home and abroad as a champion of the Catholic cause. Cecil's recommendation was effectively implemented in a series of clandestine pamphlets which expressly and violently attacked Mary's character and activities. Such pamphlets apparently had a wide circulation in England and on the Continent, but because they lacked any indication of license or even of place of publication, they could be and frequently were officially disclaimed by Elizabeth as "unauthorized." However, the circumstances under which they were produced leave little doubt that they were allowed to appear with the tacit approval of Elizabeth and her councilors. On at least one occasion, Elizabeth's ambassador in Paris indicated that he would distribute such a book gratis, rather than charge for it, since, as he wrote to Walsingham, "it is not past a four pounds matter. I had rather be at a greater charge than have anything that toucheth her Majesty come out of my house otherwise than gratis." [21] A Catholic defender of Mary, complaining bitterly about one of these pamphlets attacking her character, gives a clear and probably accurate account of how Cecil's "kind of semi-publicity" operated; there is, says the writer,

. . . small likelyhood, that either the writer or the Printer of this lewde Libell . . . would or durst endaunger them selves, with publishing such matters of State, and of such importance, if they were not sure of good authority to backe them. . . . Againe, behold how long it is, sins the first of these libells have bene in print commonly solde: how daily new and more do freshly come foorth to confirme ye former: how all come without name of Maker, Printer, or Privilege, or perused according to your [i.e., Englishmen's] owne Constitutions, & all sold without controlment: and with what severitie likewise all books, al writings, yea all speaches and words, that might answer the same, or shew you any truth, be forbidden, holden and kept backe from you . . .[22]

Apparently the earliest of these "unauthorized" tracts was *A Discourse touching the pretended Matche between the Duke of Norfolke and the Quene of Scotes*. This attack on the proposed marriage appeared with no indication of license, authorship, or place and date of publication—with no title page of any sort, in fact. But it has been established that the pamphlet was written in 1569, was printed in London in that year or early in the following, and had as its author no less a person than Francis Walsingham, then chief of Elizabeth's intelligence service and a bitter foe of the Queen of Scots throughout his career.[23]

In seeking to discredit the marriage proposal, the *Discourse* strives mainly to give publicity to the misdoings of the intended bride. Although observing that her Catholic faith and her claims to the crown of England would make her marriage to an English nobleman a threat to the nation, the author emphasized more his belief that her personal character and history would make her a perilous threat to Norfolk himself as well as to the realm. Walsingham cannot believe that the proposed match could be based on love; for one thing, he asserts, the parties involved had never seen each other, and further, it would be unlikely "that anie man that regardeth his owne safety, would match with one detected of so horrible crimes in respect of love." [24] For "how like is it," he continues, "that one ambitious, a borne Scott, a defamed person, who hath made shipwracke of her honour and reputation, and lastlie a branche of the howse of Guise whose profession is to keepe none Edict never so solemnly promised will keep faith?" [25] Walsingham does not go to the extremes of the Scots before him, or other writers in England afterward, in directly assailing Mary's morals to discredit her political and religious aspirations. Nonetheless, his *Discourse* serves to demonstrate the continuity of the Protestant propaganda attack in these first years of Mary's residence in England.

The political schemes and plots charged against Mary are the burden of the attack made on her in the second of the tracts published "unofficially" in England at the time of the Norfolk affair. Printed in 1571, again without license, title page, or imprint, the tract was presented as a letter which began *Salutem in Christo* and which was signed "R. G." [26] R. G. was probably Richard Grafton, an ardent Protestant and the author of those same *Chronicles* of the following year which, "Seen and Allowed," in dealing with Norfolk made no mention of Mary. The pamphlet appears to have been printed by John Day, a Protestant publisher active in London who had produced the first edition of Foxe's *Martyrs.* The *Salutem* was allowed to go through three editions in the one year with no official interference, thereby prompting the complaint of the Catholic writer quoted above that this particular work enjoyed government protection.[27] Since R. G. was mainly concerned with justifying the trial and execution of Norfolk, he devoted most of the tract to cataloguing instances of the Duke's treasonable activities. Mary is introduced as only an accomplice; her political activities linking her with the Duke, rather than her personal character, are the target of the attack. According to R. G., "the said Scottish Queene hath bene the most dangerous ennemy against the Queenes Majestie our Soveraigne Lady, that lyved," and he charges her—for the first time in print—with inspiring the Northern Rebellion.[28]

There was nothing incidental in the semipublicity given to the misdoings of Mary in the third and by far most celebrated of the unauthorized pamphlets published under English auspices between 1569 and 1572. This was the work by George Buchanan commonly known as *A Detection of the Doings of Mary Queen of Scots.*[29] Contrary to the impression given by most of Mary's subsequent biographers, this work, admittedly the fountainhead of all later attacks on the Scottish Queen's character and conduct, was completely a product, in its published form, of English activities to discredit Mary without violating Elizabeth's official attitude of benevolent neutrality toward her reluctant guest.

Buchanan apparently wrote the *Detection* originally in Latin as a covering letter to accompany the notorious Casket Letters that were presented in evidence against Mary at the conferences at York and Westminster.[30] In this original form, the *Detection* simply chronicled, from the Protestant point of view, the events in Scotland leading to the murder of Darnley and the marriage of Mary to Bothwell. It was designed to leave little doubt in the reader's mind that Mary was privy to all these events, including an earlier abortive effort to do away with Darnley by poison. The document was not published at that time, however, and, having served the purpose of discrediting Mary at the conferences, the manuscript remained in London, apparently unused, for the following three years.

Then in 1571, after the arrest of Norfolk for his part in the plot to release, marry, and enthrone the Queen of Scots, some of Elizabeth's councilors suddenly began to take a new and active interest in the document. Some time before November 1 of that year the original Latin version of the *Detection* was printed in London by John Day without any indication of place or date of origin.[31] Appended to it was a Latin essay entitled *Actio contra Mariam,* that is, an "Action" in the legal sense of an indictment, and three of the more incriminating Casket Letters. The *Action,* which added much rhetorical abuse but no new evidence to the case against Mary, was allowed to pass as Buchanan's work, but actually it had been written, with Cecil's knowledge, by Thomas Wilson, the scholar-diplomat who subsequently became secretary of state in Elizabeth's Privy Council. At the same time, Wilson, again with the knowledge and possibly the prompting of Cecil, translated both the Latin *Detection* and *Action* into what he was pleased to refer to, in a letter to Cecil, as "handsome Scottish," and added all eight of the original Casket Letters to the volume. This production, entitled *Ane Detectioun of the duinges of Marie Quene of Scottes,* appeared in two different editions within a month of the Latin original, and, although without indication of place of publication on the title page, it, too, had clearly been printed in London, probably by John Day.[32] Meanwhile, a version of the same work in somewhat more authentic Scottish than Wilson's was published openly at St. Andrews by Robert Lekprevik, the printer of the

Sempill ballads, and two editions of Buchanan's work were printed and circulated in Germany.[33] Finally, Cecil himself arranged for a French translation that appeared with an Edinburgh imprint, but actually was published at the great French Huguenot center of La Rochelle.[34]

In the light of Cecil's own recommendation of semipublicity for Mary's misdoings, the purpose of this elaborate series of bibliographical deceptions seems clear. By making it appear that Buchanan's attack, in any language—including the pseudo-Scottish—emanated from Scotland, and that the celebrated Scottish humanist himself was responsible for the virulent *Action* as well as the *Detection,* the English were able to blast Mary's character without violating their official attitude of protection and defense. They could always blame Mary's Scottish subjects—and they usually did. No one seems to have been completely fooled by the device, but no one seems to have been able to do much to stop it. When Mary herself asked the French ambassador in London, M. de Fénelon, to remonstrate with Elizabeth about permitting the publication of such libelous attacks on the Queen of Scotland, the ambassador wrote back to Mary that he could get no satisfaction from Elizabeth, "as she pretended that the book had been printed in Scotland, not in England." [35] The protest lodged against Buchanan's book by the French king, Charles IX, was equally futile; Elizabeth claimed innocence in the matter, and, although deploring the publication of such libels against anointed sovereignty, she explained that they had been printed beyond her control in Scotland and in Germany.[36] Mary was apparently no more deceived by these explanations than anyone else. One John Bateman, who took to her a copy of the published *Detection,* wrote back to Cecil on December 12, 1571, reporting in detail on the Scottish Queen's reaction to the book:

She said then it was a shame to suffer it abroad. I answered that there appeared no authority either from the Queen's majesty or any of the Council for the printing thereof, because there is no mention made either of privilege or allowance, but only being a book written and set out by some of her own countrymen, and spread abroad in many men's hands, I thought good to bring down one, and show it to my lord [i.e., Cecil]. Then she said she knew G. Buchanane was the author thereof, 'a vile athiest', at whom she is not a little offended for the same, and for that he is schoolmaster to her son.[37]

That the Norfolk marriage proposal was the immediate provocation for this elaborate scheme to discredit Mary in the eyes of the world was perhaps most clearly recognized by Alexander Hay, a Scottish councilor, in a letter to John Knox reporting the publication of the *Detection* in England. "In appearance," he wrote, the English "leave nothing unset out, tending to her infamy, and to make the Duke of Norfolke odious, who has a great benevolence of the people." [38] This point and purpose of the Buchanan publications was not left to be inferred by readers, however. The pamphlets made explicit their contention that the queen portrayed by Buchanan was the Queen whom Norfolk tried to put in Elizabeth's place. Appended to the English editions of the translated *Detection* was an exhortation that began, "Now judge Englishmen if it be gud to change Quenis." It was, again, probably Cecil himself who, as a further precaution against any misunderstanding of his propaganda, arranged at the same time for the publication of an anonymous pamphlet entitled *The Copie of a letter written by one in London to his frend concernyng the credit of the late published detection of the doynges of the Ladie Marie of Scotland.*[39] Although mainly concerned with establishing the credibility of Buchanan's "little book," the *Letter* also makes it perfectly clear that the denunciation of Norfolk's treason is the principal purpose of these publications. As the writer concludes, one marvels that the Duke should seek to marry a woman such as Buchanan describes and thus risk "so great a danger to hymselfe to be sent after his predecessours."

For making the Duke of Norfolk "odious" by making his intended wife infamous, no work was better suited than the amplified *Detection*. Buchanan's method, like Sempill's, was to avoid an attack on the real points at issue—Mary's faith and her attempts to claim the throne of England—and to concentrate on the reputed immorality of her personal character. The main charges brought against Mary are too familiar to require detailed description—her infatuation for Bothwell; her infidelity to Darnley; her connivance

with Bothwell in schemes to discredit Darnley politically, to trap
him in an affair with Murray's wife, to poison him, and finally to
blow him up; and her hasty marriage to Bothwell under the guise
of "abduction." Fortunately, we are not obliged here to enter into
the endless controversy as to the truth or falsehood of the charges.
What is relevant is that Buchanan spared no effort to crowd the
document with details of incident and characterization, whether
real or imagined, designed to intensify the effect of total depravity,
and thus to render Mary totally unacceptable as a queen in the
eyes of God and man.

For example, by way of illustrating the degree of Mary's adulterous passion for Bothwell, Buchanan observes that she took a private house adjoining one occupied by the Earl in Edinburgh.
Although she tried to make it seem that she had been trapped
into doing this, her real purpose, says Buchanan, was obvious to
everyone. His version of what happened provides one of the few
scenes of pure low comedy in the whole of the battle of the books.
Mary, he says (as modernized) :

... laid all the blame upon my lady Rerese, a woman of most vile unchastity who had sometime been one of Bothwell's harlots, and then
was one of the chief of the Queen's privy chamber. By this woman, who
now in her age had from the gain of whoredom betaken herself to the
craft of bawdry, was the Queen, as herself said, betrayed. For Bothwell
was through the garden brought into the Queen's chamber, and there
forced her against her will, forsooth. But how much against her will
Dame Rerese betrayed her, time the mother of truth has disclosed. For
within few days after, the Queen intending as I suppose to requite force
with force and to ravish him again, sent Dame Rerese (who had herself
also before assayed the man's strength) to bring him captive unto her
highness. The Queen with Margaret Carwod, a woman privy of all her
secrets, did let her [Dame Rerese] down by a string over an old wall
into the next garden. But in such weirlike affairs, all things cannot ever
be so well foreseen, but that some incommodious chance may over-
thwartly happen. Behold, the string suddenly broke, and down with a
great noise fell Dame Rerese, a woman very heavy both by unwieldy age
and massy substance. But she, an old beaten soldier, nothing dismayed
with the darkness of the night and the height of the wall, nor with the
suddenness of the fall, up she getteth, and winneth into Bothwell's

chamber; she got the door open; and out of his bed, even out of his wife's arms, half asleep, half naked, she forcibly brings the man to the Queen.[40]

A further indication of Buchanan's effort to emphasize the depravity of Mary is the character he attributes to Darnley. So far as we know, not even Mary's worst foes in Scotland, in private correspondence and expressions, could find much to praise in the weak, spoiled character of Mary's consort. But in the *Detection,* as in the Sempill ballads earlier, Darnley becomes the noble and innocent victim of a designing woman, the Sampson of Mary's Delilah and the Agamemnon of her Clytemnestra. Thus Buchanan dwells at length on the miseries and injuries with which the Queen repaid the tender affection and loyalty of Darnley, in order, as he writes, that she might "make empty bedroome for Bothwell."

It might seem that the English councilors scarcely needed add anything to Buchanan's original *Detection* when they arranged to publish and adapt it to discrediting Mary and Norfolk in 1571. Yet the English determination, as Catholics regarded it, "to leave nothing unset out, tending to her infamy," is nowhere better revealed than in Wilson's *Action,* appended to the published Latin and English editions of the Buchanan tract. For the most part, the *Action* simply develops as positive assertions charges against Mary's character and conduct that Buchanan left as hints or conjectures. For example, where Buchanan had suggested, naming no names, that an attempt was made to poison Darnley "by treachery," the *Action* states flatly that Mary herself administered the poison and then followed him so that "she might herself in presence satisfy both her cruel heart and her eyes with sight of his present miseries." [41] Elsewhere the writer resorts to negative suggestion to intensify the effect achieved in the *Detection.* Having professed, for example, his disinclination to discuss the physical attractions in Bothwell that aroused Mary's passion, Wilson continues:

Neither do I affirm the rumors spread of her in France in time of her first marriage: howbeit the wickedness of the rest of her life make some proof that they rose not all of nothing. And many things that have been noised of her since her return into Scotland, I have no lust to believe.

As for me, I am content they be buried in forgetfulness, or if that cannot be, let them be discredited, let them be taken for false and feigned.[42]

After having thus "buried" and "discredited" these accounts at some length, he then proceeds with his analysis of Mary's relations with Bothwell and her complicity in the murder of Darnley.

The *Action* concludes with a paragraph that is as frank a statement as can be found in the period of what Cecil and Wilson sought to achieve by publishing not only Buchanan's "little book" but all of the "unauthorized" publications directed against the character of the Queen of Scots. Answering those who would, and did, plead for Mary because of her sovereignty, her age, her dignity, and her beauty, the author, who of course continues to speak in the guise of the Scotsman Buchanan, writes:

Be it so, if she have spared him [i.e., Darnley] in whom all these respects were greater, or at least equal. Let the Majesty of royal name avail her. How much it ought to avail to her preserving, her self hath showed the example. May we commit our safety to her who, a sister, hath butcherly slaughtered her brother, a wife her husband, a Queen her King? May we commit our safety to her, whom never shame restrained from unchastity, womankind from cruelty, nor religion from impiety? Shall we bear with her age, sex, and unadvisedness, that without all just causes of hatred, despised all these things in her kinsman, her King, her husband? . . . her we have touched with no other punishment, but only restrained her from doing more mischief. For we deprived her not of liberties, but of unbridled licentiousness of evil doing.[43]

Elizabeth's government obviously succeeded in creating the effect it desired in publicizing Mary's misdoings, especially on the predominantly Catholic Continent, where the need to counteract projected support for the Queen of Scots was acute. The English ambassador to France immediately recommended that "some of Buchanan's little Latin books should be presented to the King of France and also the noblemen of his council, as they will serve to good effect to disgrace the Queen of Scots." [44] Sir Henry Killegrew, on a roving ambassadorial assignment in France at the time, distributed copies of Buchanan's work around the French court—to the Venetian ambassador there, among others, and to "one

Montagne of Montpellier, that writeth the universal story of our time." [45] Another English agent reported to Cecil from France that Buchanan's book had "done no hurt but made the matter so plain that they were ashamed to defend her that fain would." [46] Needless to say, Mary's efforts to have so damaging a book suppressed were ceaseless, though futile. As late as 1583 she apparently was desperate enough to try a kind of blackmail, for Elizabeth was informed in that year that Mary desired "that certain books printed, as she said, in London, to her great dishonor—meaning Buchanan's action—might be by her majesty's order suppressed, and she would upon her honour promise within a twelvemonth to do somewhat that her majesty should have good liking to have suppressed, which otherwise would be published." [47]

The Mary Stuart who emerges from the "unauthorized" literature is indeed odious—perhaps far more so than the worst of the factual evidence against her would warrant. Since history has tended to place most of the blame for this portrait of Mary on Buchanan alone, it might be noted, for the sake of his reputation, that he probably did not originally write his *Detection* for publication, although he may subsequently have agreed to this, and that he certainly did not write the far more sensational and less substantiated *Action* added by Wilson at Cecil's behest but passed off at the time as the work of the Scottish humanist.

But to conclude that Mary was the completely innocent victim of English hypocrisy, vindictiveness, and jealousy, as too many of Mary's historians have done, is neither fair nor accurate. Whatever the degree of her guilt or innocence in the Darnley and Bothwell affairs, Mary's very presence in England, her activities there, and the activities of her partisans, made her a very real threat to the peace and security of that realm. As Archbishop Parker put it, Elizabeth indeed had a wolf by the ears in the person of a Catholic queen who claimed the throne of Protestant England and who was appealing to Catholic Europe to support her cause with armed intervention. Political necessity demanded, in the interests of preserving the realm, that Mary's supporters both at home and abroad be discouraged by every means possible, and the defamatory literature was, as the ambassadors attested, an effective means to this end.

Meanwhile, however, Elizabeth remained firm in her insistence that no attack on Mary should appear in any work licensed to be published in England. Striking evidence of this continuing policy is found in the publications of chronicle history at this time which inevitably had to deal with events in which Mary was involved. Since, as Conyers Read has observed, the history writers had an important function as propagandists in the day, their treatment of the Queen of Scots and her affairs is significant. John Stow, for example, in the 1570 edition of *A Summarie of the Chronicles of England,* reported only the barest facts of her birth and her marriages. He noted noncommittally that Darnley "was shamefullye murthered, the revenge whereof remayneth in the mighty hande of God," [48] but in the 1579 edition of his work he dropped even this bit of speculation.[49] Holinshed's *Chronicles,* as first published in 1577, were similarly cautious. He goes so far as to say, with regard to the Scottish Queen's marriage to Bothwell, that "the suspition which men had alreadye conceyved that shee should be also privie to the murder, was nothyng diminished," but then, apparently feeling that he had stepped on dangerous ground, he hastily adds, "I have not to deale in that matter," and retreats into the relative security of a detailed analysis of the military actions at Carberry Hill.[50]

Those writers who, without unofficial sanction, violated official policy, were severely dealt with. In 1579 a Puritan named John Stubbs wrote and had published a tract entitled *The Discoverie of a Gaping Gulf.*[51] The main point of Stubbs' attack was Elizabeth's proposed Catholic marriage with the French Duc d'Alençon, which the English Queen seemed to be considering at this time. In the course of his pamphlet, however, he openly charges Mary with involvement in the Northern Rebellion and concludes with the blast: "She hath already cost us ynough of our Englishe blood, and she cares not though she make havock of nobilitye & people: she seekes hyr own turne by hooke or crooke. . . . TAKE HEEDE OH ELIZABETH OF ENGLAND, AND BEWARE OF SCOTTISH

MARY." [52] Since both the Alençon marriage proposal and Mary Stuart were forbidden subjects for published discussion, it is not surprising that Elizabeth's wrath against *The Discoverie* was immediate and great. Not only was the book promptly suppressed by proclamation, but also Stubbs and his printer paid for their temerity by having their right hands cut off.[53]

George Buchanan, despite services previously rendered to Elizabeth's "unofficial" policy of publicizing Mary's misdoings, fared little better when he returned to attack Mary Stuart on his own in his celebrated political treatise on government in Scotland, *De Jure Regni apud Scotos*, in 1580, and in his massive history of Scotland entitled *Rerum Scoticarum Historia*, in 1583. Both works, originally published in Edinburgh, were also published in London, although with no indication of the fact on their title pages.[54] The former is mainly a defense of the doctrine of popular sovereignty and the right of subjects to depose a ruler—ideas sufficiently odious to Elizabeth to account in themselves for her suppression of the work. But in his opening account of Mary's character and conduct, which in his view made her deposition necessary, Buchanan reiterates most of the charges originally set forth against her in his *Detection*. The same charges of adultery and murder are developed at much greater length in that section of his *History* that deals with the Scottish Queen's last years in her own realm. There is no evidence that Elizabeth's government had "unofficially" sponsored either work in England as they did the *Detection*. In fact, letters of the day indicate that the books were very coolly received in English officialdom.[55] When Mary herself protested against the circulation in England of Buchanan's new attacks against her, Elizabeth dutifully maintained her official attitude of protective benevolence by prohibiting both.[56]

Although we do not know that, after the fall of Norfolk, Elizabeth's government directly inspired any further "semi-publicity," nevertheless a number of books designed for the same purpose were published on the Continent at this time. They were well suited to publicizing abroad Elizabeth's reasons for holding Mary Stuart in custody, and those that found their way to England were apparently allowed to circulate there, with little interference, to provide the same publicity at home. All these works were the product of the Protestant Huguenot party in France, which Elizabeth's government had been secretly supporting and encouraging since the St. Bartholomew Day massacre in 1572.[57] As a result of the massacre, the Guise party in France—ardent Catholics and ardent supporters of their kinswoman, the Queen of Scots—had become the ascendant influence over the somewhat vacillating Henri III, who had succeeded his brother Charles IX in 1574. As Conyers Read notes, "It must never be forgotten that Mary Stuart, the heir-presumptive to the English throne, was the first cousin of the Duke of Guise, and that they [the Guise party] had everything to hope for if by any means whatsoever she could be placed upon the English throne."[58] The Huguenot party, or what was left of it after the massacre, accordingly made Mary a central issue in its propaganda to discredit the Guisean Catholics in France and to bid for continued support from Protestant Elizabeth in England. In each instance the argument against Mary was ultimately turned against the Guise party, yet the works also indicate those issues, moving to the fore in anti-Marian propaganda, that subsequently were to appear in works published in England against the Queen of Scots.

The first and by far the most important of these books produced by French Protestants was a pair of dialogues now considered the work of Nicolas Barnaud, a French physician and zealous Protestant who fled to Geneva after the massacre. There, in 1574, under the pseudonym of Eusebius Philadelphus, he published his two dialogues in both French and Latin versions.[59] To make it appear that his attack on the Queen of Scots originated in the British Isles, Barnaud issued his books with a false imprint of Edinburgh and dedicated the French version to Queen Elizabeth. The device fooled at least the Spanish agent in London, who was convinced that the work had been written in the English capital and who concluded that "it is so malicious that it once more proves the wickedness of these [English] people."[60]

The purpose of Barnaud's work, as he states it, is to persuade Elizabeth to execute without delay the woman whom he regards as a tool by means of which the Catholic party in France seeks to extend its control to England and Scotland.[61] Accordingly, he marshals for the first time in print the legal and philosophical arguments for the execution of Mary that were subsequently to become fixtures in anti-Marian propaganda both in England and abroad.[62] In Barnaud's dialogues, the case in favor of Mary is presented by "Historiographe," a kind of straw man set up to play the devil's advocate; his arguments are of course demolished by Barnaud's spokesman, "Le Politique," who presents in detail the case against the Queen of Scots. To the claim that Mary's sovereignty placed her beyond Elizabeth's jurisdiction and control, "Le Politque" responds that her sovereignty is valid only in her own realm; when she crossed into England she automatically acknowledged the sovereignty of Elizabeth over herself. To the plea that Mary be shown humane treatment as a refugee he replies that she lost her status and rights of a refugee when she began plotting against the life and throne of her benefactress. The argument for Mary's right as a prisoner, under the law of nations, to seek any means of escape, he counters with the argument that the same law allows Elizabeth, who holds the prisoner, to use any means to prevent and punish escape attempts. Finally, against the plea that Elizabeth show mercy and pity as becomes a representative of God's justice, he argues at length to show that Elizabeth cannot place mercy before justice when her own person, her realm, and above all, the true church of God are threatened with destruction.[63]

"Le Politique" develops this last point in great detail, and in so doing establishes one of the principal arguments employed by later propagandists in advocating the execution of the Scottish queen. Basing his reasoning on a fundamental doctrine of Renaissance political theory, he argues that Elizabeth as a queen was appointed by God to administer His justice on earth, and that she would be failing in her duty if she placed her personal feelings for Mary—clearly demonstrated, he says, by her widely advertised protective benevolence—before the requirements of God's law. The prince who refuses to execute justice is answerable to God, Barnaud wrote, and, as translated, he added:

To conclude, the punishment of the Queen of Scots for this conspiracy [i.e., the Ridolfi plot]—assuming that she is guilty, whatever her partisans say—is just and legitimate by all the laws divine and human:

essential to the welfare and preservation of Elizabeth of England, and of those whom Elizabeth has occasion to favor most. On the other hand, refusal to punish Mary is an abnegation of justice and of Elizabeth's duty to protect her subjects, a disdain for the welfare of her people, and a peril to the preservation of the church of God and its unblemished service, which ... would be completely overthrown if the death of Elizabeth should occur before the execution deserved by Queen Mary.[64]

Two others works by French Protestants published in this period develop similar themes in the attack against Mary, but with slightly different emphases. Domination of the Scottish Queen by the evil and ambitious house of Guise is the theme of the first of these, *A Legendarie conteining an Ample Discourse of the life and behauiour of Charles Cardinal of Lorraine, and of his brethren of the house of Guise.* Written by Louis Regnier de la Planche, a zealous Calvinist historian, under the pseudonym of François de L'Isle, this work appeared originally in French in 1576; the preparation of an English translation in 1577 suggests that the attack was intended to find its way across the channel, and that it did so is attested by no less a person than Edmund Spenser's friend, Gabriel Harvey, who refers to the *Legendarie* in a marginal note in his own copy of Buchanan's *Detection*.[65] Mary Stuart appears in the *Legendarie* as only one of the many instruments that, Regnier de la Planche charges, were employed by the Guises to extend their political and religious control to Britain. Among the tales he tells to prove his point of the influence the Guises exercised over Mary is the story that her two Guise uncles caused her first husband, Francis II, to "be wrapped in his wifes swathing cloutes, to the end to yealde him the more supple and delicate to their handling"; then, further to weaken his reputation and increase their own power, they caused the rumor to be spread that Francis, a sickly youth, "could neither hoake nor spit forth," and that he was thought to be a leper.[66] Thereupon, according to the author of the *Legendarie,* the brothers Guise persuaded Mary to take up the claim to the title and arms of England, in the hope that they might finally appropriate that realm to themselves.[67]

Less sensational, perhaps, but nonetheless damaging to Mary's name were the *Memoires*—describing conditions in France under Charles IX—sometimes attributed to Simon Goulart, a French Protestant minister who fled to Geneva after the St. Bartholomew massacre.[68] The first of his three volumes published in 1578 is largely filled with reprints of anti-Marian propaganda already mentioned—notably the French translation of Buchanan's *Detection* and the second dialogue by Nicholas Barnaud, calling for the immediate execution of the Queen of Scots. Thus the *Memoires* draw together both the older and the newer elements of the attack on the Scottish Queen—the charges against her personal character and conduct on the one hand, and the charges against her religious and political intrigues as a tool of the house of Guise on the other. After reviewing these charges, the author is strongly of the opinion that Mary should be burned alive, and at once.

As these French works indicate, the anti-Marian propaganda campaign began to take a new direction after 1572. Her claims to the succession in England remained one of the principal targets of the propagandists, but in these French tracts it was her Catholicism and her connection with the Guises that made her claims intolerable, and not, as in the earlier literature, the reputed immorality of her character. Something of this shift has already been noted in the ill-fated attack published by Stubbs, where both lines of argument were apparent. However, where the aim of earlier literature had been merely to justify continued detention of Mary in England, the avowed purpose now was to justify her execution.

The threat that Mary's religious and political connections represented to Protestants in general and to Elizabeth in particular was sharply increased in 1583. In that year the "Enterprise of England," a vast scheme promulgated chiefly by her kinsman, the Duc du Guise, and the Pope and Philip of Spain for an invasion to restore Catholicism in England, began to manifest itself in specific conspiracies to assassinate Elizabeth and to release the Queen of Scots.[69] In November of that year, Francis Throckmorton was arrested and his part in a plot to invade England and release Mary in conjunction with the assassination of Elizabeth was revealed. In the following year, Dr. William Parry, a lawyer and member of Parliament, was found to be involved in a similar project. In 1586,

Elizabeth's agents disclosed and broke the most elaborate design of them all, the Babington conspiracy. Without tracing in detail the involutions of each of these plots, we can accept two conclusions about them with some certainty: first, they were undeniably inspired by Catholic forces on the Continent, including English Catholic refugees; and second, Mary Stuart, in two instances at least, was not only aware of the plans but approved of them as well.[70]

It is not remarkable, therefore, to find a change coming over Elizabeth's attitude toward Mary. The change was signaled in 1584 by official English action that, although still not mentioning the Queen of Scots by name, was obviously meant to place her and her political activities in jeopardy. This was the so-called Bond of Association proposed by the Queen's council in October, and passed by Parliament, with some modification, as the Act of Association in November. The Act of Association decreed that should any attempt be made on the life of Elizabeth with a view to advancing "some person" to the throne—Mary was not mentioned by name—not only should that "person's" claim to the throne be disallowed, but he—or she—should be tried and put to death.[71] This was the law under which the Queen of Scots was subsequently tried and executed. There were also other signs of a shift in Elizabeth's policy. After the discovery of the Throckmorton plot and Mary's part in it, Elizabeth removed the Earl of Shrewsbury as the guardian of the Scottish Queen and replaced him with Sir Ralph Sadler. The change meant that Mary was subjected to closer confinement, to more restricted activities, and, for what it meant psychologically, to a guardian of less exalted social rank. The significance of the change, as Conyers Read points out, was that "Elizabeth began to lift the veil of pretended hospitality with which for some sixteen years she had shrouded her detention of the Scottish queen." [72]

Insofar as anti-Marian propaganda literature was concerned, however, Elizabeth indeed only began to lift the veil. Although there were some indications after 1583 of a slackening of her injunctions against printed attacks on Mary, there was no example of an open and allowed propaganda attack on the Scottish Queen herself before sentence was passed against her in December, 1586. This reticence is all the more remarkable in view of the highly effective use being made at the time of Catholic pro-Marian propaganda literature in connection with the plots and conspiracies that now harried Elizabeth. For example, William Parry admitted on several occasions after his arrest that he had been persuaded to the rightness of killing Elizabeth and setting Mary on the English throne by reading the *Defence of English Catholics,* a vigorous polemic in support of Mary and the Catholic cause in England by William, later Cardinal, Allen.[73] Parry confessed that this work, which had been sent to him out of France, had "redoubled my former conceites. . . . Her Majestie [Elizabeth] may do wel to reade it, & to be out of doubt (if things be not amended) that it is a warning, & a doctrine ful dangerous." [74] Out of doubt, Elizabeth did read it, and others like it. In authorizing counterpropaganda against such works, however, she still saw fit to ignore the involvement of Mary in these affairs and to concentrate the attack on Catholics in general.

Characteristic of the attitude of Elizabeth's government at this particular juncture was *The Execution of Justice in England* by William Cecil, now Lord Burghley, published with license by the Queen's printer in 1583 and widely circulated abroad in Latin, Dutch, French, and Italian translations.[75] Burghley nowhere mentioned the Queen of Scots in his treatise, but his basic argument to justify the government's admittedly strict measures against Catholics in England was the same one employed by later propagandists to justify Mary's trial and execution—after Elizabeth's policy against open attacks on the Queen of Scots was relaxed. This argument said, in effect, that any punitive action taken against Catholics was taken not because of their religious beliefs per se, as it had been in the reformation under Henry VIII, or against Protestants under the counterreformation of Mary Tudor, but was taken rather when the activities of Catholics constituted treason against the state in the form of plots to alter the present government or remove Elizabeth or tamper with the established succession. The point of difference may seem to be a fine one to the modern eye, but apparently Burghley, like most Protestant Englishmen of the day, sincerely regarded it as a real one.

For the time being, however, English propaganda directed against the Catholic plots in which the Scottish Queen was involved preferred to stress the guilt of Catholics in general rather than of Mary in particular. In connection with the Throckmorton plot, for example, Mary, as Conyers Read observes, was "cognizant of the whole matter and probably assistant to it"; what is perhaps more important for the present purpose, Elizabeth's government certainly thought that she was.[76] Nevertheless, authorized English publications dealing with the conspiracy were reticent as usual in openly implicating the Queen of Scots. Although Mary is incidentally referred to in an anonymous but authorized account of the Throckmorton plot published in 1584, entitled *A discouerie of the treasons practised . . . by Francis Throckmorton,* the focal point of this blast against Catholic treason and rebellion is the activity of Throckmorton himself as an agent of the Duc du Guise and the Pope.[77] Being "somewhat pinched" on the rack, he confessed that he was a "privie conveiour and receivour of letters to and from the Scottish Queene" and that, although the pretention of the plot was simply to restore Mary to liberty, its real intention was to "remove her Majestie [Elizabeth] from her Crowne and state." [78] The Duc du Guise is repeatedly referred to as the prime mover in this plot, with able assistance from agents of the Pope, but Mary remains a tool, and nowhere is the attack directed against her character, her religious faith, or her conspiratorial proclivities.

Sometime later, when George Whetstone came to deal with the Throckmorton conspiracy in *The English Myrror* (1586), he similarly held the Duc du Guise, the King of Spain, and the Pope responsible for this and all other plots against Elizabeth.[79] He made cautious allusion to the efforts of Throckmorton to kill Elizabeth and "to possesse he knewe not whome with the Crowne," but beyond that hint there is no reference to Mary Stuart by name or title at any point.[80]

Meanwhile, Mary again received only incidental treatment in the propaganda blasts against papal and Guisian conspiracies published with official license in connection with the arrest and execution of Dr. William Parry. Parry, originally an agent of Burghley's on the Continent, subsequently became a Catholic and was accused of plotting to restore Catholicism in England by assassinating Elizabeth and putting Mary on the English throne. He was tried and executed early in 1585. As a matter of fact, Mary herself does not seem to have been aware of the existence of Parry's conspiracy, nor did Elizabeth and her councilors themselves think that she was.[81] Nevertheless, the episode made clear once again that, whether Mary participated or not, she remained the focal point of actions that the English had good reason to regard as treasonable, and the propaganda literature officially licensed to defend the execution of Dr. Parry made the most of the actions if not of their real point. Parry was portrayed in a number of pamphlets as attributing his untimely end mainly to his ill-spent youth and to the "Ill Company" which had persuaded him to aid Philip of Spain and the Duke of Alva, together with France, in the scheme to enthrone Mary Stuart. Mary herself is rarely mentioned and never attacked.[32] In fact, in a letter he wrote to Elizabeth after his confession, and which was published in *A True and Plaine declaration*, Parry observed that "the Quene of Scotland is your prisoner, let her be honorably entreated, but yet surely garded." [83] These words may have been put in his mouth for official publication, or he himself, consciously or unconsciously, may have been reflecting something of the official attitude governing the treatment of Mary in the propaganda literature at this time—for while surely guarded she seems indeed to have been honorably "entreated."

Nowhere does Elizabeth's policy in this respect make itself more evident than in the voluminous literature published upon the disclosure of the Babington plot in August, 1586. The silencing effect of Elizabeth's propaganda controls at this time is especially remarkable when it is recalled that Mary's involvement in the Babington conspiracy was to be made the direct cause of her trial and execution.[84] Anthony Babington, a friend of Mary's, had, along with a priest named Ballard, worked out a plan to assassinate Elizabeth and to free and enthrone Mary Stuart. Babington wrote Mary a letter outlining the scheme, and Mary replied with a long letter which certainly welcomed the plot for her liberation and—if one section is actually hers and not a forgery inserted by her enemies— explicitly approved of the plan to kill the English Queen. Both letters were intercepted by Elizabeth's agents, the plot was broken, Babington and his fellow conspirators were executed, and Mary was brought to trial on October 11, 1586. She was found guilty. Not until December 4, however, and then only after numerous postponements and under enormous pressure from both Houses of Parliament, could Elizabeth bring herself to publish the sentence of death against the Queen of Scots.

Nevertheless, until the pronouncement of this sentence in December, 1586, gave a kind of legal sanction to published attacks on Mary, Elizabeth continued to play her role of the careful guardian of Mary's honor and position. After December, Mary was assailed violently and openly as the principal villain in the Babington conspiracy, but until then propagandists had to content themselves with attacking other scapegoats and, as in the Throckmorton and Parry literature, ascribing this latest conspiracy simply to the wicked influence of Rome as exercised through prominent parties unspecified. Such was the tenor of Thomas Deloney's *A proper new Ballad breefely declaring the Death and Execution of fourteen most wicked Traitors ... To the tune of Weep, Weep;* and similarly of his *A Most ioyfull Songe ... which was made in London at the taking of the late trayterous Conspirators ... To the tune of: A man in desperation.*[85] The frequently anthologized "lamentation" beginning "My prime of youth is but a frost of cares," by Chidiock Tychborne, one of the conspirators, was first published at this time. In it Tychborne makes no reference to the Scottish queen whose cause he served, but, like Parry, blames his downfall rather on a misspent youth and bad company.[86] The propagandists were particularly careful to point out, from the example of Babington's fate, that the tempting bribes offered by the Pope to would-be traitors and rebels against Elizabeth turn to ashes in the mouth. Such attempts to discourage future conspiracies emerge as a principal element in the literature published before the sentence in 1586.[87] All the writers, however, regarded the detection of this latest plot as certain evidence of the inevitable end to which all rebels against an anointed sovereign are brought by a just and vengeful God, and also, of course, as an infallible indication of which church God considered His own. In the *Proper New Ballad* he wrote on the subject, Deloney adds a refrain that summarizes as well as anything else both the spirit and the substance of the Babington literature:

> O praise the Lord with hart and minde,
>   sing praise with voices cleere;
> Sith traiterous crue have had their due,
>   to quaile their parteners cheere.[88]

"Their parteners cheere" probably refers to Mary and her part in the plot, as well as to the Pope, the King of Spain, and the other Catholic powers usually considered inimical to Elizabeth. The vagueness of the reference is typical of the caution made necessary by Elizabeth's injunctions against direct attacks on the Scottish Queen before pronouncement of sentence against her. On the few occasions when Mary was more or less explicitly referred to in the Babington literature licensed before December, 1586, it was with a brevity and allusiveness suggestive of the force of Elizabeth's policy.

The English Queen herself, practising what she preached, may have set a model for literature dealing with the Babington conspiracy and Mary's part in it. In *The Arte of English Poesie,* published in 1589 when all was over, a poem beginning "The doubt of future foes exiles my present joy" is presented as having been composed by Elizabeth while Mary was still alive. In introducing it into his volume, the sixteenth-century editor, probably George Puttenham, explains that:

... our sovereigne Lady, perceiving how by the S[cottish] Q[ueen's] residence within this Realme, at so great libertie and ease (as were skarce meete for so great and dangerous a prisoner) bred secret factions among her people, and made many of the nobilitie to favour her partie ... The Queen our soveraigne Lady to declare that she was nothing ignorant of those secret practizes, though she had long with great wisdome and pacience dissembled it, writeth this ditty most sweet and sententious, not hiding from all such aspiring minds the daunger of their ambition and disloyaltie....[89]

But with the same caution and indirection that she required of her subjects, Elizabeth avoided mentioning the Queen of Scots by name in her poem, and emphasized rather the evils of treason and foreign plots in general. With her rival obviously in mind she wrote:

> The daughter of debate that eke discord doth sow
> Shall reap no gain where former rule hath taught still peace
>   to grow.
> No foreign banished wight shall anchor in this port;
> Our realm it brooks no stranger's force, let them elsewhere
>   resort.[90]

Reflecting the royal policy thus exemplified, Thomas Nelson, in a very long poem entitled *A Short Discourse: expressing the substance of all the late pretended treasons against the Queenes Maiestie,* simply remarked in passing that among the many evil designs of the Babington conspirators was one to kill Elizabeth "and to proclaime the Scottish Queene, and set her in her place." [91] Similarly brief and incidental is the refrence to Mary in one of a series of Latin poems published at Oxford in 1586 to mark Elizabeth's delivery from Catholic traitors. After prolonged rejoicing at God's punishment of rebels who have been seduced by the Pope to turn against their anointed sovereign, the poet, one "H. D." noted that, among their other crimes, they sought to crown Mary as queen.[92]

Perhaps the most curious references to Mary at this critical time are those in which she was rather thinly disguised as Circe, Jezebel, a siren, or some other tempting seductress. In the eyes of the propagandists, Mary seemed to exercise an attraction stronger than mere religious piety and political persuasion in starting traitors and rebels on the road to destruction. The whole tenor of Dr. Parry's *Last Words,* it will be recalled, was his regrettable susceptibility to such seduction. Throckmorton, being again "somewhat pinched" on the rack, confessed to the same weakness; "Nowe I have disclosed the secrets of her who was the deerest thing unto me in the worlde," he exclaims with reference to Mary, and he concludes, "I care not if I were hanged." [93] One of the Latin poems published at Oxford to celebrate the breaking of the Babington plot chided the conspirators for seeking to kill Elizabeth when they might better seek to kill the "Circe" who misled them.[94] In Lodowick Lloyd's *Certaine Englishe Verses,* composed and published on the occasion of the execution of the Babington conspirators, the labored and muddled allusiveness of the poem to such mythological and Biblical figures makes painfully evident the caution with which writers were still handling the problem of Mary on the very eve of pronouncement of sentence against her. Lloyd begins with a general rejoicing at the triumph of Elizabeth over her enemies, but he soon turns to the evil designs of the enemies themselves:

> What thought *Pyragmons* sprats to do, we know,
>   their Romish *Jesebell Naboths* vineyard sought,
> Who like *Medusa* bends her cursed Bow
>   the onlie *Circes,* which hath this mischief wrought.[95]

Having thus branded Mary by association with three of the chief female villains in classical and Biblical literature long since made familiar in anti-Marian propaganda, Lloyd concludes his poem in similar vein by rejoicing that:

> *Circes* cup is falne, *Calipsos* sauce is shed
>   *Balims* blood is bard, their *Harpies* are descried,
> *Cerberus* soppes are found, *Cirens* songs are red
>   thus is *Accaron* knowen, and *Romane* Idoll tried.[96]

If this means anything at all, it indicates that Lloyd knew that after the Babington plot had been disclosed, Mary Stuart's days were numbered. But obviously he wrote before it was permitted to say such a thing in plain English verse.

William Fulke, a Puritan divine, was somewhat more outspoken in the incidental attack he made on Mary in a work published at Cambridge in 1586.[97] Fulke was mainly concerned, even at this late date, with replying to the charges brought years before against Protestant political activities by Peter Frarin in the oration he delivered and published at Louvain at the time of the Rizzio assassination in 1565.[98] Fulke remarks in passing, however, that "the *Scottish Queenes* behaviour hath so much dishonoured her Person, that *Frarine* is to be pardoned, if he spake any thing in her praise, before the uttermost of her reproch was made manifest to the worlde." [99] It is possible that Fulke's attack was published after the pronouncement of sentence in 1586, but even had it appeared before then, such incidental reference was scarcely dangerous for the author of a book mainly concerned with an attack on all Catholics.

From the arrival of Mary in England until final pronouncement of the sentence against her in December, 1586, then, Elizabeth carefully maintained her official attitude of protective benevolence insofar as publicity about the Queen of Scots was concerned. Even in this last year of Mary's life, the English Queen intervened to suppress the publication in London of John Knox's *History of the Reformation in Scotland,* with its highly unflattering portraits of her Scottish cousin.[100] Yet despite this official veil, during these years one can trace the development of the opposition's portrait of Mary in the attacks published openly abroad and surreptitiously in England, and in the allusive references that appeared with increasing frequency as the veil was gradually lifted. At the outset of this long period of Mary's "protective custody" in England, the political necessity of explaining her deposition in Scotland and her detention in England resulted in a highlighting of murder, adultery, and other indications of personal unfitness to rule. Subsequently, to intensify the Protestant campaign against Catholic political action in general, the picture of Mary was enlarged to show her as a treasonable schemer and political enchantress. The result was a portrait that combined the features of Clytemnestra the murderess, and Circe the seductress. If Circe tends to overshadow Clytemnestra toward the end of this period, it is probably because English propagandists were reacting defensively to Mary's increasing involvement in Catholic plots inspired on the Continent. Accordingly, special emphasis was given to her role as the agent of the Catholic powers of Europe who sought to invade England in her name and to restore Catholicism by force. In this connection the propagandists also set forth rather explicitly the legal arguments in favor of executing Mary, arguments for the most part based on the relative sovereignty of the two queens.

Thus it was that when the sentence against Mary was finally

published and Elizabeth's propagandists went to work openly to justify to the world the execution of the Queen of Scots, the themes and materials were ready at hand. Almost overnight the full portrait of Mary as the English saw her, Clytemnestra and Circe together, was licensed for publication to the world.

Meanwhile, during these same years of Mary's stay in England, quite different political and religious forces were working to create a quite different portrait of the Queen of Scots. Before considering the culmination of the English propaganda effort, we must turn back to trace the origin and development of a picture of Mary that is probably no less exaggerated than the English version, but is considerably more attractive.

IV THE DEFENSE OF MARY:

1569-1586

Mary's defenders in England and on the Continent reacted swiftly and strongly to the propaganda attacks launched against her after she came to England. Between 1569 and 1572 alone her supporters produced some half-dozen works in direct reply to the "unauthorized" publications inspired by Elizabeth's government, and the production increased as Mary's imprisonment continued. Like the English attacks on Mary, the works published in her defense were probably more concerned with the basic political and religious situation in Europe than they were with the personal problems of the Queen of Scots herself. Where the English propaganda was primarily to discourage an alliance embracing English Catholics, the Pope, Philip of Spain, and the King of France against England in the name of releasing Mary from Protestant imprisonment, conversely the propaganda in Mary's defense was ultimately to encourage just such an alliance for the restoration of Catholicism in England.

A brief glance at the wavering attitudes toward Mary revealed by many of the Catholic leaders in England and Europe after her flight to England will explain why her zealous Catholic partisans found it essential to counter the English propaganda campaign as strenuously as they could.[1] In England, many Catholics had apparently developed serious reservations about Mary as a result of her hasty marriage to Bothwell following the Darnley murder, and these reservations had not been lessened by the "semi-publicity to her misdoings" disseminated in England and Scotland.[2] When Mary was first taken into English custody, Charles IX of France made sufficiently menacing protests and threatening gestures against the English to cause Elizabeth real concern, but he was obviously hesitant to act against England in the name of the Queen of Scots. As a principal councilor of France told the English ambassador in Paris at this time, "We care not so much as you think what you do with her." [3] Charles himself, when told of Mary's involvement in plots to put her on the throne of England, remarked, "Ah, the poor fool will never cease until she lose her head! In faith they will put her to death. I see it is her own fault and folly. I see no remedy for it. I meant to help, but if she will not be helped, *je ne puis mais*." [4] In Spain, similarly, Philip II's threats to attack England in the name of Mary regularly ended in failure to act at crucial moments; for example, his promises to support the Ridolfi conspiracy were never carried out and the scheme collapsed because, in part at least, of Philip's personal pique against the Pope, who, he complained, "has taken this step without communicating with me in any way, which certainly has greatly surprised me." [5] In the light of such attitudes, Mary's brave hopes of support appear pathetic if not naïve. The realities of international politics undoubtedly had a great deal to do with the lukewarm attitude of the Catholic princes of Europe toward her cause, but English propaganda against her may also have had as much effect as the English ambassadors reported, in making those ashamed to defend her who would. If so, counterpropaganda in favor of her and of the cause of Catholicism in Britain was clearly in order.

The conduct of such a campaign for Mary was not easy, however. In England, while Elizabeth was refusing to authorize books attacking the Scottish Queen, she was at the same time, and far more effectively, also prohibiting the publishing or importing of

books defending her. Proclamations against such books were so
stringently enforced that one Catholic writer, apologizing for the
lack of propaganda support for Mary among the English, could
describe without much exaggeration the

> ... thral, state and servitude, that presently they [Mary's English de-
> fenders] susteyne, having (by severe searches, by suborned accusations,
> by sodaine arrests, by sharp imprisonments, by fraudulent examina-
> tions, and penalties) their handes bounde from writing, sending, or
> receiving.[6]

Abroad, Elizabeth, through her agents, protested so strongly against
the appearance of books in defense of Mary that the governments
concerned, fearing an open break with England, generally agreed
to suppress them.[7] Consequently, Mary's adherents were forced to
resort to such devices as anonymous and pseudonymous authorship,
false imprints, and smuggling. Nonetheless, they managed to secure
remarkably wide circulation for their counterpropaganda, even in
England. A manuscript book defending Mary's right to the succession in England, for example, was surreptitiously "dropped by a
stranger in a place near Guildford Park" and was duly reported
by the finder to an alarmed Privy Council shortly after the Scottish
Queen's arrival in England.[8] As Thomas Norton, one of Elizabeth's
most prolific anti-Catholic propagandists, complained, these "heretical, seditious and traiterous bookes" were licensed abroad, whereupon "good sure men at home, receive these goodly bookes, sprede
them abroade, rede them in audiences and corners, commend
them, geve them great praises for learning and substantialnesse,
as matters unanswerable, they amplifie them, they set them
out. . . ."[9]

   Thus it was that Mary's Catholic supporters at home and abroad
effectively joined the battle of the books on the Queen of Scots.
First in every sense of the word among their publications was
*A Defence of the honour of the right highe, mightye and noble
Princesse Marie Quene of Scotlande and dowager of France, with
a declaration as well of her right, title & intereste to the succession
of the crowne of Englande, as that the regimente of women ys con-
formable to the lawe of God and nature,* written by John Leslie,

Bishop of Ross, and published anonymously in 1569, shortly after
the Queen's arrival in England.[10] Because the *Defence*, which was
to reappear frequently in revised editions to the end of the century,
stands in relation to pro-Marian propaganda much as Buchanan's
Detection stands in relation to anti-Marian propaganda—in each
case the fountainhead of all subsequent argument—the circumstances and content of Leslie's work deserve consideration in some
detail.

John Leslie, among all those who wrote in defense of Mary,
probably was motivated more by personal feeling for her and less
by general concern for the Catholic cause than any of her other
adherents—although certainly the larger political significance of
her situation did not escape him. Through most of his career he
devoted his not inconsiderable talents as clergyman, jurist, and
poet completely to her service and her cause. Born in 1527, he was
educated in Scotland and France. Appointed Bishop of Ross in
1566, he had been one of Mary's closest spiritual and political
advisers since her return to Scotland in 1561. He followed her to
England in 1568, was her chief representative at the conferences
of York and Westminster, served as her agent at Elizabeth's court,
where he repeatedly and at no small risk interceded in her behalf,
and was continuously engaged in schemes to effect her release by
one means or another. Imprisoned and closely examined after the
disclosure of the Ridolfi plot in 1571, in which he was confessedly
deeply involved, he was finally released and allowed to leave England in 1574. The rest of his life—he died in 1596—he spent on
the Continent in ceaseless propagandizing and politicking in behalf of his patroness and her faith.[11]

As its full title indicates, Leslie wrote the *Defence* as a reply to
widely circulated English attacks on Mary's character and career,
on her claim to the succession in England, and on her right as a
woman to rule.[12] Obviously he had in mind, among other specific
books, Buchanan's *Detection*, with its charges of adultery and
murder, for although it was not published until later, the manuscript of the *Detection* had been produced in evidence against
Mary at the York and Westminster conferences, where Leslie was
her principal representative. Leslie testified later, under cross-

examination by Burghley's agents, that a number of Mary's adherents had collaborated in preparing the *Defence,* and there is good reason to believe that she herself had read the manuscript and suggested additions to it, but there seems little doubt that the book in its published form and its numerous revised editions was largely the work of the Bishop of Ross.[13]

Leslie's difficulties in getting his work published provide a case history of the Catholic effort to conduct the campaign of counter-propaganda for Mary in the face of English attempts to suppress such a campaign. The 1569 edition of the *Defence* bears a London imprint, and a few of its pages may have been printed there. But the printing in London had no sooner begun than government agents raided the press and seized what had been started of the work.[14] The book in its final form was probably produced on a Catholic press in Rheims and smuggled back into England.[15] As the harassed printer apologized in an address to the reader, "if thou diddist knowe with what difficulté the imprinting hereof was atchived, thou woldest rather curtouslye of frendlye faueur pardon many greate faultes, than curiouslye withe rigorouse censure to condemne one litle." [16]

The book, which was eventually published despite these difficulties, presented the case for Mary, as the title suggests, in three parts. First, in the *Defence* proper, Leslie seeks to refute the charges of immorality that Scottish and English Protestants had brought against her. He reviews the events in the Darnley-Bothwell affair and attempts to shift the blame from Mary to her accusers, and particularly to her half brother, the Earl of Murray. For the most part he argues from her character and her sex, both of which make it inconceivable, he feels, that such a creature could commit the crimes charged against her. "Thys sexe naturallye abhorrethe suche butcherlye practizes: suerly rare yt ys to heare suche fowle practizes in women," Leslie writes, conveniently ignoring the examples of Jezebel, Clytemnestra, Delilah, and the host of others who crowd the pages of Scottish and English propaganda literature against Mary. Therefore, he continues, "maye we find in our harte to beleave, that yt ys nowe at lengthe fownde in, and practized, by suche a ladye and Princes, from whose person, her noble byrthe, her honorable state, and vertuouse lyfe past, do farre repell and drive awaye, all such suspition and conjecturall presumptions?" [17]

In the same vein he seeks to refute the more specific arguments for Mary's guilt. Against the charge that she hated Lord Darnley and wished him dead, Leslie sets a touching account of the almost motherly affection he claims she bore towards her husband, difficult and undeserving as Leslie admits that Darnley was. The very short mourning period and speedy marriage to Bothwell, which Mary's enemies claimed was proof that she rejoiced in Darnley's death, Leslie explains—rather naïvely, it would seem—as ordered by Mary's doctor, who feared that prolonged grief would impair her health.[18] To refute the charge that she wrote the Casket Letters that implicated her with Bothwell in the murder, Leslie argues that the letters must have been forged by her enemies, for epistles of such coarse obscenity could never have been written by one so wise, so virtuous, and so refined as the Queen of Scots.[19] As for her marriage to Bothwell, Leslie explains that Mary agreed to it only because she was frightened by the violence around her, was misled by her enemies into believing Bothwell innocent of the murder, and was generally bewildered by villains the like of which her innocent nature had never before had to deal with.[20]

While demonstrating to his own satisfaction that Mary was by character incapable of committing the crimes charged against her, Leslie at the same time tries to show that Murray in particular, and the heretic rebels in general, were quite capable of doing just such things. Leslie makes much of the Earl's illegitimate birth as a basis for arguing that so disreputable a character might well be expected to have committed all the crimes falsely charged against Mary.[21] More specifically, he asserts that Murray directed the murder of Rizzio, persuaded Bothwell to kill Darnley, and then urged Mary to wed Bothwell so that, public opinion being thereby revolted, Murray would have excuse to drive the Queen from her throne—all in order, Leslie concludes, "to turne the blame of the fault from him selfe upon his good ladie and Quene, from whose person yt ys farthiest." [22]

Although Murray may be the one "whom above all other, we

have to charge and burden," Leslie assigns no little of the blame to the political theories and practices he regards as characteristic of rebel heretics in general. He assails their notions of popular sovereignty and the rights of a subject people to depose a ruler as ideas contrary to all the laws of God and Nature. Where in Scripture, he asks, is there authority to depose kings?

I find there that kinge David was both an adoulterer, and also a murtherer, I finde that God was highelie displeased with hym therefore. Yet finde I not that he was therefore by his subjects deposed.[23]

In view of his vehement denial of the charges of murder and adultery brought against Mary, Leslie's choice of David as an example of royal inviolability seems unhappy, to say the least. It served, however, to emphasize the extent of the crime against divine law which in his opinion the rebel heretics had committed when for any reason they deposed the Queen of Scots. The deposing of Mary he regarded as a blow to royal sovereignty everywhere, and he was convinced that the kings of the earth—the Catholic kings in particular—would not tolerate such a threat to their own authority:

. . . other Princes will judge and take yt to towche them to nighe, to suffer suche a villainie to passe and escape unrevenged, and so good a ladye to be left destitute and desolate. The emperour will not beare yt: France will not beare yt, Spaine will not beare yt . . .[24]

From this defense of Mary's character and sovereignty in the first part of his treatise, Leslie turns in the second part to a somewhat more technical and legalistic justification of her claims to the succession in England. Written mainly as an answer to John Hales' manuscript *Declaration of the Succession,* and to the anonymous, printed *Allegations against the Surmisid Title of the Quine of Scots,* Leslie's reply is organized as a refutation of the two principal points raised in these attacks on Mary's claim.[25] The two earlier tracts had argued, first, that she was excluded from the succession in England because she was a "foreigner"; and second, that she was also excluded by the will of Henry VIII, who, according to the argument, fixed the succession in England, should his own line fail, in the line of his younger sister Mary and not in the line of his elder sister Margaret, grandmother of the Queen of Scots. Leslie begins his rebuttal by asserting that, regardless of her rights, Mary Stuart has the excellence of character that would make her worthy to succeed to the throne in any realm, including England. Then he turns to the legal and historical arguments that prove, as he sees them, that Mary is not an alien nor ineligible on that score. Finally he proceeds to show that the will by which Henry was supposed to have determined the succession was either a forgery or, if not that, had been tampered with after his death by parties interested in excluding Mary. Thus, Leslie concludes, it is as natural for Mary to return to rule England, in the event of Elizabeth's death without issue, as it is for a spring to return to its source.[26]

The third part of Leslie's *Defence,* dealing with the right of women to govern realms, needs little attention here. In the main it is a point-by-point refutation of the arguments advanced against women rulers in John Knox's celebrated and ill-timed *First Blast of the Trumpet against the Monstruous Regiment of Women,* published in 1558 as an attack on Catholic Mary Tudor a few months before the Protestant Elizabeth came to the throne. As even Leslie himself admits, refutations of the *First Blast* were unnecessary by 1569.[27] Certainly Queen Elizabeth's Protestant subjects were not going to make a point of Mary's sex in arguing against her right to rule. Queen Elizabeth herself had long since made it emphatically clear that arguments based on femininity were not in order.

Such was the threefold nature of Leslie's major contribution to the defense of Mary in the literary warfare. In its insistence on the innocence and moral uprightness of the Scottish Queen, the legitimacy of her claims to the English succession, and the villainy of heretic rebels in general and of Murray in particular, the 1569 edition of the *Defence* develops the main lines of argument introduced in the literature defending Mary during her last years in Scotland. Here, as earlier, the Queen of Scots appears as the innocent victim of sinister forces, a devoted wife, a loving mother, a woman too pure to be capable even of conceiving the crimes charged to her, and a queen concerned only with what she and her supporters considered her legitimate claims and the happiness and welfare of others.

In the light of subsequent developments in the propaganda campaign, however, certain features of the argument peculiar to this earliest version of the *Defence* need special note. In the first place, Leslie avoided at this time making an issue of Mary's religious faith. Although reviling the political theories and practices of the Scottish Protestants, he did not present Mary's case explicitly as a religious issue between Protestant and Catholic faiths, as he was to do later, but rather as a political issue between rebel subjects and a sovereign queen. Second, in arguing for Mary's right to succeed to the English throne, Leslie in 1569 did not question Elizabeth's right to occupy that throne as long as she lived; he insisted that Mary's claim would become operative only if and when Elizabeth died without issue. And third, he is practically obsequious in his reference to the English Queen in this earliest version of the *Defence*. She is "our most dreade sovereigne" and "our gratiouse Queene" whom he hopes that God will long preserve and bless with happy issue.[28] On each of these points, Leslie himself, and all of Mary's apologists after him, were soon to experience a considerable change of heart.

Meanwhile, the arguments developed by Leslie and the picture of Mary portrayed by him were reproduced in a number of other works published during the first years of her imprisonment. Many of the same points were made, for example, in a pro-Marian account of the Northern Rebellion published in France early in 1570 with the announced purpose of arousing the French government to support "the reestablishment of the Catholic religion in England" and to relieve "the piteous and deplorable state of the Queen of Scots."[29] This account was effective enough as propaganda to cause Elizabeth's government to make strenuous efforts to have the work suppressed in France, and to inspire Burghley himself to write a reply to this "false and scandalous book lately published in France."[30]

Even more distressing to the English—and especially to Burghley —was *A Treatise of Treasons against Q. Elizabeth and the Crowne of England* which appeared anonymously without any indication of place or privilege of publication in January, 1572.[31] Written mainly as a reply to R. G.'s attack on Mary and Norfolk in his *Salutem in Christo,* the tract seeks first to exonerate the Queen of Scots of any complicity in the Northern Rebellion and the Ridolfi conspiracy, with which some English accounts had charged her. Then, in a second part of his treatise, the author "discovereth greater Treasons committed that are by few perceived." It is here that he departs in one important respect from the line of argument developed by Leslie and earlier writers. These latter, it will be recalled, had made the Earl of Murray the villain of the story of Mary. But the Earl had been assassinated in 1570, and, since Mary's troubles continued in spite of this removal of her alleged worst enemy, a new villain had to be found. The "greater Treasons" discovered by the author of the *Treatise,* accordingly, are presented as those of Burghley himself, and of Nicholas Bacon, Lord Keeper of the Great Seal and father of the celebrated Sir Francis Bacon. Both these advisers of Elizabeth are blamed for fomenting all the seditions and rebellions attributed to Mary, and both are accused of scheming in their "greater Treasons" to overthrow Mary and Elizabeth alike in favor of the house of Suffolk, descended from Henry VIII's younger sister Mary and kinsmen of the two privy councilors named in this accusation.

So far as the Queen of Scots was concerned, the author of the *Treatise of Treasons* was more interested in discrediting those who had attacked her than he was in defending her character and honor as Leslie had done. Obviously he was well read in English propaganda literature about Mary, for he cites specifically, in addition to the *Salutem in Christo* of R. G., such works as *A Discourse touching the pretended Matche,* Fleetwood's *The effect of the declaration,* Knox's *First Blast of the Trumpet,* Buchanan's *Detection,* a variety of occasional ballads and songs, and other literature published officially or unofficially by the anti-Marian parties. He was also quite aware that, despite Elizabeth's disclaimers, the "unauthorized" publications were officially inspired, and that their ultimate purpose with regard to Mary was "to spot her honour, to reproche and defame her for an Aduoutresse, a murderer, a

Papist, a Competitour to [Elizabeth's] Crowne, and whatsoever els could be thought on more odious." [32] In reply to such charges, the anonymous writer, like Leslie, shifts the blame for the crimes imputed to Mary to Protestant villains in general and in particular, but in so doing manages to maintain a conciliatory attitude toward Elizabeth. He insists that Mary's claim to succeed Elizabeth does not derogate from Elizabeth's present right and title, and he goes beyond Leslie in expressing concern for Elizabeth's welfare and confidence in her essential justice. He is even persuaded that once freed from the baleful influence of Burghley and Bacon, she would of her own accord return to the fold of the Catholic church.[33] Finally, although he again goes far beyond Leslie in excoriating Protestant heretics in general, he is as careful as Leslie to avoid the outright charge that Mary is being persecuted because of her religion. Rather, she and Elizabeth alike, according to the author of the *Treatise*, are victims of the purely political schemes and ambitions of two men who seek to gain for themselves the complete control of Britain.

As one would expect, reactions to the *Treatise* from the English government, in which Burghley was virtually prime minister and Bacon an eminent adviser, were explosively prompt and violent. Elizabeth issued a proclamation vigorously denouncing the book, forbidding it to her subjects, demanding that it be burned, and reaffirming her faith in her two maligned councilors.[34] Burghley adopted a tone of injured innocence. In an unsuccessful protest to Catherine de' Medici, the queen mother and power behind the throne in France where he suspected the book had been published, he conveniently forgot his own conspicuous part in the publication of Buchanan's *Detection* and remarked indignantly that "this licentiousness, to inveigh against men by name in printed books, who did not themselves use by books to provoke any, was in all good estates intolerable." [35] Despite such protests as these, however, the *Treatise of Treasons* apparently had a considerable circulation in England as well as on the Continent. As the historian Camden wrote some years later, after describing English efforts to suppress copies of the book, "Notwithstanding, through a speciall vice, very incident to the naturall curiosity of men, they were frequently read, till (as it ordinarily falls out) coming at last to be neglected and contemned, the use of them grew out of request." [36]

The language of the *Treatise of Treasons* and a lengthy prefatory address to the English reader demonstrate beyond doubt that the work, though published perforce on the Continent, was directed mainly to whatever reading public in the British Isles it could reach. Meanwhile, Mary Stuart's apologists apparently deemed it expedient to distribute in Europe a work similarly designed to counteract the English propaganda against Mary. Accordingly, an anonymous publication in French appeared very shortly after the *Treatise* in 1572 with the descriptive title, *L'Innocence de la Tres-illustre, Tres-chaste, & Debonnaire Princesse, Madame Marie Royne d'Escosse.*[37] The authorship of *L'Innocence* is still uncertain, despite strenuous efforts by English agents at the time to determine it. One of those suspected of writing it denied the charge successfully with the indignant remark, "If I had been a participant thereof, it would have carried some mark of greater learning." [38] Two of the three parts of the work are literal translations of the *Treatise of Treasons;* to these is joined a detailed, point-by-point reply to the French translation of Buchanan's *Detection*, which had been published in the same year.

The author-translator of *L'Innocence*, in assembling his diverse materials, was thoroughly aware of the larger political issues at stake in the defense of Mary. Realizing that the English propaganda attacks had been published for the purpose of making Mary odious to the French King and thereby of dissuading him from acting against England in her behalf, the author expressly designed *L'Innocence* to counteract this influence.[39] To an even greater degree than Leslie, he places much of the blame for Mary's troubles on the seditious political theories of rebel Protestants, and points to their treatment of the Queen of Scots as a warning to sovereign princes everywhere against tolerating heretics.[40] Accordingly, his picture of Mary is more clearly calculated to stimulate sympathy and support for her than any that had appeared thus far.

To this end he adds some original and colorful details to arouse

French sensibilities in her behalf. In *L'Innocence* she is the naïve, helpless, and somewhat bewildered heroine who, ignorant of Bothwell's participation in the murder of her husband, accepted the Earl because she had nowhere else to turn. Somewhat contradictorily, however, her apologist observes, in arguing against her authorship of the Casket Letters, that she was too shrewd a woman to have committed to paper such ideas as the Letters contained, even had she been capable of entertaining them.[41] Elsewhere he argues that if Mary received Rizzio privately in her chambers, as her enemies charged, it was only because, according to the author, she had been reared in France where the "Honneste liberté des Dames Françoises" prevailed.[42] The "estrangement" between Mary and Darnley, which her enemies exploited as evidence of her motive in participating in his murder, the author does not deny; he explains it as merely a petty quarrel, such as is common to every domestic arrangement. He goes on to add, again somewhat contradictorily, that any real trouble that did exist between the two was fomented by the rebel Protestants.[43] On the subject of Mary's rather truncated period of mourning for Darnley, the author disagrees with Leslie, who blamed her doctor and her precarious health; according to *L'Innocence,* a longer period of mourning for Darnley would have been inappropriate, since he was not a king in his own right, and Mary, says the author, was always nicely sensitive to matters of protocol, as befitted a true queen.[44] Finally, he remarks, with an appearance of logic, that it is odd of Mary's detractors to accuse this "lone, weak woman," without forces of her own, of causing more revolts and bloodshed than the whole Scottish army.[45] He does not refer, however, to the large Catholic forces that fought for her at Carberry hill, brought about her release from Lochleven, and fought again for her at Langside—all with considerable bloodshed.

Leslie's *Defence,* the *Treatise of Treasons,* and *L'Innocence* were the principal works that carried the counterattack against English propaganda between 1569 and 1572, but they were by no means the only works issued by Mary's Catholic apologists in these years. A number of slighter publications developed special aspects of the case for the defense. Thus in what was purported to be a copy of a letter written by the Queen of Scots from her prison at Sheffield, published at Paris "Avec Privilege" in 1572, Mary is made to describe the afflictions she claimed to suffer at the hands of Protestant heretics in an apparent bid for sympathy and support from the French King.[46] Meanwhile, in Scotland there were still active elements supporting the Queen, and accordingly a need for propaganda that might rally support for her friends there. The years from 1570 to 1573 were especially crucial for Mary's party in Scotland. Under the militant leadership of William Kirkaldy of Grange and William Maitland of Lethington, her followers seized control of Edinburgh Castle in 1571. In this key position, which they held until the Castle was besieged and taken by English forces in 1573, Mary's followers could hope to regain power and restore her to her throne in Scotland. It was probably to justify their cause and to win support both at home and abroad that two brief works in defense of the Queen of Scots were published in this period.

The first of these was published in 1572 with the title *The Copie of a Letter writen out of Scotland, by an English Gentleman . . . unto a frind . . . that desired to be informed of the truth and circumstances of the slaunderous and infamous reportes made of the Quene of Scotland, at that time restreined in maner as prisoner in England, upon pretense to be culpable of the same.*[47] Characteristically, the lengthy title describes the content and purpose of the book far more accurately than it designates the authorship and circumstances of publication, for it was apparently written not by "an English Gentleman," but by the ubiquitous John Leslie, a good Scotsman, and it came not from Scotland, but in all probability from the great Catholic center of Louvain. In content, the published letter is a summary of the arguments for Mary's innocence in the Darnley murder and Bothwell marriage much as Leslie had set forth the case in his earlier *Defence.* A concluding "Exhortation to those Noblemen of Scotland, that remaine yet mainteiners and defenders of the unnatural and dishonorable practices against the Queene" strongly suggests that Leslie, by making his defense of Mary appear to come from a neutral Protestant source, hoped to win support for her party in Scotland by subverting at least some of her foes.

An earlier defense of Mary's party in Scotland based on slightly different grounds had been widely circulated in manuscript form in 1571. This was "Ane Ballat of Ye Captane of the Castell," an analysis of the reasons that Mary's party continued to hold Edinburgh Castle against English attack in a last desperate stand in her behalf.[48] The author was probably William Kirkaldy of Grange, one of her most ardent supporters and a principal defender of the Castle. In his "Ballat" Kirkaldy mainly develops the familiar theme that Mary was unjustly deposed by rebel heretics whose doctrines of popular sovereignty are a threat to kings everywhere. He frankly admits Mary's misdeeds, but he explains that they were God's punishment on the Scottish people for fostering the Protestant heresy; God then punished Mary, in turn, by raising the Protestant lords as His scourge against her. Now that she is penitent she must be restored and the scourges themselves destroyed. Kirkaldy clearly penned his "Ballat" with the propagandistic intention of attracting aid from abroad for Mary's party in Scotland. Professing to be divinely inspired, he says:

> I heard one say within this place:
>   'With help of God and France
> I shall, within an little space,
>   Thy dolours all to dress.'

Like most of the appeals by Mary's supporters for foreign aid, Kirkaldy's great expectations were in vain. The only foreign intervention in the struggle for Edinburgh Castle came in 1573 in the form of an English army, under Sir William Drury, which ended the siege and also the hopes for Mary's party in Scotland.

Compared with what was soon to appear, the literature to arouse action in Mary's behalf during the first years of her imprisonment in England was relatively moderate and restrained in its treatment of both the Queen of Scots and the Queen of England. Mary is portrayed as the archetype of injured innocence, but culprits other than Elizabeth are found. In the vindication of Mary's character and conduct there is little reference to her Catholic faith and piety. The touchy subject of her religion is carefully avoided for the most part. At this stage, she is presented as a sovereign queen illegally deposed for false political reasons, and not as a martyr for her faith. Moreover, regarding her claim to the succession in England, the writers insist (contrary to what the plots confessedly hoped to accomplish) that her right to succeed must not be interpreted as the right to possess the throne that is still regarded as legitimately Elizabeth's. Apparently the hope continued to be held at this time that Elizabeth herself might be won over to the cause of Mary, and perhaps even to the cause of Catholicism. Hence the English Queen is praised in terms that on occasion rise to the level of the most sycophantic Elizabethan court poetry. She is addressed as a possible associate and not, as later, as the target of a coalition of Christian princes called to redress the injuries to sovereignty that the treatment of Mary by Protestant foes represented in Catholic eyes.

But by 1572 it was apparent that in terms of arousing the desired reaction this kind of propaganda campaign had failed. There could have been only small consolation in the knowledge that these early works had at least frightened and enraged Elizabeth's government. The fact remained that in 1572 Mary was still a prisoner in England, more strictly held than ever. At crucial moments—during the Northern Rebellion and the Ridolfi conspiracy, for example— France, Spain, and even the Papacy had failed to act in the cause that Mary represented. Elizabeth's gestures in the direction of releasing and restoring her royal cousin had come to nothing. It was also apparent by this time that the English Queen had no intention of forsaking either her Protestant councilors or her Protestant faith, and that she was taking increasingly severe measures against Catholics in general. Accordingly, as the campaign for Mary and for Catholicism continued in the pro-Marian literature after 1572, the conciliatory attitude toward England and Elizabeth gave way rather rapidly to increasing hostility and indignation.

Evidence of the changing propaganda line can be found as early as 1571 in Leslie's revision of his *Defence*, published under the title *A Treatise concerning the Defence of the Honour of . . . Marie*.[49] When he had published his original *Defence*, in 1569, he had apparently foreseen the need for continued revision and adaptation of the work to meet changing condtions. Shortly after the original treatise appeared, one of his henchmen confessed to English authorities that the Bishop had retained a copy of the manuscript "to be amended, translated, or changed as occasion should require." [50] The new version that appeared was admittedly prepared as propaganda to bolster the Ridolfi conspiracy in 1571. A number of copies were found on one Charles Bailley, an agent of Mary, when he was seized upon trying to enter England with final plans for the projected uprising, and Bailey subsequently confessed that the new version had been timed, at Leslie's own behest, to justify the Catholic action.[51] Needless to say, English agents rigidly suppressed all the copies they could find, and, although Leslie had sought to cover his tracks by publishing the book abroad under the pseudonym of "Morgan Philippes," they quickly detected the author and threw him in prison.

The English seem to have been as much disturbed by the increased hostility toward Elizabeth and her right to the throne manifested in the new edition of Leslie's treatise as by its connection with the Ridolfi conspiracy. William Cecil, now Lord Burghley, complained, after comparing the two editions, that the text was altered "from the former copy, and there are sundry points in it that maketh against the Queen's majeste, in the book of the successione, and sundrie untrewthis in the defens of the honour." [52] Actually, the text of the three main parts of the work remained very much as it was in the original *Defence*, but in two striking ways Leslie displayed a markedly cooler attitude toward the Queen of England. In the first place, he deleted all the ingratiating epithets that characterized his reference to her in the original. For example, the addresses to "my gracious sovereign" and "our gratious Queene" became simply "the Queen," or, more ominously, "the Queen that now is." These and others like them were minute changes, of course, but their total effect on the tone of the book is remarkable, and this is probably what alarmed Burghley. In the second place, Leslie completely rewrote, and greatly expanded, his original preface "To the Reader" in such a way that, although not yet suggesting that Elizabeth was a usurper, still he indicated that he regarded Mary as Elizabeth's *only* heir, whatever issue the English Queen might have.[53] Again, the resulting change in tone is sufficient to reveal not only Leslie's intention of fortifying the Ridolfi conspiracy, but also what must have been his dawning awareness by this time that Catholics in general and Mary's supporters in particular could expect little aid and comfort from the English Queen.

In addition to the increased hostility to Elizabeth and England revealed in his revision of the *Defence,* Leslie also now began introducing into his new propaganda the suggestion that Mary was being persecuted for purely religious reasons; that she was suffering for her faith and not for political reasons alone—subjects hitherto left implicit in pro-Marian literature. In 1574 Leslie was released from the Tower of London, where he had been held because of his revised *Defence* and his part in the Ridolfi conspiracy. He went at once to the Continent, probably at the request of English authorities, and there promptly resumed his publishing efforts in Mary's behalf. The first of his works was a series of Latin poems, purportedly exchanged between Mary and Leslie during his imprisonment, and published in Paris in 1574.[54] Although mainly illustrating the fundamental truth that misery loves company, the poems also celebrate Mary's piety and her loyalty to her faith in the face of hostile circumstances. Leslie emphasizes her fortitude and patience under trial as evidence of her piety, and, after citing numerous examples of Biblical martyrs who were sustained by their faith, he concludes that Mary, too, will find within herself the faith that will enable her to triumph over her enemies in this world.[55] In a shrewd thrust obviously aimed at recent Protestant propaganda against Mary in the English-inspired publication of Buchanan's *Detection,* Leslie also quotes here the lines of praise Buchanan himself had written in 1566 before he turned against the Queen of Scots.[56]

The assurance that if Mary remained loyal to her faith she could expect eventual release from her imprisonment is found, strangely enough, in an *Oration* Leslie addressed to Elizabeth and published in this same year.[57] The *Oration* is a formal expression of gratitude for his own release from the Tower, apparently prepared in the naïve hope that Elizabeth would respond with some kind of financial assistance, which Leslie, fresh out of prison, desperately need-ed.[58] But the work, being mainly a catalogue of Mary's pious virtues, is so obviously an appeal for the release of the Queen of Scots that one wonders how seriously Leslie could have hoped for rewards from Elizabeth for his efforts.[59] Appended to the *Oration* is a poem addressed to Mary herself, again praising her religious fortitude and promising her release; such lines could hardly have been reassuring to the English Queen to whom the volume was addressed.[60] Judged in terms of Elizabeth's completely negative response to its twofold request for money for himself and release for his Catholic patroness, Leslie's *Oration* is probably the most remarkably unsuccessful piece of literature that he produced.

From this emphasis on Mary's fortitude and patience under ad-versity it was only a short step to emphasis on the faith for which she suffered and the inevitable theme of religious martyrdom. This step Leslie took firmly and definitely in 1578 when he published in Rome his celebrated Latin *History of Scotland*.[61] In dedicating the last three books of this history to Mary, Leslie practically traces his own development as a propagandist, reminding her that:

When many, Most Illustrious, knew by me in how great misery was your grace, how fraudfully ye were invaded and closed with calamity on every side, they were, surely, sorely moved. But when they understood all your trouble chiefly therefor to be, that in the Catholic Religion ever ye remained so constant, ever with such courage the self religion defended, not only your case lamented they not, but setting aside all dolor, rejoiced of your piety, your constance, your courage.[62]

Adhering to the Renaissance notion that history should be written to teach political lessons, Leslie explains to Mary—and, in a sep-arate address, to the nobility and people of Scotland—that his account is designed to show that Scotland has always prospered when it remained loyal to the Catholic church and that the country should therefore return to the old faith. For Mary's benefit in particular he emphasizes the stories of Scottish kings who suffered for their faith, and who were rewarded by God with greater bless-ings and dignities, both spiritual and temporal. Thus, he concludes, the history is designed not only for her profit, but also for her com-fort and consolation in adversity.[63]

As he had foreseen, Leslie also continued through the years to revise and republish parts of the *Defence* for wider and more influential audiences. In 1580 he rewrote in Latin both the second part, the defense of Mary's claim to the English succession, and the third part, the defense of government by women, for publication at the great Catholic center of Rheims.[64] Thereafter, he concentrated on Mary's English title, translating his own Latin treatise on the subject into English in 1584, and into both French and Spanish in 1587.[65] By this time he was expressly seeking to arouse the most powerful of the Continental Catholic princes to fight for the restoration of Catholicism in England in the name of the martyred Queen of Scots.

Again, there are a number of points about Leslie's successive revisions that are indicative of the whole trend of pro-Marian writing after 1572. First and most obvious is that in these later versions he dropped his original defense of Mary against the charges of murder and adultery. On both sides of the battle, the question of her moral conduct was receding before more immediately relevant political and religious issues. As we have seen, Protestant propaganda against Mary was shifting its emphasis to a denunciation of her activities that could be called treasonable. Correspondingly, her Catholic defenders were shifting their emphasis to her faith, and her sufferings for her faith. In this connection, a second feature of Leslie's later revisions becomes significant. He explicitly directs these new versions to the Catholic princes of Europe in the hope that, moved by pity for the plight of a suffering coreligionist, they will come to her aid with either political or military pressures, or preferably with both. Thus in 1580 and 1584 he addresses both the Latin and the English versions of his treatise on Mary's title to the crown of England not only to the Emperor Rudolph and the Catholic princes of Europe but also to the Pope who, Leslie argues, should "defend her as his daughter, whiche neyther by straitnesse of prison, nor by any kinde of affliction could be hitherto seduced from honoring him as her father." [66]

Finally, it should be noted that during the early 1580's Leslie, like other Catholic propagandists, held high hopes that Mary's son James, King of Scotland, might be won over to the Catholic cause and thus become as firm a foundation for the restoration of the faith in Britain as his mother. Accordingly, Leslie included James in all his revised arguments for Mary's right to the succession in England and, in the 1584 English version of his work, even went as far as to include the young Scottish King in the main title of *A Treatise tovvching the Right, Title and Interest of the most excellent Princesse Marie, Queene of Scotland, And of the most noble king James, her Graces sonne, to the succession of the Croune of England.* James's brief flirtation with Rome and France, which lay behind these high hopes, was short-lived, however, and in 1586 he became a pensioner of the English Queen, beyond Catholic control or interest. Accordingly, in the revisions of his treatise that appeared after 1586, Leslie withdrew his support of the Scottish King's right to succeed his mother.[67]

Considering Leslie's exaltation of Mary's faith and piety in his later reworkings of his material, it is not surprising to find that at the same time he heightens even more the hostile attitude toward Elizabeth that had characterized his first revision of the *Defence* in 1571. Although still not claiming that Elizabeth was a usurper of the throne that rightfully belonged to Mary, as some of his contemporaries were doing, Leslie nonetheless continued to qualify his original declaration that Mary's right depended on Elizabeth's death without issue. His hostility is pointed up by some Latin verses signed "T. St." which prefaced the 1580 version of his treatise on the title, and which were translated by one "T. V. Englishman" in the English version of the work that appeared in 1584.[68] The unidentified contributor to Leslie's volumes, after sketching Mary's genealogical right to the succession in England, proclaims the Scottish Queen as heir to Elizabeth whether the latter has issue or not, and hints that the change will probably be for the better. Referring to Mary, he urges the "Nobility and people of England and Scotland" to

> Regard the right of her, who once may ryse
> And rule in state: your Quene to heavens resigned.
> That onlie Realm is in most happie state,
> Whiche beares no Tyrannes rule, nor blody hand:

> And whose renowmed Prince doeth evell hate,
> And rules in peace the people of her land.

Leslie's contributor clearly felt as strongly as Leslie himself that Elizabeth, whatever her rights of present possession, stood in the way of the blessedness of Britain.

John Leslie's propagandistic efforts for his patroness and benefactress apparently ended with the publication of his French and Spanish translations of the defense of her title to England, in 1587, the year of her death. His subsequent silence perhaps attests the measure of personal devotion that lay behind his previous activities. Unlike many of her apologists, who continued to use Mary's glamorous name in the cause of Catholicism long after she was dead, Leslie gave up the fight when the Queen herself was gone. His defense of her honor, his justification of her claims, and his arguments in behalf of a woman in politics seem to have sprung as much from a regard for her personal well-being as from a concern for the church in which he was bishop. It does not diminish his devotion to his faith to emphasize this devotion to his Queen and friend. Rather, the intensity of his personal feelings may go far to explain the forcefulness that made his publications a determining influence in Marian literature in his own day, and a considerable factor in the historical writing about Mary ever since.[69]

The alteration in Mary's situation which had progressively moved Leslie to his more impassioned expression was meanwhile similarly affecting other writers at home and abroad. Ronsard, for example, who a decade before had eulogized both Mary and Elizabeth in equally glowing terms in a single poem, had by 1578 taken a decidedly hostile attitude toward the English Queen. In a volume of poems published in that year and dedicated to the Queen of Scots, he threatened that, unless Elizabeth mitigated her wrath, the heroes of France would take up the cause of the beauteous Scottish Queen now so barbarously treated in England.[70]

The true successor to Leslie as Mary's principal sixteenth-century apologist, however, was already beginning to come into prominence while the Bishop of Ross was still at the height of his activity in the 1570's. This was Adam Blackwood, whose classic account of the martyrdom of the Queen of Scots, *Martyre de la Royne d'Escosse,* published in the year of Mary's death, was to stand side by side with Leslie's *Defence* as a principal source of pro-Marian argument for future historians. Yet even before the appearance of his *Martyre,* Blackwood's published poems and pamphlets had established him as the propagandist destined to develop to new extremes the main lines of argument laid down by Leslie.

Blackwood's life was almost as closely linked with Mary's in a personal way as was Leslie's.[71] Through most of his varied career as student, poet, lawyer, and Catholic apologist, Blackwood enjoyed the friendship, the literary patronage, and the generous munificence of the Queen of Scots. Born in Dumferline in 1539, he was brought up there by his uncle, the Catholic Bishop of Orkney. Thanks to a gift from Mary, who was then the queen of Francis II, Blackwood was able to complete his education at the University of Paris. After two years of law study at Toulouse, he returned to Paris in 1560 to teach philosophy. Except for brief visits abroad, usually in Mary's cause, he spent the rest of his life in France.

At about the time that Mary abdicated and fled to England in 1568, Blackwood began to emerge as a prominent spokesman in her party on the Continent. He worked closely with her ambassador in Paris, Archbishop Beaton, and made frequent trips to England to visit her. According to the publisher of his complete works in 1644, nothing was done by her agents and representatives without the advice and participation of Blackwood.[72] In a series of Latin poems written during the first few years of Mary's imprisonment, Blackwood excoriated the heretics who had deposed her, appealed to the French and to Catholics everywhere to rise in her defense, and stoutly argued for the title and the honor of the queen whom he later referred to as "the Queen who considers me her own poet." [73] Blackwood's efforts must have been very effective as propaganda for Mary even at this early stage of his career, since the Privy Council in Scotland found it necessary, in February, 1573/4, to include him in a list of "traitors abroad" who stirred up trouble against King James by actions, letters, and books on behalf of the King's mother.[74]

Unperturbed by such strictures, Blackwood increased his activities in defense of Mary. In 1575 he dedicated to her his first major published work, the first two books of *De Vinculo,* a treatise arguing the necessity of Roman Catholicism as a state religion.[75] This work so impressed Mary's ambassador, Archbishop Beaton, that he prevailed upon the Scottish Queen to reward Blackwood with the post of judge in the parliament of Poitiers, the disposal of which Mary had received as part of her dowry settlement with the French.[76] Blackwood's literary efforts for Mary during her lifetime culminated in 1581 with the publication of his celebrated *Pro Regibus Apologia,* an apology for kings written in reply to George Buchanan's equally celebrated defense of the right of the Scots to depose and elect their kings, *De iure regni apud Scotos.*[77] Blackwood's treatise still stands as one of the important documents in the development of the theory of the divine right of kings, just as Buchanan's stands in the development of republicanism and resistance to royal authority. More specifically, as Buchanan's work was a justification of the deposition of Mary by her subjects, so Blackwood's reply was a defense of her sovereignty and her cause against attacks by those he considered rebel heretics.

Blackwood's most important and influential publications in behalf of the Queen of Scots and her Catholic cause were to appear after her death in 1587, and will be considered in their proper place below.[78] But the main outlines of his later and sensationally effective propaganda campaign were already visible in the works he produced during the Queen's imprisonment. Given the circumstances, we should perhaps not be surprised to find that the themes and arguments he developed in these earlier poems and treatises were substantially those that Leslie was emphasizing at about the same time. Blackwood's works, however, reflect something of the growing bitterness and violence of the propaganda battle during the decade before Mary's death. More angrily and at greater length than Leslie, Blackwood excoriates the heretics who betrayed her. Such, for example, was the theme and mood of one of his earliest poems on Mary Stuart, bearing the descriptive title, "For the Queen of Scots when, her son being taken from her by impious rebels, she fled to England in hope and expectation of promised aid." [79] More openly than Leslie he praises Mary's Catholicism and hints that she is being persecuted only because of her religion and not because of her political activities. More urgently than Leslie he calls on the Catholic powers of Europe to release the Queen of Scots and restore Catholicism to Britain. One of his poems, for example, is addressed "To the most Christian King Henri III of France, that, moved by brotherly affection, he undertake the liberation of the Queen of Scots, for so many years cruelly and tyrannically held in England against the law of nations." [80] Finally, although not yet reviling Elizabeth in the opprobious terms he was to use after 1587, Blackwood is hostile in the few references he makes to the English Queen, and, like Leslie in his later works, drops all pretense of seeking to win aid and comfort for Mary by flattering Elizabeth.

Blackwood's works reflect the mounting fury of the campaign for Mary which, even before her execution, reached its climax in the accounts of the Queen of Scots given in Catholic martyrologies. These collections of the lives of faithful Catholics who had suffered at the hands of Protestants began to appear with increasing frequency after 1572. At the outset they were probably intended as the Catholic answer to John Foxe's enormously successful book of Protestant martyrs, the *Actes and Monuments*. But as the English began to apply stronger pressure against Catholics in the realm, the martyrologies came increasingly to support the Catholic argument that English members of the faith were persecuted not for political reasons, as Elizabeth's government claimed, but solely for their religious beliefs. Mary Stuart, as the most celebrated of such cases, inevitably occupied a prominent place in all these Catholic martyrologies.

One of the first and most influential of the Catholic martyrologists was Nicholas Sanders, an English recusant who taught at Louvain and Rome, worked in Madrid for the dethronement of Elizabeth, and died in Ireland while seeking to arouse Irish Catholics against the English. As early as 1571 he had recounted the sufferings of Mary in England in a martyrology, published at Louvain, which has been described as the first attempt to compile a descriptive list of the clergy and laity who endured exile or imprisonment for the Roman faith.[81] Then, before he died in 1581, Sanders completed another work that presented Mary's history in the same light; published posthumously in 1585 and again in 1587, his "Rise and Growth of the Anglican Schism" is ostensibly a history of the progress of heresy in England, but it is presented mainly in terms of the sufferings endured there by loyal Catholics, Mary Stuart prominent among them.[82]

In both of his accounts of the Queen of Scots, Sanders exercises a martyrologist's privilege in taking certain liberties with facts. Perhaps the most striking example of this appears in his treatment of Queen Elizabeth. Where Leslie and even Blackwood were cool but cautious in their references to the English Queen, Sanders makes her the chief villain of the piece. He publishes for the first time, and as fact, a mixture of fact, legend, and conjecture about her that was to become basic material in much of the literature produced by Mary's apologists after her execution. He was, for example, probably the first propagandist to print the story that Elizabeth was the child of a union that was not only adulterous, as all Catholics have held Henry's connection with Anne to be, but bigamous and incestuous as well. This complex state of affairs came about, according to Sanders, because Anne Boleyn was the offspring of an affair Henry VIII had with the wife of Thomas Boleyn; then, while still married to Katherine of Aragon in the eyes of the Catholic church, Henry proceeded to have an adulterous affair in an incestuous relationship with his daughter Anne, a union later disguised as a marriage that was at best bigamous. To Sanders, the most surprising feature of the whole business was the fact that Henry should have been attracted to Anne in the first place, since, according to the martyrologist, she had "a projecting tooth under the upper lip, and on her right hand six fingers." [83]

In view of the widespread use that was to be made of this story in subsequent literature about Mary, Sanders' account of Elizabeth's origins deserves a comment in passing. From an orthodox Catholic point of view, Henry's union with Anne can only be regarded as adulterous. His divorce from Katherine had never been recognized by the Roman church, and hence his marriage to Anne—especially when performed by a clergy branded as heretical

—could never be recognized. However, there is no historical authority to support the charge that Anne was Henry's own illegitimate daughter, or, for that matter, that she was bucktoothed and six-fingered. These last were apparently charges either invented by Sanders or picked up from current gossip to support his case.[84]

Needless to say, after presenting his arguments, Sanders has little difficulty in going beyond Leslie and Blackwood to proclaim Elizabeth's illegitimacy and Mary's natural right to the English throne. In addition, he charges Elizabeth with a cruelty and heartlessness he asserts are characteristic of heretics. Mary, he says, made a mistake in ever trusting the word of a heretic queen in the first place, for "as she had not thoroughly learned that they are not to be trusted who have abandoned the faith of Christ, she went to England against the will of her people, to another prison, to be guarded there by other soldiers." [85] In view of Mary's own letters denouncing the Scottish subjects who drove her from her realm, Sanders' claim that she went to England against the will of her people is a half-truth at best. It is the kind of presentation that, in conformity with the theme and purpose of his account of heresy in England, served admirably to heighten the portrait of Mary as the suffering martyr.

On the other basic points in the case for Mary, Sanders was an equally effective propagandist. He did not hesitate, for instance, to juggle the facts in order to dramatize the unswerving nature of the Queen's faith. When she first came to England, he wrote, she was offered the free succession to the English crown if she would renounce her Catholicism and become, in Sanders' words, a Protestant heretic. But, he exclaims, she refused, thereby revealing that she chose to die a Catholic martyr rather than reign as a queen.[86] The truth seems to be that Elizabeth had indeed made such an offer, but instead of rejecting it Mary had gone through the motions of appearing to consider it, to the extent of asking for a book of common prayer and of studying with an Anglican cleric; only when Elizabeth even then refused to commit herself formally on the succession issue did Mary abandon this effort to secure her ends.[87] In a similar attempt to heighten the impression of Mary's piety, Sanders asserted that the Earl of Shrewesbury "treated her always with excessive harshness because of her unwavering profession of the Catholic faith," yet actually Mary praised him for his leniency and kindness as her guardian, and his wife became her friend.[88]

Explicit throughout his two martyrological accounts of the Queen of Scots, and implicit throughout his own career, was Sanders' demand that the Catholic powers of Europe rise to release Mary not only for the faith but also for their own protection against the subversive activities of rebel heretics. As one modern historian puts it, Sanders "argued zealously for the validity of the bull of Pius V excommunicating and deposing Elizabeth and did his utmost from that time onwards to bring about a crusade against his heretic fellow-countrymen."[89] His activities in Madrid to this end, and above all his death in Ireland in the same cause, substantiate the claim that his campaign for Catholicism in the name of Mary Stuart was completely sincere. However, in terms of his influence on subsequent propagandists for Mary and her cause, Sanders' major contribution must remain the vivid coloring he gave to her name as a martyr for the Catholic faith. The legends to this effect that he recorded, if he did not create them, were to reappear regularly in the pro-Marian propaganda that followed her execution. By his adroit mixture of selected facts and the familiar devices of the propagandist, he helped notably to shift the emphasis from the naïvely innocent and somewhat domestically moral creature that Mary was portrayed to be in the literature of 1569 to something approaching the martyred saint that was to emerge after 1587, and of course he had brought the literary picture of Mary a long way from the pantheon of pagan deities that comprised her character in the epithalamia of 1558.

After the appearance of Sanders' first martyrology in 1571, works of this type, in which Mary Stuart was eulogized principally for her faith, were produced with increasing frequency.[90] New impetus to their production was provided by the publication and widespread translation of Burghley's *Execution of Justice in England*, in 1583, and by the Parliamentary Act of Association adopted in 1584. The latter, it will be recalled, had virtually assured Mary of martyrdom if she persisted in her political activities against the life and throne of Elizabeth. Burghley's treatise, although not mentioning the Queen of Scots by name or title, had made every effort to justify English treatment of Catholics in general, and—by implication, at least—of Mary in particular, on the grounds that they were punished for their political activities as traitors to the state, and not persecuted for their religious beliefs. Needless to say, Catholic propagandists on the Continent would have none of such explanations, and they set to work on new martyrologies designed to show to the world that English Catholics were being persecuted for their faith alone. As the celebrated geographer Richard Hakluyt, who was at the time a preacher in Paris, reported to Walsingham, "The Papists will shortly set forth a confutation of the 'Defence of the Execution of Justice in England.' "[91] Hakluyt's "Papists," in fact, set forth several such confutations.[92]

Foremost among the replies to Burghley's pamphlet was William, later Cardinal, Allen's tract, *A True Sincere and Modest Defence of English Catholiques that Suffer for Their Faith both at home and abrode: against a false, seditious and slanderous Libel intituled: The Execution of Iustice in England,* a work subsequently circulated also in a Latin version.[93] As head of the English seminaries at Douay and Rheims, and founder of the English Jesuit College in Rome, Allen had a prestige among English Catholics living abroad that made Elizabeth's agents bend every effort to prevent the circulation of his reply to Lord Burghley. But as Stafford, the English ambassador in Paris, wrote to Walsingham, there was little point in trying to suppress the reply, "first, because they are very secretly sold; secondly, because they would make men believe it is because we are touched to the quick [by Allen's work]...."[94]

Although not strictly a martyrology, Allen's defense of English Catholics includes accounts of their sufferings, and he devotes considerable space to a description of the trials and tribulations of Mary at the hands of Protestants both in Scotland and in England.[95] While emphasizing, in the martyrology tradition, the sufferings of Mary for her faith, he reiterates at the same time the other arguments in defense of the Queen of Scots that had become standard by now. He attacks the Protestant political theories that condoned the deposing of kings, and he blames the rebel heretics of Scotland for all of Mary's troubles. He defends the Queen of Scots' claim to the succession in England, and, in line with the Catholic hope then prevailing that James might be won back to the faith, he includes the son in this claim to Elizabeth's throne. Lastly, giving a curious turn to the mounting attack on the English Queen as Mary's persecutor, Allen charges that Elizabeth's virginity (a condition scornfully questioned by many of her foes) is one of the signs of God's wrath against England for its treatment of Catholics.[96]

The effectiveness of martyrological accounts, like those of Sanders and Allen, as propaganda for Catholics in general and Mary in particular is attested by the strenuous efforts made by the English to prevent their circulation. We have already noted Stafford's admittedly futile attempts to suppress Allen's *Defence*. He was more successful in suppressing a work the Catholics apparently intended to be a major contribution to the martyrological literature. In January, 1584, he came upon the printed sheets and the molds of a book describing the persecution of Catholics in England and illustrating their sufferings with pictures. The doer thereof, he reported, was one "Verstingham"—probably Richard Verstegan, whose illustrated martyrology subsequently received wide distribution after the execution of the Queen of Scots in 1587.[97] In 1584, however, Stafford prevailed upon the French King to have "Verstingham" thrown into prison, warning the King that unless he punished such attacks on Elizabeth she would have no choice but to permit the publication in England of similar attacks on him. The King yielded, but shortly thereafter, to Stafford's dismay, changed his mind. Submitting to pressures by William Allen and the Papal Nuncio, both of whom argued that "it was not a thing fit for him, being a Catholic prince, to hinder that the persecution of Catholics so tyrannically should be manifested publicly," the King released Verstegan, who boasted openly that he had got out in spite of Elizabeth's ambassador. By the time Stafford persuaded the French King to change his mind once more and reimprison Verstegan, the author had been spirited off to Rome by the Papal Nuncio. Stafford consoled himself and Walsingham by reporting that the French King had agreed to read Burghley's *Execution of Justice*—apparently as a kind of penance—in order to get a true account of why English Catholics were punished on grounds of treason and not of faith. A curious and revealing footnote to this skirmish in the battle of the books was a request by Elizabeth, who had supposed all along that Verstegan and his accomplices had been reimprisoned, that Stafford intercede in her name for their release, "so as it may appear that they are rather discharged at her Majesty's suit than otherwise." [98]

Stafford's efforts at least postponed the appearance of Verstegan's propaganda piece, but the English agent apparently had no success in trying to suppress certain obscene placards posted around Paris at this time as part of the campaign to vilify Elizabeth as a persecutor of heretics. According to Stafford,

a foul picture of the Queen was set up here, she being on horseback, her left hand holding the bridle, with her right hand pulling up her clothes; upon her head written *La reine d'Angleterre;* verses underneath signifying that if any Englishman passed that way, he could tell what and whose the picture was.[99]

The angry obscenity of this placard suggests the violence of the campaign in Mary's behalf as the two decades of her imprisonment in England approached their inevitable climax. The treatment of Elizabeth had shifted from sweet reasoning to excoriation. In the portrait of Mary, where her innocence and morality had been highlighted in the literature from 1569 to 1572, now—although the earlier elements are not absent—she was shown mainly as a radiant martyr for her faith. Since the basic facts concerning the Queen of Scots herself had not changed correspondingly in the meantime, the change must be regarded as largely a semantic one induced by the historical context and the necessities of propaganda. Certainly she was no less innocent of criminal charges in 1586, and no less a devout Catholic in 1568; and although her claims to the English throne were shifted from a right to succeed Elizabeth to a right to replace her, nothing had happened to change the actual legal status of either woman in this respect.

Through the years Mary's cause had come increasingly to be

identified with the Counter Reformation, the Catholic effort launched at the Council of Trent to resist the spread of Protestantism, just as in England and in the Protestant countries of Europe her cause had come to symbolize the Catholicism against which the Protestants were fighting. In the hands of her apologists, Mary's situation became a propaganda issue designed to arouse the Catholic leaders of Europe to military action against Protestants, and her sufferings to inspire and inflame the feelings of Catholics everywhere. To accomplish this larger end the propagandists did not hesitate to select from the complex pattern of her life those facts best suited for their purpose, and, where facts were lacking, to create them. As the Counter Reformation gained momentum, and resistance to it in England increased, the propagandists accordingly stepped up the intensity of their efforts. Yet it must be said that in comparison with the tremendous outburst that was to follow the execution of the Queen of Scots in 1587, their activities even as late as 1586 strike one as being relatively restrained.

V THE ENGLISH CAMPAIGN FOR

THE EXECUTION OF MARY:

1586-1588

Despite the increasing boldness and hostility of the Catholic propaganda in favor of Mary, Elizabeth persisted in her policy of refusing to allow any kind of authorized attack on the Queen of Scots herself until the very end of 1586. Then, in the last months of that year, a swiftly moving series of events led to a complete reversal of English policy. As a result of the Babington conspiracy, Mary was brought to trial at Fotheringay Castle on October 14 and 15 under the Act of Association. On October 25 in Star Chamber at Westminster she was found guilty of complicity in a plot to overthrow Elizabeth. Immediately thereafter, Parliament began pressing Elizabeth to pronounce and execute the sentence of death at once. The English Queen hesitated until December 4, but on that date she signed the Proclamation of Sentence and had it published by her official printer. Not until February 1, 1587, however, could she be persuaded to sign the Commission which authorized Mary's execution. Even then, she stoutly maintained that her last-minute verbal orders had been countermanded when the axe ended Mary's life in the morning hours of Wednesday, February 8, 1587.

It was apparently the Proclamation of Sentence on December 4, 1586, that signaled the lifting of the ban on direct propaganda attacks against Mary and the beginning of the authorized campaign to publicize the English case against her. The change is strikingly reflected in the pages of the Stationers' Register, where a record of licensed books was kept. All of the works described above in Chapter III, in which Mary's role in the conspiracies against Elizabeth was treated circumspectly if at all, were licensed or published before December 4, 1586, whereas the works about to be discussed, in which Mary is openly and violently attacked, were licensed and published after that date.[1]

Public acknowledgment of the old, protective policy, and an implied defense of the attack now authorized was made, shortly after the change in official attitude, by George Whetstone in *The Censure of a Loyall Subjecte,* a book licensed by "the Bishop of London and bothe ye Wardens" on January 4, 1587, and first published while Mary was still alive.[2] Whetstone probably wrote the bulk of this tract even before the Proclamation of Sentence, for he describes in detail the Babington conspiracy with no mention of the Queen of Scots. Then, on two leaves added at the end of the volume, he appended a section headed, "The Scottish Queene the root of all these treasons," in which he referred to the "bloody devices" promoted by this "Idolatrous Prince" in spite of Elizabeth's kind efforts to protect and defend her.[3] It is here that he remarks that Elizabeth had even gone so far as to forbid "the bookes of her faults, to be conversant among her english subjects: which almost in every other nation were made vulgar"— an obvious reference to the ban against published attacks just recently lifted. Whetstone was evidently trying at the last minute to adapt his account of the Babington conspiracy to the new order that permitted open assault on the Scottish Queen.

The new order was marked by the immediate appearance of a number of licensed publications like Whetstone's which openly and specifically charged Mary with misdeeds that had been only hinted at in earlier works. Several bear indications of official inspiration. Leading the attack was Elizabeth's Proclamation of Sentence itself, printed in London before the end of 1586 by her printer, Christopher Barker. Detailing the numerous counts of conspiracy against the throne charged to Mary, it was soon published abroad in a variety of translations, including Dutch, German, and Latin.[4]

Meantime, as early as November 25, 1586, no less a person than Burghley's son, Sir Robert Cecil, had assembled for publication the Parliamentary petitions beseeching Elizabeth to execute Mary, together with Elizabeth's evasive speeches in reply. The collection was ostensibly designed for private transmission to the Earl of Leicester under a covering letter that explained the justice of Elizabeth's necessary action, but the whole was made public almost immediately following the Proclamation of Sentence, and under the highest official auspices. Robert Cecil's initials appeared under the covering letter, and Elizabeth herself elaborately amended and polished her own speeches. The result was published by the Queen's Printer under the title, *The Copie of a Letter to . . . the Earle of Leycester,* and within a few months had been published abroad in Latin, German, Dutch, and French translations. As Neale remarks, "In other words, Elizabeth knew about this piece of propaganda and revised her speeches for publication. Perhaps the idea was hers, though she clearly did not wish to be associated with it." [5] Whether she wished to be associated with the new attitude toward Mary or not, Elizabeth had unquestionably given her consent to a reversal in official propaganda policy following her decision to proclaim the death sentence against the Queen of Scots.

Further officially inspired propaganda against Mary was probably prepared at the same time by Richard Crompton in a pamphlet entitled *A Short Declaration of the End of Traitors,* although it was not published until four days after the execution of Mary in February, 1587.[6] The work, which was "Seene and Allowed" and was dedicated to the Archbishop of Canterbury, refers to the execution only briefly in a last-minute postscript. The body of the pamphlet is little more than a recasting of materials, obviously borrowed from *The Copie of a Letter,* that linked Mary with all the plots and conspiracies in England after 1568 in order to justify her sentence and execution.

At the same time, publications less officially connected were setting forth in more lurid fashion the same justifications of Elizabeth's action against Mary. One of the earliest of these was a versified tract by William Kempe—the Elizabethan schoolmaster and not the celebrated Shakespearian clown—entitled *A Dutifull Invective against the moste haynous Treasons of Ballard and Babington: with other their adherents, latelie executed. Together with the horrible attempts and actions of the Q. of Scottes; and the sentence pronounced against her at Fodderingay.*[7] Kempe first details the practices of each of the traitors, and charges them with being agents of "that most lewd Italian Frier / I meane the Pope." He rejoices that by preventing such conspiracies and rebellions, God had indicated that He is pleased with Elizabeth and her Protestant government. The archvillainess is the Queen of Scots, who, according to Kempe, seduced these men into treason. If there had been any doubt in the minds of contemporary Englishmen that Mary was thinly disguised as Circe in the earlier and more circumspect literature, Kempe now removed it. Addressing the traitors he exclaims:

> Now may you all with open crie, the hower and time both
> > curse
> That ever you lent your listening eares, to her, whose words
> > have worse
> Bewitcht your wretched senceless mindes, that you could not
> > foresee
> The guerdon alwaies incident, to workes of treacherie:
>
> Then ever Circes wicked charmes, did anye wight enchaunt:
> For God forbid, that traitor should, of good successes vaunt.
> The *Scottish* Queene, with mischiefe fraught for to perform
> > the will
> Of him (whose Pupil she hath bene) hath used all her skill.[8]

Probably the most elaborate of these immediate attempts to justify Elizabeth's action against Mary was an anonymous tract now generally ascribed to Maurice Kyffin, and licensed by the Bishop of London on February 11, 1587, three days after the execution of the Queen of Scots. It bears the descriptive title,

A Defence of the Honorable sentence and execution of the Queene of Scots, Exempled with analogies, and diuerse presidents of Emperors, Kings, and Popes: With the opinions of learned men in the point, and diuerse reasons gathered foorth out of both Lawes Ciuill and Canon. Together with the Answers to certaine objections made by the fauorites of the late Scottish Queene.[9] The work, translated and published in France in the following year, is significant mainly because it sought to document the case against Mary by reprinting the letters, reputed to have passed between her and Babington, that were the immediate cause of her downfall. Kyffin returned to the same theme later in the year with a work published to celebrate the anniversary of Elizabeth's accession, *The Blessedness of Brytaine, or A Celebration of the Queenes Holyday.* With clear reference to Mary under the now familiar guise of Circe, and to the Roman Catholic role in the actions against Elizabeth in her name, he wrote:

> O wretched Wights, that would this Queene enharme,
> By close contryving of her Cruell Death;
> What cursed Circes, could their mindes so charme,
> As not to recke to reave their Liege of breath?
> Fell raging Rome, all this is long of thee,
> From whome, no Troubling Treasons, here are free.[10]

The relaxation of controls against anti-Marian propaganda after December, 1586, revealed itself in every type of publication. Latin treatises published at the universities supported Elizabeth's decision to execute the Queen of Scots; broadside ballads, heretofore limited to, at most, only covert references to Mary, were now issued with such titles as *An excellent dyttye made as a generall rejoycinge for the cuttinge of the Scottishe queene.*[11] The second edition of Holinshed's *Chronicles* appeared in January, 1587, but not without certain vicissitudes directly related to Elizabethan propaganda policies at this critical juncture. A number of leaves in this edition, dealing principally with Anglo-Scottish relations, were apparently ordered cut from the volumes before the edition was permitted to appear. The suppressed leaves were for the most part those which might have given offense to King James in Scotland—including, for example, a detailed account of the sad ends to which Scottish rulers bearing the name of James had come.[12] However, extensive materials dealing with Mary Stuart, added since the first edition of Holinshed in 1577, were not affected by the suppression order. These included reprints of the pamphlets that implicated Mary in the Throckmorton and Parry plots, reproduction of the letters alleged to have passed between the Scottish Queen and Anthony Babington, and the reprinting of the Parliamentary pleas and charges against her which had been published in *The Copie of a Letter to . . . the Earle of Leycester*. Moreover, the editors of the revised Holinshed drew heavily on Buchanan's anti-Marian *History of Scotland* for much of their material in amplifying the story of the Queen of Scots, and they did not hesitate to point up the significance of the story for English readers with such marginal notes as "The Scotish queene is an actor in this purposed conspiracie," and "The Scotish queenes advise in this mischiefous plot savoring altogither of inhumanitie." In other words, it was not so much a desire to spare Catholic Mary as it was a necessity to placate Protestant James that seems to have determined which leaves the government chose to censor. Badly as the editors may have misjudged official sensitivity in England about the feelings of James, they seem to have been fully aware of the new order that permitted attacks on the Queen of Scots.

Within a period of little more than three months, then, Elizabeth authorized the publication of what by sixteenth-century standards might be called a flood of literature explicitly directed against the Scottish Queen. In thus lifting the ban against published attacks on Mary, Elizabeth, of course, was not concerned simply with giving writers like Whetstone and Kempe an opportunity to release pent-up feelings. Her pose of protective benevolence having necessarily ended with the official announcement of her intention to execute the Queen of Scots, Elizabeth was now under enormous pressure to justify her proposed action both abroad and at home. Abroad, she had to explain affairs in such a way that Mary's death could not easily be made the excuse for a threatened military coalition of the Catholic powers against England; and at home, the English Queen who sought to keep her own claim to divine sovereignty intact had to justify the execution of another queen who also claimed divine sovereignty.

It would be impractical to describe here in detail the masses of argument and evidence adduced in these works to defend the action taken against Mary—the long lists of precedents in Biblical, classical, and modern history for executing a sovereign ruler; the elaborate expositions of political theory; the citation of laws from every land and age; the rhetorical arguments, the appeals to religious and nationalistic emotions, and the overall tone of unwilling necessity. From this welter of propagandistic materials, however, there emerge several basic themes in terms of which Elizabeth's campaign was developed.

Foremost among these, of course, is the effort to justify the sentence by making clear and emphatic the nature of Mary's treasonable activities that brought about her downfall. The charges of immorality in personal character and conduct, employed in earlier literature to justify her detention in England, are by no means dropped. Certainly the references to Circe, the enchantress who leads men to their doom, and the inclusion of much of Buchanan's material in Holinshed's *Chronicles*, served to keep the old allegations alive. Foreseeing quite accurately, however, that the martyrdom of Mary for her faith was to be the principal theme of Catholic counterpropagandists after the execution, the English sought to meet this claim in advance by insisting that she was executed for treason, not for her religion. They bent every effort to make her treasonable actions as manifest as possible, and, when referring to her Catholicism, to do so primarily in a political context. Kyffin, summarizing the case against Mary, made this attitude and treatment clear when he wrote:

What man of reason, in whom there is any naturall love to his countrie or apparance of an honest man would not counsell by justice to remove the Scottish queen; the very plague & calamity of our countrie, the very groundworke & chiefe impulsive cause of all these treasons & conspiracies; the hope of discontented subjects; & the very cause, for whom the Pope thundereth & keepeth this stir, for whom so many monsters have aduentured themselves to destroy her Majestie, & for whose sake others pretende to have just cause offered to invade this land.[13]

Richard Crompton even went so far as to argue that these treasons and conspiracies in which Mary was implicated were "pretended to bee for matters touching Religion," suggesting thereby that Mary's political ambition alone, and not her faith, was the real cause of the disturbances.[14]

To charge Mary Stuart, a Catholic woman, with treason was one thing; legally to charge the sovereign Queen of Scots with treason, let alone to bring her to trial and condemn her, was quite another. A second task of the Elizabethan propagandists, then, was to persuade a hostile and critical world of the legality of the proceedings against an anointed queen. To this end, the propagandists reiterated legal points, first advanced ten years before in French works demanding Mary's execution, to the effect that when she came to England she lost her own sovereignty and came under Elizabeth's sovereign jurisdiction.[15] Numerous historical and Biblical precedents were cited to show that the execution of one ruler by another does not violate the laws of God or nature; perhaps most frequently mentioned as an example was the execution of Conradin, King of Sicily, by Charles, King of Naples, for in this instance Pope Clement himself had confirmed the judgment in favor of Charles in words quoted frequently in support of Elizabeth's action: "The life of Conradin is the death of Charles, the death of Conradin the life of Charles." [16] The substance of all the legal precepts and precedents was expressed by Kyffin when he concluded that the trial and the sentence were legal:

Sithens the like sentence and execution of life and death, as the Scottish Queene hath received is testified, confirmed and warranted by the testimonies, reasons, & examples of so many Emperours, Kings, and Popes. Since no lawe will save so high a trespasser, the law of Nations, of Nature, and of every kingdome and countrey would inflict death on so great offenders.[17]

A third theme constantly reiterated in the literature published following the Proclamation of Sentence was that of Elizabeth's personal reluctance to act against Mary, and her grief and anguish when she was finally persuaded by her council and Parliament to do so. Considering her strong views on the sovereignty of queens,

Elizabeth's reluctance was probably sincere enough, but the effort to relieve her of personal responsibility for Mary's death in the eyes of God and of Catholic Europe is also evident in these works, as is the effort to add ingratitude to the charges against the Queen of Scots. The propagandists made much of the fact that at great personal risk Elizabeth consistently treated Mary well and winked at her repeated conspiracies. As Whetstone said of Mary:

During the whole course of her abode in England which may be properly called a protection, and no imprisonment: ther is nothing more manifest, then that her mallice thirsted the death of her own life . . . but our most gracious Queene, not withstanding these continuall advertismentes, with a magnanimous hearte, digested all this danger: yea, she was so far from revenge, as she yeelded not to make her subjects partakers of these forraine counsels whom next under her, they principally concerned . . .[18]

Elizabeth's own expressions of reluctant grief were given wide circulation in *The Copie of a Letter . . . to Leycester* and its numerous translations published abroad. She denied that her delay in signing the Proclamation of Sentence was simply "to make a shew of clemencie," as some of her enemies had charged, but was rather a last effort to find some other way of dealing with her "sister." [19] The propagandists contended that Elizabeth was so disregardful of her own personal safety that her lords and commons practically had to force her to act against Mary. The English Queen, wrote William Kempe, "with wonted grace and mercie beinge moved, / Was lothe to yealde consent thereto, for that shee well her loved," and then it was "with fainting breath" that she finally confirmed the sentence and had it published.[20]

The fourth theme consistently developed in post-Proclamation literature represents a somewhat different attempt to clear Elizabeth of personal responsibility in the matter of sentencing Mary and to justify her action in terms of political philosophy. According to a basic doctrine in the political thinking of the sixteenth century, as has been noted earlier, a ruler is appointed by God primarily for the purpose of administering His justice among men. In the language of the period, a monarch is God's lieutenant,

God's vicegerent, the image of God on earth. Therefore, a ruler who fails to execute God's judgment against violators of His laws fails in his vocation and is in danger of being punished or overthrown by God. A similar line of argument, it will be recalled, had been introduced into the play *Horestes* in an effort to justify Elizabeth's detention of Mary on her first arrival in England.[21] By this reasoning, the propagandists of 1587 could argue that Elizabeth, regardless of her personal feelings of mercy and forgiveness, was obligated to sentence and execute Mary, for the Scottish Queen had been found guilty of breaking the laws of God and man, and Elizabeth, as the representative of God's justice on earth, was forced to act against her sister queen or be punished for neglect of duty. Sir John Puckering, Speaker of the House of Commons and possibly the author of *Horestes,* was one of several to make this the culminating argument; as he told Elizabeth, in the widely published Parliamentary petitions to the Queen:

Lastly, your Majesties most loving & dutiful commons doubt not, but that as your Majestie is duely exercised in reading the Booke of God, so it will please you to call to your princely remembrance, how fearefull the examples of Gods vengeance bee, that are there to bee founde against King Saul for sparing King Agag, and against King Achab for saving the life of Benadad: both which were by the just judgment of God deprived of their kingdoms, for sparing those wicked Princes, whome God had delivered into their handes of purpose to be slaine by them, as by the ministers of his eternal and divine justice: Wherein full wisely Salomon proceeded to punishment, when hee tooke the life of his owne naturall and elder brother Adonias, for the only intention of a marriage, that gave suspition of treason against him.[22]

The example of Solomon, which recurred frequently in anti-Marian propaganda literature at this time, was of course particularly useful and appropriate, for it gave precedent for the trial and execution by one sovereign of a kinsman of the blood royal whose principal crime was treason.

The picture of Mary that emerges from this literature is inevitably a sinister one. Her treachery, her political conniving, her callous ingratitude, her wickedness as a violator of the laws of both man and God, and her operations as an agent of a foreign power

are the principal elements in the portrait as the English propagandists now painted it. Despite the abusiveness of a Whetstone
or a Kyffin, however, the predominant tone is that of sorrow rather
than anger, and necessarily so. For above all other considerations,
the English had to convince Catholic Europe, if they could, that
the execution of Mary was no act of religious or personal passion,
but rather was an obligation forced on them by the unanswerable
logic of universal, divine law.

All this publication activity, occurring for the most part between December 4, 1586 and February 8, 1587, was of course
mainly designed to prepare the world for the news to come out
of Fotheringay Castle when Mary was executed there on the latter
date. In view of such careful preliminary efforts, it is not surprising
to find that Elizabeth's government had also made elaborate
preparations to insure that their own version and justification of
what happened on that fatal morning would be the first to reach
the world. The story of these preparations, and of the resultant
official English version of the execution of the Queen of Scots,
has never been fully told. It is perhaps worth telling here in some
detail, not only because the authorized nature of this account
has not hitherto been recognized, but also because the circumstances under which the account was prepared and released are
preëminent in revealing the methods of literary propaganda in the
sixteenth century.

Well before the day of the execution itself Elizabeth's government took steps to block any effort by Mary's friends and adherents
in England to send abroad their own version of what happened
and why. Both in London and at Fotheringay Mary had followers
who were ready and anxious to write about what they considered
her martyrdom for the faith and not her execution for treason.
Notable among these were the French ambassador Chateauneuf—
who ultimately did send such an account when he could con-
trive to do so—and Dominique Bourgoin, Mary's physician, who
was among the few members of her personal retinue permitted to
witness the execution itself. Not only were these followers eager
to write on behalf of what they regarded as Mary's martyrdom, but
they also had her specific injunction to do so, for, according to

all the accounts of her last hours, she requested the presence of her servants that they might report in "their Countries, that she died a true constant Catholique to her religion." [23]

To prevent just such reports as this from reaching Europe, the English arranged to hold all of Mary's favorers strictly incommunicado after the execution. Chateauneuf complained, in a letter he was able to smuggle out of England some weeks later, that his house was closely guarded, that he was not allowed to send dispatches to his royal master, and that neither he nor Mary's servants at Fotheringay could obtain even the promise of passports to leave England. To add insult to these injuries, Chateauneuf was forced, he says, to contribute wood for the bonfires with which Londoners celebrated the news of Mary's execution.[24] Meanwhile, at Fotheringay the doors were locked on Mary's servants even before her body was removed from the scaffold.[25] Their subsequent and reiterated pleas for release were turned off with the reply that surely they would not want to leave before the funeral services for their beloved mistress. On this pretext they were held at Fotheringay for six months awaiting the promised service which was finally held on August 1, although meanwhile the servants complained bitterly that "the dead corpse putrifieth." [26]

Whatever the excuses offered by the English, their real motives, in terms of the propaganda race, were perfectly clear to the frustrated spokesmen for Mary. Chateauneuf, in describing his own guarded state to Henri III of France, explained that Elizabeth "willed that your Majesty be advised of this execution by no other than one whom she would send to you." [27] An even more perceptive analysis of the situation, and of the propaganda purposes on both sides, was given by an apologist for Mary writing after the release of her followers later in the year. He explains that their long imprisonment showed the fear of the English lest what he called the real truth, that Mary died not for political treason but as a martyr for her religion, should get back to France. He concludes by asserting that when the English had established their "faulces suppositions, faulces lettres, & impostures, procedures & preves apostees" in France, then and then only did they feel it safe to release the servants.[28]

The English thus succeeded fairly well for the time being in blocking at the source pro-Marian accounts of the execution, but the need for a more positive propaganda in defense of the English position became almost immediately apparent. Although Mary's Catholic supporters in Europe, and particularly in Paris, lacked details of what had happened, they promptly made religious and political capital of the fact of the execution itself when the word reached Paris on March 1. Especially among the Leaguers, those arch-Catholic followers of the house of Guise, was the death of Mary made the occasion for violent pressure campaigns to force the French King to invade England in the name of the martyred Queen and the Catholic church.[29] The English ambassador sent word of a demonstration in Paris by five thousand people on behalf of all martyrs in England and of "the Queen of Scots death, whom they will have a martyr, added in the end, and their conclusion to their purpose to mutiny the people, both against the Huguenots, the succession of the Huguenots, and the Catholics associate on their part."[30] Similarly, a contemporary French reporter described the mass demonstrations that took place when the bare news of the execution reached Paris, and he added:

Her death was regretted and lamented without end by the Catholics, particularly by the Leaguers, who loudly proclaimed that she died a martyr for the apostolic Roman Catholic faith, and that the Queen of England had caused her death for no other reason than religion, whatsoever other face Elizabeth strove to put upon it. In which opinion [the Catholics] were skilfully and carefully encouraged by the preachers, who canonized [Mary] daily in their sermons.[31]

From Scotland too came reports of a similar reaction among what was left of Mary's party there. In March, an English agent wrote to Walsingham about the libels set up in the streets of Edinburgh against the preachers (i.e., the Presbyterians) and against Elizabeth, because of the execution of Mary. He sent along one such libel as a sample, a little cord of hemp, tied halterwise, with the epigram:

> To Jesabell that English whore
> Receive this Scottish chain
> As presages of her great malheur
> For murdering of our queen.[32]

The English, however, had apparently foreseen reactions such as these in France and Scotland and had anticipated the need for some positive statement to support their case for executing the Queen of Scots. From such foresight there promptly sprang an account of the affair, widely disseminated throughout Europe, not only describing the execution in detail, but also setting forth the argument that Mary died for treason, not for religion, and that Elizabeth had acted, as any monarch would under the circumstances, for the security of her realm and people.

The prime mover in the preparation of this official English account seems to have been no less a person than William Cecil, Lord Burghley, a major force in the field of anti-Marian propaganda since he sponsored the publication of Buchanan's *Detection* many years before. It is perhaps worth pausing here to pay tribute to Burghley's long and continuing career as a kind of director of propaganda for Elizabeth's government. Conyers Read observes that Burghley was not really equipped as a writer of English prose to be an effective producer of propaganda on his own, but possessed remarkable instincts for discovering skillful writers of influential propaganda and for laying down the general lines of policy and emphasis they were to follow.[33] His role in the production of Buchanan's *Detection* indicates his talent in this respect, and the same talent is revealed in the choice of his son, Robert Cecil, to edit the officially authorized publication of arguments for executing Mary contained in *The Copie of a Letter to . . . Leycester.* Occasionally he seems to have written the propaganda himself, as he apparently did in the *Execution of Justice in England,* or, much later, in *A True Report of Sundry Horrible Conspiracies,* an account of the plot purportedly concocted by Dr. Lopez to assassinate Elizabeth. Whether he wrote the material himself or directed others in writing it, Burghley's characteristic handling of the publicity was always apparent. A contemporary, the celebrated Sir Edward Coke, acknowledged Burghley's special genius as a propagandist when he remarked, with reference to the pamphlet on Dr. Lopez, that "the Lord Treasurer . . . thought best to rely principally upon the confessions of the delinquents without any inferences or arguments. This book was never answered to my knowledge, and this is the best kind of publication." [34] Burghley's method, "to rely principally upon the confessions of the delinquents, without any inferences or arguments," can be observed in some degree in all the works he wrote or sponsored, but nowhere more strikingly, perhaps, than in the arrangements he made for publicizing the execution of the Queen of Scots.

In what today would be called a plan for handling publicity about the execution of the Queen, Sir Francis Walsingham prepared a memorial on February 2, 1587, that was not only endorsed by Burghley but was also heavily interlined with additional recommendations by the Lord Treasurer himself.[35] Where Walsingham had recommended that "her servants . . . be stayed for a time in this realm," Burghley added the sterner injunction that they were "to remain also in the Castle until further order." It becomes apparent later that he was anxious to prevent Mary's servants from carrying or sending out their own version of what was to happen at Fotheringay. Burghley also limited to two or three the number of servants with whom Mary might be allowed to converse privately, and he outlined in some detail the points that should be made by the Earls of Kent and Shrewesbury, who officiated at the execution, in formally announcing to Mary and to the world the reasons for the event—points that were to reappear almost verbatim in the account of the affair subsequently circulated throughout Europe by the English.

The memorial also specified that "some especial person . . . be appointed to note her speech." In this connection, we learn from other sources that Burghley independently arranged to have sent to himself the eyewitness report of the execution upon which the account subsequently published throughout Europe was apparently based. Although the Earls of Kent and Shrewesbury had been directed by the Queen's Privy Council to send a detailed report of what happened, Burghley nevertheless privately commissioned one "R. W."—probably his own kinsman Robert Wingfield—to send an independent description of the event.[36] Burghley apparently wanted a far more circumstantial account of the affair than he felt that the two Earls might send posthaste to the Council—or, as it turned out, than they actually did send. Wingfield's commission is attested by the fact, for example, that in closing the report that he sent, he explained to Burghley somewhat apologetically that "many thinges might well have bin omitted, as not worthy noting, yett because yt is your Lordshipps faulte, to desire to knowe all, & so I have certified all it is an offense pardonable." [37]

The account of Mary's final hours as Wingfield promptly dispatched it to Burghley is indeed remarkably detailed. After a brief prelude describing her calm reception of the news on the night of February 7 that she was to die on the following morning, Wingfield begins a minute-by-minute report of her last moments on earth. He describes with almost cold objectivity her various statements on the scaffold before the axe fell: her successful argument with the Earl of Kent as to whether her servants might be with her to the end, her sharp and loyally Catholic exchange with the Dean of Peterborough Cathedral, sent by Elizabeth to minister to her and to try to convert her to the Anglican faith, and her final words, "In manus tuas." Wingfield even records Mary's grim jest when she remarked to the executioner who disrobed her that "she never had such groomes before to make her unready, nor ever did put of her clothes before such a company." Every detail of her clothing and appearance is set down, including the facts that "her lipps stirred up & downe almost a quarter of an hower after her head was cutt off," and that one of the executioners then "espied her little dogge which was crept under her clothes which could not be gotten forth but with force & afterwardes could not depart from her dead corpes, but came and laye betweene her head & shoulders a thing diligently noted." Not only all that Mary did and said, but all that everyone else present did and said he apparently tried to set down in this report to Burghley.

Considering the propaganda use to which it was immediately adapted, Wingfield's original account is remarkable for its objectivity as well as for its detail. He makes repeated and even admiring reference to the courage and self-control with which Mary conducted herself. She entered the execution hall, he says, "with unapauled countenaunce," and listened to the reading of the sentence against her "with so careles a regard as if it had not concerned her at all." He duly reports her repeated affirmations of the faith in and for which she claimed to die, and he quotes her long final prayers in apparent entirety. Only occasionally does he reveal his own Protestant bias, as when he refers to her rosary and crucifix as "superstitious trumpery" and describes the "lattine book of vaine prayers" which she held in her hand. But he seeks to make it clear that in trying to convert Mary to Anglicanism the English professed to have only the good of her immortal soul in mind. In this connection he also notes, contrary to subsequent Catholic claims that she could have saved her life by embracing Protestantism, that she was doomed to be executed for treason, whether converted or not.

The exact process by which Wingfield's report was transformed into the official published account of the execution and its causes is not clear. Indeed, if such an account was actually published in English, or even in England, as it seems to have been, no copy survives and no trace of it remains in the English book lists of the time.[38] But the fact that a version of the affair closely resembling Wingfield's report was officially prepared in England for publication abroad is attested by a number of Continental writers at the time. The French historian Brantôme, for example, indicated that one of the sources he used in preparing his own story of the Scottish Queen's end was "a book on this death and its causes" written by the English.[39] Adam Blackwood, in a belated account of Mary's death, also asserted that "the English have described this execution in their own language, and have added the reasons which moved their mistress to this cruelty."[40] Two other Catholic writers at the same time described what was clearly the same account and stated positively that it had been printed in London by command of the Queen of England herself.[41]

The report these writers mention can be almost certainly identified with a printed account that appeared in a variety of languages in a variety of the capitals of Europe shortly after the end of March in the year of Mary's death. All are identical in outline and detail, within the limits of translation, and several of them indicate on the title page that the original was written in English and published in England. In all these versions the author's reference at the end to these events "here in England" seems further to attest the common source as English in origin. Three editions of the account were published in Germany, presumably under Protestant auspices, including one at Cologne with an indication on the title page that it had been translated from the English.[42] Still another German version of the same account found its way into the archives of the celebrated German merchant family, the Fuggers, and has since been translated, somewhat mutilated and abbreviated, back into English.[43] Meanwhile, Catholic apologists for Mary, denied access to reports of their own from Fotheringay, fell back on publishing Latin, German, and Dutch versions of this same account. All credit the English source of the original, the Latin edition going so far as to say that the report was written in London on March 27; but all add to it introductory material and marginal notes designed to counteract the Protestant bias they detected in the English account.[44] A curious fact that further links these widespread translations to an authorized English original is the appearance in some of them, Protestant and Catholic alike, of a Latin epitaph on Mary Stuart that was published separately as a licensed broadside in London at this time; the same epitaph appeared in a German broadside accompanied by a highly colored portrait of the Scottish Queen.[45] Explaining Mary's fate in terms of the Renaissance commonplace of fickle fortune and the uncertainty of high place, without reference to political or religious issues, the epitaph was apparently sent abroad together with the English version of what happened at Fotheringay as suitable to the theme and purpose of the narrative itself.

By translating and collating these extant Continental editions of the execution account, we can obtain what is probably a fairly accurate and complete reconstruction of what was an English original prepared and possibly printed in London. Then it becomes clear that the heart of this document, the description of the execution itself, follows in outline and in all essential details the report written for Burghley by Robert Wingfield. A few details not found in Wingfield appear to have been drawn from the report of the event sent by Kent to the Privy Council, and a few others from a manuscript description of the execution by one Edward Capell, an attendant upon Shrewesbury.[46] The result is an account of what happened at Fotheringay differing markedly in detail and emphasis from subsequent Catholic reports. Because this composite account is not easily available, and because its official status has not hitherto been recognized, the work deserves rather detailed description.

The first of the three sections into which it is divided reviews the circumstances that led to the execution, emphasizing Mary's treasonable activities in the face of Elizabeth's demonstrations of hospitality and kindness. This introductory section opens with the statement that plots to seize Elizabeth's throne, take her life, and supplant her with Mary Stuart had recently been discovered. The author of the account acknowledges that Mary had been detained in England for many years in "free custody" ("in libera custodia"; "in einer freyen Gefengnuss"), but he suggests that Elizabeth was thereby doing Mary a kindness, for the Parliament of Scotland frequently demanded that she be returned to stand trial for the murder of her husband, whom she had had strangled, he says, because of her great passion for Bothwell. These Scottish demands, following Mary's flight to England, created a difficult situation for Elizabeth, according to the author; nevertheless,

[Mary] retained her life by the kindness of her Majesty, who, although she did not wish to judge her who was so closely related to her by blood, yet nevertheless, because on other occasions Mary might usurp to herself the title of the realm of England, Her Majesty, as much for avoiding peril to her person and realm and for retaining the flourishing peace and security of religion, as for keeping peace with the Scots, was not able to set her completely free.[47]

Still, Mary was given unusual freedom by Elizabeth, "being granted attendants in accordance with her dignity, and allowed hunting and fowling for her pleasure, as much as she wished."

But despite this hospitable treatment, the account continues, Mary was "little content" and devoted all her time to participation in plots and schemes which, under the pretext of religion, sought her own liberation and the death of Elizabeth. To such ends she had seduced the Duke of Norfolk, and more recently she had conceived a scheme whereby Elizabeth was to be murdered, the realm invaded by foreigners, and herself placed on the throne of England—a reference by the author to the Babington conspiracy. He added that Mary persuaded herself and others that in this manner they would be "deserving of heaven, etc."

Having thus sought to establish the treasonable behavior of the Scottish Queen, the writer of the account returns to the theme of Elizabeth's reluctance to act against her. After the plots and schemes were exposed, he says, Elizabeth was forced to preserve her kingdom by bringing Mary to trial "before the nobles and ministers of her realm," and these found the Queen of Scots guilty. Even then, Elizabeth, according to the narrator, ordered her Parliament to find some means of preserving not her personal safety but the safety of the realm without taking Mary's life, because Mary was "joined to her by strong bonds of consanguinity and was a queen and princess not subject to the jurisdiction of any other." When Parliament demanded the execution despite these arguments, Elizabeth still refused to approve the action, says the writer, and even went so far as to allow foreign ambassadors to intercede with her on Mary's behalf.

At this critical juncture, the account continues, further evidence of Mary's treasonable activities forced the issue of her execution. New plots which "tended toward the liberation and enthronement of the Queen of Scots" were discovered, and this time not only members of Mary's retinue but even some of the ambassadors who had been allowed to intercede for her were implicated.[48] Thus Elizabeth was forced to decree that "the source and cause of so many evils must be removed from her midst, and she set forth the order effecting the final execution of the Queen of Scots."

The writer has yet another word for Elizabeth's personal grief and reluctance in decreeing Mary's death, for he concludes this introductory section of the official account with the statement that

... although the sentence was given and signed by Her Majesty, yet again Her Majesty resolved to deliberate. But in this she was prevented by her ministers, who had already obtained the signed sentence. This was not without great sorrow upon the part of Her Majesty (indeed, for this reason Secretary Davison was thrown into prison, and many others fell under Her Majesty's displeasure, and she herself from this time assumed black garments of mourning).

After this thorough exposition of the themes of Mary's treason and Elizabeth's personal concern, the author proceeds to describe the execution itself. Here, both for detail and often for wording, as I have indicated above, the author relies mainly on the letter written by Wingfield to Burghley, supplemented by material from the reports by the earls and by Edward Capell. Like Wingfield's letter, the London account begins with a brief description of the announcement of the sentence to Mary by Kent, Shrewesbury, and her two keepers, Sir Amias Paulet and Sir Drew Drury, on the night before her fatal morning. Mary received the news calmly, says the writer, whereupon the lords "proceeded to propound the great necessity, which impelled Her Majesty and the whole realm to this resolution."

The account then describes the execution hall in Fotheringay Castle, and gives the details of the scaffold exactly as they appear in Wingfield's letter. It explains at some length how Mary, who was still in her own chambers praying with some of her followers, had to be sent for three times before she indicated that she was ready to descend to the hall. Finally, coming out and seeing Melville, her major-domo, in the group awaiting her in an antechamber, she addressed him in words substantially the same as those reported by Wingfield, although markedly different from those reported in subsequent Catholic accounts of the execution:

My faithfull servant Melville, although I believe that you are one of the Protestants, while I am a Catholic, yet there is only one Christ. And I am your Queen, born and anointed, of the lineage of Henry VII. I command you that as you wish to present yourself freely before God, you will truly report to my most beloved son these things which I tell you, namely, that I pray him to serve God, and maintain the Catholic church; that he govern his realm in peace, and not subject himself, as I have done, to anyone else, although I desired to unite this island in one realm. I freely leave it to him, that he may so strive. Let him not rely greatly on worldly prudence, for that indeed will not always be profitable, but let him rather put his hope in God, and diligently take heed that he offer no occasion for evil suspicion by the Queen of England, and then God may bless him. And thou Melville will bear witness for me that I died a faithful Scot, Frenchwoman, and Catholic, as I have always professed.

Melville having declared his eagerness to do her bidding, Mary, according to the account, then turned to the English lords with a series of requests. Her plea that her priest might be with her on the scaffold was denied (a detail taken from the report of Kent and Shrewesbury), but her request that some of her servants, at least, might accompany her, in order to "report to the King of France and to others that she had died a Catholic," was granted after Mary had promised that they would cause no emotional disturbance in the execution chamber.

Thereupon Mary was led to the scaffold set up in the great hall, and, "because she was not able to stand comfortably," she sat down on a chair that had been provided for her. At this point, says the account, Secretary Beal read the order for the execution "in a loud voice," after which the Protestant Dean of Peterborough Cathedral approached Mary and began to exhort her, at the command of the English lords, to "put her faith in Christ and die a Christian." Then, in a passage that closely parallels Wingfield's report, the official account says that Mary interrupted the Dean, asserting that she was sufficiently prepared for death. When he persisted, she exclaimed, "Silence, Master Dean, I will not listen to you; you disturb me"; whereupon the earls ordered the Dean to desist "that she might not be perturbed." Kent broke in at this point to say that he grieved to see in Mary's hands "these vain and superstitious articles"—her crucifix, rosary, and prayerbook. Mary replied that she carried the crucifix in her hand that she might, in beholding it, think of Christ crucified. Whereupon Kent retorted, in a passage found only here and in Wingfield's letter, that it rather became her to carry Christ in her heart.

After this interchange, the Dean led the entire assembly in "an efficacious prayer suitable to the occasion," while Mary, refusing to participate or even listen, prayed her own prayer in Latin. Then having granted the pardon asked of her by the executioners, Mary slid from the chair to her knees and began to pray very loudly in English.

There are many versions of this celebrated prayer in contemporary and later records, but only those given in the reports by Wingfield and Capell are identical in their main elements with the version found in this official English account of the execution. According to the English account, Mary prayed first for her own salvation through Him at the foot of whose crucifix she was shedding her own blood. She prayed "for the happy state of the Queen of England," for the prosperity of the whole island, and for the afflicted Church of Christ. She prayed for her son, and for his conversion to the Roman Catholic faith. She prayed that God "might deign to avert his rod from this unhappy island," and, finally, that the saints might intercede for her and that God might receive her soul in heaven.

Then, the account proceeds, Mary began to disrobe for the execution. When one of the executioners started to help her, she exclaimed, in a passage reported elsewhere only by Wingfield, that she was not accustomed to undress before such an audience, nor with the help of such grooms as these. Having finished, she turned to say farewell to the two women servants who were on the scaffold with her. When one of them began to weep loudly, the Queen, reminding her of the promise made to the earls that there would be no disturbance, ordered her not to weep but rather to rejoice. After blessing her ministers, Melville, Bourgoin, and Gorion, who were standing by, and commanding them to witness that she died a Catholic, Mary fell on her knees "with great and intrepid courage, and without any change of color, nor giving any sign of fear of death." While one of her women covered the Queen's eyes with a handkerchief, Mary recited the Seventieth Psalm, *In te Domine*. And as she placed her head on the block, she began crying in a loud voice, *In manus tuas Domine commendo spiritum meum*.

Exactly as reported by Wingfield, the official account next relates that while one executioner held her hands, the other struck twice with the axe before her head fell. When the executioner held her head up before the spectators and cried, "God save the Queen," Mary's headdress fell off, "and they saw that it was already very white-haired, and that the hair had not very long before been cut off up to the scalp." Although Wingfield's detail about Mary's dog is omitted here, the official account explains, as does Wing-field, that all of her clothing and anything sprinkled with her blood was carried away and burned, "that nothing might serve for super-stition." The members of her entourage were immediately placed under detention. The reason given for this is in itself evidence that the report indeed reflects official English attitudes, for it is the very reason given at Fotheringay to Mary's servants themselves. As the writer of the account expresses it, "Her servants and ministers were ordered to remain there, maintaining her former state and splendour, nor was anyone permitted to leave until she might be honorably buried somewhere."

The third and last section of the official account is devoted to a reiteration of the principal themes of the English propaganda lit-erature against Mary. The writer admits that she had been "a most beautiful princess, surpassing all of her time in beauty." But he hastens to remind his readers of the immorality of her personal life by referring to Darnley, "a most handsome youth whom she caused to be murdered" because of her passion for Bothwell, "who being imprisoned in Denmark, died there insane." He also reminds his readers of the popular demand for the execution by describing the celebrations in London and by explaining that the citizens "were joyful to be liberated from the imminent danger to which on her account they had been exposed for so long a time." Finally, he turns once more to Elizabeth's attitude and role in the proceedings. After describing the rejoicing in London, he adds that only Eliza-beth "felt great sorrow of spirit, that contrary to her expectation the execution of the sentence had been hurried, whereas she had been determined to deliberate more fully upon it." Whatever her feelings, he continues, events have proved the justice, wisdom, and necessity of the execution, for from that time

... up to March 18, 1587, at which date these things were written, everything here in England is tranquil; we hope also that peace and quiet will thus continue, and that not in vain has the execution thrown great fear into the enemies of Elizabeth and the realm. Therefore, let this be an example to Princes and Rulers, that they turn not away from God and from righteousness, thinking that, under similar circum-stances, they are not subject to punishment in this world.

Thus with a clear indication that, in executing Mary, Elizabeth was simply administering God's justice on a fellow sovereign as she was ordained to do because of her position as God's vicegerent, and with a clear warning to the Catholic princes of Europe not to risk Mary's fate by taking up her cause, the official English account of the execution of the Queen of Scots ends.

In general, the account seems to be admirably adapted to its propaganda purposes, both in emphasizing Mary's treason and in minimizing any suggestion that she was executed because of her Catholic faith. To dissuade the Catholic kings of Europe from undertaking retaliatory action, the first and last sections of the work in particular develop the theme of urgent political necessity which these monarchs themselves, as sovereigns concerned with the security of their thrones and realms, could be expected to understand. Hence the constant emphasis on the threat to civil peace and order which Mary's treasonable conduct represented. Especially significant in this respect is the complete absence from the account, and from Wingfield's letter, of any suggestion that on the scaffold Mary declared her innocence of the charges of treason upon which she was being executed, as subsequent Catholic reports were to state. She had certainly done so at her trial, according to official reports of those proceedings, and she had done so on the night before her execution, according to the report sent to the Privy Council by Kent. However, any statement of innocence that she made might well have been omitted from a document designed to emphasize the fact that Mary died for treason, if only on the grounds that her apparent silence on this point would be taken by readers as an admission of guilt.

At the same time, the official account was carefully developed to show that although Mary died true to her faith, she did not die because of it or for it. Without omitting completely the elements of Protestant bias, the account tones down the Wingfield report to a considerable degree in this respect, deleting, for example, all of his editorial comments on the Queen's "superstitious trumpery" and "vaine prayers." Her Catholicism, accordingly, is not assailed as such, but rather, when referred to at all, is hinted to be simply an excuse that she and her coconspirators used to cloak her political treason, the real point at issue. In this connection, the efforts made on the scaffold by the Dean and by Kent to convert Mary to Protestantism are presented as honest attempts by sincere Anglicans to save the soul of one who was going to die for treason in any event. The point had been made clear to Mary herself when, according to Wingfield's account, the Dean told her that Queen Elizabeth had, "notwithstanding this preparacion for the execution of justice to be done upon you, for your manie trespasses against her sacred person state and government, a tender care over your soule. . . ." Although denying that Mary died *because* of her faith, the English propagandists had nothing to lose by admitting that she died *in* it. In fact, their contention that she died for treason, and not for religion, was probably better served by reporting that no serious or successful effort was made to alter her firmness in her faith.

In all respects, then, the official English account of the execution of Mary was the inevitable culmination of the propaganda campaign against the Queen of Scots that began officially on December 4, 1586, with the Proclamation of Sentence against her, but that had its beginnings long before in the "kind of semi-publicity" encouraged by Elizabeth and her ministers. Although there are sufficient suggestions and reminders here of the earlier charges against her personal character, the argument is now focused on her political activities which left a reputedly grief-stricken Elizabeth no alternative but to execute the judgment of God on a violator of His law.[49] From the point of view of an Elizabethan Englishman weary of the disturbing effects of a Northern Rebellion, a Norfolk plot, a Throckmorton, a Parry, and a Babington conspiracy—all in the name of the Queen of Scots—such a case was not without a certain realistic validity. In any event, Elizabeth's government for the moment rested its case with this explanation to the world of Mary's execution. Meanwhile, despite Elizabeth's precautionary efforts to see that no account of the affair contrary to her own should get abroad until hers had been widely disseminated, Mary's apologists contrived to launch, almost immediately, a counterpropaganda campaign of their own.

VI CATHOLIC COUNTERPROPAGANDA

ON THE EXECUTION: 1587

The official news of Mary's execution reached Paris on March 1, 1587, when a special courier arrived from Elizabeth with instructions to "explain to the King viva voce the true reasons which had rendered this step necessary." [1] The outward reaction to the news was one of universal anger and sorrow because, as the Venetian ambassador rather shrewdly analyzed the situation, "she was a Queen of France, and also because all the Catholic hopes in England are dashed." [2] The King himself at once ordered the court into mourning, and arranged for an elaborate memorial service in Notre Dame Cathedral. Meanwhile, as Pierre L'Estoile recorded in his *Journal,* Paris was the scene of daily mass demonstrations and sermons that canonized Mary. The English ambassador reported to Walsingham that he had watched five thousand angry Frenchmen flock to St. Severin to see posters and placards reviling Elizabeth and the English.[3]

Despite these outward manifestations of grief and rage, however, the total response in France was less than unanimous and wholehearted. Divergent reactions to the news of Mary's death were determined now, as in earlier situations involving her, by the different political and religious factions that existed in France and that tended to affect the rest of Europe as well. As always, Mary's cause was the particular concern of the extreme Catholic party represented by the house of Guise, by the members of the ardently pro-Catholic League who supported the house of Guise, and by the English and Scottish Catholic adherents of Mary who were in exile on the Continent. These parties saw in Mary alive, and even more so in Mary dead, the supreme occasion for rallying the Catholic powers of Europe to an attack on heresy in general and on English heresy in particular. To this end they had already formed an alliance with Philip of Spain, and they were constantly active in trying to force Henri III of France to their will.[4] It may have been, as the English ambassador observed to Burghley of the Guisian Catholics, "that religion is but a colour and worldly pride and ambition [at] the bottom of their hearts."[5] Whatever the motive, the principal demonstrations on Mary's behalf came, as L'Estoile noted at the time, from "the house of Lorraine and Guise, to whom the said deceased Queen of Scots was so closely related."[6]

The French King, on the other hand, despite his public protestations of anger and grief, was disinclined to take the positive retaliatory measures against England being urged by the Catholic extremists. As the Spanish ambassador wrote to Philip on March 7, "The King speaks publicly of all these things but gives no indication as to what measures he will take to resent them."[7] Henri's reluctance to act in the matter is generally explained by historians in terms of his continuing hostility, under the influence of his mother, Catherine de' Medici, to the house of Guise and the control that party sought to exercise over him; even before the execution, as well as after it, he was making pacific overtures both to England and to the German principalities as part of an effort to free himself from domination by the Guisian Catholic party.[8] Nor was Henri alone in this hostility toward the Guisian and League Catholics, for, as L'Estoile reports, the more moderate Catholics throughout France were inclined to view the Leaguers and their ambitions with similar suspicion.

It was clear, then, that if the partisans of Mary were to succeed in their effort to rally Europe to a suppression of heresy in her name, they would have to overcome the apathy represented by Henri and the more moderate Catholic party. Moreover, Mary's propagandists had to face the fact, as they admitted, that Elizabeth's government had meanwhile succeeded in creating further division of feeling by blocking any other detailed account of the execution while the authorized English version circulated throughout Europe. As Blackwood himself lamented later, many Frenchmen and others who had originally been well affected toward the Scottish Queen were misled at this time by what he called the libels spread through Europe by the artifices of the English.[9] A measure of the desperateness of Mary's propagandists is seen in their frantic efforts to correct the opinion of the Pope himself, who had apparently succumbed momentarily to rumors about the execution already spreading through Europe. Upon learning at the end of March, 1587, that "his Holiness will not consent to celebrate the exequies for the Queen of Scotland, being in doubt as to whether she died a good Catholic," Mary's partisans sent Dr. William Allen to Rome with instructions

... to banish his Holiness' suspicions, which he has conceived from evil reports, that the queen of Scotland did not die a very good Catholic; he having been told that she recommended her son very warmly to maintain his friendship and dependence upon the queen of England. The statement is entirely false, and there are many reasons for presuming that she died, not a Catholic alone, but a holy martyr.[10]

As a matter of fact, the Pope could not have learned from the London account that Mary "recommended her son very warmly" to Elizabeth, unless he misconstrued her message recorded there to the effect that James should "offer no occasion for evil suspicion by the Queen of England," a recommendation that sounds more like an ironic warning. However, a rumor that Mary had urged James to love Elizabeth as a mother was, as we shall see, circulating at this time, and it may have been this rumor that reached the Pope. Whatever the source of His Holiness' information, an attitude such as his made it urgently necessary for Mary's Catholic supporters that the Protestant English representation of her death be counteracted and her martyrdom established in some way, and at once.

One could brand the official account as false and malicious, condemn it as Calvinistic heresy, sneer at it as tedious and long-winded nonsense—all of which Mary's partisans tried to do.[11] But it was obvious that something more positive in the way of counterpropaganda was immediately needed to establish in Catholic Europe a belief in the religious martyrdom and the political innocence of the Queen of Scots.

Although the stimulus for this counterpropaganda came from the Guise-League party in France, most of the actual work involved in producing and disseminating the literature that resulted seems to have fallen to the group of exiled English and Scottish Catholics then living in France. It was natural that these exiles should ally themselves with the Leaguers, since a professed objective of the latter was the restoration of Catholicism in Scotland and England. Moreover, the most active propagandists among the exiles had had personal connections with the late Queen which reinforced their political and religious feelings about her death. Thus John Leslie, now in France and about to make a final effort in Mary's name, had been one of her most faithful servants and ardent apologists. Second only to Leslie among her supporters abroad was Adam Blackwood, who had visited Mary several times during her imprisonment in England, and apparently had last seen her just a few days before the execution.[12] Leslie and Blackwood were soon joined by two other Scottish Catholics closely identified with the house of Guise and the League in the effort to release Mary and return Britain to the Roman Catholic faith. These were the ubiquitous Scottish Jesuit William Crichton, who arrived in Paris in May, 1587, following his release from the Tower of London where he had been imprisoned since 1584 for suspected implication in the Parry Plot; and Blackwood's own son-in-law, George Crichton (or Critton), apparently no kin of William, but an ardent Leaguer who was teaching in Paris at the time and was a prolific composer of occasional poems in Latin. One of these two (it is not clear which) was to contribute, under the initials "G. C. S.," the most obscene of the anti-Elizabethan poems to the propaganda favoring the late Queen of Scots.[13]

The crucial problem faced by these loyal proponents for a

Catholic uprising in the name of their Queen was getting access to firsthand material. Because of the English blockade on information from Fotheringay, Mary's supporters had only the barest facts out of which to build their case for her martyrdom. Their plight in this respect, and the only solution available to them at the moment, were candidly described by Blackwood in the following year when he looked back on this problem. Noting the suppression of letters and messengers from England, he says:

For that reason both the Catholics and those others who wished her well, in England as well as in France, wanting to describe her conduct, both on that last occasion and earlier, but not knowing what had happened, could only publish what they conjectured and imagined took place; while the English did not fail to spread abroad rumors and writings to their own advantage.[14]

Considering the source, this is a remarkably frank and honest explanation of exactly what Mary's propagandists were forced to do from the time of the execution in February until October of the same year, when the Scottish Queen's retainers returned to France with ample eyewitness accounts of her death from the Catholic point of view. During these months the Catholic presses of Europe poured forth a steady stream of "what they conjectured and imagined took place." Specifically, Mary's supporters resorted to three stopgap measures designed to counteract the English accounts of her political guilt and to develop the theme of her martyrdom.

The Catholic propagandists first sought to exploit a sketchy and admittedly hearsay report of the execution which managed to slip through the otherwise tight English blockade. This account was contained in a letter that Chateauneuf, the French ambassador in London and an ardent Guisian, succeeded in getting smuggled out of England sometime after February 27, 1587, and that reached Paris on March 6 or 7.[15] The bulk of his letter was devoted to apologies for his delay in getting a report to his royal master, but the first two pages describe the proceedings at Fotheringay as the ambassador had heard them reported.

Chateauneuf, who was being held under surveillance in London at the time, apparently got his information for this account from a member of his staff who was present at the execution.[16] The ambassador admits the hearsay nature of his report by prefacing many of his statements with the phrase, "l'on dit." His account, although agreeing in general outline with the reports of Wingfield and of the earls, records totally different details of the setting, the action, and —most significantly—the speeches. Thus Chateauneuf wrote that when Mary was told of the impending execution, she remarked that she welcomed it after so long an imprisonment, although she had never believed that Elizabeth would go to this extreme. He also recorded such circumstantial details as the fact that she ate a little food before leaving her chamber, and that on mounting the scaffold she asked Paulet, her English keeper, to support her as the last request she would make of him.

More important, he records a version of the speech delivered by Mary to Melville, her major-domo, different in substance and language from that found in Wingfield's letter and in the official English published account. In the latter, it will be recalled, Mary had urged her son to maintain the Catholic church, to give Elizabeth no cause for evil suspicion, and to understand that she had "desired to unite this island in one realm." Chateauneuf reported simply that she charged Melville to find her son, give him her blessing, and serve him faithfully, and that James would be better able to reward the major-domo's faithful service than she. Chateaneuf also emphasized the report that when Mary was approached on the scaffold by "an English bishop," she protested that she was a Catholic and would die a Catholic. Then, according to the ambassador's letter, Mary addressed various requests to the English earls, and, according to a detail not recorded elsewhere, she asked about her former servants—Nau, Curll, and Pasquier, all of whom were in prison. Finally, he reported the actual beheading in one sentence without detail, after which he described Elizabeth receiving the news while riding horseback, and noted the general rejoicing in London when the news was announced there.

At this point Chateauneuf interrupted his account with his complaint to the French King that Elizabeth was holding Mary's servants and himself incommunicado until she could send her own report of the execution and its causes abroad. Then he returned briefly to the execution itself to add a detail singularly notable because of its absence from any of the published English reports, and because of its usefulness to the Catholic cause. He observes that according to rumors he had heard, the Scottish Queen, as she died, persisted in saying that she was innocent of the political charges brought against her, and that she had never thought to cause the Queen of England to be killed.[17] Here was a detail understandably omitted from English accounts designed to emphasize Mary's political guilt, but essential to the case for her political innocence and religious martyrdom that her friends wanted to make. As events proved, they were to make the most of the item. At the same time, they were to ignore another observation that Chateauneuf appended at this point, simply as a doubtful rumor, to the effect that the Scottish Queen had recommended that her son respect the English Queen as his mother and do nothing to lose her friendship.

Incomplete and secondhand as Chateauneuf's account necessarily was, it at least had the virtue of being timely and available for Mary's Catholic supporters on the Continent. Almost immediately they lifted bodily those sections that dealt specifically with Mary's death and had them printed verbatim in a slight, hastily produced pamphlet entitled *Discours de la Mort de . . . Marie Stouard Royne d'Ecosse*.[18] The paragraph reporting her protestations of innocence, appearing as the climactic finale of this account, revealed at least one of the lines the pro-Marian propaganda literature was inevitably going to develop.

The Chateauneuf account was timely, but in at least some quarters its adequacy and its accuracy alike were questioned. The Parisian diarist, Pierre L'Estoile, for example, recorded in his *Journal* that although it was immediately printed and widely accepted as true because of its official source, it "contained almost as many errors as lines, and occupied only about a page and a half of writing."[19] Moreover, from the point of view of the Catholic party's main line of defense, the account was completely lacking in those details of Mary's conduct and speeches that could be made to enhance the case for her religious martyrdom.

These shortcomings were apparently obvious to the propagandists themselves, and steps were soon taken to circulate an account of the execution that, while reproducing all Chateauneuf's report, added to it a number of details to strengthen the impression that Mary died a martyr for religion, innocent of the political charges the English brought against her. The versions of this amplified account bearing the earliest dates—none after March 13, 1587, and hence all before the published English account was available—are found in the papers of three ambassadors resident in Paris at the time: James Beaton, Archbishop of Glasgow, who was Mary Stuart's representative there; Giovanni Dolfin, the Venetian ambassador; and Bernardino de Mendoza, the Spanish ambassador.[20]

In these three reports, Chateauneuf's basic account is reproduced in substance and often verbatim, but it is supplemented with the information that, on the night before her death, Mary, although protesting her innocence of plotting against the life of Elizabeth, nevertheless confessed that she had indeed striven for the propagation of the Roman Catholic religion. She felt, according to one of these accounts, that she "was dying chiefly for the Catholic cause, than which nothing is more glorious." [21] All versions of the report also add that Mary spent her last night praying before a eucharist smuggled in to her cell secretly from the Pope, and that she had received her final communion from a priest who was with her in disguise. On the scaffold, these amplified accounts go on to say, Mary not only professed again her political innocence but also confessed that she had always striven for the restoration of Catholicism to England and Scotland. All the reports, significantly, omit Chateauneuf's mention of the rumor that Mary urged her son to regard Elizabeth as a mother. Finally, Chateauneuf's original statement that Elizabeth was riding horseback when she received the news of Mary's death becomes the assertion that, upon hearing the tidings, she *took* to her horse and rode through the streets of London to receive the acclaim of her subjects.

Whether these supplementary details were obtained from a communication now lost, or were transmitted orally by the courier who brought Chateauneuf's letter, or were created out of the whole cloth to reinforce the case for Mary's martyrdom is not certain.

Some of the details, at least, seem to have been rather freely adapted to the execution account from earlier diplomatic reports on Mary's reception of the news in December, 1586, that sentence had been passed against her. It is not improbable that Adam Blackwood, Mary's most ardent apologist, supplied the details from whatever sources he could lay hands on, including earlier printed accounts of the pronouncement of sentence. He had been in the party of Pomponne de Bellièvre, the French secretary of state whom Henri III sent to England in November, 1586, to deliver a final plea to Elizabeth in behalf of Mary, and he was probably still there when the sentence was published in December.[22]

Whatever their sources, the means by which these consistently pro-Catholic additions came to be incorporated into the Chateauneuf report to form an account that was soon to be widely published under the highest auspices can at least be tentatively suggested. At the head of Archbishop Beaton's copy of the manuscript is a note which seems to explain where he got the amplified account, and, presumably, where the other ambassadors got their almost identical versions. Beaton's copy is entitled: "Epitome of those things which were written from England to the Most Christian King [Henri] by his Ambassador [Chateauneuf] concerning the manner of the most lamentable death of the Queen of Scotland and Dowager of France, reported by order of his Majesty to the Most Christian Lord, the Archbishop of Glasgow, sometime Ambassador of the said Queen, by the Sieur de Gondy, Agent of the Ambassadors." Now as we have just seen, the amplified account given to Beaton, like that given to Mendoza and Dolfin, is not, as claimed in its heading, Chateauneuf's report exactly as he wrote it and as it was published in the *Discours de la Mort*. Apparently the "Sieur de Gondy," acting as a kind of minister of information under the orders of the French King, prepared or caused to be prepared this amplified version of the letter intended to be placed in the hands of the ambassadors of the chief Catholic powers of Europe.[23] In a sense, then, the Chateauneuf-Gondy account, as we may call it, is as much an authorized French Catholic account of Mary's execution as the Wingfield-based report is the authorized English account.

While the Chateauneuf-Gondy account was being transmitted by the ambassadors to their respective capitals, it seems also to have been put to almost immediate use in Paris. At least two of the funeral sermons preached in France in commemoration of Mary's death appear to have relied on it for much of their detail concerning the execution. The first of these was delivered by Renauld de Beaune, Archbishop of Bourges, at the funeral services held for Mary in Notre Dame cathedral on March 13, 1587. A published version of the sermon appeared in the following year.[24] The service was ordered by the French King himself and, according to L'Estoile, was sumptuously set and was attended by all the notables of Paris. As published, the sermon was mainly an elaborate eulogy of Mary's life and character that developed the principal themes of the earlier literature in her behalf—her personal and political innocence, Elizabeth's perfidy, the threat to royal authority contained in Elizabeth's treatment of Mary. Above all, the oration stressed her martyrdom for her religion. As de Beaune cried, "But accused of what crime? Accused of being a Catholic! O happy crime! O desirable accusation!" To illustrate this thesis, the Archbishop gave a detailed description of her conduct on the scaffold. Here his reliance on the Chateauneuf-Gondy account is most apparent, for he describes her remarks to her attendants, her professions of religious faith and political innocence, the barbaric pleasure of Elizabeth in taking to horse when she received the news, and similar details exactly as they appeared in the French account. Then, in his peroration, de Beaune made explicit one of the principal motives behind most of the Catholic literature written on Mary's death. Branding the event as the death of royal sovereignty everywhere, he demanded that the "Christian princes" of the world invade England and avenge the death of the martyr. In other words, he directed his remarks to achieving precisely what English propaganda had been designed to prevent.

The second of the two funeral orations followed the authorized execution account even more closely than did de Beaune's in developing the established propaganda themes. This was delivered by Mary's most faithful apologist, John Leslie, the Bishop of Ross, although where and exactly when is not indicated. Leslie, who was probably in Rouen at the time of the execution, apparently gave the oration in Scots, but it survives only in a French translation published in the year following the execution.[25] Leslie began by saying that he intended only to honor one of God's servants dead, and to remind his listeners of the vanity of this world. And indeed, the early part of his oration is an impressively simple and moving tribute by one who had served Mary faithfully and well. As he proceeds to review her career, however, the familiar themes begin to appear, and in an extended account of her execution he draws on all the resources offered by the Chateauneuf-Gondy report to develop these themes to the full. He cites her repeated professions of political innocence and confessions of activity for her church. As proof of her piety he describes the night spent in prayer before the smuggled eucharist and her secret communion received from the disguised priest. He quotes her joyful exclamation that she was to die for her religion. In all of the circumstantial details of the episode, he follows the official French account exactly. A long section toward the end of his "Harangue" is devoted to castigation of Elizabeth so violent that Leslie himself must apologize: "I pray you forgive me," he says, "if I am constrained to make an invective of a funeral lament." He concludes, in a characteristic appeal to Catholic princes, that this execution is a violation not only of innocence, not only of true religion, but of "the right of scepters," and until the serpents of heresy are stamped out, he adds, no throne anywhere will be safe.

Meanwhile, the same official French account of the execution upon which these sermons seem to have drawn was receiving circulation abroad exactly as Gondy had apparently hoped it would when he made it available to ambassadors and other foreign residents in Paris. Especially in Italy the account served as the basis for frequently reprinted reports of the affair at Fotheringay. Some half-dozen versions were published in as many Italian cities early in 1587. All purport to be original letters written from Paris, but all actually or substantially reproduce the Chateauneuf-Gondy account.[26] Usually some distinctive introductory or concluding remark in epistolary manner is added to emphasize the propagandistic point of the original. One of the more striking of such touches appears in a version attributed to Sartorio Loscho and printed in separate editions at Bergamo, Parma, and Vicenza.[27] Loscho prefaced the body of his report, which is for the most part a literal translation of the Chateauneuf-Gondy account, with a sketch of Mary's earlier history. Referring to her flight from Scotland in 1568, he reports that the Queen of Scots arrived in England against her wish, her ship having been driven off its course by a storm while she was seeking to escape from Scotland to France.[28] Actually, Mary had, according to her own statements, gone to England of her own free will. With this legend Loscho apparently seeks to undermine the English argument that Mary, by her activities in England, had violated a hospitality she had deliberately sought, and to heighten the impression that Mary was the innocent victim of English villainy. He continues his prefatory statement by admitting that the Scottish Queen made numerous efforts while imprisoned in England to gain her liberty that she might establish the true faith there, but he asserts that she never plotted in treasonable fashion against the throne or life of Elizabeth. Finally, he says, Mary was brought to trial and found guilty, despite her protests that she was not subject to the jurisdiction of the English Queen. By such mixing of fact and fancy, Loscho, like many of his Italian counterparts who used the Chateauneuf-Gondy account, succeeded in creating the impression that Mary was imprisoned and punished not for political reasons, as the English contended, but purely because of her faith and of English hatred of the Catholic church.

With the publication in 1587 of these Italian versions, together with the two funeral orations and whatever reports the three ambassadors in Paris may have sent back to their respective capitals, the account of the execution prepared by Gondy on the basis of Chateauneuf's smuggled letter received remarkably wide distribution. Considering that at the same time Chateauneuf's original unamplified report was also being widely circulated in printed form, the zeal as well as the sense of urgency that marked the activities of Mary's Catholic apologists in France becomes unquestionable. For Chateauneuf's letter could not have arrived before March 6, if Mendoza's report to Philip is true. Yet by March 13, the supplemented account had been handed to all the ambassadors, was available to the Archbishop of Bourges and the Bishop of Ross, and was on its way to widespread publication in Italy. In this manner, Mary's defenders, making the most of what information they could get through Elizabeth's blockade, had spread their own story of the execution over a large part of the Continent even before the official English account, dated in London on March 27, could have appeared there.

In addition to the Chateauneuf-Gondy account, however, Mary's supporters very soon had available a second means of spreading the story of her death as, in Blackwood's words, "they conjectured and imagined it to be." This was the official English account itself, which Mary's Catholic apologists immediately began to adapt to their own purposes and to publish widely. Judging from the versions that survive, such use of the English account was the practice of Mary's defenders particularly in the Low Countries and in Germany, where—perhaps because Chateauneuf's reports were not readily available—adaptation of the English report was the only choice open to the Catholic propagandists. Those who thus resorted to the London version were fully aware of its origin and acknowledged that it was a "Calvinist" account, as they generally termed it. But, as one of them explained, even through the report of heretics Mary's martyrdom for her religion seemed obvious.[29] However, lest any Catholic reader of the official English account miss this point, the adapters devised various ways of emphasizing the principal pro-Marian propaganda themes in their presentation of the report.

One method employed by Mary's partisans, as exemplified in two similar versions, one German and the other Dutch, was to substitute a new, ardently Catholic introduction and conclusion for the corresponding first and last sections of the English account, but to leave the London description of the execution itself intact. The German adaptation was published in Munich in 1587 with the imperial privilege. It bore a lengthy title which clearly revealed its theme and purpose: "A brief and well-founded report of how Mary Stuart, the noble and pious Queen of Scots, and by her mother and the House of Guise, also of the royal blood of France, was executed in England on February 18 [n.s.], and how she met a holy death." [30] Here, in place of the extended English explanation of Mary's treason and Elizabeth's kindness and grief, the German account substitutes a shorter resumé of Mary's career that gives a very different impression. According to the German introduction, Mary was driven from her throne and realm by rebel heretics because of her religion. Contrary to Mary's own account of her flight to England, the German adapter avers that she had planned to escape into France, and in fact had already boarded ship to do so. But in a version of this episode differing from that of his Italian counterpart Loscho, he says that Elizabeth, hiding her hatred under words of pretended friendship, offered to help Mary regain her throne if she would come into England. Mary believed her, but no sooner had her ship put in at an English harbor than she was taken prisoner. Then, the German writer continues, she was held at Fotheringay Castle for twenty years until, at the order of Elizabeth and her Parliament, the Queen of Scots "willingly died with great and steadfast faith in the Holy Roman Catholic religion."

Following this introduction, the German account then reproduces verbatim the official English description of the execution itself, beginning with Mary's reception of the announcement on the eve of her death. It ends, however, with the description of the blow struck by the executioner, omitting the concluding details about her appearance in death, the clearing of the hall, and the announcement of the news in London. In place of the lengthy English summary of the major Protestant propaganda themes, the German account has only one short paragraph which explains that Mary was killed because the heretics feared that she would succeed Elizabeth and restore Catholicism to England. It concludes that Mary died innocent, a martyr to her faith, and that God would render final judgment.

The Dutch account is in many respects identical with the German version just described. It was published at Antwerp in 1587 "Met Consent," and, like the German publication, it bore a lengthy title that revealed its Catholic auspices and point of view.[31] The opening lines of the account differ curiously from the German. Instead of the story that Mary was lured into England from Scotland under false pretenses, the Dutch account, like the Italian account by Loscho, offers the odd piece of misinformation that the ship on which she was trying to escape to France was blown off its course by tempestuous winds and forced to take refuge in an English harbor, where Mary was recognized, promptly seized, and thrown into prison.[32] From this point on, the Dutch version follows the German exactly verbatim, even in paragraphing. It reproduces the London report of the execution, and it concludes, like the German account, with a reiteration of Mary's religious martyrdom, which it calls on God to avenge.

A second way of turning the official English account of the execution into propaganda for Mary's martyrdom is exemplified in a version published in Germany in 1587 and 1588. Here all three parts of the original are translated exactly and in entirety, according to an assertion on the title page which is substantiated by comparison of the text with versions of the report published under Protestant auspices. But it is accompanied by a mass of commentary and critical apparatus designed to offset, for the Catholic reader, the "Calvinistic" bias of the original and to make clear the idea that Mary was martyred for her religion.

The best extant example of this version is probably the earliest that appeared, a Latin pamphlet headed *Mariae Stuartae . . . Supplicium & Mors,* printed at Cologne in 1587.[33] Its full title provides a complete description of the source, the method, and the nature of the work. Translated, it reads:

The Execution and Death, for her most steadfast Catholic faith, of Mary Stuart, Queen of Scots, Catholic princess recently killed by Queen Elizabeth and her Council of England, after imprisonment for 19 years at the castle of Fotheringay. First written in England in the vernacular: and therefore tainted in many respects by the prejudices of this Queen's enemies; which things she never any time confessed, nor which have yet been properly proved. Now translated and edited faithfully for the benefit of Catholics, with absolutely no omissions: in order that the fervor of the most holy martyred princess, and the undaunted constancy of her spirit, confirmed by the testimony of her very adversaries themselves, may enlighten the whole world. Hereto are added certain brief animadversions and notes, and a short chronology of the whole life of the Queen, collected out of some of the best authors.

In spite of the assurance that here is "testimony of her very adversaries themselves," it is still rather surprising to find, in this arch-Catholic publication, the entire official English account of the execution. Everything is here, word for word, including the introductory and concluding defenses of Elizabeth's actions. The pro-Marian propaganda themes, however, are developed in the apparatus that accompanies the account. First of all, to show the Catholic reader how he should interpret the English report, the editor adds to the text a series of pro-Catholic marginal comments and numbered "Animadversions." For example, when Mary, according to the text, tells Kent that she would rather die than live, the marginal note observes, "Worthy voice of the martyr aspiring to Heaven." On the Dean of Peterborough's efforts to convert Mary, the marginal note comments, "Diabolical temptations by the Calvinist minister." As the account approaches its climax, the notes become correspondingly more emphatic in pointing up Mary's martyrdom. Thus, when the London account reports that Mary forgave the executioners, the note exclaims, "Voice of the queen after the example of Christ." The "Animadversions" following the text itself similarly emphasize the themes of Mary's martyrdom, of Elizabeth's perfidy, and of warning to princes against heretics. Typical of these is the gloss on the executioner's cry for Elizabeth, "God Save the Queen," which reads, for Mary, "Vivat Regina martyr cum Christo in secula."

In addition to these notes and comments, the Cologne publication contains a number of Latin poems to enhance the Catholic propaganda value of the work. The Latin epitaph signed "I. H. D.," which was prepared in England and seems to have accompanied the official English account as it circulated over the Continent, is reprinted here intact, but following it is an altered version which, for the "Sic transit Gloria" theme of the original, substitutes the theme of Mary's glory in heaven. Thereafter appears a series of six Latin poems headed, "On the Martyrdom of the Most Serene Mary Queen of Scots, Murdered in England for the Catholic Faith." In the most curious of these poems, Mary is presented as congratulating her husband Darnley, who "was strangled by heretics," on his own glorious martyrdom.

At the end, the Cologne edition provides a "Chronologia," a year-by-year summary of Mary's life. The "best authors" upon which, according to the title page, this sketch is based, are principally John Leslie, whose appearance in this context is not surprising, and George Buchanan, whose presence here is very surprising indeed. By selection of detail, however, the writer constructs an account of Mary's career consistent in tone and attitude with the editorial policy of the publication, and with Leslie's theme if not with Buchanan's. Indeed, the "Chronologia" is far less the story of Mary's life than it is a general account of the rise and menace of the Protestant heresy. Where it does deal with Mary specifically, it tells the story made familiar in earlier Catholic accounts of her troubled career, blaming the Earl of Murray for her difficulties in Scotland, Elizabeth for those in England, and the Calvinist heresy throughout.

By and large, the Cologne pamphlet is a remarkable demonstration of the way in which Mary's supporters, with little new material at hand, could make propaganda capital of secondhand and even hostile reports. The pamphlet's effectiveness was extended when it was republished at Ingoldstadt in the following year, together with a translation of *The Copie of a Letter to . . . Leycester* and a series of pro-Catholic answers to the English reasons for Mary's death set forth there.[34] Thus in at least two widely separated parts of Germany the propaganda materials of the English were turned back against the English themselves.

Meanwhile, in addition to the versions of the English account published with new introductions at Antwerp and Munich, and the annotated texts published at Cologne and Ingoldstadt, there was still a third way in which Catholic propagandists turned the London narrative to their own purposes. This technique was merely to work into the Chateauneuf-Gondy account those elements and details from the authorized English report that would make the authorized French account a more circumstantial and effective presentation of the case for Mary's innocence and martyrdom. Such, at least, seems to have been the procedure involved in the preparation of an account published in Italy in 1587, although apparently later in the year than the Italian accounts previously described. This work, edited by one Francesco Dini da Colle and printed in different editions at Genoa, Vico, Milan, and Florence, bore the title, "A true and complete account of the execution of the most Christian Queen of Scotland." [35] In dedicating his work to the Mother Superior and the Sisters of the Order of Santo Clemente, Dini points out that the story of Mary's heroic, Catholic end, and especially her rejection of a heretical minister offered to her by Queen Elizabeth, will serve as an eternal example to the Sisters and to all Catholics everywhere.

Like the earlier Italian treatments of the French account and the Antwerp and Munich versions of the London, Dini's work opens with an introductory sketch of Mary's last years. In this respect, however, his account seems to be totally independent of the other reports and their sources. He tells of Mary's removal from "Essex's palace" (Chartley) to Fotheringay castle after Catholic plots to rescue her had been discovered by the English. He then explains that she was brought to trial, adding that she refused to answer or to speak because she did not consider herself under the jurisdiction of Elizabeth. This point of Elizabeth's lack of jurisdiction was by this time, as we have seen, a standard argument in pro-Marian propaganda, but, contrary to Dini's inference, Mary spoke, and spoke at extraordinary length, in her own defense at the trial.[36] After the trial, he continues, sentence of death was passed on the Queen of Scots, and the news was taken to her (presumably in November, 1586) by Lord Buckhurst, who, according to the Italian writer, added insult to injury by removing all the royal trappings from her chamber and draping it in black. Meanwhile, the ambassadors of France and Scotland interceded with Elizabeth for Mary and were assured, he says, that the sentence would not be carried out. However, Elizabeth went back on her word, and on February 16 [sic] Mary was told that she was to be executed the following day.

In his account of the execution itself, Dini seems to follow in the main the pro-Catholic version of the story which Gondy fashioned on the basis of Chateauneuf's report. But the Italian amplifies the narrative with details which, although particularly adaptable to Catholic propaganda themes, were apparently lifted out of the official English account of the execution. For example, as in the English account, Dini says that Mary charged her major-domo Melville to tell James to trust not worldly prudence but only God, to give no offense to Elizabeth, and to embrace the Catholic faith—all injunctions notable for their absence from the Chateauneuf-Gondy accounts hitherto considered. Perhaps most indicative of Dini's source and his way of using it is his handling of Mary's verbal exchange with Kent regarding the crucifix she carried. In the London version, it will be recalled, Mary, replying to Kent's reference to her crucifix as "superstitious," retorted that it served to keep Christ in her mind, whereupon Kent, having the last word, remarked that it would become her instead to carry Christ in her heart, and not in her hand. This whole episode was apparently missed by Chateauneuf's reporter and Gondy's sources of information alike, for no trace of it appears in other versions of the official French account. Properly handled, it could be the kind of detail essential to Mary's Catholic propagandists. Dini apparently recognized this possibility. He borrowed the episode but revised it so that, after Kent's remark on her idolatrous superstition, the interchange ended with Mary asking that she be left in peace to contemplate the passion of her Savior. Thus, by allowing Mary instead of Kent to have the last word, Dini added considerable vividness to the portrait of the Christian, Catholic martyr.

In such fashion Dini made out of the Chateauneuf-Gondy narrative what is probably the most detailed of the Catholic execution accounts published before the return of Mary's servants from England with their own eye-witness stories. His work illustrates again the remarkable ingenuity with which Catholic propagandists, deprived of adequate materials of their own, used all available sources, including the official English propaganda report itself, for their own advantage.

While the official French account of Mary's execution was circulating over the Continent and the official English account was being adapted for distribution in her cause, the more ardent of her admirers were producing still a third type of interim propaganda to arouse Europe against England in the name of Mary and of the faith for which they claimed she died.

A series of poems on the death of Mary, the first group of which began to appear before the return of her servants, made up in violence of feeling and expression what they lacked in factual information about the execution and its attendant circumstances. Here in literal truth Mary's propagandists resorted, as Blackwood said they had to, to "what they imagined took place," and their imagination was reinforced by emotional attitudes that make these poems the best indication of the state of mind Mary's execution produced among her loyal followers. As Pierre L'Estoile, who made a collection of some of the poems, observed rather sardonically in his *Journal:* "The pasquils, the placcards, the epitaphs, and the discourses on this death flew about Paris and everywhere, and were used according to the feeling and the passions of the parties." [37]

Altogether, some fifty poems of this sort, in a variety of languages and by a variety of authors, were ultimately published in a series of closely related collections or anthologies that appeared throughout 1587 and 1588 all over Europe.[38] From the outset Adam Blackwood appears to have been the prime mover in the preparation of these collections, as well as one of the principal contributors. On the day of Mary's funeral service at Notre Dame, a Latin poem that extolled her martyrdom and scurrilously abused Elizabeth as her murderer was posted at the door of the cathedral. Now known to have been written by Blackwood, the work bore a title that might be translated as, "A Poem Concerning the Parricides of the Jezebel of England, Addressed to the Pious Ghost of Mary Queen of Scots." Shortly thereafter the same poem, somewhat revised, appeared with others of similar nature in two small collections, both entitled, as translated, "Latin and French Poems of Various Kinds Concerning the Parricide [Committed] by the Jezebel of England." Subsequent collections, incorporating these earlier poems and adding new ones in the same vein, continued to appear frequently in France and Belgium, and were circulated, if not published, in Italy and Spain as well. The poems are of many types, as the title indicates, including funeral odes, invectives against Elizabeth, proposed inscriptions for Mary's tomb, sonnets and epigrams on the execution, and ingenious anagrammatic poems on Mary's name. Although most of the pieces are anonymous, a number are signed by such figures as Malherbe, Robert Garnier, and Cardinal du Perron. But the major contributions are by Blackwood. In addition to his poem that was first posted at the Cathedral, he included in the collections a longer Latin poem on the same theme, a Latin epitaph on the Scottish Queen, and a *Monumentum Regale* intended for her tomb in Peterborough Cathedral, where Elizabeth finally had her interred.

Varied as they are in other respects, the *De Jezabelis* poems—as they may be termed on the basis of Blackwood's Latin poem that appeared first in most of the collections—have in common the central theme and purpose of arousing Catholic Europe against England and Protestantism in the name of the martyred Queen of Scots. As the somewhat cynical Pierre L'Estoile remarked, the verses "cried and shouted that she died a martyr for the Roman, Catholic, and Apostolic faith, and that the English queen killed her for no other reason than religion." [39] At the same time, the Spanish ambassador in Paris apparently recognized the same purpose of the poems when he sent to King Philip "a book of various poems which have been written on the death of the queen of Scotland, as it contains some smart epigrams on the life of her of England." [40] The poems themselves, indeed, are quite explicit as to their purpose, and often shrill in their calls for action. To this end they continue to develop the basic themes characterizing the campaign for Mary during the preceding twenty years. But where formerly a certain caution and moderation had ruled, now no holds were barred.

The principal theme developed in the poems is the charge that Elizabeth, in executing Mary, revealed herself as an English Jezebel. Mary's propagandists have come a long way since John Leslie first introduced the theme of Elizabeth's culpability with the cautious suggestion that she was a well-meaning and admirable queen, but possibly misled by wicked advisers. The original Jezebel herself would have blushed to behold the woman now portrayed in the poems of 1587. Assuming with little argument and less evidence that Elizabeth was personally responsible for the death of Mary, the poets proceed to revile the English Queen in terms of her alleged adulterous and incestuous ancestry, her licentious life, and her wolfish cruelty.

The poems elaborately develop the story, first published in Marian literature by Sanders a decade before, that Elizabeth was both the daughter and the sister of Anne Boleyn. The original "De Jezabelis" posted at the door of Notre Dame begins by denouncing the bastard (Murray) who drove Mary from her Scottish throne, and then proceeds to excoriate the other bastard (Elizabeth) who has now taken Mary's life. The poem explains in some detail that Anne Boleyn slept not only with her own brother and with Henry VIII but also with so many other men that Elizabeth's parentage was considerably obscured.[41] The "Vers Funèbres" attributed to Cardinal du Perron develop the same theme, describing Elizabeth as "this monster, conceived in adultery and incest, her fangs bared for murder, who befouls and despoils the sacred right of scepters, and vomits her choler and gall at heaven." [42]

Not only on the grounds of her ancestry, but also of her character and conduct, Elizabeth was frequently and violently reviled in the poems. The title poem by Blackwood, for example, alleges that Elizabeth personally tried to administer poison to Mary—on the altar table—and, failing in this, sought to murder James, so that the English throne would be left secure for what were described as Elizabeth's illegitimate offspring. Other poems explain, in terms of obscenity forbidding translation, that these illegitimate children were the fruit of Elizabeth's promiscuous conduct with most of the members of her Privy Council, and with the Earl of Leicester in particular. One poem charges that Elizabeth deliberately avoided marriage because she wanted to be free to enjoy these licentious pleasures.[43]

In reviling Elizabeth, the De Jezabelis poems also assail what they describe as her motiveless and malicious cruelty toward the Scottish Queen. For this purpose, the poets regularly employ the figure of the she-wolf. Much literary sport is had with the tradition that there are no wolves in England; as a French "Quadrain," frequently reprinted in the collections, puts the point:

> Englishmen, you say that there
> A single wolf cannot be found:
> No. But you have there a she-wolf,
> Worse by far than a million.[44]

The poems charge Elizabeth with such cruelties, for example, as murdering out of sheer jealousy any man who showed more than passing interest in the beauteous and helpless Queen of Scots, and placing the corpses of these victims outside Mary's window to rot, just for the nuisance value they would afford.[45]

The high-pitched fervor of this attack on Elizabeth in the *De Jezabelis* poems is well sustained in the development of the second major theme of the collections, the eulogizing of Mary the martyr. Occasionally, to be sure, preoccupation with literary ingenuity seems to get in the way of pure zeal, as in the one Italian poem that appears in the collections. Here each triad of the terza rima verse is accompanied in the margin by a phrase from the Ave Maria, so that one reads panegyrics to Mary of Scotland and Mary the Virgin at one and the same time.[46] For the most part, however, rapture and reverence rather than ingenuity are the tones that prevail when the poems deal with Mary's death for her religion.[47] Robert Garnier prays to Mary as a saint already established in heaven to protect France against the encroachments of the heretical German barbarians.[48] More than once Mary's sufferings are identified with those of Christ Himself; thus in "Les Derniers Parolles de la Royne d'Escosse," an elaborately imagined version of Mary's words on the scaffold, she is made to exclaim: "I, by Thy will, O Lord, both night and day, have traced the path that leads to martyrdom. But is this martyrdom, that for Thy sacred name leads me by this degree to mount to Thee, and follow Thee, my God, along this way?" [49]

Perhaps the most unusual expression of the theme of Mary's martyrdom appears in a "Pindarelle en faveur de la feu Royne d'Escosse." [50] This curious piece, which quite understandably has baffled its one modern editor, is in the form of a short Pindaric ode that manages in its brief compass to link Britain's King Arthur with the martyred Mary Stuart. The ode is built on an anagram printed in its entirety at the head of the poem:

> Marie Stuart
> Tu as martire,
> Artus a temir
> Artus merita
> Artus te mira.

In view of the fact that Elizabeth, like earlier Tudors, based her claim to the throne of England in part on the well-publicized contention that the family was descended from King Arthur, the reference in this poem to Mary's claims based on the same descent perhaps provides a key to its meanings. The poem then proceeds to develop the general idea that the English treatment of Mary is a disgrace to the chivalric tradition established by King Arthur. But the "Pindarelle" cannot go far without returning to the theme of religious martyrdom. Thus, in a typical stanza woven around one of the anagrams on her name, "Tu as Martire," the poet apostrophizes Mary as one whose devotion to the faith has given her name a holy renown.

Almost as fully and consistently developed in the *De Jezabelis* poems as the martyr theme is a third element already familiar from earlier propaganda literature but now carried to a new intensity. This is the theme of Mary's personal and political innocence, first introduced by Leslie in 1569 to counteract English charges of immorality and treason. A number of the poems sketch the story of her trials and tribulations in the customary terms of her victimization by rebel heretics. The title poem, Blackwood's "De Jezabelis," makes the Earl of Murray, aided and abetted by Elizabeth, the principal villain; in the words of a French paraphrase of the poem, "La bastarde au bastard promet un bonsecours." [51] Another poem in the collection charges that Elizabeth fomented the troubles in Scotland simply to force Mary to fly to England, where the English Queen could more conveniently murder her.[52] Mary, says Blackwood, steadfastly refused to do any wrong; accordingly, the English could only trump up the accusation that she was a Guise by birth. On this basis, they deliberately allowed her to become involved in the Babington plot. Blackwood admits that she participated in this scheme to assassinate Elizabeth, but he expresses indignation at what he calls the nefarious English trick by which

Mary was enticed to do so. In his opinion, the moral responsibility for Mary's participation fell on Elizabeth. Thus trapped, Mary was hastily convicted in a mock trial and condemned to death. Blackwood ends his versified biographical sketch with a brief account of the execution, emphasizing Mary's protest of her innocence and her confession that she had labored only for her own liberation and the restoration of the Catholic faith in England. The poet, after surveying the whole of human history for a parallel to this barbarous cruelty and injustice, can find none—not even among the cannibals who, he explains, eat human bodies.

It was inevitable that the poets of the *De Jezabelis* collections, having thus portrayed Mary as an innocent, sovereign queen who was martyred because of her Catholic faith by a Jezebel of Elizabeth's background and character, should interpret these circumstances as a warning to sovereigns everywhere against tolerating Protestant heretics in their realms. This theme, already familiar before Mary's execution, found emphatic new expression in these later collections. It was the sum and substance of the Latin prose *Monumentum Regale,* published repeatedly in the collections, which Blackwood wrote for Mary's tomb in Peterborough Cathedral. Having eulogized Mary and assailed her enemies, Blackwood concludes that "with the sacred herse of Saint Mary here lieth violate and prostrate the majestie of all Kings and Princes." [53] Another poet—probably the Scottish Catholic George Crichton, Blackwood's son-in-law—deplored the execution of a sovereign queen as the inevitable consequence of doctrines of popular sovereignty and regicide such as the heretics expounded. Choosing to ignore for the moment the fact that many of his fellow Catholics were expounding similar doctrines of rebellion and regicide when these doctrines could be directed against Elizabeth, he concluded that God would not tolerate those who put themselves above kings and queens in this mutinous fashion.[54] Similarly, in the title poem of the *De Jezabelis* collections Blackwood provided a versified "summary" of Buchanan's treatise on popular sovereignty, *De Jure Regni,* to illustrate the iniquitous and dangerous doctrines embraced by Protestants. Mary herself is made to sound the same warning to kings in the "Derniers Parolles." She calls on the kings of Europe to witness the wrongs done to her by heretics, and her death for the cause of religion, urging them to suppress heresy, that her fate might not be theirs. Then in a lengthy excursion into numerology, which the poet claims she made while on the scaffold awaiting the axe, she demonstrates that the name "Calvin" is the equivalent of the mystic number "666" in the Book of Revelation, and hence clearly a threat to universal peace and order.[55]

From such warnings there inevitably followed an appeal to Catholic kings to avenge Mary's death—by invading England, deposing Elizabeth, and restoring Catholicism. A few of the pieces are content to appeal generally to "all Christian kings everywhere" in this cause.[56] One poem, addressed to Elizabeth in threatening terms, exclaims, somewhat petulantly, that it is time for Catholic kings to stop talking and start taking action to avenge such crimes.[57] A few other poems appeal more specifically to Philip of Spain and James of Scotland to come in the name of Mary to the defense of religion and the right of kings.[58] By far the largest number of the poems direct their appeal for vengeance to Henri III of France. In view of Henri's wavering attitude towards the Scottish Queen and her party in France this concentration of effort is perhaps not surprising. The De Jezabelis poems sought to move the French King to act by appealing to him directly, and by arousing French public opinion to force him to do so. One of these poems, for example, opens by urging France to take punitive action against the English murderess of a French queen.[59] The poet then attempts to shame the French, and Henri in particular, by speculating on the reactions to these events that Mary's first husband, Francis II, must now be experiencing in heaven. Three times Francis tries to embrace Mary, says the poet, and three times, embracing only a headless body, he curses the French for permitting this affront to himself as a husband. Against this macabre background, the poet develops his main point. He calls on the French to forget their quarrels and bickering and to unite against England to avenge this deed by ravaging the land, sinking the island, and sending Elizabeth to a deservedly monstrous death. Finally, he sums up the central idea of his own poem and of most of those in the De

Jezabelis collections by demanding that Henri lead the fight to avenge the honor of Mary and of France by stamping out the heresy of a queen who does not respect the authority of princes. He points out, as an added practical inducement, that Henri can thereby join the crown of England and Scotland to the crown of France. Similar appeals to French national pride appear in poems warning that if France does not act, Spain or Germany may move first to avenge the honor of a Catholic queen.[60]

The *De Jezabelis* poems, like the adaptations of the execution accounts, indicate that Mary's Catholic supporters on the Continent managed, despite the obstacles presented, to propagandize her death as the supreme occasion for a Catholic action against the English Queen and the Protestant heresy. The English blockade on information from Fotheringay may have put the writers abroad at some disadvantage, but it by no means frustrated them completely. Circumstances were such that they could not afford to let themselves be frustrated, as the English no doubt hoped that they would be. Such factors as the acknowledged success of the English propaganda campaign in justification of the execution, the wavering opinion of the Pope, and the lukewarm attitude of Henri III at this critical juncture forced Mary's supporters to act quickly and positively with whatever materials they could lay their hands on. Hence within six months after the execution they had managed to flood Europe with printed material designed primarily to set in motion a great crusade against England in the name of the Scottish Queen.

The immediate response to this first effort must have been disappointing. James of Scotland, having already tacitly agreed not to interfere for his mother if Elizabeth would assure him the succession in England, contented himself and most of his people with verbal protests.[61] In France, Henri III, despite protestations of grief and anger at the death of his "sister," appeared to be moving steadily toward a reconciliation with the Protestant Henry of Navarre and away from the Guise-League faction which had espoused Mary's cause.[62] In Germany, the Catholic elements apparently were inclined to believe the English charges against Mary, and were not moved to act against England or Protestantism in her name.[63] Of course, the Pope and Philip of Spain were contemplating action, but differences between the two great Catholic leaders had so far produced only delays and hesitation.[64] But such apathy in France, Germany, Spain and Rome—in all of Europe, for that matter—did not deter Mary's supporters in their continuous efforts to arouse Catholics everywhere, and when her servants, released from English control, returned to France with eyewitness accounts and fresh material, the propagandists went to work again with new zeal.

VII THE CATHOLIC PERORATION:

1587-1603

It was late in October of 1587 when Mary's servants arrived in Paris after their long detainment at Fotheringay.[1] They included, to name the most important, Dominique Bourgoin, her physician; Pierre Gorion, her surgeon; and Elizabeth Curle and Jane Kennedy, the two ladies-in-waiting who were allowed on the scaffold with her.[2] As the English had anticipated, and as Mary's Catholic supporters had hoped, these attendants brought with them in their memoirs and their memories detailed reports of their mistress's words and actions in her last days. Bourgoin, for example, had prepared a written memorandum that, in addition to providing some new details of the execution itself, gave a full account of the Queen's activities on the night before the execution, when she was left alone with her retainers.[3] His fresh material was particularly important. Except for a confused rumor that she had taken a secret communion, little or nothing had been published about Mary's final hours the night before her death, since the English, having had the tact to leave her alone with her friends and servants, had not been able to describe what went on, and Chateauneuf's reporter was apparently not among those present.

Dr. Gorion evidently brought back an account, similar to Bourgoin's, which he gave to the Spanish ambassador for transmittal to Philip II.[4] Meanwhile, all the servants of every rank were interviewed and questioned. Blackwood claimed that he talked at length with the two women who had been allowed on the scaffold, and had secured from them information that, like Bourgoin's, he used in his published accounts of the Scottish Queen's martyrdom.[5] The information thus supplied by Mary's servants, grafted on to what was already available to her apologists from English sources or their own, was to become the basis for practically all the literature published in Mary's cause to the end of the century.

The man chiefly responsible for fusing these various materials into what might be called the definitive presentation of the Catholic case for Mary was Adam Blackwood himself. He merits this distinction on the basis of two works published immediately after the return of the servants. The first was the *Martyre de la Royne d'Escosse,* a detailed and impassioned account of Mary's mistreatment at the hands of the English from her arrival in Scotland in 1561 to her burial at Peterborough Cathedral in August, 1587.[6] Published anonymously toward the end of 1587, the work appeared in at least five separate editions before the end of 1589. In each successive edition Blackwood added supplementary material, drawn mainly from the imaginative *De Jezabelis* anthologies, to enhance the effect of his book.

As Blackwood himself candidly confessed in the *Martyre,* there was still strong need for further propaganda. Despite the earlier efforts of himself and his associates, few of the Catholic powers in Europe, as we have seen, had been moved to act against heretics in general or English heretics in particular. The hope for support that Catholics held in Mary's son, King James of Scotland, was thoroughly blasted. They had apparently sought to win him over to their cause by preparing a work called a "Book of Complaint from the Queen of Scots to her Son," but if, indeed, the book was ever published, or was ever seen by James, it had little effect on him. He persisted in his Protestantism and in his disinclination to lead a crusade in the name of his martyred mother.[7] Blackwood expressly blamed such inaction as this, especially in France, on the influence of English propaganda. The defection of Henri III, and of the Protestants and moderate Catholics who followed him, Blackwood explained, was brought about because these Frenchmen had been misled by the lies the English spread abroad concerning the causes and circumstances of the execution. It was his announced objective in the *Martyre* to correct this state of affairs for, as he says in an address to the reader, his book "is not prejudiced by false information as I know many of our Frenchmen are, who although they are not otherwise evilly disposed in this cause, nevertheless because they are not well informed, have allowed I don't know how many libels to be spread through France by the artifice of the English. . . ." [8] He then proceeded to make it clear that he was referring here to that wavering faction in France that had so far hesitated to take immediate action against England in the name of Mary. Accordingly, he concluded, he was moved to set forth the true account of how Mary was persecuted throughout her life by heretics, and how, contrary to the claims of the English that she died for the political crime of treason, she was in fact executed by heretics because of her Catholic faith.

The character and tone of Blackwood's effort is accurately reflected in the full title of the work which, translated, reads: "The Martyrdom of the Queen of Scotland and Dowager of France, containing the true account of the treasons practised against her at the instance of the English Elizabeth, by which discourse the lies, calumnies, and false accusations raised against this most vertuous, most catholic, and most illustrious princess are revealed and her innocence demonstrated." Most of the *Martyre* may have been prepared even before the return of Mary's servants, for, although Blackwood refers to "many faithful witnesses," he makes relatively little use of the details they brought with them, and, in contrast to a second work which he published early in the following year, his account of the actual execution in the *Martyre* is a bare sketch. Rather, by careful selection of facts, by liberal use of legend, and by free exercise of an inflamed imagination, Blackwood sought to accomplish his purpose. As one commentator has observed, Blackwood's *Martyre* is not so much a history of the Scottish Queen as it is "an eloquent panegyric on the virtues of his royal mistress, an indignant exposure of her sufferings, and an unsparing invective on the atrocities of [Elizabeth]." [9]

The *Martyre* opens with a statement that, in effect, is the thesis of the entire volume. Elizabeth, says Blackwood, is a bastard and a usurper; knowing this, and fearful of Mary as the rightful heir to the English throne, the English Queen plotted from the outset to destroy her rival. To show how completely illegitimate Elizabeth was, Blackwood elaborately embroiders the legend, already familiar in pro-Marian propaganda literature, of Henry VIII's adulterous relationship with his own illegitimate daughter, Anne Boleyn. It was remarkable that Henry should have been attracted to Anne in the first place, says Blackwood (here probably surpassing Nicholas Sanders), for she had buck teeth, six fingers on her left hand, and a large lump under her double chin; she was used as a whore by the principal courtiers of England and France, and was a Lutheran. In fact, says Blackwood, when Elizabeth was born six months after Henry and Anne were married—bigamously, in his opinion—Henry was not at all sure that Elizabeth was his offspring, for Anne had slept with many men, and Henry was especially suspicious of her brother George. On the basis of all this, Blackwood concludes that by all the laws of God, Nature, man, and the realm, Elizabeth had no right to the throne of England and Mary was the true queen there. Because Mary and all Catholics everywhere knew the truth of these matters and could thus expose and dethrone Elizabeth, the English Queen feared, hated, and sought to destroy them all.

Having thus established Elizabeth as the principal villain of the piece, Blackwood next turns to a discussion of Mary's troubles in Scotland. Closely following John Leslie at this point, Blackwood explains that all her difficulties were caused by an unholy alliance between Elizabeth, who feared and hated Mary for political reasons, and the Scottish heretics, led by Murray, who feared and hated her for her religion. Murray, according to Blackwood, was additionally motivated by the ambitions of his mother—a whore, of course—who had dreamed that he would some day control all Scotland.

Blackwood develops the section of the *Martyre* dealing with Mary's imprisonment in England mainly in terms of what he charges were Elizabeth's efforts to involve Mary in activities that could be called treasonable and hence pretended grounds for legally executing her. Elizabeth's first efforts in this direction almost backfired, according to Blackwood's version, for the commission she appointed at York in 1569 to find Mary guilty of murdering Darnley concluded, despite the efforts of Murray to the contrary, that the Scottish Queen was quite innocent and so reported to Elizabeth. But Elizabeth, who, according to Blackwood, "wanted Mary one hundred feet under the ground together with her son," and whose chief entertainment at court was listening to evil things said of her cousin, dissolved the recalcitrant commission and ignored their report. Failing in further schemes to destroy Mary, such as poisoning her food and drink, Elizabeth hit on the plan of passing a law (the Act of Association) making plots against her own life punishable by death, and then arranging to trap Mary in just such a plot. To this end the Babington plot, Blackwood alleges, was arranged by the English themselves. He considers this a particularly nefarious trick, for he says that the English knew when they passed the law that Mary was already in correspondence with foreign powers and domestic conspirators for her liberation and her restoration to her rightful throne in England. Thus without denying her involvement in the Babington plot, Blackwood here, as in his *De Jezabelis* poem, indignantly shifts the criminal responsibility from Mary, who participated, to the English, who, knowing that she would thus execute herself, allowed her to participate.

When he comes to the trial and execution of Mary, Blackwood develops the now familiar theme that whatever the false charges of treason trumped up against her, the real and only cause of her death was her religion. To this end he quotes in its entirety the sentence of execution and analyzes it in detail to make it appear that the real cause of all Mary's troubles was the English desire to destroy Catholicism and establish the Protestant heresy. Then he describes at length what he regards as Mary's exemplary conduct throughout the ordeal of her trial and her three-month wait before the execution—her quiet and uncomplaining suffering of the indignities and miseries he alleges Elizabeth deliberately heaped upon her; her sweetness and good will to Elizabeth in everything; and her steadfast refusal to blame the English Queen for anything that happened. Somewhat inconsistently, Blackwood concludes this eulogy by quoting the last letter Mary wrote to her priest, in which she complains bitterly of the injustice and the indignities she has suffered in England because of her religion.

Blackwood describes the execution itself only in the barest outline; as we shall see, he was about to deal with the death of the Queen in far greater detail elsewhere. Insofar as he discusses the event in the *Martyre,* he presents it wholly in terms of what he regards as Mary's martyrdom for her faith. To heighten this effect he now had access to, and made use of, details of the scene that could only have been supplied by Mary's servants. Thus in a passage found elsewhere only in the report Bourgoin brought back with him, Blackwood tells how Mary, on the night before the execution, read the story of the Passion to strengthen her soul for the ordeal that was to come. Similarly, only the servants could have supplied Mary's last letter to her priest, which Blackwood quotes to show that she, at least, believed that she was dying for her religion. To such details as these and an outline sketch of the execution that includes details from both the English and the earlier Catholic accounts, Blackwood adds touches of his own to enhance the atmosphere of martyrdom. For example, he describes the Protestant Dean of Peterborough who prayed for Mary as a "minister of Satan" whom Elizabeth sent to destroy Mary's soul, together with her body. And the three strokes of the executioner's axe, reported by many of the observers, were necessary, he says, "pour rendre le martyre plus illustre."

Blackwood concludes the *Martyre* with a final angry and violent excoriation of Elizabeth, and a prolonged warning that God and the kings of Europe—the French King in particular—will not let her crimes against religion and royal sovereignty go unpunished. He admits that Mary often plotted for her own freedom, but he denies again that she was ever involved in any treasonable plots against Elizabeth, although he argues that Elizabeth's tyranny

would have justified Mary in so involving herself. He closes the
work with two Latin poems addressed to Elizabeth, both in the
form of epitaphs prepared for what he believes is the imminent
and deservedly horrible death of this she-wolf at the hands of
Mary's avengers.

Blackwood's efforts to turn the death of Mary to his propaganda
purpose were not limited to the *Martyre.* Shortly after the first
publication of this work late in 1587 there appeared a substantial
volume on the execution itself entitled *La Mort de la Royne
d'Escosse.*[10] Like the *Martyre, La Mort* was published anonymously,
but Blackwood's authorship seems certain and is now generally
granted. In any event, this most detailed of the accounts of her
death was clearly regarded at the time as a companion piece to
the *Martyre,* and on one occasion was printed as such with the
Martyre in a single volume. *La Mort* was frequently published and
widely distributed. At least four separate editions appeared in
1588 and 1589, one containing an elaborate series of folding
woodcuts depicting the execution. The work was known, and
frequently borrowed from, in such widely separated places as
Germany, Italy, and the Netherlands, and it drew the inevitable
complaint from the English ambassador in Paris, who wrote to
Walsingham in August, 1588, that the Catholic party in France
"now print afresh all things that may touch her Majesty, for
instance matters touching the Queen of Scots death. . . ." [11]

By Blackwood's own repeated admission in the text, *La Mort*
is the execution account that Mary's Catholic supporters had been
unable to write earlier because of the English counterpropaganda
tactics. He is as candid here as he was in the *Martyre* in describing
the discomfiture of his party, the relative ineffectiveness of their
stopgap efforts, and the success of the English in deluding, as he
put it, the French King.[12] Now, he says on a note of triumph, Mary's
faithful servants who were so long detained by the English for
fear they would report the truth in France, have returned with
eyewitness accounts of what happened and why.[13] With equal can-
dor he confesses that, although his original aim had been simply
to tell in *La Mort* the true story of Mary's death, he decided to take
this opportunity to prove the innocence of the Queen of Scots, her

constancy, her virtue, and her willingness to die solely for the cause of her religion.[14] In terms of this not-too-surprising decision, *La Mort de la Royne d'Escosse* is developed.

For the details of his account of Mary's last twenty-four hours, Blackwood acknowledges that he drew freely from both the official English and the official French reports of the execution, but amplified the story at all points with material obtained from Mary's servants.[15] Whatever his sources, Blackwood consistently selected those details that would best document his thesis. For example, he acknowledges the official English report as his source for the account of Mary's charge to Melville, with its detailed explanation of how the Queen bade Melville tell James of her firm faith and her request that James be urged to maintain the Catholic church.[16] He could not find there, however, her speech on the scaffold protesting her innocence of treason and charging that she is dying for her religion; for that, he apparently turned to the Chateauneuf-Gondy report, transcribing almost verbatim her remarks as they were reported there.[17] In one way or another, he thus works into his narrative practically all the details already published, pointing and shaping them for his larger purpose.

For this purpose the new material provided by Mary's servants, most of which now appears in print for the first time, was of incalculable value. Blackwood states that he obtained this information in personal interviews, but he seems also to have had before him Bourgoin's memorandum, for he incorporates into his own account occasional word-for-word passages from the physician's document.[18] Again Blackwood selected details that were especially effective in developing the theme of religious persecution. Mary's letter to her priest, already used in the *Martyre,* is introduced here as evidence from Mary herself that the English tried to destroy her soul together with her body by attempting to convert her to their own false doctrines. The English argument that Mary was to be executed for treason, converted or not, is ignored. From the servants also must have come numerous details of Mary's pious behavior during the night before the execution, when she was alone with her followers—such as how she rejoiced with them in her triumph over the Earl of Kent's efforts to convert her, and how his efforts proved that she was being killed not for treason but for her religion; how she read selected lives of the saints with her maids, choosing the story of the worst sinner and proclaiming that her sins were greater than his; how she made her will and generously took care of all her servants—all, that is, except two who, according to Bourgoin, thought they had been slighted and remained disgruntled until the Queen remembered them in a marginal notation on her last testament. Finally, the servants were able to provide Blackwood with an account of events immediately following the execution. In *La Mort* he describes for the first time the detailed autopsy that was performed on Mary, revealing the poor health she had endured and, according to Blackwood's interpretation, demonstrating beyond doubt the extent of the English mistreatment of her. On the basis of the same interviews, Blackwood also describes the cruelties suffered by the servants themselves in their long detention after the execution, and the numerous attempts he says were made by the English to subvert and destroy their religious faith.

By thus combining extant accounts and fresh, firsthand information, Blackwood was able to produce in *La Mort* the fullest and most circumstantial narrative of the execution that had yet appeared. But for all this narrative detail, by far the larger part of his book is devoted to his own running commentary on the affair, and it is here that the fundamental propagandistic bias of the account becomes most apparent. He misses no opportunity to excoriate the English in general and Elizabeth in particular, or to expound at length on the sanctity and innocence of Mary. Here, as in the *Martyre*, for example, Blackwood notes the religious significance of the three strokes of the executioner's axe, but in *La Mort* he adds that the circumstance was further proof of the cruelty of heretics, for, he charges, the English deliberately sent an inexperienced apprentice executioner to do the job, and, to make matters worse, supplied him with a blunt axe.[19] Blackwood certainly cannot be accused of trying to conceal his bias or disguise his purpose. Occasionally his digressive outbursts become so long and impassioned that he himself feels called upon to account for them. At the end of the narrative, after hurling a series of epithets at the English and warning the kings of Europe against heretics such as these, he apologizes for the violence of feeling that has led him to digress from his "simple narrative." As he himself concludes, every story he heard moved him to write more passionately and at greater length.[20]

It would be difficult to overestimate the importance of the *Martyre* and *La Mort* in the history of sixteenth-century literature dealing with Mary Queen of Scots. Taken together as the single effort of a single man, they stand as the culmination of all that had gone before in the defense of Mary—the final, angry extreme of the arguments that had begun so diplomatically with Leslie's restrained *Defence* in 1569. As the following pages will show, they also stand as the largest single determining influence on all that was to follow. Of the large number of pamphlets, martyrologies, occasional poems, biographical sketches, and dramatizations dealing with Mary's story and appearing before 1603, at least half reveal their direct indebtedness to the materials Blackwood's widely published books made available; the remainder, if not directly indebted to Blackwood, effectively served to carry on the campaign to which he had given principal impetus. Nor should it be forgotten that Blackwood's works, to which innumerable latter-day historians of all parties and faiths have turned for source material, were by the author's own frank admission passionately written for ardent propagandistic purposes.

Meanwhile, legal and philosophical support for Blackwood's campaign against Protestantism and England was provided by the delayed publication, in 1588, of the oration that Pomponne de Bellièvre, French secretary of state, had delivered before Elizabeth on November 28, 1586, in a futile effort to deter the English Queen from executing her sister sovereign. Entitled, as translated, "Harangue Addressed to the Queen of England to Dissuade Her from Undertaking Any Jurisdiction on the Queen of Scots," the oration was twice published in 1588 with the apparent purpose of setting forth the legal principles and precedents that Elizabeth and the English were supposed to have violated.[21] As printed and widely circulated, Bellièvre's *Harangue* marshaled the principal Biblical and historical injunctions against the execution of sovereigns. He reiterated the old arguments that Mary had come to England in search of promised aid, and that as a sovereign she was not subject to the laws of England, or of any other land, for that matter. He added new arguments to the effect that, as a virtual prisoner, Mary had a right, under the laws of mankind, to seek to escape. Like a true Frenchman, he appealed to Elizabeth's mercy—and to her vanity—which he claimed to see revealed in "la doceur et beauté de votre face vrayment royalle." He argued that the death of Mary would not settle the succession issue in England, but would only serve to open the door to countless conflicting claims. Finally, he hinted that killing Mary would not remove the threat of an invasion of England by Catholic powers, but would rather make that danger a certain probability. Such pleas and threats may have been lost on Elizabeth, but they were to prove useful in the campaign waged by Mary's Catholic partisans to arouse Europe to avenge her death.

The theme and tone of the campaign led by Blackwood's works and supported by Bellièvre's were perhaps most clearly echoed in the Catholic martyrologies which now gave Mary a permanent place in their rosters, and usually the place of principal distinction. One of the first of such treatments to appear after the execution was Richard Verstegan's Latin "Theater of the Cruelties of Heretics in Our Time." [22] Probably an amplified version of his martyrology that had been suppressed in 1584, the *Theatrum* was apparently completed about the time of the return of Mary's servants. It was published in Latin at Antwerp in 1587, and in a French translation in the following year. Numerous editions in both languages continued to appear for the rest of the century.

Verstegan, whose real name was Rowlands, was an English printer and engraver educated at Oxford but denied a degree there because of his Catholicism. He fled to Paris in 1582 and later moved to Antwerp, where he set up a printing press that became a principal center for the transmission of Catholic literature to and from England. The *Theatrum* was probably his most important production of this sort. It is a collection of prose accounts by Verstegan himself and by others about the sufferings of Catholics at the hands of Protestants all over Europe, but mainly in England. Each account is accompanied by an engraving, probably done by Verstegan, depicting the persecution of the martyr, usually in grim detail, and his or her pious endurance.

The account of Mary, with engraved pictures of her execution, stands at the end of the collection as the culmination. As an English agent wrote to Burghley, the rest of the book is only an "induction" to the portrait of the Scottish Queen.[23] There is a brief sketch of her sufferings for the faith at the hands of Elizabeth, "that inhuman murderess of saints," but no detailed account of her execution. In a note, however, Verstegan indicates, possibly with Blackwood's activities in mind, that Mary's story "will be more fully written in another place." [24] The propaganda aim of the book is made explicit in a verse epilogue signed "I. B. S."—probably James Beaton, Scot, the Archbishop of Glasgow, who was Mary's ambassador in Paris, a co-worker with Blackwood in her cause, and a contributor to the *De Jezabelis* collections. In these lines the poet promises:

A new Hercules will be called up who, flushed with victory, will erase the memory of her criminal oppressors, and will avenge the Queen who was wickedly murdered by her foresworn hostess. He will boldly lead his ships across the sea, and will purge that land so cruelly stained by Mary's kindred blood. Nor will he ever fear the Boleyn's scepter, an incestuous lineage drunk on human blood.[25]

A propagandistic treatment of Mary's story similar to that in the *Theatrum* is found in another martyrology published in Latin about this time. This was the voluminous *Concertatio*, or "Disputation of the Catholic Church in England against 'Calvinopapistas' and Puritans under Queen Elizabeth...." [26] Originally compiled by a Jesuit priest, John Fenn, in 1583, the *Concertatio* was taken over and considerably amplified in 1588 by Dr. John Bridgewater, an English Catholic divine who at one time had been domestic chaplain to Elizabeth's favorite, the Earl of Leicester. Maintaining Fenn's original thesis that English Catholics were martyred because of their faith and not for treason, Bridgewater added numerous case histories to the original, most notably the account of the martyrdom of the Queen of Scots.

Although not directly linked with Blackwood's accounts, Mary's story as it is told in Bridgewater's martyrology uses many of the same sources of information and was obviously inspired by the same motives and feelings. For his brief sketch of Mary's sufferings up to the execution Bridgewater quotes with acknowledgment from Nicholas Sanders's somewhat fictionalized account in *The Rise and Growth of the Anglican Schism*. For the account of the execution he adapts, again with acknowledgment, the official English report as it had been translated and annotated for Catholic purposes in the *Mariae Stuartae . . . Supplicium & Mors* published at Cologne.[27] Bridgewater does not hesitate to rewrite his sources, the English one in particular, where to do so will better serve the purposes of his martyrology. Thus he cuts from the London account of the execution those paragraphs seeking to explain Elizabeth's political reasons for executing Mary and describing Elizabeth's grief and remorse. In the same vein, he does a great deal of retouching; for example, where his English original, in explaining why Mary's bloodstained belongings were burned, had read, "that nothing might serve for superstition," Bridgewater wrote, "that nothing might serve as a relic for the piety of Catholics." [28]

Similar to these martyrology accounts in the ardor of their indignation and the themes they develop are the numerous occasional poems written throughout Europe in the year or two immediately following Mary's death. Seldom published at the time, and hence of little possible influence as propaganda, they nonetheless serve as an index to the uniform and widespread existence of the attitudes and materials characterizing the more widely circulated publications. A sonnet by Giulio Cortese, for example, calls upon Rome to rise and avenge the cruel murder of a holy martyr at the hands of English heretics.[29] A Latin poem by the youthful Maffeo Barberini, later Pope Urban VIII, proclaims that although Mary died without the royal honor due a queen, the shadows of night that cover half the earth are her funeral drapes, and the stars that shine in the heavens are her funeral tapers.[30] The mood and point of such poems is illustrated in the work of the English Jesuit, Robert Southwell, who wrote verses in both Latin and English on

Mary before he died in 1595. Distinct echoes of Mary's last words as reported by her servants, and as recorded by Blackwood, are found in such lines as these:

> Alive a Queene, now dead I am a sainte;
>   Once Mary called, my name nowe Martyr is;
> From earthly raigne debarred by restraint,
>   In liew whereof I raigne in heavenly blisse.
> My life my greife, my death hath wrought my joye,
>   My frendes my foyle, my foes my weale procur'd;
> My speedy death hath shortned longe annoye,
>   And losse of life an endless life assur'd.
>
> . . . .
>
> By death from prisoner to a prince enhaunc'd
>   From crosse to crowne, from thrall to throne again;
> My ruth my right, my trapp my stile advauncd
>   From woe to weale, from hell to heavenly raigne.[31]

Somewhat more restrained and qualified in their lament for the dead Queen are several Latin epitaphs written soon after the execution by Patrick Adamson, the Scottish prelate who had asserted Mary's political claims to England more than twenty years before in his *Genethliacum* on the birth of James. Despite his Catholic sympathies and frequent tangles with the Kirk, Adamson managed to remain in Scotland as a trusted adviser to young King James.[32] Under the circumstances of James's ambiguous attitude and conduct regarding his mother's death, Adamson necessarily wrote with delicate caution, but still, in his Latin verses, one catches echoes of such familiar Catholic themes as the cruel ignominy of her death, the piety of her conduct, the right to the crown of England which she was denied, and the royal sovereignty which had been impugned by this execution of a queen.

Like the martyrologies and the occasional poems, a number of biographical accounts of Mary, or "histories," appearing in the years immediately following her death, similarly embodied the main elements of the propaganda campaign stimulated by Blackwood and his associates. Of these, the one that relies most heavily and directly on Blackwood's own work for its material is the oft-reprinted, and more often quoted, account of Mary given by Pierre de Bourdeille, Abbé de Brantôme, in the work now commonly known as *Vies des Dames Illustres*; in fact, Brantôme candidly admits that he has "learned much from a book which has been published, entitled 'The Martyrdom of the Queen of Scotland, Dowager of France.' " [33] Since the sketch by Brantôme, who died in 1614, was not published until 1665, its interest, like that of the occasional poems, is less that of effective contemporary propaganda than of an index and measure of the influence of the propaganda disseminated by others. Considering the authority that it has assumed for subsequent historians, novelists, and dramatists in the romantic tradition, however, his account deserves special attention.

Brantôme, as the Lytton Strachey of Renaissance biographers, was far more interested in describing Mary the amorous and romantic woman than Mary the queen and martyr. His work, accordingly, remains the principal source of those stories of her tender relations with the youthful Francis and the poet Chastellard that have graced so many latter-day accounts of the Scottish Queen. Picking up once again the themes of the earliest literature on the Queen of Scots, he rhapsodizes over her beauty, "for the fairness of her face contends with the whiteness of her veil . . . and the snowiness of her white features effaces the other . . ."; he also observes, with a Frenchman's characteristic interest and condescension, that she looked like a goddess even in the barbarous costume of her native country. He describes her devastating effect on all men who beheld her, and he reports in this connection that the King of Navarre desired to abandon his wife for Mary. Mary would not consent, however, "making a great scruple of marrying a man already married," Brantôme says.[34] Navarre's passion was apparently not strong enough to move him to divorce his wife, as Bothwell was to do later under similar circumstances.

Although this often richly sentimental account of Mary would seem to have little connection with the Catholic campaign to make of her a holy martyr and a cause for holy war, Brantôme's romantic sketch nevertheless appears to have been written under the direct and acknowledged influence of this campaign. Over half of his narrative is devoted to a detailed description of the execution, the material for which, he asserts, he obtained from the "very lips of her maids who were present." Perhaps he did talk to them, but the text of his account is taken word-for-word from Blackwood's *La Mort de la Royne,* which of course had acknowledged the servants as among its principal sources of information.[35] In fact, Brantôme reproduces all the essential features of the religious and political propaganda literature concerning Mary, and even strengthens the central theme of this material by adding a prediction of his own (still to be fulfilled) that "in years to come some good Pope will canonize her as a martyr who suffered for the honor of God and His law."

In the sketch as a whole, however, Brantôme does not seem to have been primarily concerned with the political purposes that determined the portrait of Mary in his source. Instead, he seems to have been more interested in the resultant portrait itself—the heightened and moving account of Mary's piety, beauty, innocence —and, above all, the pathos of her fate. As he states at the outset, he desires to describe a good and beautiful woman whose life was "tres mal accompaignés de la bonne fortune." For this essentially sentimental and romantic purpose, Blackwood's portrait of the beautiful martyr was no less appropriate and suggestive than the earlier literature describing the beautiful woman and queen. Brantôme's use of Blackwood is perhaps typical of one kind of influence both the *Martyre* and *La Mort* were to have for a long time to come. In such almost casual fashion as this did the political propaganda literature dealing with the Queen of Scots come to shape a work regarded as a principal source by a long line of subsequent dramatists, poets, novelists, and biographers who dealt with Mary.

Another biographical account of Mary written before the end of the century develops more deliberately than does Brantôme's the propaganda purposes and methods of the Catholic apologists' tradition. Entitled *Maria Stuarta . . . Innocens,* the work was published by Robert Turner, under the pseudonym of "Obertus Barnestapolius," in 1588.[36] Turner was one of Mary's English Catholic supporters who had fled to the Continent to carry on the struggle.[37] Given the momentous events that were now taking place in this struggle, it is surprising to find that Turner was solely concerned, at this late date, with exonerating Mary of any complicity in the murder of Darnley two decades earlier. The author himself was apparently aware that this resuscitation of ancient history might seem gratuitous, because he explains that it is not his purpose to describe the sufferings of only one woman, but to reveal through this example the way in which Calvinists generally persecute innocent women, even sovereign queens. Mary's death, he continues, is the inevitable consequence of toleration of heretics in a kingdom, as were her sufferings at the time of the murder of her husband in Scotland.[38]

Having thus struck the keynote of pro-Marian propaganda literature, he proceeds to clear Mary of guilt in the Darnley affair in the way that the literature written in her defense had long since made familiar. His narrative, in fact, is often very close to Blackwood's in the *Martyre,* although just as often even more vividly colored. After chronicling the events, Turner takes up the arguments advanced by heretics to prove Mary's guilt in the Darnley murder. To their charge that she murdered her husband, he replies that one so beautiful and so pious could not have thus quenched "so great a flame of love." [39] To their charge that she wrote letters—the controversial Casket Letters—to Bothwell, which implicated her in the crime, Turner, like Blackwood, makes a somewhat ambiguous reply. He says on the one hand that the letters contained nothing that was incriminating, thereby implying that Mary indeed wrote them; but he says in the same breath that the letters were forged by George Buchanan at Murray's behest so that Mary might falsely be accused of the crime.[40] Finally, Turner argues that the concluding evidence offered by heretics to prove Mary's guilt, the love poem ostensibly addressed by her to Bothwell and found in the casket along with the notorious letters, is inadmissable, because it is written in a low style of which the talented Queen would have been incapable.[41]

Untimely as it may seem at first encounter, Turner's work is nevertheless a revealing document in the history of the literary war over Mary Stuart. For one thing, he admits quite candidly that the continuing influence of Buchanan's attack on Mary as the murderer of Darnley, especially in Germany where Turner published his book, had inspired him to produce this effort to refute what he calls the lies and calumnies of the Scotsman. In other words, as late as 1588 Turner is disturbed because Buchanan's *Detection* had been twice published in Germany, with the result that Mary's well-wishers there "are infinitely displeased, that a Queen so Catholic has had attached to her reputation a crime so detestable." [42] Apparently Burghley's foresight in sponsoring the publication and translation of Buchanan's work was not in vain if we can trust the testimony of the opposition itself. On the other hand, Turner's work was just as discomforting to the English, for they acknowledged its potential influence on public opinion when they placed it first on a list sent to Walsingham in 1588 "of certain seditious books newly published." [43]

Walsingham might well have regarded this first of "certain seditious books" with concern. In the following year, 1589, there was further evidence of the influence and popularity of Turner's work. His Latin text was not only translated into French, but was amplified and brought up to date with a lengthy appendix describing the execution and martyrdom of the Queen of Scots. Published in Paris as *L'Histoire et Vie de Marie Stuart,* this expanded version of Turner's defense was the work of Gabriel de Guttery.[44] An adherent of the Catholic house of Guise, Guttery has also been described as "principally a man of spirit and pleasure, who passed his life among the most fashionable social circles in Paris." His *Priapeia,* a set of dialogues in the style of Aretino, seems to justify this characterization.[45] Whatever his playboy tendencies may have been, Guttery spared no effort to reinforce the religious and political purpose of Turner's original. In adding the account of Mary's execution Guttery explained to the patroness to whom he dedicated his translation that he hoped to show the extremes to which Protestant heresy could go. For the account of the execution he had to rely, as he admits, on the official English report—"the very memoirs themselves which were printed in London at the commandment of the Queen of England." [46] Like other Catholic editors of the English version, he compensates for the Protestant bias of his source with introductory warnings and passing comments to direct attention to the piety and martyrdom of the Queen of Scots. The bells and the bonfires that marked the rejoicing in London when she died, says Guttery, were really portents of the destruction that awaits England for this crime, for her death is a threat to all kings, and her blood cries for vengeance.[47]

Of all the works—martyrologies, poems, histories—written about Mary in the years following her execution, those that show most effectively the influence of Blackwood's campaign in her behalf are the dramatizations of her story. Four plays are known to have been written before 1603 on the tragedy of Mary—the vanguard of hundreds that were to follow in succeeding centuries.[48] One of these, Montchrestien's *Escossoise,* may more properly be dealt with in the next chapter. Another—Campanella's *Tragedia della Regina di Scozia*—has not survived, although from what the author himself tells us about it, it appears to have belonged in the Blackwood tradition. The two remaining plays, both Latin dramas by Catholic teachers, reveal direct and heavy indebtedness to the information and arguments circulated by Blackwood and his associates.

The earliest known drama on the subject of the Queen of Scots is *Maria Stuarta Tragoedia,* a manuscript Latin school play written in 1589 by Jean de Bordes, a French Jesuit who was teaching at the time in Milan.[49] Like the authors of the *De Jezabelis* poems, the *Martyre,* and the Catholic execution accounts, Bordes wrote his tragedy primarily to put the history of Mary to propaganda purposes in the larger battle against heresy. In fact, such a motive was imposed upon him by the requirements of the peculiar dramatic form within which he worked. Plays written with the double purpose of instructing schoolboys in right Latinity and right piety had become a regular feature of the Jesuit educational system by the end of the sixteenth century. Seneca was the model in style and form for these Jesuit dramas, but scriptural story and church history were the only authorized subjects. As a seventeenth-century Jesuit educator who was himself such a dramatist explained, "The tragedy ought to serve to form the *moeurs*. Thus the poet must choose his subjects from the vast and fertile domains of Holy Scripture and the annals of the Church, where he will find a great number of remarkable events and precious instructions." [50]

Bordes clearly considered the martyrdom of Mary suitable material for this general instructional purpose and, more particularly, for showing his charges the evils of heresy. In an Italian prologue to his Latin drama he explains, with a schoolteacher's characteristic despair, that because the boys have complained of failing to understand completely what previous Latin school plays have been about, he is taking the trouble to summarize the action of this play in their vernacular; thus, he concludes, they will be able to comprehend the ravages of heresy.[51] Similarly, in Italian prologues affixed to each act, he reiterates this instructional point which the Latin drama is designed to convey.

The action of the play covers the last twenty-four hours of Mary's life on earth and turns on the efforts of her friends to save her while her foes trick the hesitant Elizabeth into agreeing to the execution. In Act I, Leicester, Cecil (as he is called here), and a Protestant minister[52] reveal that they want Mary executed because they fear that, if she lives, Catholicism will be restored in England and the false religion upon which their own political power depends will be destroyed. However, in Act II, the ambassadors of France, Spain, Scotland, and Germany plead so persuasively with Elizabeth to spare Mary that the English Queen decides against the execution. She agrees with them that Mary is the innocent victim of plots by her enemies, that the Scottish Queen is not subject to English jurisdiction in any event, that the execution of Mary would destroy the whole principle of royal sovereignty, and that the English Queen herself would be punished by God and by all Christian kings if she killed Mary.

Learning in Act III that Elizabeth has thus changed her mind, the three heretical councilors decide to resort to lies, calumny, and fraud to win her back again. Accordingly, they summon three Furies from hell—namely, Ambition, Heresy, and Calumny. The Furies disguise themselves as Cecil, the Minister, and Leicester, respectively, and, by arguing with Elizabeth that her own safety, the safety of the realm, and the safety of the new religion require the death of Mary, they succeed in persuading her to agree to the execution. The news is announced to Mary in Act IV after she has summarized at length the sufferings she has undergone at the hands of heretics for the sake of her religion. She receives the news of her impending execution cheerfully, proclaiming her innocence of the charges of treason that have been brought against her by fraud, and rejoicing in this opportunity to die a martyr for her faith.

In Act V, her faithful Doctor describes her exemplary conduct during the night before the execution, including her prayers and the secret communion she had to administer to herself when the English heretics denied her the ministrations of her priest. As the Doctor concludes his narrative, the English officials arrive to lead Mary to the place of execution. Rejecting the last efforts of the English to persuade her to renounce her faith, she proclaims again her innocence of any treasonable attempts against Elizabeth's life or throne, asserting that she sought only her own liberty and the liberty of her religion. She commands Melville to tell James how she died in and for her faith, and to urge her son to renounce the heresy into which he has been misled. An Angel then appears to her, assuring her of an eternal reward as a blessed martyr in heaven. The executioner strikes three blows, and a herald announces that the Scottish Queen is dead.

In a long epilogue, James arrives on the scene to discover that he is too late to save his mother. Over her body he bursts out in grief at his loss and in rage at the barbarity of the English heretics. When the efforts of his attendants to restrain and console him are unavailing, the Ghost of his mother appears. She tells him that he must rejoice, for she has won the heavenly crown of a martyr. Again she urges him to renounce heresy and to be faithful to the church of Rome. Thus consoled and converted by Mary, James and his followers depart for Scotland, leaving—as they put it—England and heresy to the inevitable punishment of God.

It is no accident that in material and in tone Bordes' drama should seem to reflect so clearly the pamphlet literature disseminated by Mary's partisans, and by Blackwood in particular. The Jesuit dramatist apparently had before him as he wrote several of the propaganda publications that emanated from the Catholic party in France. His general treatment of Mary's last night and morning follows in its main outlines and in innumerable details—the latter including many exact verbal parallels—the account given in Blackwood's *Martyre* and the subsequent *La Mort*.[53] There are also specific and unique parallels that suggest his use of Dini's compendium of official French and English accounts of the execution, which was published in Milan at the time Bordes was teaching and writing there; and similar parallels in details can be found between the play and the published version of the *Harangue* which Bellièvre delivered to Elizabeth in a final and futile effort to forestall the execution.[54] In a work that is so complex a medley of fact, fiction, and fantasy, it would be impossible to trace all the specific authorities the author might have had before him. Nevertheless, on the basis of discernible parallels and general tone, Bordes' indebtedness to the Chateauneuf-Gondy-Blackwood propaganda can be safely assumed.

However, it is in the episodes and incidents that Bordes' creative imagination added to his sources that we see most clearly the impact on the Catholic mind of Mary's death as it was presented by Blackwood and his fellow propagandists. The central device of the three Furies disguising themselves as the Protestant leaders who trap Mary is typical of Bordes' ingenuity in devising incidents to emphasize a major theme of the pro-Marian propaganda. Similarly, quite contrary to the facts of history and the evidence of his own sources, Bordes makes James a vehement spokesman against Protestant heresy and even sends him to England for this purpose. The young King's supposed attitude is revealed with somewhat lugubrious sentimentality when, at the end of the play, he beholds his mother's headless, bleeding neck and recalls the days when he used to hang from it as a child. Since, as a matter of historical fact, James had agreed not to intercede actively for his mother if he were assured the succession in England, his demonstrations of filial concern in the play must stand among the more remarkable of Bordes' imaginative achievements. In the same imaginative way the Jesuit playwright dramatizes Blackwood's account of Mary's heroic fortitude and serenity in receiving the news of the sentence. In Act IV, Bordes, with considerable sense of theater, creates the episode where the English come to announce the sentence only to find that Mary has disappeared. Thinking that she has escaped with the ambassadors who had come to intercede for her with

Elizabeth, the officials indulge in mutual recriminations and launch a frantic search for the condemned Queen of Scots. In the midst of this confusion Mary quietly enters from the garden where she had gone to pray, serenely assuring them that she had no intention of seeking to escape the martyr's death she welcomes.[55]

The materials and arguments dramatized by Bordes in the first Mary Stuart play are similarly used in the second, the *Stuarta Tragoedia* by Adrian Roulers, professor of rhetoric in the Dominican Gymnasium Marcianense at Douai.[56] Long but erroneously regarded as "the oldest Mary Stuart tragedy," Roulers' drama was published at Douai in 1593, some four years after Bordes' work was produced in Milan. Except for the very obvious fact that Roulers was a far better poet and playwright than Bordes, the two dramas are remarkably similar in their features and circumstances. Like Bordes, Roulers wrote his play for performance by and before schoolboys, to inculcate in them right piety and right Latinity. Like Bordes, moreover, Roulers was strong in his conviction that piety with regard to Mary Stuart involved assailing the Protestant heresy which he believed had martyred her. Such a conviction was probably inescapable at Douai, which has accurately been described as the center of the battle against the inroads of Calvinism, and especially the base of Catholic operations against the England of Queen Elizabeth.[57]

The action of the *Stuarta Tragoedia*, like that of Bordes' play, concentrates on the last few hours of Mary's life, and turns, although far less spectacularly, on the conflicting efforts of Mary's friends and foes to sway Elizabeth in her final decision as to the fate of the Scottish Queen. In developing this action, Roulers employs all the machinery of Senecan drama to set forth the familiar themes of Marian propaganda. At the opening of the play, the Ghost of Henry VIII enters to describe the turbulence and terrors brought to England by the Protestant heresy which he fostered and which is maintained by Elizabeth, who, he confesses, is the offspring of his incestuous and adulterous union with his own illegitimate daughter, Anne Boleyn. In the following scene, Elizabeth herself, by way of explaining why she hesitates to execute Mary, reviews the major arguments advanced by the Scottish Queen's defenders—her sovereignty, her right to hospitality, her kinship with Elizabeth, and her innocence of the crimes charged against her. Nevertheless, with encouragement from Leicester, Elizabeth decides that if she is to save her throne and her false religion, she must execute Mary.

Many of the same themes and arguments are reviewed in Act II, when Mary recounts to Bourgoin, her physician, her sufferings at the hands of heretics, and then, in a debate with her English keeper, Sir Amias Paulet, refutes point by point the charges of treason brought against her by her Protestant captors. Thereupon a "Chorus of captive boys and girls compares the evils in Scotland resulting from neglect of religion with the ancient evils of Judea." [58] In Act III, Paulet and Drury discuss their efforts to involve Mary in the Babington conspiracy and trap her with false charges of treason. Confronted with these charges, Mary replies that she sought only her own liberty, and never Elizabeth's life or throne. When informed that she is to die, she answers that she knows she dies for her religion, and rejoices to do so.

She continues to proclaim her innocence in Act IV, and to develop at length the theme of her religious martyrdom as she seeks to console her wailing servants, represented by the Chorus. Act V is devoted to a detailed account of Mary's preparation for the execution—her prayers, her messages to her son and to the Catholic kings of Europe, her assurances to all that she will wear a martyr's crown in heaven. The decapitation itself is announced by messenger in Senecan fashion, not shown, as it apparently was in Bordes' more lurid drama, and the play concludes with a choral excoriation of the heretics in general and in particular who have brought about this tragedy: "Murray, an Ishmael born of Hagar, encircling serpent-like the cities and all Scotland, pressed the lion's head beneath his foot: but soon this evil spirit departed, sundered from his hatreds, and preceded the Jezebel [Elizabeth] to Stygian darkness." [59]

The marked similarity in material and attitude between this play and Bordes' is accounted for by something more than the pedagogical purpose and sectarian zeal the two dramatists had in common. Both relied heavily, if not exclusively, on the principal propaganda documents produced by Mary's supporters on the Continent, and particularly on those written by Adam Blackwood. In the general argument prefixed to his play, Roulers specifically names some of his sources—Leslie's *History of Scotland,* Natalis Comes' universal *Historiae,* Giliberti Genebrardi's *Chronographiae,* and, as the basis for the execution account in Act V, the "scriptum datum Londini 27 Martii 1587." [60] This last, of course, turns out to be, as Roulers' modern editor has indicated, the account of the execution emanating from London and annotated for Catholic readers in 1588 by "Romoaldus Scotus"; it is, as we have seen above, the straight English official version of the affair, with running commentary in Mary's favor. However, as Roulers' modern editor points out, the dramatist does not mention the work that was clearly his main source of material and argument—Blackwood's *Martyre de la Royne d'Escosse.* After a detailed analysis of the striking verbal parallels between Roulers' text and that of the *Martyre,* the editor concludes that, "in short, except for the 'London account,' Blackwood is the principal—indeed, perhaps the only—source for Roulers." [61]

These two earliest Mary Stuart plays appear to be little more than extensions in dramatic form of the propaganda campaign launched by Blackwood and Mary's ardent Catholic supporters abroad. Campanella's *Tragedia della Regina di Scozia,* written in 1598 but now lost, was very probably of the same order, for the celebrated philosopher describes enough of its general nature to suggest that he gave a strong political bias to his dramatization of Mary's story; the play as he refers to it even carries the subtitle, "For Spain Against England" (*per spagna contra Inghilterra*) .[62] In any event, the early plays on Mary bear additional testimony to the far-reaching nature of the efforts to arouse Catholic Europe in her name.

The Spanish Armada of 1588 was, in some respects at least, a consequence of these efforts. In the National Library at Madrid is the manuscript of a contemporary document apparently intended to be issued as a pamphlet to the men who sailed with the Armada. It is a fervid and violent exhortation to action, reciting in inflammatory language the whole case against England,

and is headed: "An Address to the Captains and Men on the Armada." Its abuse of Elizabeth equals that of the *De Jezabelis* poems. It assures the seamen that the persecuted saints of England —Fisher, More, Campion—will be waiting there to aid the cause. It concludes, in a stirring peroration, that "with us, too, will be the blessed and innocent Mary, queen of Scotland, who, still fresh from her sacrifice, bears copious and abounding witness to the cruelty and impiety of this Elizabeth, and directs her shafts against her." [63]

Blackwood's part in these efforts is truly remarkable both for its extent and for his apparently tireless zeal. His contributions to the *De Jezabelis* collections and his possible association in the production of the influential Chateauneuf-Gondy execution account suggests that he was a principal figure in the early stages of the campaign. [64] After the return of Mary's servants, his leadership in the cause cannot be disputed. Not only did his *Martyre* and *La Mort* catch up all the main themes of Marian propaganda to 1587, but his works brought together and intensified data from the various execution accounts that would enhance the development of these themes. The fruits of his labors were widely and immediately apparent throughout Europe—in the variety of editions in which they were published, in martyrologies, in numerous epitaphs and occasional poems, in the highly sentimentalized manuscript pages Brantôme was writing at this time, and in at least two plays enacted by schoolboys in centers as far apart as Milan and Douai. [65]

If the measure of effective propaganda is successful action, Blackwood must go down to defeat with the Spanish Armada in the futile effort to supplant the heretic Jezebel of England with a Catholic monarch. In fact, the whole great cause that had been championed with such admirable vigor, courage, and imagination by Blackwood, and before him by Leslie and a host of other devoted adherents to Mary and her church, achieved a bitterly ironic victory when the succession of Mary's line in England, for which they had fought so long and so hard, brought a Protestant king to Elizabeth's throne. But if propaganda literature is evaluated in terms of the variety and numbers of people reached, and in terms of the lasting impression it creates in the imaginations of men for generations to come, then Blackwood can be ranked close to John Leslie, if not with him, as the most effective spokesman for Mary Stuart and the faith for which she claimed to die.

For it is mainly to Leslie and to Blackwood that we owe the portrait of the Queen of Scots as it was finally drawn by her partisans in the sixteenth century. In their works and those they influenced, Mary becomes not an individualized, historical human being, but a symbol, or perhaps, more accurately, a complex allegorical figure, designed to arouse men to political and military action for the cause she came to represent. To this end, those elements in her character and history best suited to enhance her appeal are highlighted, while the rest are dismissed or ignored. The result is a composite created out of elements drawn from the literature of forty years on the Queen of Scots. She is, even at the end, made radiantly, even youthfully, beautiful. It is curious that, despite the evidence of both English and Catholic accounts that on the scaffold the middle-aged Mary was sick and worn, the impression of her freshness and loveliness at the end pervades most of this literature, the plays and poems especially, and survives to the present day in literary treatments of the Scottish Queen. Moreover, she is portrayed as the faithful and devoted wife, to at least two of her three husbands, and as the loving mother of an adoring son, despite the historical fact of James's singular lack of concern for her fate. In addition, she is the innocent, patient, and uncomplaining victim of her own brother and her own royal cousin, her ceaseless escape efforts and letters of outraged protest to the contrary notwithstanding. Always, of course, she is supremely regal —dowager of France, Queen of Scotland, and, in the opinion of her partisans, rightful Queen of England. But above all, in this literature, she is the martyr—pious, humble, and already one of the radiant company of saints, although the ruthlessly objective church for which she claimed she was killed has as yet—despite numerous proposals and the fond hopes of Brantôme—to accord her that supreme honor.

VIII THE ENGLISH DILEMMA:

1588-1603

While Mary's partisans on the Continent continued to proclaim her martyrdom, Protestant propagandists both in England and abroad were forced to make an abrupt about-face in their treatment of the now defunct Queen of Scots. From the time of her death until the end of Elizabeth's reign, the attitude of Protestant writers toward Mary was governed by one very large political consideration—the growing certainty that her son James would succeed Elizabeth on the throne of England. James himself was aware of this, to the extent of refusing to adopt a policy that could have saved his mother's life at the risk of forfeiting his right to the succession. Elizabeth too was aware of it, for although she declined to name him explicitly until she was literally on her deathbed, she nevertheless made it clear that she would offer no impediment to James's succession if he remained friendly to England, to Elizabeth, and to Protestantism. Elizabeth's most influential councilors were of the same opinion; as Conyers Read observes, they "were convinced that in the natural course of events James would be the next king of England," and, with a practical eye to their own futures, they treated him accordingly.[1]

Political wisdom therefore required some modification of the hostile attitude, toward the mother of the prospective king, that had dominated Protestant propaganda about Mary Stuart up through the early months of 1587. It was not just the fact that the mother of the prospective heir had been reviled on grounds of personal immorality and religious nonconformity that had to be explained away by the English. Far more important to James himself, as he soon made known, was his fear that Mary's right to the English throne, and hence his own right through her, had been impugned by the widely publicized charges of treason under which she had been tried and executed. He had some reason for this apprehension, for by the Act of Association, under which Mary had been found guilty, not only was the person thus convicted excluded from the succession, but also his or her heirs.[2] Accordingly, whatever his personal feelings about his mother may have been, James had very practical reasons for demanding reassurances about his own title when his mother, ostensibly accused of treason, was executed on these grounds. As he wrote in a personal letter to Elizabeth upon receiving the news of Mary's death, "I looke that ye will geye me at this tyme suche a full satisfaction, in all respectis, as sall be a meane to strenthin and unite this yle, establish and maintaine the treu religion, and obleig me to be, as of befoire I war, youre most loving." [3] With all Catholic Europe urging him to join in an attack on England in the name of his martyred mother, James was in a strategic position to press his demand for reassurance that he would succeed Elizabeth. It clearly behooved the English Protestants, then, to modify those charges against the Catholic mother that might seem to make the Protestant son unwelcome as Elizabeth's successor in England or block his title altogether.

Signs of a modified English attitude toward Mary began to appear in authorized literature about her shortly after the execution.[4] In 1589, for example, an elaborate description of the funeral Elizabeth had given the Queen of Scots two years earlier was published in London. Entitled *The Scottish Queen's Burial at Peterborough upon Tuesday, being Lammas Day 1587,* the account put special emphasis on the high honors accorded Mary at her last rites.[5] It describes in detail the lavish trappings of her hearse and the rich heraldic devices that accompanied it. It gives facts and figures on the number of mourners employed for the occasion, and it lists by name the distinguished noblemen and noblewomen in attendance. On the cause and circumstances of her death the account remains diplomatically vague; in the words of the Bishop of Lincoln, who preached the funeral sermon, "Of [her] life and departure, whatsoever shall be expected, I have nothing to say: for that I was unacquainted with the one; and not present at the other. Of Her Majesty's faith and end, I am not to judge." He would not have been Bishop of Lincoln if he had not added at this point, "It is a charitable saying of the Father Luther 'Many a one liveth a Papist; and dieth a Protestant.'" But without pressing the issue of Mary's faith, the Bishop quickly concluded, "Only this I have been informed, That she took her death patiently; and recommended herself wholly to Jesus Christ." [6] In general, *The Scottish Queen's Burial* was effectively designed to create the impression that Mary had been accorded every honor befitting the mother of James, and that royal sovereignty had been accorded all due respect, despite Catholic charges to the contrary.

The English were apparently aware that James's sensitivity about his mother's death was mainly inspired by a concern for his right, through her, to the succession in England, since they now spared no effort to put his mind to rest on this score. When James complained in 1595 that one William Leonard had "spoken slanderous words to the dishonour of the King and Queen of Scotland, as also of his mother," Elizabeth's government took prompt action to appease the King. Under questioning by the English, Leonard confessed that indeed he had said that the Scottish King was impotent, that Bothwell "commonly went to bed with" Mary, that "the late Queen was a whore," and that he—Leonard—"could show a book in his study which proved it." His English interrogators replied that whoever wrote this book was a knave. Leonard retorted that then their "great poet Buchanan was one, for he wrote it, and it had been translated into the Northern tongue, so that it might be known." If Leonard's examiners were embarrassed by this reminder that they themselves had sponsored the dissemination of Buchanan's *Detectioun of the duinges of Marie* when circumstances were different, they did not record the fact. Rather, in the spirit of the new order, they simply reported that

We ... have strictly examined all circumstances of this case, and do find the man to have spoken foolishly of the State of Scotland, but far from malicious, slanderous humour, for which (if it could have been so proved), he should dearly have paid for it, according to Her Majesty's absolute direction given to us; but being not proved so, he hath been only committed for his busiosity in matters beyond his calling, a fault very usual in this age.[7]

Far more celebrated evidence of Elizabeth's conciliatory policy is found in the case of James's well-known complaint against the treatment accorded "himself and his mother deceased" in Canto ix, Book V, of Edmund Spenser's *Faerie Queene*. When the work was published in 1596, James promptly recognized, as has every reader since, the highly unflattering and practically unveiled account of his mother in the trial of Duessa before Mercilla.[8] Like Mary in the earlier English propaganda literature, Duessa is here accused of a variety of public and private sins. "Zele," the prosecutor at the trial, charges her with

> Abhorred *Murder,* who with bloudie knyfe
> Yet dropping fresh in hand did her detect,
> And there with guiltie bloudshed charged ryfe:
> Then brought he forth *Sedition,* breeding stryfe
> In troublous wits, and mutinous vprore:
> Then brought he forth *Incontinence* of lyfe,
> Euen foule *Adulterie* her face before,
> And lewd *Impietie,* that her accused sore. [V, ix, 48]

Like the writers against Mary in 1586, Spenser indicates, however, that Duessa is being tried not for these crimes, nor for her false religion, but solely for the political crime of treason, for conspiring

> . . . .   to depryue
> *Mercilla* [i.e., Elizabeth] of her crowne, by her aspyred,
> That she might it vnto her selfe deryue,
> And tryumph in their blood whom she to death did
>   dryue. [V, ix, 41]

Finally, Spenser's account of the grief and reluctance of Mercilla in sentencing Duessa to death closely echoes the insistence in earlier propaganda literature on Elizabeth's sorrow and hesitation regarding the Queen of Scots:

> But she, whose Princely breast was touched nere
> With piteous ruth of her so wretched plight,
> Though plaine she saw by all, that she did heare,
> That she of death was guiltie found by right,
> Yet would not let iust vengeance on her light; [V, ix, 50]
>
> ·　·　·　·　·　·　·　·　·　·　·　·　·　·　·　·　·　·
>
> Till strong constraint did her thereto enforce.
> And yet euen then ruing her wilfull fall,
> With more than needfull naturall remorse,
> And yeelding the last honour to her wretched corse. [V, x, 4]

Spenser's thinly veiled portrait of Mary in her final days is, in its essential elements and in much of its specific language, little more than a highly poetic version of officially condoned Protestant literature that had appeared in the months preceding the Scottish Queen's death.

Upon reading these lines, James immediately registered a protest against this presentation of his mother. Robert Bowes, one of Elizabeth's agents in Edinburgh, wrote to Lord Burghley on November 12, 1596, that "the King hath conceived great offence against Edward Spencer [sic]. . . . He alleged that this book was passed with privilege of her majesties commissioners for the view and allowance of all writings to be received into print." Bowes tried to explain to the King that *The Faerie Queene* was "not given out with such privilege," but James still desired "that Edward Spencer for his faulte, may be duly tried and punished." [9] The Scottish King indeed had some grounds for assuming that *The Faerie Queene* had been printed with the approval of Elizabeth's government. It had been duly entered in the Stationers' Register, carried a clear indication of the responsible publisher in the imprint, and otherwise met the requirements imposed by governmental licensing authorities. Bowes, in his reply, may have been trying to convince James that the book had not been printed with "privilege" in the special sense of that term, that is, with exclusive rights conferred by the Crown suggesting active and official sponsorship of the work.[10] In any event, the fact that this minor tempest was closely linked to sensitive feelings, on both sides, about the succession seems to be indicated by all the circumstances. James's complaint, focused as it was on Elizabeth's licensing policies, suggests his fear that her government, by allowing Spenser's work to be published, was thereby condoning an attack on the Scottish right and title to the succession in England. The ambassador's efforts to reassure him that the attack on Mary was not officially sponsored suggests, in turn, the English concern for James's feelings in this matter.

Such an interpretation of his complaint is confirmed by the fact that he promptly assigned the job of preparing an answer to Spenser to one Walter Quin, a prolific writer who defended the King's English title on other occasions.[11] Quin's rejoinder to Spenser, if he actually wrote one, has not survived.[12] But that James requested an authority on succession matters to answer Spenser's poem suggests that the King read the epic attack on his mother primarily as an attack on his own rights. Eventually, however, James must have decided that no defense of his title against Spenser was necessary. Apparently he accepted Bowes' explanation that The Faerie Queene had not been printed "with priviledge," and therefore did not represent a shift in English policy in the direction of attacking the Scottish right to the succession by authorizing attacks on his mother. In any event, the English seemingly did nothing to punish Spenser, and James did not press the point. And, significantly, once he himself was secure on the throne of England, he allowed the portrait of Mary that had at first so offended him to appear in all the editions of Spenser's work published during his reign.

The Spenser affair, like the Leonard affair and the publication of the Peterborough funeral account, make it clear that Elizabeth was anxious to appease James by forbidding or disclaiming attacks on his mother after 1587. On the other hand, it is equally clear that the Queen of England was not willing to go so far in appeasing James as to tolerate published defenses of his right to succeed her, or even to allow defenses of his mother designed to reaffirm his

right and title. This apparently ambivalent attitude toward the late
Queen of Scots was dictated largely by Elizabeth's well-known disinclination to permit any public discussion of the succession which
she tacitly admitted would occur. As her godson, Sir John Harington, wrote, one of Elizabeth's ladies-in-waiting told him that the
Queen "hath taken occasion to speak of [the succession] herself,
and then hath not stuck plainely to say that they were fooles that
did not knowe that the lyne of Scotland must needes be next heires,
but for all that no bodie dares ever sooth her when she saith it." [13]
Elizabeth's attitude in this matter was not composed all of feminine
vanity and Tudor perversity. As her ablest modern biographer has
pointed out, "To have done otherwise would have been to invite
all rivals and enemies to set about forestalling [James's] accession,
thus jeopardising both his rights and her domestic peace." [14]

In line with this policy, Elizabeth, while disallowing published
attacks on Mary, at the same time rigidly suppressed works written
in England that tried even incidentally to defend James's right to
the succession by defending his mother against the charges that
might have clouded his title. With equal vigor, she protested
against the production of such works in Scotland. In 1594, for
example, she objected strenuously to the printing of a Latin poem
by Andrew Melville, on the birth of James's first son, Prince Henry,
because it called James "king of all Britain in possession." [15] A
somewhat more touching example of the dilemma in which pub-
lishers in Scotland found themselves as a result of pressures from
two monarchs—and, incidentally, an illustration of Elizabeth's
superior pressure—involves the Latin treatise defending the King's
right and title to the English succession; the treatise was prepared
in 1598 by Walter Quin, to whom James had earlier assigned the
task of replying to Edmund Spenser. According to a report received
in England by Robert Cecil, King James had ordered Robert
Waldgrave, an Englishman who had moved to Scotland to become
the King's Printer there, to publish Quin's tract. Waldgrave, who
as an Englishman was fully aware of Elizabeth's strictures against
the publication of such works, had the courage to refuse, although
not without obvious distress:

... lamenting his hard fortune, that ether he must printe it, stayenge here, or be undon, and he feares quarrelled for his life if he refuse it, and printing it greve his conscience, offend her Majestie & utterly loose his contry: all most weping, and wishing that for avoyding of this he might have libertie to returne to his owne contrye; which being granted him he wold returne and leave all here to themselves to printe as they coulde.[16]

The dilemma of the unhappy printer was the dilemma of most Protestant writers caught between the ambivalence of Elizabeth and the aspirations of James. They were damned if they did, and damned if they did not, seek to clear the way for Protestant James by defending his Catholic mother. They dared not attack Mary in the old, familiar way for fear of offending not only James, the hope of all Protestants in England, but the reigning Queen as well, who tacitly regarded him as her successor. On the other hand, they dared not attempt to exonerate Mary for fear of appearing to press the forbidden question of the succession. Their dilemma is poignantly revealed by Sir John Harington, who prepared but refused to publish an elaborate treatise in defense of James's right to the succession. In the course of the treatise he sought to exonerate Mary of the charges that had been brought against her. But he concludes that, "having ventured upon more dangerous matter in this booke," he would never dare to express what he has to say except that he does not intend to publish it.[17] Most Protestant writers, and especially those in Britain, who dealt with Mary after her death appear to have been governed by a similar wariness. They tried in various ways and by various means to present the subject without giving offense to either party, but for the most part their efforts are accompanied by indications that through the end of Elizabeth's reign the story remained a difficult one to handle.

The most forthright expressions of the adjusted attitude toward Mary produced by the new political circumstances are found in treatises on the succession question written between the time of her death and the beginning of her son's reign in England. So forthright were these tracts that, like Harington's, they usually remained unpublished at the time, and hence their effectiveness as popular propaganda was minimal. But as documents revealing the motives and methods of the modified Protestant attitude, they are invaluable.

These treatises make it clear that Protestant writers, generally speaking, now shifted to a defense of Catholic Mary in order to defend the succession of her Protestant son. They were forced to do so, in part at least, by a corresponding shift in the opposite direction on the part of extremists among English Catholics. After the death of Mary, the Jesuits in particular found themselves obliged to attack the Scottish Queen, their heroine until her death, in order to support their arguments against the succession of her Protestant son. Even John Leslie, his hopes for a Catholic succession in England ended with Mary's death, prepared a book designed to prove Philip of Spain to be the true heir "since the king of Scotland is incapacitated by heresy"; and later, Cardinal Allen projected a book defending the claims of the Infanta of Spain and attacking those of James and the Stuart line.[18]

This paradoxical shift on the Catholic side appears most strikingly in *A Conference about the next succession to the crowne of England,* written by the Jesuit Robert Parsons under the name of "N. Doleman," in support of the claims of the Infanta of Spain to the throne of England, and published—perforce, abroad—in 1594.[19] In arguing against the right of James to succeed Elizabeth, Parsons found it necessary to argue against the right of his mother before him. In so doing, he had to reverse the major arguments advanced in Catholic Marian literature of the preceding quarter-century, and even the arguments he himself had advanced just two years before in Mary's favor when he was attacking Elizabeth's anti-Catholic edict of 1591.[20] For example, in the earlier treatise he had argued, as had most of the Catholic literature supporting Mary throughout the century, that she was the legitimate heir to the throne of England should Elizabeth die without issue.[21] Now, in his *Conference,* he carefully reconsidered the arguments for Mary's right that had been advanced by no less a defender than John Leslie; Parsons now concluded that James, "who pretendeth al his right to the crowne of Ingland by his said mother, can haue none at all." [22] In the earlier work he had charged that Mary was executed against all law and royal sovereignty for crimes falsely attributed to her by heretics.[23] But now he accepted without rejoinder the arguments of the chief anti-Marian Protestant writers who had earlier claimed that, because Mary was lawfully executed under the Parliamentary Act of Association for conspiring against England and Elizabeth, her son was thus excluded from the succession.[24] Although it cannot be said that Parsons in this later work ever subjects Mary to the kind of attack she had received in earlier Protestant literature, his calm acceptance of charges of her political and moral guilt and his arguments against her rights to the English throne strike a strange new note in literature issuing from a Catholic pen.

The Protestant writers who undertook to defend the claims of James against attacks like those of Parsons were quick to seize upon the about-face of the Jesuit, and, it must be added, were just as quick to execute an about-face of their own in the opposite direction. The earliest published effort to answer Parson's shift in argument with a shift in argument of its own was a tract by Peter Wentworth, published in 1598, which bore as its full title, *A Pithie Exhortation to her Maiestie for establishing her successor to the crowne. Whereunto is added a discourse containing the authors opinion of the true and lawfull successor to her Maiestie.*[25] The true and lawful successor is, of course, James, and, in defending the Scottish King's right and title, Wentworth relied heavily and with acknowledgment on the arguments advanced not many years before by John Leslie in favor of Mary's claim, and hence her son's, to the English throne. Thus the Puritan Wentworth accepts the arguments for Mary, advanced by the Bishop of Ross, that were rejected by the Jesuit Parsons. As to the private character and the political conduct of Mary, however, Wentworth maintained the hostile, even virulent, attitude that had marked authorized English publications on the Queen of Scots at the time of her death. His low opinion of Mary, as well as his effort to reconcile this opinion with his enthusiastic support of her son as Elizabeth's successor, is summed up when he exclaims:

The actions of the mother and the sonne was so farre different, as the East is from the West: the one a papist and a maintainer of superstition: the other a protestant and enemie to all superstition: the one adhering to that which was falsely called the holy league: the other puklikely [*sic*] opposed himselfe to the same, and motioned a counterleague, the one a follower and favourer of the house of Guise, the most pernicious enemie that Engl. had in their time, the other in a manner ruled and governed by our Soveraigne, the surest and firmest friend she hath in Europe, as plainlie appeared An. 1588. And brieflie the whole frame and course of their lives was in some sort one opposite to the other.[26]

Wentworth's effort here to separate feelings about mother and son in the intricate political-religious situation was not adequate, however, to save him from Elizabeth's far-reaching wrath. Having been thrown into prison when he tried to circulate his manuscript in England in 1587, he later had it published surreptitiously in Edinburgh.[27] However, its double violation of Elizabeth's ban against attacks on Mary and defenses of James's title did not escape the notice of the English agents in Scotland. Their reaction is tersely but vividly revealed in a note from Scotland recorded in the State Papers: "A book published in the name of Mr. Wentworth; flight of the compositor." [28]

Sir John Harington, the epigrammatist, translator of Ariosto, and godson of Queen Elizabeth, was more circumspect than the impolitic Wentworth in expounding similar views on the succession matter. Harington's *Tract on the Succession to the Crown,* which, as he said with a clear awareness of his godmother's feelings, "ventured upon more dangerous matter," remained in manuscript form until the nineteenth century.[29] The larger part of his *Tract,* like Wentworth's, is devoted to a defense of James's right to the succession with arguments that closely parallel those advanced by Catholic writers earlier in the century in favor of James's mother. Harington developed one new argument that is at least ingenious in its effort to resolve the dilemma of the English treatment of Mary at this point of history. Because of her, he says, the accession of James will put an end to the strife between Protestants and Catholics in England. Protestants will welcome James as one of their own, while Catholics—Harington hopes—will welcome him as the son of their beloved martyr, and will say, "Wee loved your mother. She favored us; she dyed for us, & wee dye for her." [30] In thus urging Catholics to accept the son out of loyalty to the mother, Harington reminds them of the virtues in her that they had always so admired. He quotes at length from William Rainold's *Calvino-Turcismus*, an ardent defense of Mary and eulogy of her martyr-dom published in 1597, and concludes by appealing to Catholics to "transferre all that good conceit that you had of or towardes her to hir more noble sonne, to whome by all lawes of nature and nations it is due by inheritance." [31]

If Wentworth did not go far enough in suppressing his low opinion of the personal character and conduct of Mary for the sake of her son, Harington perhaps went too far—according, at least, to his own testimony. After quoting from Rainolds to account for the misfortunes of the Queen of Scots he introduces an epigram on Mary that might well have been modeled on any one of the milder *De Jezabelis* poems published earlier by Catholics in defense of her cause:

> When doome of Peeres & Judges fore-appointed,
> By racking lawes beyond all reach of reason,
> Had unto death condemn'd a Queene anointed,
> And found (oh strange!) without allegeance, treason,
> The axe that should have done that execution,
> Shunn'd to cut off a head that had been crowned,
> Our hangman lost his wonted resolution,
> To quell a Queene of nobles so renowned.
> Ah, is remorse in hangmen and in steele,
> When Peeres and Judges no remorse can feele?
> Grant Lord, that in this noble Ile, a Queene
> Without a head, may never more be seene.[32]

Harington was well aware that such sentiments were probably more sympathetic to Mary than his royal English godmother would find acceptable. "I confesse," he wrote, "that meditating of what I had heard of the manner of [Mary's] arraignement and execution, I made this epigrammaticall epitaphe, and tould it to some good freindes bothe English and Scottish, but now, having ventured upon more daungerous matter in this booke, I will adventure also to sett it downe herewith, though it was Agraphon before." [33] Even then, however, he lost his nerve and decided against publishing the tract, with its epigram, while he and Elizabeth still lived.

Meanwhile, for the change in attitude toward Mary among Scottish Protestants as a result of the succession issue, one must again rely on a manuscript defense of James's claims that could not safely be published at the time.[34] This was an elaborate treatise written by Sir Thomas Craig, the Scottish legal authority and Latin poet, entitled, *The Right of Succession to the Kindom of England . . . against the Sophisms of Parsons the Jesuite, who assum'd the Counterfeit Name of Doleman. . . .* Although written and dedicated to James in 1603, the work apparently remained in manuscript until it was published in London in 1703. Like Wentworth and Harington, Craig was concerned mainly with establishing James's legal right to the English throne on the basis of Mary's right, and like them, too, he reiterated many of the arguments set forth earlier in defense of Mary's claim by her Catholic partisans. The awkward matter of her religion he avoided entirely—Craig, after all, was an advocate in the Kirk of Scotland. In answering Parson's charge that under the English Act of Association James was excluded from the succession because of his mother's crimes, Craig notes that James was not implicated and, he adds parenthetically, Mary in any event simply "had a mind to free herself from an imprisonment which was contrary to the Laws of Nations, by whatever means. . . ." [35] This claim that Mary had sought only her own freedom, and not the life and the throne of Elizabeth, had of course been one of the major points in the earlier Catholic defenses of her actions. Craig is cautious in advancing the point, however; he is mainly concerned, as a lawyer, with showing that the Act of Association "would not have the fact of the Mother . . . to prejudice her Son." [36]

Elsewhere in his tract Craig pays his compliments to Mary in terms of less controversial points of her career and her character. Defending the right and ability of women to rule as legitimate monarchs—John Knox to the contrary notwithstanding—he observes that "we have known two Queens in this very Age in which we live of such eminent accomplishments"; he then proceeds to write glowing tributes to the administrative abilities of both Elizabeth and Mary Stuart. Of the latter he says, for example:

I have often heard the most Serene Princess Mary Queen of Scotland, discourse so appositely and rationally in all Affaires which were brought before the Privy-Council, that She was admir'd by all ... Her other Discourses and Actions were suitable to Her great Judgment: No Word ever dropt from her Mouth, that was not exactly weigh'd and ponder'd. As for her Liberality, and other Vertues, they were well known.[37]

Elizabeth he treated with equally lavish praise. Truly, if the succession of James presented Protestants with a dilemma in their attitude towards Mary, none resolved the problem more blandly than did Sir Thomas Craig. Nevertheless, he apparently deemed it unwise to publish such compromising statements while Elizabeth was still on the throne.

As the record—including Wentworth's account—shows, Craig was probably right in deeming that Protestant defenses of Mary in the interests of James were better left in manuscript. Meanwhile, most of the authors who had the temerity to publish their works in these final years of the century show far greater caution in dealing with the Queen of Scots. Even in these, however, a modification of the former Protestant hostility towards Mary is evident. The historian Stow, for example, appears to have handled the delicate subject with an uneasy regard for the certain prospect of her son's succession to the English throne. His *Annales of England,* published in 1592, was essentially an expansion of his earlier chronicles.[38] But in what he saw fit to add concerning the Queen of Scots, and what not to add, the pressures under which publishing writers were now operating in England are evident.[39] Stow discusses the Norfolk, Throckmorton, and Babington plots in his 1592 edition, as he had in earlier editions, with no reference at all to Mary's involvement, thus diplomatically ignoring the charges that were widely and officially publicized just a few years earlier. He does go so far as to say that the reading of the proclamation of Mary's sentence on December 6, 1586, was made "to the great and woonderfull rejoicing of the people of all sorts, as manifestly appeered by ringing of bels, making of bonfiers, and singing of Psalms in every of the streetes and lanes of the citie." [40] But his account of the execution, given in less than a hundred words, does little more than state the

fact itself, and then, apparently picking up the official theme announced in the pamphlet on *The Scottish Queen's Burial*, he
observes in conclusion that "shee was (as appertained to a queen)
royally buried at Peterborough on the first of August next following." [41]

The versified history of England by William Warner, *Albions
England*, modified the earlier Protestant English attack on Mary
in somewhat different fashion. Although first published in 1586,
the poem contained no mention of the Queen of Scots by name
until the revised edition of 1596. Then she is introduced in the
course of a violent diatribe against the Catholic enemies of
England. The poet observes of her that

> . . . . the *Guizian Scot,*
> Fatal to Seas of blood, and to her owne by earned lot,
> Did with our Foes against our State and Soveraignes life
>   complot,
> Wherein King Phillip and the Pope especially weare hot.[42]

Before continuing in this fashion reminiscent of Buchanan and the
preëxecution attacks on Mary, however, Warner assures his readers
that he intends to spare her memory, out of deference to her son:
"Here, but in Reverence of her Sonne an happie Prince in all . . .
not thus of Marie should we end." [43] Despite his reluctance, he
nevertheless continues for six pages crowded with his pedestrian
fourteeners to detail what *might* be told of Mary if it were not for
this respect for James. In this curiously qualified fashion, he
manages to suggest everything that had been charged against her
in the most extreme Protestant propaganda attacks. For example,
he writes that "Her Favours unto *David Rize*, offensive to the
King / His Highness Father, but for him [i.e., James] in storie
would we bring." [44] Further, he could tell of her adultery with
Bothwell, their murder of Darnley, Mary's bloody plots against
England. "All," he says, "that *Buchanan* doth wright should
largely here be read," were it not for "th'aforesaid Reverence for
her son." [45] Warner's carefully placed disclaimers may do little to
alter the portrait of Mary, but they at least make clear the sensitivity to the political situation that now made such portraiture
dangerous.

Considering the furor aroused by Spenser's unqualified description of Mary, it is surprising to find that Warner's unflattering account apparently drew no censure from James or Elizabeth when it first appeared, or in subsequent editions, including those published quite openly in London after James became king of England. Perhaps Warner's repeated disclaimers of any intention to attack James by attacking his mother were, after all, politically if not poetically effective in preserving *Albions England* for posterity.

Meanwhile, a number of writers on both sides of the Channel—Protestants for the most part—were not slow to recognize the suitability of Mary's story for treatment as tragedy in the Renaissance sense of the term. The poets and the one playwright who handled the subject in this fashion were perhaps motivated primarily by artistic considerations, but some of them, at least, apparently also felt that presentation of the Queen of Scots as a tragic heroine offered them a way out of the dilemma created by the imminent succession of James. Such a treatment permitted them to emphasize the larger philosophical implications of Mary's history while ignoring or minimizing the more immediate and controversial political issues involved.

Tragedy, as it developed during the Renaissance in both dramatic and nondramatic forms, was originally concerned with portraying the pitiful downfall of eminent persons through the caprices of fickle fortune.[46] However, in such Elizabethan examples as *The Mirror for Magistrates,* Drayton's *Legends,* and Daniel's *Complaint of Rosamond,* the conception of tragedy, although continuing to emphasize the fickleness and uncertainty of worldly fortune, came more and more to explain the downfall of fortune's victims in terms of punishment for sin. Fortune, in other words, was one of God's ways of punishing the violation of His laws. Moreover, the transgression of these laws, or sin, came to be consistently defined as the triumph of the passions over the reason in determining individual conduct. The point of view of the writer of Renaissance tragedy, then, is not so much that of the political or religious polemicist as that of the moral philosopher. As such, he is primarily concerned with individual human conduct, and only incidentally, if at all, with specific (and more dangerous) political and religious issues. Although he never lets us forget the moral responsibility of the individual, his main purpose, as he usually reminds us again and again, is to arouse in the audience or reader pity for the tragic victim and an awareness of the uncertainties of fortune.

It was perhaps inevitable, whatever the succession predicament, that Mary's career would sooner or later have been viewed as a tragedy in this Renaissance sense.[47] The application of the concept itself is succinctly illustrated in a manuscript lyric that was probably written not long after the execution of the Queen of Scots:

> The Noble famous Queene,
> Who lost hir head of Late
> doth shew that kings as well as Clownes,
> are bound to fortunes fate,
> and that noe earthly prince,
> can soe secure his crowne,
> but fortune with hir whyrling wheele,
> hath power to pull them downe.[48]

A more extended treatment of the same theme is found in John Dickenson's *Speculum Tragicum,* a Latin prose imitation of the *Mirror for Magistrates* published at Delft in 1601 and in subsequent editions at Leyden. Little is known about Dickenson, except that he was apparently a Protestant who divided his creative energies between writing euphuistic romances in English and historical tragedies and epistles in Latin.[49] In its presentation of the tragic downfall of eminent persons, the *Speculum* covers a field wide enough to include Mary Stuart, the Marechal Biron in France, the Earl of Essex in England, and "Motexuma Mexicano, & Atabalipa rege Pervano." Dickenson's approach to these tragedies is suggested by his full title, which reads, as translated, "The Tragic Mirror, bringing together briefly the calamitous downfalls and deaths of the most celebrated kings, princes, and potentates in high worldly positions: in which both divine judgments and human folly are revealed through notable examples." [50] He makes his theme and treatment more specifically clear when he adds in an address to the reader that his tragic subjects have fallen "because of some instance of fortune, or of sin, or of some other." [51]

Such is the tragic formula, politically and religiously noncommittal, that he applies not only to Mary but also to Darnley and Bothwell, to Murray and Lennox and the Duke of Norfolk, all of whom have their tragedies recorded. Taken in order, as Dickenson presents them, the "tragedies" comprise a fairly complete history of the Scottish Queen from the beginnings of her troubles in Scotland through her execution at Fotheringay in 1587. The point of view throughout is characteristically Protestant in suggesting Mary's moral responsibility for her downfall. She married Darnley because she was captivated by his youthful appearance and manners, but, tiring of him, she turned to Bothwell, whom she admitted "in familiaritem intimam." [52] Darnley was murdered by Bothwell, according to Dickenson, with the knowledge if not the connivance of Mary, and the final ignominy marking the "tragic downfall" of the young King was his burial next to Rizzio, whom Mary, the author observes, had known "immoderately." [53] Dickenson is equally frank in placing the moral responsibility on Mary for her troubles after she fled to England. He describes Norfolk as one of those "who perished in England because of the Scottish Queen," since he and Mary conspired to wed against the will of Elizabeth. [54] Mary's own death he describes as brought about because she was involved in plots against both the life and the throne of the Queen of England. [55]

But castigation of Mary is not the major emphasis or purpose of Dickenson's *Speculum*. He stresses rather the mutability of fortune and the uncertainty of worldly position and glory which all of the "tragedies" are supposed to illustrate. He notes that Darnley was not only ignobly murdered, but also buried at night without ceremony. Bothwell, he points out, perished miserably in squalor and filth after years of imprisonment in Denmark. His account of Mary's "tragedy" itself is extremely brief. Perhaps his brevity, and his explanation that he leaves the writing of longer and fuller accounts to others, reflects some of the uneasiness that affected most of the Protestant writers who dealt with the Queen of Scots at this critical juncture. Whatever his reasons, he does little more than mention her separation from Bothwell, her escape from Lochleven, her imprisonment in England, her plots against Elizabeth, and her death. He is careful to point out that she was an offspring of the English royal line, and, by implication, that her son's claim to the English throne is good. Mainly, however, he regards her as a remarkable example of the certainties of God's judgments and the uncertainties of fortune—"a singular record of the wretched uncertainty of human affairs, and of divine justice." [56] Here, as throughout the *Speculum,* Dickenson suggests the moral responsibility for tragedy but prefers to emphasize the pity and terror aroused by the spectacle of the downfall of great and illustrious persons.

An almost identical approach to the problem of Mary is taken in John Johnston's *Inscriptiones Historicae,* a series of Latin verses on Scottish rulers published at Amsterdam in 1602.[57] The work, translated into Scots in the following year, is dedicated to James with the hope that the lessons of history found in the *Inscriptiones* will provide his son, young Prince Henry, with suitable instruction in the differences between government and tyranny. The lesson Johnston finds in the story of Prince Henry's grandmother Mary actually has less to do with government and tyranny than with the insecurity and uncertainty of high position— a lesson no Renaissance ruler was ever allowed to forget, lest he succumb to the sin of pride. In his "Inscription" on Mary, Johnston observes that she was triply eminent, as the descendant, the wife, and the mother of kings. Yet all these apparent guarantees of position were vain, he concludes, for "no one who is subject to Fortune's will may trust in greatness." [58] He puts similar words into Mary's mouth in a legend beneath a full-page portrait of her when he makes her say, "I who seemed to stand high by the will of Dame Fortune soon became the lamentable object of her mockery." [59] Unlike Dickenson, Johnston refused to place the moral responsibility for Mary's downfall upon Mary herself, a hesitancy not surprising in view of the dedication to Mary's son. Like Dickenson, however, he apparently felt that pity for Mary rather than censure provided a convenient escape from the political predicament in which he, like other Protestant writers, found himself.

Another Protestant poet who wrote about Mary in similar

fashion was Andrew Melville, a pillar in the Kirk of Scotland and, after Buchanan, one of the most distinguished Latin poets in the British Isles. Two poems by Melville on the Queen of Scots were printed by Johnston along with his own *Inscriptiones*. The shorter of Melville's two is an epitaph in which the themes of Mary's rightful place in the line of succession and the tragedy of her downfall from high place are implicit if not clearly stated; in a contemporary translation it reads:

> Issu'd from kings, I greatn'd kings, & kingly
>   crowns have worne:
> Thrise wedded, thrise a widow, I three kingdomes
>   have forgone.
> The French my wealth, the Scott my birth, the
>   English hath my tombe.[60]

The longer of Melville's two poems is an expansion of the same basic themes in more explicit terms. In the fashion of nondramatic "tragedies" or "complaints," it is the Queen of Scots herself who speaks. At the outset she emphasizes the threefold nature of her high place—by virtue of her birth, her marriages, and her son. But, as she says, she "was subject to all the fortunes of kings," and was defeated. Then, addressing James, she exclaims, "To you, my son, I gave the scepter which was rightfully yours"—a probable reference to James's claim to the crown of England through his mother. In the end, Melville, without committing himself concerning Mary's religious faith, pays a graceful tribute to her strength of character during her imprisonment and at her death when he makes her say, "Through hope I reigned steadfastly; while I could breathe, I could hope." Like Sir Thomas Craig, Melville was apparently willing to concede that Mary's plots against Elizabeth were motivated more by her desire for escape than by her ambitions to supplant the English Queen. Hence his emphasis on her indefatigable hope, as well as on her place in the succession and on the pity of her downfall.[61]

Perhaps the most curious, and certainly the most extended, treatment of Mary's history as a "tragedy" in the Renaissance sense of the term is *The Legend of Mary, Queen of Scots,* a poem attrib-

uted to Thomas Wenman, an Oxford orator and member of the
Inner Temple. Composed in 1601, the *Legend* remained in manuscript for some two centuries for reasons that were probably literary
rather than political.[62] Wenman closely modeled his poem on the
"tragedies" in the *Mirror for Magistrates*. As in the *Mirror*, it is to
William Baldwin, editor of the earlier work, that the ghost of Mary
appears with the plea that he tell her tale in verse. The nearly two
hundred rhyme-royal stanzas in which Wenman wrote his poem
are certainly no worse, but certainly no better, than most of those
that make up the *Mirror for Magistrates*. The principal theme
developed by Wenman in his *Legend* is to the effect that, although
the Queen of Scots was guilty of sins and crimes, she paid for them
by her downfall and her death, and now deserves the pity of all who
read her "tragedy." In the words that Mary's ghost addresses to
Baldwin:

> My faultes I graunte, and sorrowe with my harte,
> Yet since of gilt I have sustained the smarte,
> I might bemone the hap befalne to me,
> That in my grave must still accused be.[63]

In the fashion characteristic of the *Mirror* type of legends and
tragedies, fortune is made to share the blame with moral guilt for
Mary's downfall; in fact, Mary excuses many of her confessed sins
on the basis of a malevolent fate:

> And doe but note thou in my tender age?
> Before my eares were apte for good or ill,
> What cause I had to curse vile fortunes rage,
> Who gan so sone to worke on me her will,
> Whom ever since she hath pursued still;
> Makinge those thinges which promise greatest blys,
> My onely bane, so muche her malice is.[64]

Wenman's *Legend of Mary* contains little in the way of literary
quality to make one wonder that it has been published only once,
and then only as an antiquarian curiosity two centuries after it was
written. Nevertheless, as the fullest expression of a prevalent attitude toward Mary among Protestant writers in the crucial years
preceding the accession of James, it is a work of considerable

interest. Not only in his general conception of Mary's history as "tragedy," but also in the particular themes he develops, Wenman is drawing together and treating *in extenso* the principal elements of the solution other Protestant writers in the last decade of the reign found for their predicament. He makes much of her motherly tenderness and devotion to James. He avoids the problem of religion, and ignores the claims of martyrdom made for her by Catholic writers. He suggests that in her plots and conspiracies in England she was more concerned with her own liberty than with the life of Elizabeth. Finally, without exonerating her of the sins and crimes attributed to her by earlier Protestant writers, he gives definitive expression to the pity and sympathy her "tragedy" came, perforce, to inspire as James approached the throne of England.

Meanwhile, a similar shift in the treatment of Mary was taking place, in some quarters at least, in France. The change is probably reflected, for example, by Montaigne in his essay "That We Should Not Judge of Our Happiness, untill after Our Death," where he says with reference to Mary, "the fairest Queene, wife to the greatest King of Christendome, was she not lately seene to die by the hands of an executioner? Oh unworthie and barbarous crueltie!" [65] The context discloses that the great essayist is here less concerned with the Scottish Queen as a political or religious symbol than simply as one of several historical examples he offers to demonstrate the uncertainty of high place and the caprices of Fortune.

More striking evidence of the tragic interpretation of Mary's story as it developed in France is found in the last and relatively the most distinguished of the plays written about the Queen of Scots before 1603. Antoine de Montchrestien's *Escossoise, ou le Desastre Tragedie* was composed some time after 1597 and first published in 1601.[66] Montchrestien, a playwright acknowledged by critics to be one of the most brilliant of the age, spent the greater part of his time and energy getting into, and out of, a variety of scrapes and brawls brought about by his activities in lawsuits, dueling, and alleged counterfeiting. In more than one respect he reminds one of Christopher Marlowe. How long and how deeply Montchrestien had embraced Protestantism is not clear, although his principal modern editor feels that the individualistic playwright had been a Protestant since birth.[67] The circumstances of his death in 1621 leave no doubt that he not only died a Protestant, but for Protestantism. In the reign of Louis XIII he undertook to raise troops in support of the reformers, and it was while trapped in an ambush with these troops that he met his death.

Montchrestien's theory of dramatic tragedy, in its emphasis on pity for the tragic victim and horror at the uncertainties of fortune, resembles that of the Elizabethan writers of nondramatic tragedy. In fact, he is far more explicit in describing this concept than are any of the British writers. Dedicating his collected dramas to the young Prince of Condé, son and heir to the most illustrious Protestant family in France, Montchrestien says in a prefatory epistle that his tragedies present the various accidents of life, the strange blows of fortune, the admirable judgments of God, the singular effects of His providence, and the dreadful punishments of ill-advised kings and ill-behaved people.[68] Such, apparently, was his interpretation of the history of the Queen of Scots. He may well have been led to this reading of her story by his principal source, Pierre Matthieu's *Histoire des derniers troubles de France,* in which the author concludes a "Digression sur la mort de la Royne d'Escosse" with the exclamation: "Voila une vie bien tragicque, et un vray tableau de la vanité des grandeurs du monde." [69]

Like the earlier Catholic dramas on the subject, the *Escossoise* is concerned with the last few hours of Mary's life. The action of the play begins some time after she has been tried and sentenced. Elizabeth is portrayed as wanting to spare Mary, but the English councilors urge her to execute the Queen of Scots, who has been discovered plotting against the life and throne of the English Queen. In Act II, Elizabeth, moved by pity and mercy, by fear of killing a sister queen, and by concern for her own reputation in history, refuses to act. But her councilors, to save the Queen of England and her realm, decide that the Queen of Scots must die. In Act III, Mary delivers a long recital of her troubles, characterizing them in general as "mon malheur fatale," and concluding that she is resigned to her fate. Davison, Elizabeth's secretary, arrives at this point to read the charges against Mary; she conspired with kings against England, she aroused civil broils and factions in the realm, and she tried to poison the English Queen. Mary receives the news with philosophic calm while the chorus comments on the inevitability and commonness of death.

Act IV is one long soliloquy by the Queen of Scots on the night before her execution as she prepares herself for her approaching ordeal. Her speech is composed mainly of lengthy farewells—to Scotland, to France, to her son, to her attendants—and of expressions of piety. These latter make no reference to martyrdom for her faith, but are utterances of relief that her long and unfortunate life is about to end. Their tone and attitude are more in the tragic than the religious tradition. The chorus, in concluding the act, picks up and develops the same theme, observing in general that anyone is happy who is about to know the joys of life eternal beyond the trials and tribulations of this world.

Act V deals with Mary's conduct on the scaffold, the action being described by a messenger in classical fashion rather than shown on the stage. The act opens with expressions of indignation at English cruelty and barbarity by Mary's maître d'hôtel (Melville) and by the chorus. The messenger then proceeds to recount her behavior on the block, emphasizing her beauty, her piety, and above all her courage. The drama concludes with a final, highly eulogistic chorus which, while avoiding such issues as her religious faith and her political guilt or innocence, praises her personal virtues and attractions in a style reminiscent of Brantôme, and, long before that, of Ronsard. We are told that her mouth, once an oracle of love sweetly flowing with honeyed eloquence, is silenced, her hair of purest gold is bloodied, her visage has lost its natural grace, and her eyes, in despite of love, have been closed by death.[70]

Although there are touches throughout the play reminiscent of Catholic martyrological literature about Mary—her own reference to her heavenly crown, for example, or a comment by the chorus that one should rejoice at the death of saints and martyrs—the *Escossoise* in its over-all emphasis is far closer to the Protestant literature of the end of the century. The almost equal division of sympathy between Elizabeth and Mary, a feature of the play that has puzzled and disturbed many of its critics, resembles strikingly, in fact, the treatment accorded the two queens by British writers like Harington and Craig. The reasons given by Elizabeth and her councilors for executing Mary are presented objectively and convincingly, and are allowed to stand without argument or refutation. The cruelty of the decision is not minimized, but neither is the necessity. Elizabeth herself is portrayed in the first two acts not as the bloodthirsty Jezebel of the extremist Catholic literature, but rather with some sympathy, as a queen who cannot bring herself to execute a sister sovereign. Her councilors who order the execution against Elizabeth's will and knowledge are described, unlike the horrendous creatures found in Bordes' Jesuit drama, as men honestly convinced that the welfare of Elizabeth and her subjects depends on the death of Mary.

Mary emerges not so much the martyred victim of English duplicity and Protestant intolerance as the pitiful and awe-inspiring tragic heroine. If Montchrestien refuses to place the moral responsibility for her fate on the English, he also refuses to place it on the Scottish Queen herself. Instead, he chooses to emphasize those elements in her character and history designed to arouse sympathy for a victim of fortune and circumstance. He says little about her political and religious activities, but much about her beauty, her despair, her courage, and her piety. He misses no opportunity to stress her proneness to misfortune and mischance. To this end, for example, Montchrestien made use of the curious bit of misinformation that Mary was brought to England against her will when by chance the ship supposed to carry her to a refuge in France was blown off course. Even the seas and the elements, he concludes, conspired against her.[71] In its final and overall effect, then, the play is less a polemical and propagandistic document, like the Jesuit dramas, than a "tragedy" in the Renaissance meaning of the term.

Despite this portrayal of Mary and the understanding presentation of Elizabeth's role, Montchrestien's *Escossoise* seems to have run afoul of the Queen of England's sensitivity about public discussions of the case of the Queen of Scots. On March 17, 1602, Sir Ralph Winwood, at that time the English ambassador in Paris, wrote to Sir Robert Cecil in London that "certaine base Comedians have publicklie plaied in this Towne the Tragedy of the late Queen of Scottes," referring, it has been shown, to Montchrestien's drama. Winwood continues that he complained to the French chancellor about "so lewde an Indiscretion" and was promised that "this Folly should be punished, and that the like hereafter should not be committed." [72] The French authorities, who had their own reasons for being offended with the *Escossoise*, apparently feeling it was Guisian in sympathy, pursued the matter until February, 1604, when the English ambassador could report to England that "ye booke is suppressed, and the author and ye printer inquired after to tast of ye same cupp." [73]

But by February, 1604, the whole complex and delicate matter of the succession to the English throne had been settled for almost a year. Elizabeth had died in March of the preceding year, and Mary Stuart's son wore the crown of England. If an account of what now happened to Montchrestien, written by one of his contemporaries, is true, the French dramatist became one of the first writers to feel the effect of the dynastic change in England on literary treatments of the Queen of Scots.[74] For reasons that are still obscure but may have been connected with French disapproval of his Mary Stuart drama, Montchrestien was forced to flee from France in 1604. He made his way to England, of all places, and there presented his tragedy on the Scottish Queen to King James, who apparently had not known the editions of the work published earlier. According to the contemporary account, James was so well pleased with the treatment of his mother in the *Escossoise* that, to show his favor, he interceded with the French King to permit the safe return of Montchrestien to Paris. In view of the feelings on the succession issue during the last years of Elizabeth's reign, it probably should not be surprising to find that Montchrestien's portrait of Mary, which had proved offensive to the English Queen just two years before, was highly pleasing to the Queen of Scots' son who was now the Protestant King of England. In any event, with the accession of James the dilemma confronting Protestant writers who sought to deal with Mary Stuart while Elizabeth was still on the throne had been resolved.

EPILOGUE

The battle of the books on Mary Stuart did not end with the accession of her son James to the throne of England, nor has it ended yet. However, when Elizabeth on her deathbed finally and officially named Mary's son as her successor, there inevitably followed a period of truce in the propaganda warfare that had raged for almost half a century. For the moment, with Protestant fears of a Catholic succession allayed and Catholic hopes for a Catholic succession dashed, the primary cause of the battle was gone.

There were, to be sure, occasional echoes of the more violent warfare that had marked the preceding reign, but these were few, and most of them bore authorized imprints that indicated tacit toleration by the new king and his government. For example, Spenser's *Faerie Queene,* complete with its thinly veiled attack on Mary in the trial of Duessa in Book V, was officially allowed to be published in two new editions before 1615, despite James's outraged demands in 1596 that Elizabeth punish the poet for this presumptuous attack on the Queen of Scots.[1] With the same apparent lack of concern, the King also allowed to be published a further edition of Warner's *Albions England,* containing an invective even more outspoken than Spenser's against Mary in particular and Catholics in general.[2] On the other side, attacks on Elizabeth and Protestantism in the name of the martyred Queen of Scots also continued to appear occasionally, although in most cases abroad and thus beyond the control of James's censorship.[3] The faithful Blackwood, for instance, published two collections of poems in the decade following the accession of James; these included not only several of the more violent pieces he had composed for Mary's cause in the years just before and after her death, but also a new poem addressed to James upon his arrival in England.[4] In this last, Blackwood expressed regret that the King had shown deplorable leanings toward Protestantism, but wished him a long and happy reign anyway. Suggesting that James's error in religion could be blamed on evil advisers, over whom the King would eventually triumph, the poet then more than hints that James would do well to extirpate heresy and restore Catholicism to England if he wished to keep his throne.

Extreme expressions on the Mary Stuart controversy were, however, relatively infrequent in the first ten years of the new reign. King James was apparently anxious to achieve some kind of public settlement of the debate about his mother's life and death, one that would mollify Catholics at home and abroad and at the same time not offend or alarm his newly acquired Protestant subjects in England. A solution to the problem was at hand in the line followed by Elizabeth's authorized propaganda after 1587, when Mary was dead and her son clearly destined to succeed to the throne in England. It was a line that, to put it simply, emphasized Mary's dynastic rights and personal charms, but minimized or actually ignored the religious and political activities that led her to the block. The treatment is exemplified by a broadside ballad, published in 1603 on the occasion of the accession, that praises the new King as a foe of the Pope and all Catholics, but refers to his mother merely as "a very fayre and princelye dame . . . / By whose most sweet and happy bed our sorrowes nowe are quight stroke dead." [5]

It is not my purpose here to describe the development of this reconciliatory theme in every work dealing with Mary Stuart that was published during the reign of her son. Two episodes should serve to suggest how King James, largely through his own direct pressures, encouraged the publication of accounts of her career that were designed to appease Catholics and reassure Protestants, and that were destined to go far in shaping the image of Mary accepted by historians for generations to come.

In 1612, nine years after he succeeded Elizabeth, James arranged to have his mother's body moved from Peterborough Cathedral, where it had rested since her death, to its present place of prominence in Westminster Abbey. As the King explained to the Dean of Peterborough in a letter ordering the removal, "We think it appertains to the duty we owe to our dearest mother" that a monument be erected for her in the Abbey, and "think it inconvenient that the monument and her body should be in several places." [6] The motives of genuine love and affection that might have prompted James cannot, of course, be determined; it is hard to believe, however, that strong filial sentiment had much to do with this belated effort to honor her remains, for he had not laid eyes on his mother since he was one year old. But whatever the personal considerations might have been, political considerations seem also to have influenced his actions. For one thing, as he told the Dean of Peterborough in the same letter, he had just completed the magnificent tomb where "his dear sister the late Queen Elizabeth" now rested in the Abbey. It is characteristic of his efforts to appease both his Protestant and Catholic subjects that he should have sought to honor the royal idols of the one and the other alike.

In any event, a prominent feature of the tomb finally erected for Mary in the Abbey is a lengthy Latin inscription summarizing her career and praising her virtues. This was apparently the work of Henry Howard, Earl of Northampton. Northampton, the second son of the poet Surrey and brother of Mary's ill-fated Duke of Norfolk, had led the uneasy life of a Catholic sympathizer in the reign of Elizabeth; under James, however, he emerged as an influential favorite, and he seems to have played some part in persuading James to transfer Mary's remains to Westminster.[7] The epitaph he composed for her monument consists of a prose account of her lineage and life, and an impassioned commentary in verse on her virtues and misfortunes. The whole is signed "H. N. gemens" (i.e., Henry Northampton, mourning).[8] As it presently reads, the epitaph might well have satisfied contemporary Catholics without antagonizing contemporary Protestants. It acknowledges Mary the true and undoubted heir to the crown of England while she lived, but it does so in order to emphasize the point that through her right her son James is now the rightful king of all Britain. It extols her beauty of face and form, her wisdom, her purity and modesty of conduct, her invincible courage, and her steadfast, unviolated faith in her cause and in her God. It goes so far as to attribute her "wrongful" imprisonment—"in custodia detenta fortiter et strenue (sed frustra)"—to malevolent slanders and inimical plots, and to describe her execution as a threat to royal sovereignty everywhere. It remains vague, however, about the parties and the persons whom Catholics would consider her enemies, and about her religious and political activities which Protestants would consider the cause of her tribulations and death. Instead, it tends to emphasize the role played in her affairs by Fortune, over which, it exclaims, she has now triumphed in death. Eulogistic as it is, the epitaph in its final form minimizes or avoids completely those controversial details of her history which would inevitably have aroused strong partisan feelings at the time.

But this final form inscribed on the monument is not, it seems, the version of the epitaph the pro-Catholic Earl of Northampton originally wrote. Several drafts of the inscription surviving in manuscript indicate that he intended to describe Mary's life and death in terms scarcely less martyrological than those of Blackwood or Leslie.[9] In one of these drafts, for example, the epitaph specifically cites the "perfidious ambition" of the Earl of Murray to account for Mary's troubles in Scotland; it refers to the false promises of Elizabeth that enticed the Scottish Queen to England; and it claims that she was executed solely because of her religious faith.[10] Significantly, these explicit reminders of the earlier Catholic campaign for Mary did not appear in the inscription finally placed on her monument in the Abbey. Although there is no evidence that James personally decreed the diplomatic excisions, the editorial work is very much in the spirit of the more moderate and less controversial approach to the problem of his mother's reputation that the King demonstrated on other occasions.

The King's direct intervention in securing a more moderate treatment of Mary's history, this time from the Protestant side, is revealed by the circumstances attending the publication of William Camden's *Annales* in 1615.[11] Generally regarded as the most authoritative and objective contemporary account of Elizabeth's reign, the *Annales* are based almost entirely on state papers and official documents. The notable exception to the rule occurs, as one modern historian of history writing has observed, in the sections dealing with Scottish affairs and the history of the Scottish Queen, where Camden apparently allowed himself to be guided by the wishes of James in the choice and use of his sources of information.[12] Camden admitted as much when the celebrated French historian Jacques Auguste de Thou (Thuanus), who was about to publish his *Historia sui temporis* with an account of Scottish affairs based largely on the works of George Buchanan, wrote to ask Camden if such an account would offend James. Camden replied, in effect, that it most certainly would, and he urged the French historian to exercise moderation and caution in dealing with these affairs.[13] But since Camden failed to send an "authorized" account of Mary's career in answer to de Thou's request for such material, the latter went ahead and published his *Historia*, relying on Buchanan as he had indicated he would for the treatment of the Queen of Scots.[14] As Camden had predicted, the publication brought so violent a response from James that when de Thou's son visited England, years later, the King's explosion of wrath against the historian-father sent the young man to bed ill for three months.[15] Meanwhile, when James first read de Thou's account, he demanded that Camden draw up a list "of the falsehoods which were found in M. de Thou." Camden's list, duly drawn up and transmitted to the Frenchman, has been preserved; it suggests the moderate position between extreme Protestantism and extreme Catholicism that James wished to take with regard to his controversial mother.[16]

The de Thou affair reveals the kind of pressures under which

Camden must have worked as he prepared his own account of Mary Stuart in the *Annales*. Commenting upon the circumstances, Richard Gough, one of Camden's earliest editors, wrote in 1806 that the historian

... has been charged with being influenced in his account of the queen of Scots by complaisance for her son, and with contradictions in the informations given by him to M. de Thou and his own account of the same particulars. It is not to be wondered if James made his own corrections on the MS. which his warrant sets forth he had perused before he permitted it to be published. It was no easy matter to speak the truth in that reign of flattery in points where filial piety and mean ambition divided the mind of the reigning monarch. An English historian in such a reign could not indulge the same freedom as Thuanus.[17]

Gough perhaps exaggerates both the "filial piety" and the "mean ambition" of James at the expense of the King's quite understandable political motives, but otherwise this summary of Camden's situation is probably accurate.

It is not surprising, therefore, to find that Camden, in his effort to reach the compromise dictated by James, picked and chose rather carefully from versions of Mary's story previously published by Protestant and Catholic partisans alike. For example, in dealing with Mary's affairs in Scotland, as Camden's first biographer explained in 1691, prudence and good faith alike required that he present the case not as Buchanan had presented it, but in terms of those facts that might partly exonerate her moral character.[18] Accordingly, Camden rejected Buchanan as his source and in general accepted Leslie's account of the Darnley murder which cleared Mary of any complicity in the crime. Here, incidentally, Camden states explicitly, in defending his choice of authorities, that he was guided by King James's own opinion of the relative value of the two sources.[19] Similarly, Camden follows Leslie in blaming Murray, Morton, and their associates among the Scottish lords for Mary's involvement with Bothwell and for her subsequent abdication. Unlike Leslie, however, he minimizes the religious views of her foes and ascribes their actions mainly to political ambition. At the same time, he rejects what he terms the premature claims of Mary herself, inspired by Leslie and the Guises in France, to occupy the throne in place of Elizabeth. And he does not hesitate to record as fact Mary's involvement in the Throckmorton, Parry, and Babington plots, or to rely on the official commissions for the trial and the sentencing of Mary, in both of which she was charged with treasonable activities, to justify Elizabeth's actions.[20] Camden's account perhaps overemphasizes what he terms the efforts of the King, "out of dear love for his mother," to forestall the execution, but such overemphasis is understandable, given the conditions in 1615. On the other hand, Camden gives considerable space to a description of the doubts and perplexities suffered by Elizabeth before she was forced to take fatal action against a sister sovereign and a kinswoman.[21] For his account of the execution itself, Camden follows in general outline and in numerous details the story as related in Blackwood's *Martyre* and *La Mort*, but he consistently omits the emotional asides and comments that make Blackwood's originals two of the primary documents in the martyrology tradition.[22]

In the final impression of Mary that it creates, Camden's history probably reflects the image that King James wished to have accepted at the time, and perhaps for all time.[23] It is, first and foremost, the image of a sovereign queen whose lineage indubitably established the right of her son to the thrones of Scotland and England. It is the image of a loving mother, cleared of the charges of immoral conduct employed by her adversaries in Scotland to remove her from the throne there; she is portrayed, rather, as a victim, "much tossed and tumbled," of the antimonarchic doctrines subscribed to by her "unthankefull and ambitious subjects." It is the image of a woman "most constant in her religion," although Camden remains vague as to which religion, and "of singular piety towards God, invincible magnanimitie of minde, wisedome above her sex, and passing beauty." However, it is also the image of a person who permitted herself to "be thrust forward into dangerous designes" so inimical to the security and religion of England that Elizabeth had no alternative but to decree her death.

From all this, Camden draws a conclusion that probably indicates the way in which he and his royal master hoped these unhappy events would be regarded by all factions:

> By this most lamentable fate of so great a Princesse appeared most evidently (as some wise men have observed,) the disposition of the Divine providence. For the things which both Queenes Elizabeth and Mary most of all desired, and in all their counsailles propounded to themselves, hereby were attayned. Queene Mary, (as she sayd even at her death) desired nothing more ardently, then that the divided king-domes of England and Scotland might be united in the person of her most deere sonne: and there was nothing which Queene Elizabeth wished more earnestly, then that the true religion with the safety and security of the people, might be preserved in England. And that the high God granted to both their prayers, England now seeth with unex-pected felicity, and most joyfully acknowledgeth.[24]

Northampton's revision of his epitaph, and Camden's caution in preparing his account of Mary for the *Annales,* reveal the attitude of compromise and conciliation insisted upon by James that helped to bring a temporary truce in the battle of the books about the Queen of Scots. But readers of Schiller and Swinburne, of Dickens and Froude, of Drinkwater and Maxwell Anderson, will know that the battle did not end with the accession of James. On the basis of the foregoing survey, however, it should be evident that the main lines of strategy and much of the ammunition for the continuing battle had been supplied by the propagandists of the sixteenth century. Mary Stuart is reported to have said, "In my end is my beginning." Like so much that she was reported to have said, this was a half truth. Her beginning as a character in history and romance clearly started well before her end.

Notes

ABBREVIATIONS USED IN NOTES

Cal. Scot. Papers=Calendar of Scottish Papers
CSP Domestic=Calendar of State Papers, Domestic
CSP Foreign=Calendar of State Papers, Foreign
CSP Scotland=Calendar of State Papers, Scotland
CSP Spanish=Calendar of State Papers, Spanish
CSP Venetian=Calendar of State Papers, Venetian
DNB=Dictionary of National Biography
ELH=Journal of English Literary History
Folger=Folger Shakespeare Library, Washington, D.C.
Hist. MSS Comm.=Historical Manuscripts Commission Reports
HLQ=Huntington Library Quarterly
Huntington=Huntington Library, San Marino, California
Morgan=Morgan Library, New York
Scott=John Scott, *A Bibliography of Works Relating to Mary Queen of Scots, 1544-1700* (Edinburgh, 1896)
STC=Pollard and Redgrave, *A Short Title Catalogue of Books Printed in England and of English Books Printed Abroad, 1475-1640* (London, 1926)

NOTES TO PROLOGUE

[1] Melin de Saint-Gelais, *Œuvres Complètes* (Paris, 1873), I, 167. The pageant, apparently first published in Saint-Gelais' *Œuvres Poétiques* (Lyon, 1574), is headed: "Six Dames Jeunes et Petites Firent, par Commandement de la Royne, une mascarade, un soir, estant habillées en Sibylles, pour donner passetemps au roy à son retour d'un voyage à Sainct Germain en Laye, l'an 1554."

[2] For the political background of Mary's French marriage, see M. Mignet, *Histoire de Marie Stuart* (Paris, 1852), I, chap. ii, and T. F. Henderson, *Mary Queen of Scots* (London, 1905), I, *passim*.

[3] Mary had been referred to by name and title in earlier works published in connection with the effort to betroth her to England's Edward VI. Cf. John Scott, *A Bibliography of Works Relating to Mary Queen of Scots, 1544-1700* (Edinburgh, 1896), nos. 2, 3, 4, 5, and 6. None of these, however, does more than refer in passing to the Queen, then scarcely five years old. If any works were published in celebration of her birth, her succession to the Scottish throne, or her departure for France, they do not appear to have survived.

[4] Cf. note 2, above, and Chap. I, below.

NOTES TO CHAPTER I

[1] Cf. Prologue, note 2, above.

[2] T. F. Henderson, *Mary Queen of Scots* (London, 1905), I, 100.

[3] *Ibid.*, I, 95.

[4] "Pour la Royne Marie," in *Œuvres Complètes* (Paris, 1873), I, 220. As Saint-Gelais died in 1558, the poem was probably written before Mary's marriage in that year. Referring to Francis, the poem concludes, "Si donc heureux un chacun se peut rendre, / En voyant sans faveur

plus expresse, / Qui sauroit l'heur mesurer et comprendre / Du semidieu qui l'a pour sa maistresse."

[5] "Avant-Mariage de Madame Marie, Royne d'Escosse," in *Les Poesies de Iacques Tahureau, Du Mans. Mises toutes ensemble & dediées au Reverendissime Cardinal de Guyse. A Paris* . . . (n.d.), fol. 11[v]. The dedication (sig. Ai[v]) is dated "De Poictou" 1 May 1554. Michaud's *Biographie Universelle,* s.v. "Tahureau," says that the first edition of the poems was published at Poitiers in 1554. Both Michaud, and Brunet, *Manuel du Libraire,* assign a date of 1574 to the Paris edition. On Tahureau, who died in 1555, see George Saintsbury, *A Short History of French Literature* (Oxford 1918), p. 180.

[6] "Sonnet à la Royne d'Escosse," in *Œuvres Françoises* (Paris, 1866), I, 316, and note, I, 500. First published as No. CLXX of *Les Regrets* (1558), the sonnet was reprinted at the end of Du Bellay's *Hymne au Roy sur le Prinse de Callais* (Paris, 1559); "In futuras nuptias Francisci Gall. Delphini et Mariae Stuartae," in *Poematum Libri quatuor* (Paris, 1558), fol. 30. Scott 10. Two "Inscriptions" eulogizing Mary in similar terms were probably also written by Du Bellay about this time and published with his *Entreprise du Roy-Daulphin* (1559). Scott 25. Cf. *Œuvres Françoises,* II, 454, 463.

[7] *Nouvelle Continuation des Amours* (Paris, 1556), reprinted in *Œuvres Complètes,* ed. Paul Laumonier (Paris, 1914-1919) VI, 306. The editor notes that this poem was "la première que Ronsard adressa à Marie Stuart" (VIII, 65).

[8] Henderson, *Mary Queen of Scots,* I, 76.

[9] *Discours du Grand et Magnifique Triumphe faict au Mariage de* . . . *François* . . . *& . . . Marie d'Estreuart Roine d'Escosse* . . . (Paris, 1558). For the three editions, cf. Scott, 15, 16, 17. The *Discours* was edited by William Bentham for the Roxburghe Club (London, 1818).

[10] *In Francisci Illustriss. Franciae Delphini, et Mariae Sereniss. Scotorum Reginae Nuptias, viri cujusdam Ampliss. Carmen* ([Paris], 1558). Scott 13; cf. also Scott 27. Another edition was published in 1560. The *Carmen* was reprinted in *Michaelis Hospitalii . . . Epistolarum seu Sermonum Libri Sex* (Paris, 1585: Scott 128), and in *Œuvres Complètes de Michel L'Hospital* (Paris, 1824-1825), III, 331. It is reprinted and translated in Francis Wrangham, *Epithalamia tria Mariana* (Chester, 1837), pp. 20-29.

[11] *Ex Cuiusdam commentariis Historiarum Nostri Temporis, excerpta Oratio, quam ipsa sponsalium die Regina Scotiae ad Henricum regem habuit* (Paris, 1558). Scott 19 believes that it "was probably

written by M. L'Hospital and issued as a State paper, to support the pretensions of the Dauphin to be recognized as King of Scotland." I do not find the work as such in the *Œuvres Complètes de . . . L'Hospital.*

[12] *Carmen,* tr. Wrangham, p. 21.

[13] *Ibid.,* p. 29.

[14] *Ibid.,* p. 23.

[15] Pierre de Ronsard, *L'Hymne de Tresillustre Prince Charles Cardinal de Lorraine* (Paris, 1559), ed. Laumonier, *op. cit.,* IV, 243; *Chant de Liesse au Roy* (Paris, 1559), ed Laumonier, *op. cit.,* VI, 313.

[16] Adrianus Turnebus, *Epithalamium Francisci Valesii illustr. Franciae Delphini et Mariae Stuartae Sereniss. Scotorum Reginae* (Paris, 1558), Scott 12, reprinted in J. Gruterus, *Delitiae C. Poetarum Gallorum, Huius Superiorisque Ævie illustrium, collectore Ranutio Ghero* (Frankfurt, 1609), III, ii, 1035:

> Foedera nec populis, nec regnis firma coibunt,
> Et male concordi rumpetur gratia nexu.
> At duo perpetua constringes lege maritus
> Sceptra: dies Francis Scotisque haec foedera nunquam
> Dissolvet; convexa polus dum fidera pascet,
> Durabunt nives sic vellere Parca fidelis
> Nunquam frangendum, deduxit pollice filum.

(See Michaud, *Biographie Universelle,* "Turnèbe.")

[17] *Nuptiale Carmen Renati Guillonii Mercurium agentis, quo exhortatur Franciscū Valesium Galliarum Delphinū ad uxorem ducendam, Mariam utpote Scotiae reginam quam tandem duxit anno. 1558. Aprilis die. 24* (Paris, 1558). Scott 11. Included in the volume are a number of "Epigrammata" addressed to members of the Guise family. The passage on the union of the realms is as follows:

> Alba rosis albis nunc insere lilia, quas vel
> Gallorum plausu Scotica terra tulit.
> Euge rosalbiferam ducas Francisce puellam.
> Delphino tibi vult nubere liligero.
> Liligeros pariet patri tibi tempore natos,
> Qui nativa olim Gallica sceptra regent.
> Gallia Scotorum & Gallorum Scotia regum
> Quae nunc divisa est, tunc erit una domus.

[*Nuptiale Carmen,* p. 5]

Guillon (1500-1570) studied with Budé, translated the letters of Isocrates, and wrote a treatise on Greek prosody (Hoefer, *Nouvelle Biographie Générale*).

[18] *Carmen,* tr. Wrangham, p. 25.

[19]   Dois tu pas estre aisé,
               O peuple escossois,
               D'estre en l'obeissance
               Du petit roy Francoys.

"Chanson Nouvelle du Mariage de Monsieur Le Dauphin et la Royne d'Escosse. Sur le chant des Bouffons"; reprinted in Antoine Jean Le-Roux de Lincy, *Recueil de Chants Historiques Français depuis le XIIe jusqu'au XVIIIe siècle (Deuxieme Série. XVIe siècle)* (Paris, 1842), pp. 208-210, who notes (p. 585) that the poem was published in *Recueil des plus belles chansons de ce temps. . .* (Paris, 1559).

[20] *Ioannis Mercerii Montacutani, (Adolescentis) Dialogus, in nobilissimi gallorum Delphini, & Illustrissimae Scotorum Reginae Nuptias. Eiusdem aliquot Epigrammata* (Paris, 1558). Scott 18. Mercerius is described in the catalogue of the Bibliothèque Nationale as "Jean Mercier, élève au collège du Montaigu." The pertinent passage in the "dialogus" among the muses appears on sig. [aviii^r-v] as follows:

> *Thaleia.* Nunc viunt galli, & Scoti sub legibus iisdem,
> Et iuncti florent rege sub eximio.
> *Me.* O fortunatos Scotos sua si bona norint,
> Quos modo *Franciscus* sub ditione regit.
> *Ter.* Principe sub tanto iam scotica terra triŭphet,
> Ac armis hostes comprimat Angligenas.
> *Eu.* Iam fortis clamet sublimi Gallia voce,
> *Francsicus* vivat, coniuge cum *Maria.*

In the same work, among the *Epigrammata,* cf. "Ad Nobilissimum . . . Franciscum . . . Scotorumque Regem" (bii^v); "In Nuptias galliarum Delphini . . . Ode" (cv^v); and "In easdem Nuptias" (c vi^r).

[21] *Carmen,* tr. Wrangham, p. 29.

[22]   O mariage heureux, que Dieu veule lier
       Pour faire sous un Roy deus roiaumes plier.
       Et non deux seulement, maie sans meurdre & sans guerre
       A la France & l'Escosse alliant l'Angleterre.

Jean-Antoine de Baïf, *Chant de joie du jour des espousailles de Francois, roi daufin, et de Marie roine d'Ecosse* (Paris, 1558), p. 4. Having sent the royal couple to bed with these political prognostications, de Baïf concludes his epithalamic *Chant* with an imperialistic vision of the future:

       C'est assez pour le iour: i'ay chanté la iournée,
       Un plus hardi dira la nuit bien fortunee

De vostre chaste amour: Mais qui oseroit bien
D'une tant sainte nuit dire l'heur et le bien?
O noble sang des Roys, & du quel doivent naistre
Des enfans pour regner quand vous cesserez d'estre.   [P. 8]

Cf. *Hymne à Monseigneur le Dauphin, sur le mariage dudict Seigneur, et de Madame Marie d'Estevart, Royne d'Escosse. Par Jacques Grévin de Clermont. A Paris . . . 1558. Avec Privilege,* analyzed and extensively quoted by Lucien Pinvert, *Jacques Grévin (1538-1570) Étude Biographique et Littéraire* (Paris, 1899), pp. 206-211, who observes that, unlike de Baïf, Grévin, a Protestant, ignores the political triumph of the Guises and the political and personal attractions of the bride to write an account of mythological figures that make the poem essentially "une théogonie."

[23] *Ioannis Mercerii . . . Dialogus . . .,* sig. a-vii[v]: "P. Perpetuo Galli cum Scotis foedere iuncti / Vivant, ac hostem sedibus eiiciant. / V. Debellent Batavos, Hispanos, & simul Anglos, / Et subigant Flandros, Hesperiosque doment."

[24] *Epitalamio Di. M. Gabriel Symeoni Fior. Sopra l'utile della Pace, & la celebratione delle Nozze del Re Catolico, & de l'Illustrissimo Duca di Savoia. A i due primi Principi Christiani* (Paris, 1559). Scott 23. According to Michaud, *Biographie Universelle,* Symeoni spent a number of years in France in the service of both the brothers Guise in what was apparently a fruitless search for lucrative patronage. The passage pertinent to Mary Stuart in his *Epitalamio* appears at sig. B[i[r]] as follows:

In tanto che il tremendo
Cognato di costui si dara vanto
Nel Mar Britanno uguale
Haver Imperio al Gallican congiunto. . . .

[25] "Francisci Valesii & Mariae Stuartae, Regum Franciae & Scotiae, Epithalamium," translated in Wrangham, *Epithalamia tria Mariana,* pp. 3-17. The poem was apparently first printed in *Georgi Buchanani Scoti Poetae eximij, Franciscanus & Fratres quibus accessere varia eiusdem & aliorum Poemata . . .* (Basle, 1566). (Cf. Scott 43.) The original of the passage quoted is as follows: "Ipse tibi explorator eras, formaeque probator, / Et morum testis" (*Georgii Buchanani . . . Opera Omnia,* ed. Thomas Ruddiman [Leyden, 1725], II, 333).

[26] Buchanan, "Epithalamium," tr. Wrangham, p. 3.

[27] *Ibid.*

[28] P. Hume Brown, *George Buchanan: Humanist and Reformer* (Edinburgh, 1890), p. 171.

[29] *The Maitland Folio Manuscript*, ed. W. A. Craigie (Edinburgh, The Scottish Text Society, 1919), pp. 27-30. An account of Maitland's career and position will be found in the *DNB*.

[30] *Ibid.*, p. 29.

[31] Jacques de la Tapie, d'Aurillac, *Chantz Royaulx sur les Triumphes du mariage du Roy Daulphin, & de la Royne Daulphine* (Paris, 1558), sig. Ci[r]-iii[r]. Scott 14. An account of de la Tapie's career will be found in Michaud, *Biographie Universelle*.

[32] *Nuptiale Carmen Renati Guillonii . . .*, p. 4: "Maria in Musis Musarum maxima musa est, / Qua sine nulla modo florida musa foret"; *Ioannis Mercerii . . . Dialogus . . .*, sig. aiii[r]:

> Quos Pierides celeri iã currite gressu:
> O sacri vates, Aonidèsque Deae:
> O praecellentes Nymphae Dryadesque puellae,
> O fauni, gressus tēdite perceleres.
> Nullàque sit vobis mora, verum sedulo ad acres
> Pergite Liligeros: carpite iàmque vias.

[33] *Carmen*, tr. Wrangham, p. 23.

[34] "Epithalamium," tr. Wrangham, p. 3.

[35]
> Zeuxis voulant pourtraire une Junon,
> Fit assembler les plus belles de Grece;
> Mais maintenant id ne faudroit, sinon
> Que ma beauté pour peindre une Déese.

Jacques de la Taille, "Inscription pour la reine d'Ecosse, Marie," in *Annales Poétiques* (1779), X, 64. The inscription was probably first published at Paris in 1572 in a *Recueil des Inscriptions, anagrammatises et autres œuvres poétiques* with *Saul le Furieux*, a drama by Jean de la Taille, brother of Jacques (Hoefer, *Nouvelle Biographie Générale*).

[36] *Carmen*, tr. Wrangham, p. 27.

[37] *Ioannis Mercerii . . . Dialogus . . .*, sigs. a-iiij[r] and a-vii[r].

[38] "Epithalamium," tr. Wrangham, p. 3.

[39] M. Mignet, *Histoire de Marie Stuart* (Paris, 1852), I, 56-57.

[40] *Tumulus Henrici Secundi . . . per Ioach. Bellaium* (Paris, 1559). Scott 26; "De Sacra Francisci II Galliarum Regis Initiatione," in *Michaelis Hospitalii . . . Epistolarum seu Sermonum* (1585), where it apparently first appeared (*Œuvres Complètes*, III, 353); the inscription at Chatelleraut is reprinted in Mignet, *Histoire*, I, 56 n. 1: "Gallia perpetuis pugnaxque Britannia bellis / Olim odio inter se dimicuere pari. / Nunc Galles totosque remotos orbe Britannos / Unum dos

Mariae cogit in imperium. / Ergo pace potes, Francisce, quod omnibus ais / Mille patres armis non potuere tui." Somewhat similar sentiments are suggested in *Les Ordres Tenuz à la reception et Entrée du Roy Tres-Chrestien François II & de la Roine, en la ville d'Orleans* (Paris [1560]: Scott 29); however, there is no discernible reference to Mary in the similar *Les Triomphes Faictz à l'Entree du Roy a Chenonceau Le Dymanche Dernier Iour de Mars* (Tours, 1559; Scott 28; ed. Prince Augustin Galitzin, Paris, 1857, where it is attributed to one "Le Plessis").

[41] "A La Royne de France," ed. Laumonier, *op. cit.*, VI, 337; first published in *Second Livre des Melanges* (Paris, 1559). Cf. also the two "Inscriptions," entitled respectively "Pour la Royne d'Escosse, alors Royne de France," and "Pour elle mesme," first published in *Discours a ... le Duc de Savoye. Chant Pastoral a Madame Marguerite, Duchesse de Savoye. Plus XXIIII Inscriptions...* (Paris, 1559), ed. Laumonier, *op. cit.*, VI, 321.

[42] "Deploratio status rei Gallicae, sub mortem Francisci Secundi Regis," in *Opera Omnia*, II, 339. The poem was probably first published in the collection of Buchanan's poems that appeared in 1566. Scott 43. Cf. note 25, above.

[43] Conyers Read, *Mr. Secretary Walsingham* (Cambridge, Mass., 1925), I, 40-41.

[44] *Ibid.*

[45] Cf. *Elegie sur le despart de la Royne Marie retournant à son Royaume d'Escosse* (Lyon, 1561; Scott 31), ed. Laumonier, *op. cit.*, V, 17; "Elegie à H. Lhuillier," first published in *Recueil des Nouuelles Poësies* (Paris, 1563), ed. Laumonier, *op. cit.*, V, 15, who conjectures (VII, 466) that it was composed in 1561 and was inspired by a similar elegy composed, upon the departure of Mary from France, by H. Lhuillier, Seigneur de Maisonfleur, but never published; "Elegie à la Royne d'Escosse," first published in *Recueil des Nouuelles Poësies* (Paris, 1563), ed. Laumonier, *op. cit.*, V, 4; *"A elle-mesme"* [i.e., Mary Stuart], ed. Laumonier, *op. cit.*, V, 8, who indicates that the piece was first published in Ronsard *Œuvres* (1567) "au 3° livre des *Elegies*." The context, however, suggests that the poem was composed shortly after Mary's departure from France.

[46] Cf. Mignet, *Histoire*, I, 144; and Henderson, *Mary Queen of Scots*, I, 253-257.

[47] Mignet, *op. cit.*, I, 446 (Appendix B), reprinted from *Memoires de Michel de Castelnau* (Brussels, 1731), I, 549-550. The poem was not pub-

lished in the sixteenth century, to my knowledge, although Brantôme (*Vies des Dames Illustres* [Paris, 1868], p. 152) gives a brief prose summary of it, and of another he attributes to the same poet (*ibid.*, p. 116).

[48] Brantôme, *op. cit.*, p. 155.

[49] John Knox, *The History of the Reformation in Scotland,* in *The Works of John Knox,* ed. David Laing (Edinburgh, 1846-1864), II, 369.

[50] "Off the Quenis Arryvale in Scotland," in *Maitland Folio Manuscript,* p. 34. A similar message to the Queen is possibly implied in "A ballad of welcome to Mary Stuart," reprinted, with no source given, in E. M. Brougham, *News Out of Scotland* (London, 1926), p. 65, in which a six-year-old boy presents her with a Bible, a psalter, and the keys to Edinburgh on September 2, 1561.

[51] Cf. T. F. Henderson, *Scottish Vernacular Literature* (London, 1900), pp. 240 ff.

[52] Alexander Scott, "Ane New Yeir Gift to the Quene Mary . . .," in *The Poems of Alexander Scott,* ed. James Cranstoun (Edinburgh, The Scottish Text Society, 1896), p. 1. Cf. also p. 99 for Cranstoun's valuable note on the poem.

[53] "Maria Regina Scotiae puella," in *Opera Omnia* II, 389; "Ad Mariam Reginam Scotiae," and "Ad Eandem," II, 394; "Ad Mariam Scotiae Reginam," II, 395; "Ad Mariam Illustriss. Scotorum Reginam . . . epigramma," in *Psalmorum Dauidis paraphrasis poetica nunc primum edita. Authore Georgio Buchanano . . .* (Paris?, 1564?: Scott 35), sig. *ii[r]. Cf. also the tribute of Buchanan's close friend, the humanist Charles Utenhove, in "A la Royne d'Escosse Douariere de France, Sonnet de Char. Utenhove," first published in *Georgii Buchanani . . . Franciscanus & fratres* (Basel, [1568?]), and reprinted in Buchanan, *Opera Omnia,* I, sig. *n* 1[v].

[54] *Vicentius Lirinensis . . . for the antiquitie and veritie of the Catholik fayth . . . neulie translatit in Scottis by Niniane Winzet . . . Antwerp Decemb. 1563,* ed. J. K. Hewison (Edinburgh, Scottish Text Society, 1890), II, 9. Scott 33. Cf. also Winzet's similar appeal to Mary in his *Certane Tractatis for Reformation of Doctryne and maneris . . . Edinburgi 21 Maij 1562,* ed. Hewison (Scottish Text Society), Vol. I. Scott 32; *STC* 25860.

[55] Cf. Mignet, *Histoire,* I, 56 n. 1, for a suggestion of the multiplicity of evidence indicating Elizabeth's attitude. Cf. also Read, *Walsingham,* I, 41-44.

[56] The history of the Saconay affair can be traced in *CSP Foreign, 1561-1562;* see Index, under Mary Stuart. Cf. also Michaud, *Biographie Universelle,* "Saconay, Gabriel de."

[57] Paul Reyher, *Les Masques Anglais ... (1512-1640)* (Paris, 1909), pp. 125-128. According to Reyher, the manuscript of the masque is to be found among the Burghley papers; I have not seen it and have had to rely on the detailed synopsis and analysis that Reyher gives.

[58] Thomas Randolph to William Cecil, May 22, 1564, *CSP Foreign, 1564-1565*, p. 137: "The bruit is more common that some are in the Tower for making a book against this Queen [Mary]. By their imprisonment, though he [Randolph] told her it was not in the Tower, she thinks much kindness in the Queen [Elizabeth]."

[59] *De Bello et Pace Liber. Ad Mariam Serenissimam Scotiae Reginam*, in Bizarri, *Varia Opuscula* (Venice, 1565), fols. 26-49. Scott 39. The prose dedication (fols. 26ʳ-29ᵛ) is followed by a poem "Ad eandem" (fols. 30ʳ-31ʳ). With these should also be compared the Latin verses "Ad Mariam Scotiae Reginam," in "Poematum Liber II," *Varia Opuscula*, fol. 123ʳ. Meantime, in the same year, Bizarri dedicated his other major treatise, *De Optime Principe* (*Varia Opuscula*, Venice, 1565) to Queen Elizabeth in terms no less flattering. See *DNB*, "Bizarri," and *Bibliographica*, I (London, 1895), 455-473, for accounts of the dedications.

[60] "Bergerie dédiée à la Maiesté de la Royne d'Escosse," first published in *Elegies, Mascarades et Bergeries* (Paris, 1565), ed. Laumonier, *op. cit.*, III, 383-384, as "Eclogue I"; cf. also "Discours. A elle-mesme," ed. Laumonier, *op. cit.*, V, 13, who notes that it was published among the *Elegies* in Ronsard's *Oeuvres* (1567), but was probably written in August, 1565, and sent as an "envoy" by Ronsard to Mary together with a copy of the *Elegies, Mascarades et Bergeries*, which had just appeared. Laumonier also adds (VII, 466): "Il existe dans les *Papiers d'Etat* de l'Angleterre ... une lettre de M. de Foix, notre ambassadeur à Londres, à Cecil, secrétaire de la reine Elisabeth, mentionnant l'envoi d'un livre de Ronsard et demandant au nom du poète que ce livre puisse être présenté à la reine [date: 23 août 1565]." Although the "Bergerie" was dedicated to Mary, the volume of *Elegies, Mascarades, et Bergeries* containing it was dedicated to Elizabeth.

NOTES TO CHAPTER II

[1] Cf. M. Mignet, *Histoire de Marie Stuart* (Paris, 1852), I, Chap. III.

[2] Conyers Read, *Mr. Secretary Walsingham* (Cambridge, Mass., 1925), I, 44.

[3] Cf. "Mary Hamilton," no. 173, *The English and Scottish Popular*

Ballads, ed. Francis James Child (Boston, 1883-1898), III, 381, and V, 298. "The Queen's Marie" is a variant title of the same ballad.

[4] *DNB,* "Craig, Sir Thomas." See Chap. VIII, below, for a discussion of Craig's *The Right of Succession to the Kingdom of England* (1603).

[5] *Henrici Illustrissimi Ducis Albaniae, Comitis Rossiae, etc. et Mariae Serenissimae Scotorum Reginae Epithalamium* (Edinburgh, 1565), translated in Wrangham, *Epithalamia Tria Mariana,* p. 47. Scott 38. *STC* 5970. Buchanan apparently wrote but did not publish at the time several short poems on the marriage, including "Apollo & Musae Exules" (*Opera Omnia* [Leyden, 1725], II, 399); "Pompa Deorum in nuptiis Mariae" (II, 400-401); "Ad Salutem in nuptiis Reginae" (II, 426); and two poems addressed "Ad Regem Scotiae Henricum" (II, 393), and "Ad Henricum Scotorum Regem" (II, 426).

[6] *Iacobi Serenissimi Scotorum Principis Ducis Rothesaiae Genethliacum* (first published in 1566, according to the *DNB,* although I have found no record of the edition elsewhere), in *Delitiae Poetarum Scotorum,* ed. A. Johnston (Amsterdam, 1637), I, 221.

[7] "Genethliacon Jacobi Sexti Regis Scotorum," in *Opera Omnia,* II, 340-343. Cf. also "Pompae Deorum Rusticorum dona ferentium Jacobo VI & Mariae matri ejus, Scotorum Regibus, in coena quae Regis baptisma est consecuta," II, 404.

[8] *Genethliacum Serenissimi Scotiae, Angliae, & Hiberniae Principis, Iacobi VI, Mariae Reginae filii* (Paris, 1566), in *Delitiae Poetarum Scotorum,* I, 13-17. Cf. Scott 209. Meanwhile, the legal and historical arguments underlying the claims put forth by poets for Mary and James had received rather wide circulation throughout Scotland and England in 1565 in a manuscript entitled *Allegations in behalf of the high and mighty Princes, the Lady Mary, now Queen of Scots . . . touching the succession of the Crown.* The author of the *Allegations* was less concerned with stating Mary's rights positively than he was with denying the claims contrary to hers that were being advanced in some quarters in favor of the Lady Katherine Grey, a niece of Henry VIII. Cf. *CSP Domestic, 1547-1580,* p. 286, no. 79. The *Allegations* was published as an appendix to William Attwood's *The Fundamental Constitution of the English Government* (London, 1690), where it is attributed to T[homas] M[organ], identified in the British Museum *Catalogue of Printed Books* as a Fellow of Oriel College.

[9] *CSP Foreign, 1566-1568,* pp. 146, 148, 151, 152 (November, 1566).

[10] DeSilva to Philip II, December 16, 1566, *CSP Spanish, 1558-1567,* p. 601.

[11] *Ibid.* Cf. also *CSP Foreign, 1566-1568,* p. 172, which indicates that Adamson was still languishing in prison on January 24, 1567. Evidence of the disaster that befell Adamson as a result of Elizabeth's displeasure at his *Genethliacum* is supplied by the poet himself some years later when he addressed a poem to Elizabeth, hoping, as he wrote to her ambassador Killigrew, "to gain the goodwill of so great a Princess, whose mind he repents having once alienated from him in France, which brought disaster on his affairs" (Patrick Adamson to Henry Killigrew, June 19, 1573, *Cal. Scot. Papers,* IV [1571-1574], 589, no. 697).

[12] *DNB,* "Hales, John." The MS account is probably that referred to in Scott 62 as *A Declaration of the Succession* and described in the *DNB* as Harleian MS 550. Cf. Chap. IV, note 12, below.

[13] Cf. J. E. Neale, *Queen Elizabeth* (New York, 1934), pp. 124 ff., who observes that at this time Elizabeth probably had Mary in mind as her successor, but wanted to be sure of Mary's religious and political leanings before committing herself openly. A more detailed account will be found in Conyers Read, *Mr. Secretary Cecil and Queen Elizabeth* (New York, 1955), p. 229.

[14] DeSilva to Philip II, October 19, 1566, *CSP Spanish, 1558-1567,* p. 587.

[15] *CSP Foreign, 1566-1568,* p. 148, nos. 81, 813, 815 (November 18-19, 1566).

[16] *STC* 17564; Scott 37. A note on page 32 of the *Allegations Against* reads "Excusum S. A. 7 Decembris 1565."

[17] *Allegations Against . . .* (1565), pp. 2, 22.

[18] *Ibid.,* p. 4.

[19] *Ibid.,* p. 22. Archibald Douglas, Earl of Angus, and Margaret Tudor, widow of James IV of Scotland, were married privately in 1514, making their daughter, Darnley's mother, technically legitimate (*DNB,* "Douglas, Archibald" and "Tudor, Margaret").

[20] *Allegations Against . . .,* pp. 29 ff.

[21] John Knox, *The History of the Reformation in Scotland,* in *The Works of John Knox,* ed. David Laing (Edinburgh, 1846-1864) II, 277 ff., 331 ff., 372 ff. Cf. *STC* 15071; Scott 130, 236.

[22] Knox to Queen Elizabeth, August 6, 1561, *Cal. Scot. Papers,* I (1547-1563), 542. On the *First Blast,* which was probably published at Geneva in 1558, see *STC* 15070.

[23] Cf., for example, John Aylmer, *An harborowe for faithfull and trewe subjects agaynst the late blowne blaste concerning the gouernmēt of wemen* (London, 1559). *STC* 1005.

[24] Read, *Walsingham,* I, 44. For the violence of English feelings about the Guise influence, see *CSP Foreign, 1564-1565,* p. 438, no. 1419, and p. 458, no. 1487.

[25] *Satirical Poems of the Time of the Reformation,* ed. James Cranstoun (Edinburgh and London, Scottish Text Society, 1891-1893), I, 1. Cf. *ibid.,* I, xvii, for an account of Jeney and his subsequent switch, at the time of the Northern Rebellion in 1569, from the Protestant English to the Catholic cause. The *DNB,* s.v. "Jenye, Thomas," cites a work attributed to him in the suppressed leaves of the 1587 edition of Holinshed's *Chronicles* (see Chap. V, note 12, below), called the *Black Booke;* Holinshed says that the work was printed at "Cullen" (i.e., Cologne) in 1575, was dedicated to the Scottish Queen ("whome this deuiser intituleth high and mightie princesse"), but that "euen then it was said that the commonwealth of Scotland was past hope, &c."

[26] *Ibid.,* I, 10 (modernized).

[27] *Ibid.,* I, 25 (modernized).

[28] *Ibid.,* I, 17 (modernized).

[29] *CSP Foreign, 1566-1568,* pp. 74-75, 81, 85.

[30] "The Epistle dedicatorie To the right wurshipfull Mr. Thomas Randolphe...," in *Satirical Poems,* I, 3 (modernized). Cf. also the biographical sketch of Jeney, *ibid.,* I, xvii ff.

[31] Elizabeth to Mary Stuart, June 13, 1566, *CSP Foreign, 1566-1568,* p. 85.

[32] *Ibid.,* December 2, 1566, p. 152.

[33] T. F. Henderson, *Mary Queen of Scots* (London, 1905), II, 355 ff. (Chap. VIII: "The Murder of Riccio.") A detailed account of the murder and its motives by one of the participants will be found in Patrick Ruthven, *A Relation of the Death of David Rizzi ...* (London, 1699). For an account of Mary's affairs following the death of Rizzio until her flight into England, purportedly written by the man who became her secretary in 1575, see Claude Nau, *The History of Mary Stewart,* ed. Rev. Joseph Stevenson, S. J. (Edinburgh, 1883).

[34] Henderson, *Mary Queen of Scots,* II, 369; see also pp. 38-39, above, for Catholic efforts to refute this charge.

[35] *Kurtzer Ausszug und schlechte erzelung eines Landuerreters stucks wider die Künigin in Schottland von etlichen abfalligen mainaydigen vund Aussrürischen beschehen vermerckt auss eines hoch-ansehnlichen Herzens Schreiben trewlich verteuischt* (s.l., 1566), Scott 44; *Proditionis ab aliqvot Scotiae Perdvellibus Adversvs Serenissimam suam Reginam non ita pridem perpetratae breuis & simplex narratio ex amplissimi*

cuiusdam viri literis fideliter descripta (Lovanii, 1566). Scott 40, 41. The Latin text has a conclusion (sig. Biii^r-Biv^r), not found in the German, that reiterates the warnings to kings and princes against the rebellious political doctrines and practices of Protestants.

[36] The English version of the *Oration* was published at Antwerp in 1566. Scott 46. *STC* 11333, 11334. A translator's preface in this edition indicates that versions in French, Dutch, and Latin were published as well, suggesting unusually wide circulation in Catholic countries.

[37] Frarin, *An Oration* (Antwerp, 1566), sig. E[i]^r (modernized). In his preface the English translator states that he has appended "notes & further additions" to the original oration delivered in 1566; thus the translator himself may be responsible for this glance at Scottish affairs of 1566.

[38] *CSP Foreign, 1566-1568*, p. 205, no. 1091 (April, 1567).

[39] *CSP Foreign, 1566-1568*, p. 198, no. 1053 (March 29, 1567). Other examples of bills and placards inspired by the Protestant party will be found in *ibid.*, p. 178, no. 960 (February 19, 1567); p. 185, no. 997 (March 8, 1567); p. 191, no. 1017 (March 14, 1567). On the contemporary significance of "mermaid," cf. the *Oxford English Dictionary*.

[40] *Satirical Poems*, I, xxv-xxxviii; *DNB*, "Lekprevik, Robert."

[41] *Satirical Poems*, I, 57. Scott 55. *STC* 22192, 22192^a.

[42] *Ibid.*, I, 62 (modernized).

[43] In addition to *Ane Declaratioun*, the principal Sempill ballads attacking Mary at this time include: *Ane Exhortatioun derect to my Lord Regent* (Edinburgh, R. Lekprevik [1567]: *STC* 22194) in *Satirical Poems*, I, 52; *Heir followis ane Ballet declaring the Nobill and gude inclinatioun of our King* (Edinburgh, R. Lekprevik, 1567: Scott 52, *STC* 22196) in *ibid.*, I, 31; *Heir followis ane Exhortatioun to the Lordis* (Edinburgh, R. Lekprevik, 1567: Scott 54, *STC* 22197, 22198 [anr. ed., 1571]) in *ibid.*, I, 46; *Heir followis the testament and tragedie of vmquhile King Henrie Stewart of gude memorie* (Edinburgh, R. Lekprevik, 1567: Scott 53, *STC* 22199) in *ibid.*, I, 39. For an English ballad on the same subject in the same vein, which possibly originated at this time, see "The Murder of the King of Scots," printed in Bishop Thomas Percy's *Reliques* (1876, II, 213) from his *Folio Manuscript* (ed. Hales and Furnivall, London, 1868, II, 260,) where it appears under the title of "Earl Bodwell," as it does in Child Ballad 174, and reprinted in J. Maidment, *Scottish Ballads and Songs* (Edinburgh, 1868), II, 16; Henry Chettle's somewhat modified version of this same ballad, published in 1579, is discussed in Chap. III, note 50, below.

[44] *Ane Ballat declaring . . ., Satirical Poems,* I, 36.

[45] *Ane Declaratioun . . ., ibid.,* I, 62-63 (modernized).

[46] *The Testament and tragedie . . ., ibid.,* I, 43 (modernized).

[47] *Ibid.,* I, 42 (modernized).

[48] Michel L'Hôpital turned against his former Queen in verses entitled "In Mortem Regis Scotiae"; he describes the terrors of the night at Kirk-o-Field and does not "shrink from naming the wife and young mother as the murderer of the father of the child still at her breast" (C. A. Sainte-Beuve, *Causeries* [11 août 1851], quoted, with the pertinent lines, in P. Hume Brown, *George Buchanan* [Edinburgh, 1890], p. 205 n.). A similar attack is found in Thomas Metallanus (i.e., Maitland), "Jacobi VI, Scotorum Regis Inauguratio," in *Delitiae Poetarum Scotorum,* II, 154 ff.

[49] Read, *Walsingham,* I, 47-48.

[50] *A Newe Enterlude of Vice Conteyninge, the Historye of Horestes with the cruell reuengement of his Fathers death, vpon his one naturall Mother. by John Pikeryng* (1567). *STC* 19917. Reproduced in *Tudor Facsimile Texts* (1910). For a complete consideration of the play, cf. F. Brie, *Englische Studien,* XLVI (1912), 66-72; Carl Kipka, *Maria Stuart im drama der Weltliteratur* (Leipzig, 1907); and James E. Phillips, "A Revaluation of *Horestes* (1567)," *HLQ,* XVIII (1955), 227-244.

[51] Cf. p. 44, above, and *Satirical Poems,* I, 35-36, 43.

[52] *Horestes,* sig. A. iv^v. (Here and in following quotations, the spelling is modernized.)

[53] *Satirical Poems,* I, 42.

[54] *Ibid.,* I, 48-49.

[55] *Horestes,* sig. B ii^r, C ii^r.

[56] *Ibid.,* D ii^v.

[57] *Satirical Poems,* I, 65. The manuscript is endorsed, "An answer to ye Bills set upp against the Regẽt of Scotl."

[58] *Ibid.,* I, 68. The manuscript from which the ballad is printed in the *Satirical Poems* is dated December 11, 1568, but the content of the piece indicates that it was written before Mary's flight to England. The apologist George Chalmers (*Life of Mary Queen of Scots* [London, 1818], II, 443) reprints the poem "because it is full of historical, and useful truths." He attributes it to Thomas Bishop, who in March 1568/9 was questioned in London about "a book wrighten against the Earl of Murray, in defence of the Scotts Q., for which he was committed to the Tower." The poem itself is signed "Tom Trowth."

[59] *Satirical Poems,* I, 70.

[60] *Ibid.*, I, 74.

[61] Henderson, *Mary Queen of Scots*, II, 503; cf. Read, *Walsingham*, I, 47-48.

NOTES TO CHAPTER III

[1] For a detailed account of the political background of Mary's arrival in England and the events that immediately followed, see Conyers Read, *Mr. Secretary Cecil* (New York, 1955), Chap. XX, upon which the following summary chiefly relies.

[2] Mary Stuart to the Queen of Spain, September 24, 1568, Alexandre Labanoff, *Lettres, Instructions et Mémoires de Marie Stuart* (London, 1844), II, 184, quoted in Conyers Read, *Mr. Secretary Walsingham* (Cambridge, Mass., 1925), I, 60.

[3] J. E. Neale, *Queen Elizabeth* (New York, 1934), p. 162; Read, *Walsingham*, I, 49.

[4] Read, *Cecil*, pp. 409 ff.

[5] Mary Stuart to Guerau de Spes, quoted in T. F. Henderson, *Mary Queen of Scots* (London, 1905), II, 527.

[6] Neale, *op. cit.*, pp. 191-192.

[7] Quoted *ibid.*, p. 161.

[8] Henderson, *Mary Queen of Scots*, II, 507, observes, for example, that, when Elizabeth wrote to the Regent Murray requiring his presence at the York and Westminster conferences, she made it clear that he was to come not as a witness against Mary, but as a rebel subject bound to answer for his "very strange" doings against a sovereign prince.

[9] *Ibid.*, II, 517.

[10] *Cal. Scot. Papers*, II (1563-1569), 418, cited in Henderson, *op. cit.*, II, 518. An account and evaluation of Cecil's role as a kind of director of propaganda in Elizabeth's government will be found in Conyers Read, *Lord Burghley and Queen Elizabeth* (New York, 1960), pp. 245, 426, 431-433, 499. Cf. also p. 130, above.

[11] Something of the way in which this equivocal propaganda policy operated is revealed in an exchange of letters between representatives of Mary and Elizabeth regarding a series of sermons delivered before the Queen of Scots not long after her arrival in England. Mary's custodian, the Earl of Shrewesbury, arranged in January, 1570, for the Bishop of Coventry to preach a series of sermons before the Queen of Scots "unless the Queen's [i.e., Elizabeth's] pleasure be otherwise." Elizabeth's pleasure was obviously not otherwise. The Bishop pro-

ceeded to deliver sermons to remind the Queen of Scots of the error of her ways, both political and religious. Mary promptly complained that he "plenli prechit in veri outrageous and vild terms off me by my nom," and, protesting through her ambassador, the Bishop of Ross, to Elizabeth, the Scottish Queen added, "where I am named, except it be by some tolerance, I think it is 'to mutche.'" Elizabeth, who had allowed Cecil to encourage the attack on Mary, was quick to disclaim officially any "tolerance" of such proceedings. Through Shrewesbury, Elizabeth promised that "she would have the party known and punished." *Cal. Scot. Papers,* III (1569-1571), 58, no. 93; 62-63, nos. 101-102; 83, no. 129 (January, 1570).

[12] *STC* 8014; Robert Steele, *A Bibliography of Royal Proclamations* (Oxford, 1910), I, 68, no. 638. Cf. William Camden, *Annales* (1625), p. 216, and pp. 69-70, above. For subsequent proclamations, aimed more at forbidding books in Mary's defense than at restricting those against her, cf. Chap. IV, below.

[13] Cf. pp. 60 ff., above. Subsequent proclamations were probably also directed in part against the ballads attacking Mary which appeared in Scotland at the time of the assassination of the Earl of Murray, by remnants of the party favorable to the Scottish Queen, in January, 1570. The dominant Protestant faction, fearing the return of Mary, took this occasion, while deploring the assassination, to propagandize not only against her party in Scotland, but also against the Scottish Queen herself. The majority of these ballads are by Robert Sempill, including the following which directly involve Mary: *The Cruikit Liedis the blinde* (Edinburgh, R. Lekprevik, 1570: *STC* 22191), in *Satirical Poems of the Time of the Reformation,* ed. James Cranstoun (Edinburgh and London, 1891-1893), I, 128; *The Exhortatioun to all plesand thingis . . . to deploir the Cruell Murther of vmquhile my Lord Regentis Grace* (Edinburgh, R. Lekprevik, 1570: *STC* 22193), in *ibid.,* I, 122; *The hailsome admonitioun &c* (Edinburgh, R. Lekprevik, 1570: *STC* 22195), in *ibid.,* I, 165; *The Poysonit Schot* (Edinburgh, R. Lekprevik, 1570: *STC* 22204, as "Anon."), in *ibid.,* I, 132; *The Regents Tragedie* (Edinburgh, R. Lekprevik, 1570: *STC* 22205-22206; cf. also *STC* 22210, *The tragical end and death of the Lord James Regent of Scotland,* an Anglicized version with minor revisions of Sempill's Scottish ballad, published in London by J. Awdeley in 1570), in *ibid.* I, 100; *The Spur to the Lordis* (broadside s.l., 1570: Scott 66, *STC* 22208) in *ibid.,* I, 156; *Ane Tragedie, in forme of ane Diallog betwix Honour, Gude Fame, and the Authour heirof in a Trance* (Edinburgh, R. Lek-

previk, 1570: Scott 63, *STC* 22209) in *ibid.*, I, 82; *The Tressoun of Dunbartane* (Edinburgh, R. Lekprevik, 1570: *STC* 22211) in *ibid.*, I, 170. Cf. also *The Complaint of Scotland* (broadside, s.l., n.d. [1570]: Scott 48, *STC* 22189 [erroneously dated 1567]) in *ibid.*, I, 95; *The Deploratioun of the Cruell Murther of James Erle of Murray* (Edinburgh, R. Lekprevik, 1570), in *ibid.*, I, 108; *The Kingis Complaint* (broadside, s.l., n.d. [1570]: *STC* 22200 [wrongly dated 1567]) in *ibid.*, I, 117 (where the obvious reference to the death of Murray in 1570 is pointed out, and Sempill's authorship is denied); *Maddeis Proclamatioun* (broadside, s.l., n.d. [1570]: *STC* 17177), in *ibid.*, I, 149; *The Lamentatioun of Lady Scotland* (St. Andrews, R. Lekprevik, 1572: Scott 77), in *ibid.*, I, 226. For a ballad in a similar vein, cf. John Davidson's poem on the death of Knox, *Ane Breif Commendatioun of Vprichtnes* (St. Andrews, R. Lekprevik, 1573: *STC* 6321) in *ibid.*, I, 275.

[14] George Whetstone, *The Censure of a Loyall Subiecte* (London, 1587), sig. Gl[v] Scott 141. (Cf. p. 118, above.) Nevertheless, Thomas Randolph, the English representative in Scotland, kept London fully informed of the publications and apparently sent copies from time to time. Cf. *CSP Foreign, 1569-1571*, p. 180, nos. 663, 664; p. 196, nos. 721, 723; and *Cal. Scot. Papers*, III (1569-1571), 140-142.

[15] On Elizabethan control of the press, cf. W. W. Greg, *Some Aspects and Problems of London Publishing between 1550 and 1650* (Oxford, 1956), Chap. III, "Licensing for the Press."

[16] *Ibid.*, p. 1.

[17] The Northern Rebellion and contemporary literature relating to it are fully described in James K. Lowers, *Mirrors for Rebels* (Berkeley and Los Angeles, 1953). Folk ballads dealing with the Northern Rebellion were similarly reticent in mentioning Mary's involvement—possibly because the information, as a result of official censorship, was not generally known; cf. Child Ballads 175, "The Rising in the North"; 176, "Northumberland Betrayed by Douglas"; and 177, "The Earl of Westmoreland."

[18] *A disclosing of the great Bull, and certain calues that he hath gotten, and specially the Monster Bull that roared at my Lord Byshops gate* . . . (London, John Daye, [1570]), sig. Bi[r]. *STC* 18679.

[19] Norton, *A Warning agaynst the dangerous practises of Papistes* . . . (London, John Daye, 1570), title page (verso), which also indicates, "Seen and allowed, according to the order of the Queenes Iniunctions." *STC* 18686.

[20] William Fleetwood, *The effect of the declaration made in the*

Guildhall by M. Recorder of London (London [1571]), *STC* 11036. Scott 72; Richard Grafton, *An Abridgement of the Chronicles of Englande, newely corrected and augmented, to thys present yere of our Lord, 1572* (London, 1572; *STC* 12152: cf. Scott 59), fols. 209 through 216; Elderton, *A Balad intituled the Dekaye of the Duke* (London, [1572?]), reprinted in *Harleian Miscellany* (London, 1813), X, 270.

²¹ Stafford to Walsingham, from Paris, March 17, 1583/4, *CSP Foreign, 1583-1584*, p. 415, no. 487. The book referred to was possibly Cecil's *The Execution of Justice in England* (see p. 76, and note 75, below).

²² *A Treatise of Treasons against Q. Elizabeth* . . . (1572), fol. 73ᵛ (cf. p. 93, above). The anonymous author has reference specifically to the pamphlet *Salutem in Christo* (see p. 61, above). The English operated in the same clandestine fashion to spread propaganda against Mary on the Continent without betraying the official attitude. On January 10, 1572 Sir Henry Killegrew, then resident in France, sent to Cecil a "discourse in French" attacking the Queen of Scots "to be printed in England, and sent over here secretly" *(CSP Foreign, 1572-1574*, p. 14, no. 27).

²³ Scott 61. The authorship and circumstances of the tract have been established in Read, *Walsingham*, I, 63-79, where a manuscript version of the work is printed. *STC* 13869, which attributes the work to "T. Sampson," indicates that there were two editions, and conjectures that both were published in 1571.

²⁴ Quoted in Read, *Walsingham*, I, 70.

²⁵ *Ibid.*, I, 71.

²⁶ *STC* 11504, 11505, 11506. Scott 69. The card catalogue of the Huntington Library lists two issues of *STC* 11505, and suggests, without authority, William Cecil, Lord Burghley, as the author. The British Museum *Catalogue of Printed Books* indicates Grafton as both author and printer of the tract, but the *STC* names John Day as printer. Cf. *DNB*, "Grafton, Richard." See also *A Treatise of Treasons* (1572), sig. A4, L4, where the contemporary author of a Catholic reply to the *Salutem* shrewdly guesses at Richard Grafton's authorship and the official inspiration of the tract. (See pp. 93-94, above.)

²⁷ Cf. note 22, above.

²⁸ *Salutem in Christo* ([London?, 1571?], *STC* 11504), sig. A3ᵛ-A4ʳ.

²⁹ The fullest account of Buchanan's *Detection* in its multiform versions will be found in R. H. Mahon, *The Indictment of Mary Queen of Scots* (Cambridge, University Press, 1923). Cf. also the detailed biblio-

graphical accounts of the various editions of the work in *George Buchanan: Glasgow Quatercentenary Studies 1906* (Glasgow, 1907), pp. 439-445.

[30] Mahon, *op. cit.,* p. 3.

[31] *De Maria Scotorum Regina, totáque eius contra Regem coniuratione, foedo cum Bothuelio adulterio, nefaria in maritum crudelitate & rabie, horrendo insuper & deterrimo eiusdem parricidio: plena, & tragica plane Historia . . . Actio contra Mariam Scotorum Reginam in qua ream & consciam esse eam huius parricidij, necessarijs argumentis euincitur* (Scott 75; *STC* 3978). Cf. also Malcolm Laing, *History of Scotland* (London, 1819), I, 254; and Mahon, *Indictment,* p. 16. The work has become better known under the title given it in Ruddiman's edition (Leyden, 1725) of the *Opera Omnia* of Buchanan (I, 63-106), *Detectio: sive, de Maria Scotorum Regina . . . Historia.* Mahon *(Indictment,* pp. 24-26) argues for a number of different stages and forms of both the Latin and the English first editions, generally indicating the increasing efforts of the English to strengthen the propaganda case against Mary. Appended to the original Latin edition are two anti-Marian poems, "In Mariam Reginam Scoticam," signed "G. M.," and "In Mariam Stuarta Regina Scoticam Satyra," signed "P. R. Scotus." These are reprinted in Buchanan's *Opera Omnia,* I, 64.

[32] Scott 76, 81. *STC* 3981. A manuscript in the Morgan Library, described in that library's catalogue as "contemporary," bears the title *A Detection of the doeinge of Marie Queene of Scottes . . . .* It is an English, not a Scots or pseudo-Scots translation of the *Detectio;* it contains a number of marginal notes not found in the printed editions in any language; and the *Actio* attributed to Thomas Wilson, though not the *Detection* itself, varies considerably in wording from the printed Scots translations. Cf. Seymour De Ricci, *Census of Medieval and Renaissance Manuscripts* (New York, 1937), II, 1504, no. MA40.

[33] For the St. Andrews edition, cf. Scott 80; *STC* 3982. Authority for the German editions, of which I have found no copies, is "Obertus Barnestapolius" [i.e., Robert Turner], *Maria Stuarta . . . Innocens a caede Darleana . . .* (Ingolstadt, 1588), tr. G. de Guttery, *L'Histoire et Vie de Marie Stuart* (Paris, 1589), sig. ãvii^v: "Buccanan . . . par deux fois a esté Imprimé en Allemaigne . . ." (see Chap. VII below). In the Morgan Library there is a contemporary manuscript of the Latin *Detectio* in what is described as "German script" (De Ricci, *Census,* II, 1504 no. MA 42, who dates the manuscript "ca. 1567").

[34] *Histoire de Marie Royne d'Escosse* (Edinburgh, 1572). Scott 82.

The work was translated by a Huguenot lawyer named Camuz (or Cumez). Scott notes that Cecil apparently provided a Supplement published with the French translation which is not found in either the Latin or English versions of the *Detectio*. The elaborate deception intended to make the *Histoire* appear as a Scottish publication was immediately and accurately exposed by Mary's Catholic defenders; cf. *L'Innocence de . . . Marie* (1572), sig. a3v (see Chap. IV, below), and Blackwood, *Martyre* ("Edinburgh" [i.e., Paris], 1587), p. 261 (see Chap. VII below).

[35] Labanoff, *Lettres, instructions . . . de Marie Stuart*, IV, 9 (December 10, 1571).

[36] Mahon, *Indictment*, p. 25.

[37] *Cal. Scot. Papers*, IV (1571-1574), 65, no. 81. Buchanan had been appointed tutor to James VI in 1570.

[38] *The Works of John Knox*, ed. David Laing (Edinburgh, 1846-1864), VI, 609.

[39] Scott 84. Printed without indication of place or date, but probably from the press of John Day in 1572. Scott thinks it "probable that this letter is the production of Buchanan himself," but the Norfolk references and the London production seem to point to an Englishman.

[40] *Ane Detectioun of the duinges of Marie . . .* (London, 1571), sig. Biir-v.

[41] *Ibid.*, sig. Hiv.

[42] *Ibid.*, sig. Iiiv (modernized).

[43] *Ibid.*, sig. Niiiiv (modernized).

[44] "Robert Bele's Pamphlet," dated December 3, 1571, *CSP Foreign, 1569-1571*, p. 570, no. 2159. Apparently Beale feared that his "Pamphlet," which recommended a series of stringent measures to discredit the Scottish Queen in France, might be construed as violating Elizabeth's "injunctions" against writings that deprecated Mary. In a letter that accompanied the "Pamphlet," he wrote to Cecil that he "thinks it behoves the Queen for her own safety to disgrace [Mary] as much as she justly may, and to induce the French King to join with [Elizabeth] in good amity" (*ibid.*, pp. 570-571, no. 2160).

[45] Killegrew to Cecil, January 10, 1572, *CSP Foreign, 1572-1574*, p. 14, no. 27. Killegrew also reported that, after reading Buchanan's tract, Cavagnes and Teligny, two French Protestant leaders who were soon to lose their lives in the St. Bartholomew Day massacre, expressed surprise that the Queen of Scots was allowed to live, and they urged that Elizabeth put her to death at once (*CSP Foreign, 1569-1571*, p. 582, no. 2196).

[46] *CSP Foreign, 1572-1574,* p. 13, no. 23.

[47] *Cal. Scot. Papers,* VI (1581-1583), 425, no. 425.

[48] Fol. 410^r.

[49] *The Summarie of the Chronicles of England . . . unto . . . 1579 . . .* (London, 1579), pp. 391 ff. (Huntington Library copy; not recorded in *STC* or in Scott.)

[50] *The firste volume of the Chronicles of England, Scotlande, and Irelande* (London, 1577: Scott 99; *STC* 13568), I, 494. A further example of caution is Henry Chettle's *A Dolefull Ditty, or Sorowfull Sonet, of the Lord Darly,* published openly in London by Thomas Gosson in 1579 (*Stationers' Register,* ed. Arber, II, 349; reprinted in *Harleian Miscellany* [London, 1813], X, 264, and in *Satirical Poems,* II, 40). The ballad is simply a somewhat expanded version of the anonymous Scottish ballad, "The Murder of the King of Scots" (cf. Chap. II, note 43, above), and why Chettle chose to reopen the subject at this late date is not clear. In any event, he refrains from open attack on Mary, and even goes so far as to describe her grief at the death of her husband whom, he says, she wanted to be king. Cf. also Jean de Serres, *The three partes of commentaries of the ciuill warres of Fraunce . . . Translated out of Latine into English by Thomas Timme Minister. Seene and allowed* (London, 1574: Scott 87; *STC* 22242), where, in a passing reference, the Guises are blamed for forcing Mary to proclaim her right to the throne of England (p. 62).

[51] *STC* 23400; Scott 104. Printed without indication of author, place, or publisher, but apparently published in London by H. Singleton for W. Page. Walsingham was informed on October 26, 1579, that the book had been "translated into Italian and sent to the Pope in 'written hand' " (*CSP Foreign, 1579-1580,* p. 79, no. 73).

[52] Stubbs, *Discoverie* (1579), sig. E5^v-E6^v.

[53] The Proclamation was published September 27, 1579 (*STC* 8114). Cf. Steele, *A Bibliography of Royal Proclamations,* I, 79, no. 740, where a Dutch translation of the proclamation published at Antwerp in 1580 is also noted. On September 25, 1579, Mendoza, the Spanish ambassador in London, wrote to Philip II that "As soon as it [i.e., Stubbs's *Discoverie*] was published the Queen prohibited its possession under pain of death, and great efforts were used to collect all copies, and to discover the author, in order to prevent the circulation of the facts before Parliament meets" (*CSP Spanish, 1568-1579,* p. 700, no. 602). Considering the punishment given Stubbs, it is rather remarkable to find that he subsequently accepted employment by Elizabeth's government to prepare an authorized reply to Cardinal Allen's *A True Sincere and*

Modest Defence of English Catholiques (see Chap. IV, note 94, below). Typical of manuscript attacks on Mary that were apparently not allowed to find their way into print at this time are the following: *Againste the sscottishe Queene, that shee ought not to liue: That mercy in that case is both dreadeful and dawngerous* (Morgan Library MS, ca. 1585); *Marie Stewarde late Quene of Scotland hath defiled hir owne bodie wth many Adulteries: hathe slaine her husband consentinge unto his death: is ane open enemy to the churche of god and the greateste hope of all Idolaters, accused covicted of these crimes she hathe resigned her crowne. And for feare of iustice she is fled into England where she woorkethe dailie muche mischef. The question is weather she oughte to die or no* (British Museum MS, Cotton Caligula C, II, fol. 580 ff.); *Reasons drawne by the learned in the Romon Lawe to moue the Quens Matie to proceade against the Q. of S. accordinge to the firste Bill wch [imported? (defective MS)] the takinge awaie of hir lief & not disablemēt* (British Museum MS, Cotton Caligula C, II, fol. 583 ff.).

[54] *De iure regni apud Scotos dialogus* ("Edinburgi" [i.e., London], 1580: Scott 113, *STC* 3976; 1581: Scott 114, *STC* 3977); *Rerum Scoticarum historia* ("Edinburgi" [i.e., London], 1583; Scott 122, *STC* 3992). The original Edinburgh editions of *De iure* appeared in 1579 (Scott 110, 111; *STC* 3973), and of the *Historia* in 1582 (Scott 121; *STC* 3991).

[55] For an account of the reception of Buchanan's works in England after 1579 see James E. Phillips, "George Buchanan and the Sidney Circle," *HLQ*, XII (1948), 39-45.

[56] Mary's protest was registered through her secretary, Claude Nau, in November, 1584 (*Cal. Scot. Papers,* VII [1584-1585], 435, no. 405). Cf. also *Cal. Scot. Papers,* VIII (1585-1586), 402, no. 429, where Mary acknowledges Nau's services in obtaining "a public prohibition of the history of Buchanan." Shortly before this, Mary had made her effort to blackmail Elizabeth into acknowledging the London publication of Buchanan's *Detectio* and suppressing the work. Cf. p. 68, above. On the suppression in Scotland of both the *De Jure* and the *Historia* see W. S. McKechnie, "De Jure Regni apud Scotos," in *George Buchanan: Glasgow Quatercentenary Studies 1906,* pp. 211 ff.

[57] "Fearing to revert to the isolation from which the Treaty of Blois [with France] had rescued her, Elizabeth responded—though in view of the Massacre of St. Bartholomew, with just the right amount of coolness and restraint—to Catherine de' Medici's desire for continued

friendship . . . Yet at the same time she lent secret aid to the Huguenots who were again in revolt, deeming it essential to maintain the balance of parties in France and keep the House of Guise from ruling the roost" (Neale, *Queen Elizabeth,* p. 228).

[58] Read, *Walsingham,* II, 366-367. Two ballads by Robert Sempill published in Scotland at the time warn that the massacre was part of a plan by the Guise faction in France to accomplish the release of Mary and the restoration of Catholic power in Scotland and England; cf. *Ane Premonitioun to the barnis of Leith* (St. Andrews, R. Lekprevik, 1572), in *Satirical Poems* I, 212, and *Ane new Ballet set out be ane fugitive Scottisman that fled out of Paris at this lait Murther* (St. Andrews, R. Lekprevik, 1572), in *Satirical Poems* I, 257.

[59] *Le Reveille-Matin des François, et de Leur Voisines. Composée par Eusebe Philadelphe Cosmopolite, en forme de Dialogues* (Edinburgh, "Avec permission," 1574). Scott 89: *STC* 1464; *Dialogi ab Eusebio Philadelphio Cosmopolita in Gallorum et Caeterarvm Nationvm gratiam compositie, quorum primus ab ipso auctore recognitus & auctus: alter vero in lucem nunc primum editus fuit* (Edinburgh, 1574). Scott 88: *STC* 1463. Scott calls the author "Barnand," but "Barnaud" is the author to whom Michaud's *Biographie Universelle* and *STC* attribute the work.

[60] Antonio de Guaras to Zayas, July 4, 1575, *CSP Spanish, 1568-1579,* p. 495, no. 414.

[61] *Le Reveille-Matin* (1574), Dialogue II, p. 15. (Each Dialogue in this edition has separate pagination.)

[62] See Chap. V, below.

[63] *Le Reveille-Matin* (1574), Dialogue II, pp. 28 ff.

[64] *Ibid.,* p. 48: "Pour conclusion, la punition de ceste conspiration sur la royne d'Escosse, suppose qu'elle soit veritablement coulpable, quoy que sachent dire & alleguer ses partizans, est tres juste, & legitime, par toutes loix diuines, & humaines: vtile, voire tresnecessaire pour le salut, & conseruation de la personne de la Royne, & de tous l'estate d'Angleterre, & mesmes de ceux, que la Royne a occasion d'aimer le plus. Au contraire, l'impunite est un vray refus de iustice, & de la protection a ses suiets, un mespris du salut de son peuple, & contemnement de la conseruation de l'Eglise de Dieu, & de son pur service, lequel, comme tu as dict au commencement, y seroit de tout point renuerse, si la mort de la royne Elizabeth aduenoir, deuant le supplice deu a la royne Marie."

[65] *La legende de Charles Cardinal de Lorraine & de ses frères de la*

Maison de Guise descrite en troise Livres (Rheims, 1576). Scott 112. The British Museum copy is dated Rheims, 1579. See Scott 98: *STC* 20855, on the English translation, probably published at Geneva. Scott describes "scandalous references" to Mary in the French edition, but these do not seem to appear in the English. For Harvey's notes in his copy of Buchanan's Latin *Detectio* see William Robinson, *A Catalogue of Rare Books* (London, 1948), and *George Buchanan: Glasgow Quatercentenary Studies*, p. 441, where a copy of the pseudo-Scottish *Ane Detectioun of the duinges of Marie*, similarly annotated by Harvey, is described.

[66] *A Legendarie* (1577), sig. Eiv^v.

[67] *Ibid.*, sig. Evii^v.

[68] *Memoires de l'Estat de France Sous Charles IX* . . . (Middelburg, 1578), especially I, fols. 109^v and 181^r. Scott 103 records another edition of the work in the same year, some copies of which are dated 1579; earlier editions in 1576 and 1577 contain no material on the Queen of Scots. The *Memoires* is attributed by the British Museum *Catalogue of Printed Books* to Goulart, about whom cf. Michaud, *Biographie Universelle*.

[69] Cf. Neale, *Queen Elizabeth*, Chap. XVI.

[70] Cf. Read, *Walsingham*, II, Chap. XI, especially pp. 389 ff.

[71] Neale, *Queen Elizabeth*, p. 263.

[72] Read, *Walsingham*, II, 396-397.

[73] For an account of Cardinal Allen and his *Defence*, see p. 113, above.

[74] *A True and Plaine declaration* . . . (1584-1585?), p. 17 (cf. p. 78, above). Cf. also *A discouerie of the treasons . . . by Francis Throckmorton* (1584), sig. Aii^r (cf. p. 77, above); among the papers found on Throckmorton when he was arrested were "twelue petidegrees of the discent of the Crowne of England, printed and published by the Bishop of Rosse, in defence of the pretended title of the Scottishe Queene his Mistresse, with certaine infamous libelles against her Maiestie printed and published beyond the seas. . . ." The works of John Leslie, Bishop of Ross, which were found on Throckmorton, were probably copies of a later edition of his celebrated *Defence of the honour* (cf. Chap. IV, below).

[75] *STC* 4902 through 4907. The English edition is reproduced in *Scholars Facsimiles and Reprints* (New York, 1938), with an introduction by Franklin L. Baumer. Cf. also W. K. Jordan, *Development of Religious Toleration in England* (Cambridge, Harvard University

Press, 1932), I, 169-174; J. W. Allen, *A History of Political Thought in the Sixteenth Century* (London, 1941), p. 233; and Read, *Lord Burghley and Queen Elizabeth*, p. 251.

[76] Read, *Walsingham*, II, 389.

[77] Scott 124; *STC* 24050. Two editions of the work were published at London in 1584, both by Christopher Barker, the Queen's Printer. The tract was also reprinted by Holinshed in the 1587 edition of his *Chronicles* (cf. Chap. VII, below). The British Museum *Catalogue of Printed Books* records a Latin translation, *Iudicium Proditionum quas Fr. Throckmortonus contra Reginae Majest. suscepit, qui damnatus est— 21 maij ultimae praeteriti 1584* [London?, 1584?] (cf. W. T. Lowndes, *The Bibliographer's Manual*, ed. Bohn [London, 1869], V, 2678), and a Dutch translation, *Een warachtich eñ naect verclaers van de verschricklijcke verra derije ghepractikiert . . . door F. Throckmorton . . . Ende W. Parry die ouer zyn verraedt verwesen was tot Westminster* (Middelburg, 1585). On Mary's complicity in the Throckmorton plot, see Read, *Walsingham*, II, 389.

[78] *A discouerie of the treasons . . .* (1584), sigs Ai^v, Aiii^v.

[79] *STC* 25336. Entered in the *Stationers' Register* April 29, before the lifting of the ban against attacks on Mary Stuart in December, 1586. Whetstone must have completed the work in 1584, however, for he refers to the Throckmorton conspiracy as the last plot against the Queen of England, and he expresses the hope that there will be no more (p. 171).

[80] *The English Myrror* (1586), p. 171.

[81] Read, *Walsingham*, II, 405.

[82] *The Last Words of William Parry, a Lawyer, who Suffered for endeavouring to Depose the Queens Highness, and bring in Q. Mary and her young son James. XXVII Eliz.* [London, 1585?]. *STC* 19339. The single-sheet broadside was probably printed by Christopher Barker, the Queen's Printer; *In Gvil. Parry Proditorem Odae et Epigrammata. Oxoniae, Ex officina Typographica Iosephi Barnesij, Celeberrima Academiae Typographi. 1585.* (*STC* 19340); David Pareus [Wängler], *Pareus* [a Latin poem] *Oxoniae typis J. Barnesii. 1585* (*STC* 19193), in which the Catholic enemies of England and Elizabeth are attacked in general terms; *An Order of Praier and Thankes-Giving, for the preseruation of the Queenes Maiesties life and salfetie: to be vsed of the Preachers and Ministers of the Dioces of Winchester. With a short extract of William Parries voluntarie confession, written with his owne hand. Imprinted at London by Ralfe Newberie* (1584-1585?). *STC*

16516. The "short extract" from Parry's confession omits all of his references to the Queen of Scots; *A True and Plaine declaration of the horrible Treasons, practised by William Parry, the Traitor* ... (London, 1584). Scott 129. *STC* 19341, 19342, 19342a. Printed by Christopher Barker, the Queen's Printer, "Cum privilegio." There were three editions of the work, and a Dutch translation. *Een warachtich ende volcomen verclaers vande ... verraderijen ... by ... W. Parry ...* ([Middelburg?], 1585), is recorded in the British Museum *Catalogue of Printed Books* s.v., "Parry, William"; Philip Stubbes, *The Intended Treason of Doctor Parrie: and his comlices, against the Queens moste Excellent Maiestie. With a Letter sent from the Pope to the same effect* ... (London, [1584?]), *STC* 23396.

[83] *A True and Plaine declaration* ..., p. 19.

[84] For a detailed account of the Babington conspiracy and a judicious evaluation of the evidence of Mary's complicity, see Read, *Walsingham*, III, Chap. XII: "The Babington Plot." Cf. also John H. Pollen, S. J., *Mary Queen of Scots and the Babington Plot* (Edinburgh, 1922 [Scottish History Society, Third Series, vol. 3]). The more temperate of Mary's friends and enemies alike agree now that she was aware of the plot and involved in it; they differ on whether she entered freely or was tricked by Walsingham into participating.

[85] *A proper new Ballad* ... (London, 1586), in F. O. Mann, ed., *The Works of Thomas Deloney* (Oxford, 1912), p. 465; *A most ioyfull Songe* ... (London, 1586), in *Works*, ed. Mann, p. 460. The latter is probably the ballad entered in the *Stationers' Register* August 27, 1586, with the permission of the Archbishop of Canterbury (ed. Arber, II, 456). For an argument similar to Deloney's, cf. Michel Reniger, *A Treatise conteining two parts. 1. An Exhortation to true loue, loyaltie, and fidelitie to her Maiestie. 2. A Treatise against Treasons, Rebellions, and such disloyalties* ... (London, 1587); *Stationers' Register* December 10, 1586; *STC* 20888. Reniger was one of Queen Elizabeth's chaplains and, after 1575, archdeacon of Winchester (*DNB*, "Renniger or Rhanger, Michael"). Other ballads and tracts apparently inspired by the Babington conspiracy that were entered in the *Stationers' Register* before December, 1586, include: *A Dittie of the lord Darley somtyme Kinge of Scottes* (ed. Arber II, 454: August 15, 1586); *A new ballad of Reioycinge for the Revealinge of the queenes enemyes* (*ibid.*, II, 455: August 24, 1586): *A ballad of the three laste Traytours that suffered at Tiborne the 8. of October 1586* (*ibid.*, II, 459: November 10, 1586);

The Commons crye of England against the queens maiesties Enemyes (*ibid.*, II, 460: November 21, 1586).

[86] T. K., *Verses of Prayse and Ioye, Written upon her Maiesties preseruation. Whereunto is annexed Tychbornes lamentation, written in the Towre with his owne hand, and an aunswere to the same* (London, John Wolfe, 1586). *STC* 7605. Reprinted in *Fugitive Tracts, First Series,* ed. Henry Huth (1875), no. xxvi.

[87] John Norden, *A Mirror for the Multitude* (London, 1586), p. 32. *STC* 18613. Cf. *DNB;* T. K., *Verses of Prayse and Ioye;* Deloney, *A proper new Ballad* (in *Works,* ed. Mann, pp. 465-466).

[88] *Works,* ed. Mann, pp. 465-466; Cf. also R. Thacker, *A godlie Dittie to be song for the Preservation of the Queenes most excelent majestie's Raigne* (London, 1586); "Cum Privilegio Regiae Majestatis" (*STC* 23926).

[89] George Puttenham (?), *The Arte of English Poesie,* ed. G. D. Willock and A. Walker (Cambridge, 1936), pp. 247-248.

[90] *Ibid.*

[91] [1586]. *STC* 18425; Scott 132. Passage quoted appears in Stanza 8.

[92] "Sceptrifero Mariam insignent diademate." H. D., *Anglia Querens. Oxoniae . . . Iosephi Barnesii . . . 1586,* sig. A6ʳ. *STC* 6167.

[93] *A discouerie of the treasons . . . by Francis Throckmorton* (1584), sig. Biiiᵛ.

[94] *In Catilinarias Proditiones, Ac Proditores Domesticos, Odae 9* (Oxford, Joseph Barnes, 1586), sig. A6ᵛ, ode 7. *STC* 4838:

> Non illa Circe est, non animi impotens
> Medea, ferro, perfide, quam petis?
> Cur stringis ensem? siste, Elisa est,
> Cui properas aperire pectus.

An edition of the work published in the same year and place prints only the first six odes (*STC* 4837).

[95] Lodowick Lloyd, *Certaine Englishe Verses, presented vnto the Queenes most excellent Maiestie, by a Courtier: In ioy of the most happie disclosing, of the most dangerous conspiracies pretended by the late executed Traitours, against her royall person, and the whole Estate . . .* (London, 1586), *STC* 16617. Reprinted in *Fugitive Tracts, First Series,* no. xxvii. "Pyragmon," that is, Pyracmon, one of the Cyclops, apparently refers to the Pope and the Babington conspirators.

[96] *Ibid.* For the suggestion that the English attitude toward Mary at this time is reflected allegorically in the treatment of Tellus in John

Lyly's *Endimion* (London, 1591: *STC* 17050), probably written and first produced in 1585, see *The Complete Works of John Lyly*, ed. R. W. Bond (Oxford, 1902), III, 81-103.

⁹⁷ *An apologie of the Professors of the Gospel in Fraunce against the railing declamation of Peter Frarin* . . . (Cambridge, 1586). Scott 133.

⁹⁸ Cf. Chap. II, above.

⁹⁹ *An apologie* . . . (1586), p. 35.

¹⁰⁰ For an account of the reception accorded this work in England and of Knox's reputation there, see James E. Phillips, "The Background of Spenser's Attitude toward Women Rulers," *HLQ*, V (1941), 5-32. The hope was held in some strongly Protestant quarters in England that the printing of Knox's *History* would be allowed because "the counceil perceived that it would bring the Queen of Scots in detestation" (Calderwood MSS, quoted in Thomas M'Crie, *Life of John Knox* [Philadephia, 1898], p. 497).

NOTES TO CHAPTER IV

¹ A detailed account of the international political situation in the years covered in this chapter is contained in Conyers Read, *Mr. Secretary Walsingham* (Cambridge, Mass., 1925), I, Chap. II.

² T. F. Henderson, *Mary Queen of Scots* (London, 1905), II, 525-526.

³ Henry Killegrew to Cecil, January 10, 1572, *CSP Foreign, 1572-1574*, p. 14, no. 27. Killegrew does not identify the "great counsellor" whom he quotes.

⁴ Sir Thomas Smith to Cecil, March 22, 1572, quoted in Read, *Walsingham*, I, 186.

⁵ *CSP Spanish, 1568-1579*, p. 254, quoted in Read, *Walsingham*, I, 82.

⁶ *A Treatise of Treasons* (1572), sig. a8^r. Cf. p. 93, above.

⁷ For an account of English efforts to suppress one such work cf. Walsingham to Burghley, February 10, 1573, *CSP Foreign, 1572-1574*, p. 253, no. 767. The book referred to was probably *A Treatise of Treasons* (cf. p. 93, above).

⁸ *CSP Domestic, 1547-1580*, p. 311, no. 4.

⁹ Thomas Norton, *A Warning agaynst the dangerous practices of Papistes* (1570), sigs. Fiii^v and -Gi^v (cf. Chap. III, note 19, above). Another method of circulating propaganda for Mary is vividly described by Norton—"certaine notable and noted walkers in Paules [i.e., St. Paul's Cathedral in London] and such places of resort, so common that the very usuall places of their being there, are ordinarily knowen

by the names of Papists corner, and liers bench, sauing that I heare say now of late many of them flocke more into the middle isle, which is supposed to be done partly to shunne publike noting, partely for better harkening, and partly for more commodious publishing" (*loc. cit.*).

[10] *STC* 15505. A bibliographical account of this work will be found in Scott 62. Cf. also A. C. Southern, *Elizabethan Recusant Prose, 1559-1582* (London, 1950), pp. 438-440.

[11] *DNB*, "Leslie, John."

[12] More specifically he had in mind, in addition to Buchanan's as yet unpublished *Detection*, John Knox's *First Blast of the Trumpet*, John Hales's manuscript, *A Declaration of the Succession*, Walsingham's *Discourse Touching the Pretended Match,* and the anonymous *Allegations against the Surmisid Title of the Quine of Scots*. Cf. *A Defence of the honour* (1569), "The Author to the Gentle Reader," sig. †ii^v. See Chaps. II and III, above, for an account of the works named.

[13] The most complete account of the authorship of the *Defence* is found in James Anderson, *Collections Relating to the History of Mary Queen of Scotland* (Edinburgh, 1727), I, where the 1571 second edition of the *Defence* is reprinted. The essential details are summarized in Scott 62, and Southern, *Elizabethan Recusant Prose,* p. 439. According to Leslie's own statement under examination, "The Book of the Defence of the Queene's Honour, Thomas Busshop [Bishop] made, by the information of the Lord Harris [Sir John Maxwell, Baron Herries, one of Mary's commissioners in England], before this Examinate's comyng into England; and that Booke was reformid and encreased by Thomas Busshopp, this Examinate, the Lord Harris, and others at the Conference at Westmynster" ("Interrogatories of the Bishop of Ross, October 26 and 27, 1571," in William Murdin, *Collection of State Papers . . . left by William Cecill* [London, 1740-1759], II, 20 ff.). For Leslie's part in the preparation of subsequent editions of the work, see note 50, below. Leslie's own account of his various literary activities in behalf of Mary Stuart is contained in his *A Discourse, conteyninge A perfect Accompt given to . . . Marie, Queene of Scots . . . Of his whole Charge and Proceedings . . . from his Entres in England in September 1568 to the 26th of March 1572,* printed in Anderson, *Collections,* III.

[14] Scott 62. There is some reason to believe that Elizabeth had led Leslie to think that his *Defence* would be permitted to circulate in England. When the London printing was interrupted, Leslie wrote to Cecil that there was nothing in the book offensive to Elizabeth, and that he had sent "the principal copy" to her to be "considerit" (April

26, 1570, *Cal. Scot. Papers,* III [1569-1571], 134-135, no. 194). Cf. also Leslie's *A Discourse, conteyninge A perfect Accompt.* Camden later wrote that Elizabeth "suffered by way of connivance the Bishop of Rosse to answer" current attacks on Mary (*Annals,* 1635, p. 113).

[15] The obviously fictitious colophon is as follows: "Imprinted at London in Flete strete at the signe of Iustice Royal, againste the Blacke bell, by Eusebius Dicaeophile, anno D. 1569. and are to be solde in Paules churche yearde, at the signs of Tyme & Truthe, by the Brasen Serpẽt, in the shoppes of Ptolomé and Nicephore Lycosthenes brethren Germanes." Southern, p. 440, claims on the basis of typographical evidence that the book was printed on the press of John Fogny in Rheims; cf. Scott 62. When Alexander Hervey was arrested and examined in April, 1570, in connection with the appearance of the *Defence,* he testified that "the book was made twelve months since by the Lord Herries, Lord Boyd, and the Bishop of Ross," and, further, that "the Bishop of Ross willed that this said book should be printed," and that he, Hervey, procured it "by the direction of the said Bishop of Ross, his Maister" (*Cal. Scot. Papers,* III [1569-1571], 114-115, no. 176).

[16] *Defence* (1569), sig. [† vi^v].

[17] Fol. 3^v-4^r.

[18] Fol. 14^v.

[19] Fol. 10^r.

[20] Fol. 16^{r-v}.

[21] Fols. 35^r, 41^v-42^r.

[22] Fol. 41^v-42^r.

[23] Fol. 33^r.

[24] Fol. 49^v.

[25] For Hales's *Declaration,* and the *Allegations,* see Chap. II, above.

[26] Fol. 145^v.

[27] Sig. † iii^v. Apparently Leslie's collaborators were in disagreement as to whether this section should be included in the published volume at all; one of them thought the book "to long toward the End, and wishid the latter Part, towchyng the Defense of Women, to be cut away, sayeng he wold not subscribe it with his Hand . . ." (Murdin, *Collection of State Papers,* II, 29). For an account of Knox's *First Blast* and its reception in England, see James E. Phillips, "The Background of Spenser's Attitude toward Women Rulers," *HLQ,* V (1941), 5-32.

[28] ". . . our most dreade Soueraigne Elizabeth doth and hathe sitt in the royall seate with such peace, quietnes, and tranquilitie amoge all her subjects hitherto, that we haue greate cawse to render to God

almighty our most hartie thancks for the same: and to craue of him like continuance, whereof the singuler fruite & benefitt, as longe as it shall please God to preserue her to vs: Whiche we most humble suppliantes desier of him for manie yeares, with some happie issewe from her grace (yf it be his blessed will) we hope most fortunatlie to enjoye" (fol. 52ᵛ). For Leslie's considerably altered opinion of Elizabeth two years after this, see pp. 100-101, above.

²⁹ *Discours Des Troubles nouuellement aduenez au Royaume d' Angleterre, au moys d'Octobre 1569,* "*Avec permission.*" Scott 67: "A Lyon . . . M. D. LXX." An edition in the following year, not recorded by Scott, bears the imprint: "A Paris, Chez Nicolas Chesneau, rue sainct Iacques, au Chesne verd. 1571 Avec Privilege." The head title, sig. Aiiʳ, reads: "Discours Envoye De Londres, & dresse sur le present Estat d'Angleterre." Other works designed mainly as replies to Buchanan's *Detectio* include *Copie d'une Lettre de la Royne d'Escosse . . . touchant ses aduersitez . . .* and *The Copie of a Letter writen out of Scotland, by an English Gentleman . . .* (see p. 98, above).

³⁰ *CSP Domestic, 1547-1580,* p. 364, no. 55, dated February 1569/70; Sir Henry Norris to Cecil, February 25, 1570, *CSP Foreign, 1569-1571,* p. 193, no. 712. Cf. also *Cal. Scot. Papers,* III (1569-1571), 527, no. 692, April 11, 1571, where Thomas Randolph reports a Latin book in defense of Mary written by John Gordon, son of the Bishop of Galloway, "approving her authority, excusing the murder, and blaming the disobedience of her rebellious subjects who deposed her." Subsequently, Gordon wrote to Cecil directly to the effect that "the 'bwik' which Mr. Randel alleges me to have written against my mistress' adversaries, in Latin and Scottish, is against rebellion in general, and is not yet ended. As soon as it is finished, I promise your honour the first copy thereof, and will submit myself to your judgment, and the judgment of all the universities in Germany and England" *(ibid.,* p. 640, no. 858, August 9, 1571).

³¹ Scott 83. *STC* 7601. For a general account of the reception given the *Treatise* in England, and of Cecil's reactions in particular, see Conyers Read, *Lord Burghley and Queen Elizabeth* (New York, 1960), p. 95. According to Scott, the work was printed at Paris or Antwerp; Southern *(Elizabethan Recusant Prose,* p. 447) argues from typographical evidence that it was printed at Louvain by John Fowler, who was responsible for many of the works of Leslie. His conclusion is borne out by the fact that English agents apparently knew that Fowler was the printer of the abstract of the *Treatise of Treasons* by "G. T." described

below (Dr. Thomas Wilson to Cecil, from Antwerp, February 1, 1575, *CSP Foreign, 1575-1577,* pp. 10-11, no. 21). Southern attributes the authorship to Leslie himself, but on rather tenuous grounds; for men suspected of authorship by contemporary Elizabethan agents, see note 34, below. The arguments of the *Treastise* were reiterated in 1573 in a tract entitled *A Table gathered ovvt of a Booke named A Treatise of Treasons against Q. Elizabeth, and the Croune of England. Latelie compiled by a stranger and sent owt of France, Printed in the yeare of our Lord 1572.* See Southern, *op. cit.,* pp. 501-503, for a complete description of this work. The *Table* is not recorded by Scott. The dedicatory epistle to Elizabeth is signed "Your heighnes dailie Orator. G. T." (sig. *1-3); "G. T." has not been identified. The book was actually printed in 1573, since it contains a letter to Sir Christopher Hatton which was sent to him with the manuscript "From Antwerp. the 26. of Iune 1573" (sig. **6-7). For an Italian account of these events written from the Catholic point of view, see Emilio Maria Manolesso, *Historia Nova nella quale si contengono tutti i successi della guerra Turchesa, la Congiura del Duca de Nortfolch contra la Regina d'inghilterra* (Padua, 1572: Scott 79, who cites fols. 78ᵛ-80ᵛ).

³² *A Treatise of Treasons* (1572), fol. 117ᵛ. In another passage particularly revealing of Elizabeth's counterpropaganda methods, the author had observed that the *Salutem in Christo,* despite its anonymity, could not have been published unless powerful authority had been behind it, "in this time specially, when the searches are so straight, & the penaltie so sharpe, for any least thing uttered by writing, printing, or by word, otherwise than Authoritie would" (fol. 73ᵛ).

³³ Fol. 171ᵛ.

³⁴ September 28, 1573. *STC* 8064. Cf. also Robert Steele, *A Bibliography of Royal Proclamations* (Oxford, 1910), I, 74, no. 688; and Camden, *Annales* [1625], p. 323. The most complete account of English efforts to track down the author of the *Treatise* is found in a report Dr. Thomas Wilson sent to Cecil on February 1, 1575, from Antwerp. Wilson, after questioning a number of suspects and even trying to play one against the other, could report nothing definite; but he mentioned specifically as possibilities the Earl of Westmoreland, living in exile abroad after the collapse of the Northern Rebellion; Sir Francis Englefield, Sir Nicholas Throckmorton, Gilbert Gifford, and "Darbyshire, Stapleton, Dr. Knotte, Hyde of Louvain, and Heighynton, the Countess' [of Westmoreland's?] secretary" (*CSP Foreign, 1575-1577,* pp. 10-11, no. 21). A month later, however, he was still trying to find out, from

a Spanish agent, "the printer and author of the *Treatise of Treasons*" (*ibid.*, pp. 26-27, no. 46).

[35] Quoted in John Strype, *Annals of the Reformation* (Oxford, 1824), II, i, 264.

[36] Camden, *Annales* (1625), p. 323.

[37] *L'Innocence de la Tres-illustre, Tres-chaste, & Debonnaire Princesse, Madame Marie Royne d'Escosse. Où sont amplement refutees Les Calomnies faulces, & impositions iniques, publiees par un liure secrettement diuulgué en France, l'an 1572, touchant tant la morte du Seigneur d'Arnley son espoux, que autres crimes, dont elle est faulcement accusee. Plus un autre Discours. Auquel son descouuertes, Plusieurs trahisons, tant manifestes, que iusques icy cachees, perpetrees par les mesmes calomniateurs.* Scott 85. According to Southern (*Elizabethan Recusant Prose*, p. 446 n.) the work was probably published at Rheims by John Fogny, the printer of many of John Leslie's works. After noting that extant copies show many variations, Scott observes that "differences are caused by the addition or removal of passages offensive to many of the actors in the drama, more especially to Murray."

[38] The work was attributed to François de Belleforest, the translator of one of Shakespeare's sources for *Hamlet,* by Jacques DeLong (*Bibliothèque Historique de la France* [Paris, 1769], II, 651) with the statement "François de Belleforest est l'Auteur de cette Apologie." Scott asserts that Belleforest was, if anything, only the editor and translator. James Maitland in his *Apologie for William Maitland of Lethington* (ed. Andrew Lang, *Miscellany of the Scottish History Society* [1904], pp. 158 ff.) attributes the work to Leslie, as does Southern (p. 446 n.). On the efforts of Elizabeth's agents, cf. *CSP Domestic: Addenda, 1566-1579*, p. 444, no. 7, February 18, 1573. John Gordon (cf. note 30, above), after denying responsibility on the grounds that the book lacked learning, confessed to Walsingham that he knew the author, but thought "it not his office to be an accuser" (*CSP Foreign, 1572-1574*, p. 264, no. 789, February 25, 1573). Later, Dr. Thomas Wilson reported to Cecil that the work was "turned into French by Belforest" (*ibid.*, p. 579, no. 1612, December 12, 1574); still later he stated just as positively that "one Mownse . . . servant to the Duke of Norfolk, put the English into French" (*CSP Foreign, 1575-1577*, pp. 10-11, no. 21, February 1, 1575). The probability that Leslie was instrumental in bringing about the French publication is suggested by the following entry from his diary, dated August 30, 1571: "I wrote to 'Nicolas,' the ambassador of France's servant, and to William Lesly to place 'Jame' Broun with a

'wretar' in the French tongue in London for three months" *(Cal. Scot. Papers,* III [1569-1571], 529, no. 695).

[39] Referring to the French translation of Buchanan's *Detectio* in particular, he writes that the book was published "expres pour rendre ces Princes odieux envers le roy, & frustret ladicte Royne du benefice de la ligue susdite" *(L'Innocence* [1572], sig. aiii^v).

[40] *L'Innocence,* reprinted in Samuel Jebb, *De Vita et Rebus Gestis Mariae* (London, 1725), I, 480 ff.

[41] *Ibid.,* I, 524.

[42] *Ibid.,* I, 457.

[43] *Ibid.,* I, 518.

[44] *Ibid.,* I, 531.

[45] *Ibid.,* I, 497.

[46] *Copie d'une Lettre de la Royne d'Escosse escripte de sa Prison de Cheifeild touchant ses aduersitez* (Paris, 1572). Scott 86. Scott follows Lowndes, *Bibliographer's Manual,* in calling this work a forgery.

[47] Not included in Scott. The work appeared without imprint, but Southern argues from typographical evidence that it was probably published in 1572 at Louvain by John Fowler *(Elizabethan Recusant Prose,* p. 448). The work is attributed to Leslie by James Maitland in his *Apology for William Maitland of Lethington* (ed. Lang, pp. 158 ff.), and on this authority by Southern. Southern gives a complete bibliographical account of the work.

[48] *Satirical Poems of the Time of the Reformation,* ed. James Cranstoun (Edinburgh and London, 1891-1893), I, 174 ff. Cf. also II, 117, for Cranstoun's useful notes on the authorship and circumstances of the ballad.

[49] Scott 73; *STC* 15506; Southern, *Elizabethan Recusant Prose,* p. 442. The imprint reads "Leodii. Apud Gualterum Morberium. 1571." Southern argues convincingly that the *Treatise* was actually printed at Louvain by John Fowler, and that the "Morberium" (i.e., Walter Morbers) title page is a cancel. In this connection, it should be noted that the *Treatise* appeared with an official "Imprimatur," dated Louvain, March 6, 1571, sigs. i4^v and Dd7^v, despite the Liège imprint. Charles Bailley, who was arrested by the English when he tried to smuggle copies of the *Treatise* into England in 1571, wrote for Cecil the following explanation of the circumstances under which the book was published: having been requested by Leslie to pick up copies of the book from Sir Francis Englefield, one of Mary's partisans, in the Spanish Netherlands, Bailey was told by Sir Francis "that the Books

weare not yet ready, because he could not obtayne, at the Duke's [of Alva's] Hands, as yet, the Priviledge for the Printer, for which they had made all the Suite they coulde; the Duke and his Counsell alledging, that they could no whit intend thereunto, for that they wold not give her Majestie [Elizabeth] Cause to be discontent with him, or with the Q. of Scotts. And that therefore they had sent to Liege to cause som Parte to be imprinted; and that they weare not as yet com. . . . And so I went to Lovayn, where I found the Books trymmed as they be, in a Stationer's House, to whom Mr. Englefeld had given me a Lettre for them to be delyvered unto me" (Murdin, *Collection of State Papers,* II, 11). Bailley's statement, if true, explains why it was necessary to print the book at the great Marian center of Louvain but to give it a false imprint of Liége, the seat of the Spanish Catholic governor, the Duke of Alva. For, like Philip of Spain, and Charles of France, Alva did not wish to antagonize the English Queen by seeming to approve officially of a book that defended her enemy and raised questions about her right to the throne. It was the same ambiguity of attitude among Catholic rulers that confronted Mary's apologists and propagandists at every turn. The "Imprimatur" suggests that ecclesiastical authorities did not share the scruples entertained by political authorities about England and Elizabeth. The *DNB,* giving James Maitland's *Apology for William Maitland of Lethington* (ed. Lang) as authority, cites *Sommaire du livre de Guillaume Stewart, augmenté par Andre Mophat* (s.l., n.d.) as a publication in French of the first part of Leslie's *A Treatise;* and *Discourse sur les Affaires d'Escosse* (s.l., n.d.) as a French version of the third part of Leslie's work, dealing with women rulers. I have seen neither French work; Maitland's *Apology* does not specifically indicate that either is linked in any way with the 1571 *A Treatise concerning the Defence* but treats both as separate efforts by Leslie, under the pseudonyms.

[50] Alexander Hervey, April, 1570, *Cal. Scot. Papers,* III (1569-1571), 114-115, no. 176. See note 15, above.

[51] Cf. note 49. Leslie himself, under cross-examination by the English, confessed that he had indeed sent "over [to the Continent] certen Books concerning the Quene of Scot's Title, and the Defence of Hir Honor, in Wrytying [i.e., in manuscript]," but he denied Bailley's testimony that he, the Bishop, had requested Bailley to bring copies of the revised *Treatise* into England out of Flanders. He sought to clear himself of charges that the new edition was revised by himself to support the Ridolfi plot by insisting that "whyther the printed Books agree with

those in Wrytyng [i.e., his manuscript], he knoweth not." In the light of the actual events and Bailley's testimony, the Bishop's excuse seems somewhat lame: ". . . having commodity that Charles [Bailley] was to pass over into Flanders, he willed him to bring some of them [i.e., copies of the *Treatise*] with him, that he might consider whether they would serve in this parliament time, but afterwards, thinking the time nothing convenient, he wrote to Charles, and sent special message by tongue, which he received in Calais, to bring nothing. 'Albeit he keiped not command' " ("Examination of the Bishop of Ross," May 13, 1571, *Cal. Scot. Papers,* III [1569-1571], 569, no. 740).

[52] *Cal. Scot. Papers,* III (1569-1571), 529, no. 695: "Diary of the Bishop of Ross"; "Examination of the Bishop of Ross," June 16, 1571, *Cal. Scot. Papers,* III (1569-1571), 606-607, no. 802.

[53] The alterations and their over-all effect are summarized in Scott 73, and more fully in Anderson, *Collections,* I. Leslie admitted under examination that he did the revising himself with the "help of some yong students within the court—sic as Franceis Bishop and utheris" (*Cal. Scot. Papers,* III [1569-1571], 576-578, nos. 749, 750, May 16, 1571). Among these "utheris" who helped was Dr. James Good, who testified later that he had made corrections in the book, had "englished" some of the words, and had sent a copy to the Queen of Scots (*Cal. Scot. Papers,* V [1574-1581], 105-106, no. 105, March 14, 1575; 121-122, nos. 121, 122, April 28, 1575; 128, no. 129, April 28, 1575; 140, no. 143, May 12, 1575). But Leslie stoutly maintained, even to Elizabeth herself, that he never intended any "trouble" to herself or to her state (*Cal. Scot. Papers,* III [1569-1571], 550, no. 710, "The Bishop of Ross to Elizabeth"). Among the more significant deletions from the 1569 version is the eulogistic paragraph in praise of Elizabeth quoted in note 28, above, which does not appear in the 1571 *Treatise.*

[54] *Libri duo: Quorum uno, Piae afflicti animi consolationes, diuinaque remedia: Altero, Animi Tranquilli Munimentum & conseruatio, Continentur* (1574). See Scott 91. Leslie's dedicatory epistle to Mary is dated from the Tower of London, May, 1572. The poems attributed to Mary include a "Meditation faite par la Royne d'Escoce" (fol. 38^r), and a "Sonet," beginning "L'ire de Dieu par le sang ne s'appaise" (fol. 40^r). A French translation of the *Libri Duo* was subsequently published at Rouen in 1590 under the title *Les Devotes Consolationes et divins remedies* (*DNB,* "Leslie, John").

[55] *Libri Duo* (1574), sig. Fiij^r: "Pulchrior longe est animosa virtue / Regis ab intus. / Intus est cor, quod Deus intuetur: / Intus est, quod

punit, amat, coronat: / Intus exultat pietas, fidesque / Regis ab intus. Sperne, Regina, haec lutulenta quaeque: / Consciam recti pietate mentem / Indue: hanc serua, hanc cole, laeta viues / Semper ab intus."

⁵⁶ *Ibid.*, sig. †iiij. The lines are those beginning "Nympha Calidoniae quae nũc foeliciter ore," with which Buchanan dedicated his paraphrase of the Psalms to Mary (cf. Chap. I, note 53).

⁵⁷ *Pro Libertate impetranda. Oratio. Ad Serenissiman Elizabetham Angliae Reginam* (Paris, 1574).

⁵⁸ Leslie to Burghley, March 20, 1574, *CSP Scotland, 1509-1603*, II, 915, no. 13. Cf. also *Cal. Scot. Papers*, IV (1571-1574), 652, no. 758.

⁵⁹ *Pro Libertate impetranda* (1574), sigs. ãvᵛ and -ãviʳ: "Vnde omen capto, fore tandem eadem tua clementia (qua ego aura vescor, & in libertatem vindicatus sum), vt Domina mea, patriae, focis, laribus & sceptro, tuis auspiciis restituatur. Nihil enim in rebus humanis tuae gloriae maiorem cumulum addere possit, quam immerito exulantem, quam foeminam, quam consaguineam, quam sororem, quam denique Reginam, a te Regina clementissima, suaui indole, pacato ingenio, bonis literis, omni humanitate imbuta, erga tot exules & peregrinos, ipsos etiam hostes mitissima, tot aduersis fortunae telis petitam, atque inimica & immerita fata violentia prostratam, in pristino honoris culmine reponi. Sed de Regina Domina mea alias." Leslie concludes this "Epistola" with a direct appeal to Elizabeth herself that she restore his bishopric, incomes, and other losses (sig. ãviiiʳ⁻ᵛ). The "Oratio" proper, dated 1573, is mainly an account and defense by Leslie of his ambassadorial activities in Mary's behalf during the preceding years.

⁶⁰ "Ad Sereniss. D. Mariam Scotorum Reginam," in *Pro Libertate impetranda*, sig. [Eiiii]ʳ.

⁶¹ *De Origine Moribus et Rebus Gestis Scotorum Libri Decem* (Rome, 1578). Scott 100.

⁶² I quote James Dalrymple's 1596 Scots translation of Leslie's Latin, as printed in *The Historie of Scotland*, ed. by E. G. Cody for the Scottish Text Society (Edinburgh, 1888), II, 51.

⁶³ Mary's "pietatis honos, fidei constantia, morum Integritas" are celebrated also by Alexander Seton, the later chancellor and Privy Councilor under James I, in commendatory verses printed on the verso of the separate title page provided for the last three books of Leslie's *De Origine Moribus et Rebus Gestis* (Rome, 1578).

⁶⁴ *De Titulo et ivre serenissimae principis Mariae Scotorum Reginae, quo Regni Angliae successionem sibi juste vendicat, Libellus . . . Rhemis . . . 1580. Cum Privilegio* (Scott, 115); *De Illvstrium Foeminarum*

in Repvb. Administranda, ac ferendis legibus authoritate, Libellus ... Rhemis ... 1580. Cum Privilegio (Scott 116). The Huntington copies of these two works are bound together, but they appear to be bibliographically separate publications (cf. Scott).

[65] *A Treatise tovvching the Right, Title, and Interest of ... Marie, Queene of Scotland, And of the most noble king Iames, her Graces sonne, to the succession of the Croune of England* ... ([Rouen? Rheims?], 1584). Scott 123. *STC* 15507. The French and Spanish translations are described in Scott 137 and 138, respectively; I have not seen them.

[66] *A Treatise tovvching the Right* ... (1584), fol. 3[r-v]. The corresponding Latin passage appears in *De Titulo et ivre* ... (1580), sig. ãiij[r]. Similarly, he dedicated his 1580 Latin version of the defense of woman rulers to the Queen Mother of France in the hope that, related in marriage and faith as she was to the exiled and afflicted Queen of Scots, Catherine de' Medici might join the campaign for Mary's relief; see his *De Illvstrium Foeminarum* ... (1580), fol. 3[v]: "... nostram tibi affinitate ac pietate filiam, voluntate supplicem, acerbo casu exulem & afflictam, commendatum habeas, qua possum animi contentione, etiam atque etiam efflagito."

[67] For a detailed account of James's flirtation with Catholic powers, see Read, *Walsingham*, II, 155 ff. Other Catholic writers holding hopes for James at this time, like Leslie, included John Hamilton, who, in a dedicatory epistle to Mary, expresses the belief that her son will soon disown his Protestant misleaders and punish her persecutors (*Ane Catholik and facile traictise* ... [Paris, 1581; Scott 118; reprinted in *Catholic Tractates of the Sixteenth Century*, ed. T. G. Law, Edinburgh, Scottish Text Society, 1901]); and Jacobus Laingaeus, *De Vita et moribus atque rebus gestis Haereticorum nostri temporis* ... (Paris, 1581).

[68] "Ad Nobilitate Popvlvmque Britanniae T. St. Angli Carmen," in *De Titulo et ivre* ... (1580), sig. eiiii[v]; "To the Nobilitie and people of England and Scotland, A Poesie made by T. V., Englishman," in *A Treatise tovvching the Right* ... (1584), fol. 12[r-v]. "T. Str." also contributed a Latin prefatory poem expressing a similar attitude toward Mary and Leslie, "In Praesentem Libellum De Illustrium Foeminarum Authoritate, Carmen," to Leslie's *De Illvstrium Foeminarum* (1580), fol. 4[r-v].

[69] Leslie's arguments and materials, for example, were extensively used, with acknowledgment, in the works published in 1579 by David Chambers, Lord Ormond, a Scottish jurist who had remained loyal to

the Queen through her difficulties in Scotland (*DNB*). Cf. *Histoire Abregee de tous les Roys de France, Angleterre et Escosse* (Paris, 1579: Scott 107), where Chambers cites Leslie as one of his chief authorities for his account of Mary's troubles and his justification of her claim to the English succession; *Discours de la Legitime Succession des Femmes* (Paris, 1579: Scott 109), which is little more than a reworking of Leslie's treatise on the right of women to govern kingdoms; and *La Recherche des Singularitez Plus Remarquables, concernant l'estate d'Escosse* (Paris, 1579: Scott 108), an account of the civil disorder produced by Protestantism in Scotland, dedicated to Mary with the hope that she and other Catholic princes may soon restore Catholicism and order there.

[70] "Sonnet," in *Le Premier Livre des Poèmes . . . dediez a tres-illustre et tres-vertuese Princesse Marie Stuart, Royne d'Escosse*, in *Œuvres Complètes*, ed. Paul Laumonier (Paris 1914-1919), V, 3: Notes VII, 465. The "Sonnet" and dedication to Mary apparently first appeared in *Les Poèmes* (Paris, 1578), prefacing "Le Second Livre des Poèmes," which became "Le Premier Livre" in the reorganized edition of *Les Poèmes* in 1584. For an earlier and more restrained example of Ronsard's changed attitude, cf. *Le Tombeau de Marguerite de France, Duchesse de Savoye* (Paris, 1575), ed. Laumonier, *op. cit.*, V, 248.

[71] The following biographical sketch is based on that by T. F. Henderson in the *DNB*, and on "Adami Blacvodaei Elogium" by Gabriel Naudé prefacing Blackwood, *Opera Omnia* (Paris, 1644).

[72] Blackwood, *Opera Omnia*, p. 506. In his *Adversus Georgii Buchanani Dialogum*, sig. *ii^v (see note 77, below), Blackwood himself indicates that he was in England in 1580 on a mission concerning Mary. He was also in the party of Pomponne de Bellièvre, French secretary of state, whom Henri III sent to England in November, 1586, to deliver a final "Harangue" to Elizabeth in behalf of the condemned Queen of Scots. Cf. *Opera Omnia*, "Elogium," and Chap. VI, below.

[73] "La Roine qui me tient pour son poete," in "Paraphrase du Poeme Latin [*De Jezabelis*] sur le parricide . . . ," reprinted in G. Ascoli, *La Grand-Bretagne devant l'Opinion Française* (Paris, 1927), p. 280. See Chap. VI, below. The Latin poems are described below; to them should be added "E Gallico illustrissimae Scotorum, Gallorumque (quam dotariam vocant) Reginae" (*Opera Omnia*, pp. 478-481).

[74] *Registers of the Privy Council of Scotland*, II (1569-1578), 334.

[75] *De Vinculo: seu Conjunctione Religionis et Imperii* (Paris, 1575). A third and final book of the treatise was published in 1612.

[76] *DNB*, "Blackwood, Adam."

[77] *Adversus Georgii Buchanani dialogum . . . pro regibus apologia* (Poitiers, 1581). Scott 117. Another edition appeared in 1588. See Chap. III, above, on Buchanan's *De iure regni apud Scotos.*

[78] Chaps. VI and VII.

[79] "Pro Scotiae Regina quo tempore filio sibi per impios perduelles erepto, promissi auxilij spe & opinione profugit in Angliam," in *Opera Omnia* (1644), pp. 393-394. It was apparently first printed in Blackwood's *Sanctarum precationum prooemia* (1608), p. 39. As the title indicates, the poem was probably written at the time of Mary's flight from Scotland.

[80] "Ad Christianissimum Galliae Regem Henricum tertium, vt Schotia Reginam in Anglia contra ius gentium tot annis crudeliter & tyrannide detentam affectu fraterno motus, liberandam curet" (*Opera Omnia,* p. 481).

[81] *De Visibili Monarchia Ecclesiae* (Louvain, 1571). Cf. *DNB,* "Sanders, Nicholas." This section on Mary appears in Book VII. According to Kervyn de Lettenhove (*Relations politiques des Pays-Bas et de l'Angleterre sous la régne de Philippe II* [Brussels, 1888], VII, 469-470), the Spanish censor in the Low Countries refused to approve Book VII, for fear it would offend Elizabeth. Accordingly, although Books I through VI and Book VIII were published with approval at Louvain, Book VII appeared with a Cologne imprint (cited by Southern, *Elizabethan Recusant Prose,* p. 33).

[82] *De Origine, Ac Progressu Schismatis Anglicani. Libri Tres,* "Editus et auctus per Edouradum Rishtonum," Rheims, 1585: "Aucti per Edovardum Rishtonum," Ingolstadt, 1587. See Scott 225. Translated by David Lewis, *Rise and Growth of the Anglican Schism* (London, 1877). Cf. also, Johann Mayr Frisingensem, *Kurtzer bericht Aller gedenckwurdigen sachen, so sich in Engelland in de nechsten hundert Jaren verlauffen, auss D. Niclass Sanders, Edwuardo Risthono und andern mehr Engellandischen Historicis zusamen gezogen . . . München . . . 1600.* Scott 188. For an account of the political context of Sanders' work, cf. Read, *Lord Burghley and Queen Elizabeth,* p. 241.

[83] Sanders, *Rise and Growth of the Anglican Schism* (1877), pp. 23-25; Sanders was accused by William Camden of being the first to publish this story of Elizabeth's parenthood (*ibid.,* p. xxii).

[84] David Lewis, in his introduction to Sanders' *Rise and Growth of the Anglican Schism* (pp. xxii ff.) presents convincing evidence to show that the story was in circulation before Sanders printed it, but argues with less plausibility that the story was true.

[85] Sanders, *op. cit.,* p. 293.

[86] "Quanquam sane maius quiddam mihi esse videtur, pro fide Catholica pati, quam in fide catholica regnare," *De Visibili Monarchia Ecclesiae*, quoted in *Supplicium & Mors* (1587), sig. D8ʳ. (Cf. Chap. VI, below.)

[87] Henderson, *Mary Queen of Scots*, II, 519.

[88] *Rise and Growth of the Anglican Schism*, p. 293. On Shrewesbury as guardian of Mary, see J. E. Neale, *Queen Elizabeth* (New York, 1934), p. 256, 266; Henderson, *Mary Queen of Scots*, II, 525; and Read, *Walsingham*, II, 354-355, for accounts of Shrewesbury's lenience and the distrust it aroused in English officialdom.

[89] J. W. Allen, *A History of Political Thought in the Sixteenth Century* (London, 1941), p. 205.

[90] Cf., for example, *Illvstria Ecclesiae Catholicae Trophoea, Ex recentibus Anglicorum martyrum, Scoticae proditionis, Gallicorumq; furorum rebus gestis grauis. vivorum fide notatis. Charae Posteritati, Vt nimirum ea de praesentium errorum natura atcq; ingenio integre ac libere tandem iudicet, Erecta. Anno M.D.LXXIII.* Colophon: "Monarchii exudebat Adamus Berg." Morgan Library copy, New York City. This anonymous compilation gives accounts of the sufferings of celebrated English Catholics; then, to provide an example of "holy martyrdom" in Scotland, it turns to Mary Stuart, reprinting verbatim the 1566 Latin account of the murder of Rizzio, *Proditionis ab aliqvot Scotiae Perdvellibvs* (see Chap. II, note 35 above). In its emphasis on Mary's sufferings for her faith the Rizzio account was, among all the earlier works in her defense, perhaps best suited for reproduction in a latter-day martyrology.

[91] Richard Hakluyt to Walsingham, April 1, 1584, *CSP Domestic, 1581-1590,* p. 169, no. 1. Hakluyt was at this time the Anglican preacher assigned to Stafford, the English ambassador.

[92] Cf., for example, *De Iustitia Britannica, sive Anglica, quae contra Christi Martyres continenter exercetur* (Ingoldstadt, 1584). Scott 125. The intended irony of the title becomes evident when it is recalled that the widely circulated Latin translation of Cecil's tract bore the title, *De Iustitia Britannica.* The Catholic work relies heavily and with acknowledgment on the work of Sanders (sig. Blʳ). As Scott observes, "Foremost among the women is placed the name of Mary Queen of Scots, with a notice of some length of her devotion to the Roman Catholic faith, and an outline of her sufferings while detained in England." Similar treatments of Catholic martyrs and of Mary in particular may be found in three other works: Natalis Comes (Natalie Conti), *Universae Historiae sui temporis* (1581); Giliberti Genebrardi, *Chrono-*

graphiae Libri IV (1584); and John Fenn, *Concertatio Ecclesiae Catholicae in Anglia* (1583). On this last, cf. Chap. VII, below.

93 [Ingolstadt, 1584.] *STC* 373. Southern, *Elizabethan Recusant Prose*, p. 387, gives Rouen. On the Latin edition, see Scott 126: *Ad Persecutores Anglos pro Catholicis . . .* [Ingolstadt? Douay? 1584?].

94 Stafford to Walsingham, August 24, 1584, *CSP Foreign, 1584-1585*, p. 33. Cf. *ibid.*, pp. 68, 207, for further reports by Stafford on Allen's answer to Cecil, and *CSP Foreign, 1583-1584*, p. 522. According to Conyers Read (*Lord Burghley and Queen Elizabeth*, p. 255), John Stubbs, who lost his right hand for the unauthorized published attack on Mary and the Alençon marriage, entitled *The Gaping Gulf* (cf. Chap. III, note 53, above), was employed by Elizabeth's government to answer Allen's pamphlet. Stubbs's answer, although favorably recommended by a board of reviewers, was apparently never printed (Read, *Lord Burghley*, Chap. XIII, note 86).

95 *A True Sincere and Modest Defence . . .* (1584), Chap. IV.

96 *Ibid.*, p. 191.

97 For an account of Verstegan and Stafford's dealings with him, see A. G. Petti, "Richard Verstegan and Catholic Martyrologies of the Later Elizabethan Period," in *Recusant History*, V (1959-1960), 64-90. Cf. also Chap. VII, below.

98 Walsingham to Stafford, February 7, 1584, *CSP Foreign, 1583-1584*, p. 341, no. 408.

99 Stafford to Walsingham, November 17, 1583, *CSP Foreign, 1583-1584*, pp. 218-219, no. 246.

NOTES TO CHAPTER V

1 John Norden's *Mirror for the Multitude*, which refrains from attacking Mary, although licensed on December 5 was obviously prepared, and probably submitted, with the ban in mind. See Chap. III, note 87, above.

2 London, Richard Jones, 1587; *STC* 25334; Scott 141; *Stationers' Register*, ed. Arber, II, 462. The first issue refers to Mary as sentenced but still alive. A second issue, printed in London by Jones but without date (*STC* 25334ᵃ; Scott 141), indicates on the title page and in a note on the last leaf that Mary had been executed. According to an address to the "Curteous Reader," the text for both issues was prepared for the press by Thomas Churchyard. The first issue is reprinted in *Collier Reprints* (Red Series), XX, no. 2 (Huntington Library copy).

[3] *The Censure of a Loyall Subiecte* (1587, 1st issue), sig. GI^v.

[4] *A true Copie of the Proclamation lately published by the Queenes Maiestie, vnder the great Seale of England, for the declaring of the Sentence, lately giuen against the Queene of Scottes, in fourme as followeth. Richmond: 4 December 1586.* (London, C. Barker [1586].) Scott 134; *STC* 8160; Robert Steele, *A Bibliography of Royal Proclamations* (Oxford, 1910), I, 85, no. 790. For the published translations of the proclamation, see *By de Coninginne De waerachtighe Copie van de proclamatie* (s.l., n.d.), Scott 135; *Een warachtich verhael van seeckere requesten* ... (Leyden, 1587); *Copye wan eenen brief* ... (Middelburg, 1587), cf. note 5, below; *Copey Vonn Einem Brieff* ... *Auch ist hierbey ein warhafftige Copey* ... *von der Sentenz* ... (Cologne, 1587), cf. note 5, below; Romoaldus Scotus, *Summarium Rationum* (Ingoldstadt, 1588), Scott 171; cf. Chap. VI, below.

[5] J. E. Neale, in *Elizabeth I and Her Parliaments 1584-1601* (London, 1957), pp. 129 ff., has established the facts that Robert Cecil, not Richard Crompton, as hitherto assumed, was the compiler of the materials and author of the letter to Leicester signed "R. C."; and that Elizabeth herself participated in the preparation of this propaganda venture. Recorded versions of the resultant pamphlet include: (1) *The Copie of a Letter to the Right Honorable the Earle of Leycester* ... (London, 1586: *STC* 6052; Scott 131); (2) *Copey Vonn Einem Brieff an den Grafen von Leycester* ... (Cologne, 1587; not in Scott; the edition also includes a translation of the Proclamation of Sentence and of four of the letters alleged to have passed between Mary and Antony Babington); (3) *Een warachtich verhael van seeckere requesten* ... (Leyden, 1587; Scott 142; the edition also includes a translation of the Proclamation of Sentence; the "priuilegie" is dated "in Sgrauenhage ... Ianuarius 1587"); (4) another Dutch edition, entitled *Copye wan eenen brief aen den E. den Grave van Leycester,* published at Middelburg in 1587, is recorded by Scott 143; (5) *La Copie d'une Lettre inscrite a monseigneur le comte de Lecestre* ... (London, Christopher Barker, 1587; *STC* 6053. It should be emphasized that this French translation was prepared under official auspices in England by the Queen's Printer for distribution abroad.); (6) *Recueil de Certaines Requestes et declarations* ... (printed, with a separate title page, in Kyffin *Apologie ou Defense* ... [Paris?, 1588], p. 125; [see p. 121, above]); (7) the substance of the *Letter,* and of the Proclamation of Sentence, was also reproduced, along with suitable Catholic replies to the charges, in Romoaldus Scotus, *Summarium Rationem* (Ingoldstadt, 1588; see Chap. VI, below).

[6] London, 1587; *STC* 6055; Scott 140. The dedication is dated February 12, 1587.

[7] London, 1587; *STC* 14925; Scott 139; entered in the *Stationers' Register,* December 23, 1586 (ed. Arber, II, 462); reprinted in *Fugitive Tracts, First Series,* no. xxviii. On Kempe, cf. *DNB.*

[8] *Ibid., Fugitive Tracts, First Series,* no. xxviii.

[9] London, J. Windet [1587]; *STC* 15098; Scott 145; Arber, II, 464; all of which attribute the anonymous publication to Kyffin. Under the same date in the *Stationers' Register* is entered, to Windet, a work entitled *An Analogie or resemblance between Johane Quene of Naples and Marye Queene of Scotland;* the title is identical with that of the first chapter of Kyffin's *A defence of the Honorable sentence.* The French translation, entitled *Apologie ou Defense de l'Honorable sentence & tres-juste execution de defuncte Marie Steuard* . . . (Paris?, 1588; Scott 163) acknowledges Windet's edition as its source, and also appends a translation of the substance of *The Copie of a Letter to* . . . *Leycester* (see note 5, above).

[10] Maurice Kyffin, *The Blessedness of Brytaine* (London, 1587, "Published with Authoritie"); *STC* 15096; a second edition appeared in 1588: *STC* 15097. The work is reprinted in *Fugitive Tracts, First Series* (1875), no. xxix, and by the Cymmrodorion Society (London, 1885). According to the *Stationers' Register,* ed. Arber, II, 478, the work was entered as allowed by the Archbishop of Canterbury on November 10, 1587.

[11] Cf., for example, *De legato et absoluto principe perdvellionis reo. Oxoniae, typis Iosephi Barnesii, 1587, STC* 15387; on *An excellent dyttye,* see *Stationers' Register,* ed. Arber, II, 464 (entered February 27, 1587). Cf. also *The sorowfull sobbes and sighes of England &c, ibid.,* II, 465 (entered March 8, 1587).

[12] *STC* 13569. For an account of the castrations in the 1587 edition of Holinshed, see Conyers Read, *Bibliography of British History, Tudor Period* (Oxford, 1933), p. 23, no. 289; and *The Bardon Papers,* ed. Conyers Read (Camden Third Series, Vol. XVII: London, 1909), p. 97, where criticism of the Earl of Shrewsbury for favoring his charge, Mary Stuart, in the unexpurgated Holinshed is presented as another reason for the censorship. The suppressed leaves were reprinted as a unit in 1722-1723, and twice before the end of 1728 (cf. *Cambridge Bibliography of English Literature,* "Holinshed"). The leaves also appear in the six-volume Holinshed edition of 1807-1808. A discussion

of Anglo-Scottish relations that determined Elizabeth's concern for James at this time will be found in Chap. VIII, below.

¹³ Kyffin, *A Defence of the Honorable sentence* (1587), sig. K4ᵛ.

¹⁴ *A Short Declaration of the End of Traitors* (1587), sig. aiiᵛ; cf. also Holinshed, *Chronicles* (1587), II, 1577, 1578; Whetstone, *The Censure of a Loyall Subiecte* (1587), sig. G1ᵛ; Kempe, *A Dutifull Invective (Fugitive Tracts, First Series)* no. xxviii.

¹⁵ In a marginal note, Whetstone reminded his readers of "a booke long since written in french to sentence the blody proceedings of the Q. of Scottes with death" (*Censure of a Loyall Subiecte,* sig. G2ʳ). Whetstone probably refers to Barnaud's *Le Reveille-Matin* (1574), described in Chap. III, note 59 above. Cf. also Kyffin, *A defence of the Honorable sentence* (1587), sig. I3ʳ.

¹⁶ "Vita Conradini mors Caroli, mors Conradini vita Caroli," in Kyffin, *A Defence* (1587), sig. 14ʳ.

¹⁷ *Ibid.,* sig. K4ʳ.

¹⁸ Whetstone, *The Censure of a Loyall Subiecte* (1587), sig. G1ᵛ.

¹⁹ *The Copie of a Letter* (1586), pp. 27-29.

²⁰ *A Dutifull Invective* (1875), n. p. Cf. also, *The Copie of a Letter* (1586), *passim;* and Kyffin, *A Defence of the Honorable sentence* (1587), sig. K3ᵛ.

²¹ J. W. Allen, *A History of Political Thought in the Sixteenth Century* (London, 1941), Pt. II, chap. ii. On *Horestes,* cf. Chap. II, above.

²² *The Copie of a Letter* (1586), p. 6. Similarly, Whetstone wrote that "God deliuered the Scottish Queene unto the sword of [Elizabeth's] iustice: as he did many Idolatrous princes, into the hands of the kings of Israel" (*The Censure of a Loyall Subiecte* [1587], sig. G1ᵛ. Cf. also *Agaynste the Q. of Scottes for her aduouterie,* British Museum MSS, Cotton Caligula C, II, fol. 528 [580]).

²³ *A true narracion of the execution of Mary* . . . (British Museum MSS, Cotton Caligula C, IX, fols. 589, 599), quoted in A. F. Steuart, *The Trial of Mary Queen of Scots* (Edinburgh and London, 1923), p. 175. Cf. also her letter to Preau, her confessor: "You will hear from Bourgoin and others that I at least faithfully made protestation for my faith, in which I wish to die" (quoted in Mrs. Maxwell Scott, *The Tragedy of Fotheringay* [London, 1905], p. 184).

²⁴ Chateauneuf to Henri III, February 27, 1587, in A. Labanoff, *Lettres Inédites de Marie Stuart* (Paris, 1839), p. 219. See Conyers Read, *Lord Burghley and Queen Elizabeth* (New York, 1960), p. 365, for an

account of a conspiracy purported to have been hatched in January, 1587, by Des Trappes, one of Chateauneuf's staff, and William Stafford, renegade brother of the English ambassador to France, to murder Elizabeth and free Mary—a conspiracy that served the English as an excuse to hold Chateauneuf incommunicado until after the execution.

25 Earl of Kent, *et al.*, to the Council, February 8, 1587, *Cal. Scot. Papers*, IX (1586-1588), 273, no. 266.

26 "Peticion of the Scottish Queenes People to her majestie," *Cal. Scot. Papers*, IX (1586-1588), 443, no. 257; cf. also nos. 326, 369, for similar requests from the servants. Passports were eventually issued to them in August (*Cal. Scot. Papers*, IX [1586-1588], 471, no. 378), but according to Mendoza, the Spanish ambassador in Paris, the servants did not arrive there until October (*CSP Spanish, 1587-1603*, p. 158, no. 159).

27 "... la Royne ne vouloyt pas que vostre Majesté fust advertie de ceste exéqqution par aultre que par celluy que elle vous enverroyt ..." (Labanoff, *Lettres Inédites*, p. 218).

28 Adam Blackwood, *La Mort de la Royne d'Escosse* (1588), pp. 107, 110. For a detailed account of this work see Chap. VII, below.

29 Ch. Labitte, *De la democratie chez les predicateurs de la Ligue* (Paris, 1841), pp. 31-32; and Chap. VI, below.

30 Stafford to Walsingham, June 22, 1587, *CSP Foreign, 1586-1588* (Vol. XXI, Pt. I), p. 316, describing a Catholic martyrology he calls *Advertissement des Advertissements*. I have not been able to identify this work, although it may possibly be an *Avertissement aux catholiques sur les abus des hérètiques, par F. B.* [Olivier De Douzac] (s.l., 1587); or *Advertissement des catholiques anglois aux catholiques francois* (s.l., 1586, 1587, 1588), attributed to Louis Dorléans. (See Barbier, *Dictionnaire des Ouvrages Anonymes.*)

31 Pierre L'Estoile, *Registre-Journal ... de Henri III*, ed. MM. Champollion-Figeac and Aime Champollion fils (Paris, 1837), pp. 217-218: "Sa mort fut infinment regrette et plainte par les catholiques, principalement par les Ligueurs, qui crioient et disoient tout haut, qu'elle estoit morte martyre pour la foy catholique, apostolique et romaine, et que la roine Angloise, n'l'avoit fait mourir pour autre chose que pour la religion, quelque couleur d'ailleurs elle se fut efforcee d'en enquerir et rechercher. En laquelle opinion ils estoient dextrement et soigneusement entretenus par les predicateurs, qui la canonizoient tous les jour en leur sermons."

32 Robert Carvell to Walsingham, March 6, 1587, *Cal. Scot. Papers*, IX (1586-1588), 330-331, no. 310. (I have Anglicized the original Scots

spelling.) So general were hostile reactions in Scotland to the execution of Mary that the Presbyterian government there decreed severe punishment for pro-Marian writers and speakers of libels against the King and his Protestant council (cf. *Reg. of the Privy Council of Scotland,* IV, 141, February 1, 1586/7).

[33] Read, *Lord Burghley and Queen Elizabeth,* p. 245.

[34] Quoted in *ibid.,* p. 499.

[35] "Memorial from Secretary Walsingham Touching the Execution of the Queen of Scots," *Hist. MSS Comm., Hatfield House Papers,* pt. iii, no. 471, quoted in Maxwell Scott, *The Tragedy of Fotheringay,* pp. 251-253. Cf. Read, *Lord Burghley and Queen Elizabeth,* p. 369.

[36] Most editors of the report identify "R. W." as Wingfield, who was listed among the official witnesses present at the execution (Scott, *The Tragedy of Fotheringay,* p. 250). *Cal. Scot. Papers,* IX (1586-1588), no. 270, however, attributes the report to Robert Wise. See J. E. Neale, *The Elizabethan House of Commons* (London, 1949), p. 208; and *Elizabeth I and Her Parliaments, 1584-1601* (London, 1957), pp. 353, 363, for reference to the Robert Wingfields, senior and junior, as political allies of their kinsman Lord Burghley. The account exists in a number of manuscript copies and has been widely reprinted. I refer throughout to the copy in British Museum MSS, Cotton Caligula C, IX, fols. 589, 599, reprinted in Steuart, *Trial of Mary Queen of Scots,* pp. 173-184. The full report of Kent and Shrewsbury to the Privy Council is printed in *Cal. Scot. Papers,* IX (1586-1588), 269-273, no. 266; a shorter account signed by the earls and the official witnesses is printed in Scott, *Tragedy of Fotheringay,* pp. 248-250, from Ashmole MS 830, fol. 18, in the Bodleian Library.

[37] Steuart, *op. cit.,* p. 184.

[38] In British Museum MSS, Cotton Caligula B, V, fols. 175[b] through 177[a] [179[b] through 181[a]], there is a document in English that appears to be the central portion of the official account. It contains a description of the execution identical with that published abroad and attributed to an English original, but lacks the introductory explanation of the reasons for the execution and the concluding section on Mary's marital career and the reaction in London to news of her death.

[39] *Vie des Dames Illustres* (Paris, 1868), p. 139. Cf. Chap. VII, below, on Brantôme.

[40] *Martyre de la Royne d'Escosse* ("Edinburgh" [i.e., Paris], 1587, p."421" (i.e., 431).

[41] John Bridgewater, *Concertatio Ecclesiae Catholicae In Anglia . . .*

(1594), fol. 207ᵛ: "Caeterum ne minus, candide rem gestam narrare, aut quippiam affingere videamur, sanctissima Reginae & martyris mortem, quemadmodum a Caluinista quodam crudelissimi facti spectatore in lucem edita est, referemus . . ." *L'Histoire et Vie de Marie Stuart . . . faicte Françoise, par Gabriel de Gutterry* (Paris, 1589), sig. ã iiijʳ: ". . . ie me suis aydé des memoires mesmes qui ont esté imprimez a Londres par le commadement de la Royne d'Angleterre, & de ce qui en a esté receu en France pour tres-docte & tres-veritable." A complete account of both of these works will be found in Chap. VII, below.

⁴² *Grundliche und Eigentlich Warhaffte Beschreibung Von der Konigen in Engellant warum sie die Konigin von Schottlandt hat enthaupten lassen . . .* (Cologne, 1587); the title page bears the statement, "Auss Englischer Spraach in Teutsch vertirt oder gebracht und in Druck verfertiget"; *Execution oder Todt Marien Stuart* (Konigsberg, 1587; Scott 157). Scott 162 notes another edition of this last, published at Magdeburg in 1588.

⁴³ *The Fugger News Letters, First Series,* ed. Victor von Klarwill, tr. Pauline De Chary (London, 1928), pp. 107-116. The editor notes that "on the report is a note in old handwriting: From a Calvinist Source." More important, the Fugger version ends with the statement: "Described by Emanuel Tomacson, who was present at the happenings." This attribution appears in none of the other versions of the account that I have seen. The account attributed to Tomacson is reprinted in E. M. Brougham, *News out of Scotland* (London, 1926), and R. M. Douglas, *The Scots Book* (New York, 1935). I have not been able to identify or explain Tomacson.

⁴⁴ See Chap. VI, below.

⁴⁵ The London broadside is entitled *Mariae Scotorum Reginae Epitaphium. Londini. Excudebat Ioannes Charlewood pro Roberto Wallie* [1587?] and is signed with the initials "I. H. D.," that is, Iohannes Hercusanus Danus (*Stationers' Register,* ed. Arber, V, no. 3386; *STC* 13194; Scott 156). The epitaph appears in the Konigsberg *Execution oder Todt* (see note 42, above) and in the pro-Catholic *Supplicium & Mors* (see Chap. VI, below). It also appeared, together with a highly colored portrait of the Scottish Queen, in a broadside published in Germany, *Marie der Konigin auss Schotlandt eigentliche Bildtnuss* (s.l., [1587]; Scott 154).

⁴⁶ The report to the Privy Council is printed in *Cal. Scot. Papers,* IX (1586-1588), 269, no. 266; Capell's report is in British Museum MSS, Stow 159, fols. 108 through 111.

[47] Passages quoted in English are my own translations, based on the Latin edition, *Mariae Stuartae . . . Supplicium & Mors* (Cologne, 1587 [see Chap. VI, below]), and the German text printed at Konigsberg in 1587, *Execution oder Todt Marien Stuart*. I have collated these texts with the other extant versions of the account which, for convenience of reference, I am calling *The English Account of the Execution and Death of Mary Stuart*.

[48] See note 24, above.

[49] Similar statements of the case against Mary had been prepared by ardent Elizabethans and presented to the Queen's Council in manuscript form; cf., for example, the document attributed to George Puttenham (*Hist. MSS Comm., Second Report* [1871], p. 39) and reprinted in *Accounts and Papers Relating to Mary Queen of Scots* (Camden Society, 1867), pp. 65-134, entitled "A Justification of Queen Elizabeth in Relacion to the Affair of Mary Queen of Scots."

NOTES TO CHAPTER VI

[1] Giovanni Dolfin, the Venetian ambassador to France, to the Doge and Senate, March 2, 1587, *CSP Venetian, 1581-1591*, p. 249, no. 477.

[2] *Ibid.*

[3] Pierre L'Estoile, *Registre-Journal . . . de Henri III*, ed. MM. Champollion-Figeac and Aime Champollion fils (Paris, 1837), p. 217. (L'Estoile's reports may be colored by the fact that he belonged to the Catholic party that was bitterly opposed to the Guises and the Ligueurs); Stafford to Walsingham, June 22, 1587, *CSP Foreign, 1586-1588* (Vol. XXI, Pt. I), p. 315. Cf. also René Radouant, *Guillaume du Vair* (Paris, n.d.), Chap. VII, for a detailed account of these events.

[4] Conyers Read, *Mr. Secretary Walsingham* (Cambridge, Mass., 1925), III, 193. Cf. also Scott 166 which describes an anonymous pamphlet "par gens d'auctorité" apparently written to persuade the French King that James was ready to join with France and Spain in an attack on England in the name of his mother: *De la Guerre ouuerte entre le Roy d'Escosse & la Royne d'Angleterre . . . A Paris . . . 1588. Auec permission*. Cf. also Claude de la Chastre, *Discours. Contenant les plus Memorable faits . . . en l'annee 1587* (Paris, 1588), which develops the theme that the house of Guise will avenge the death of Mary.

[5] Read, *Walsingham*, III, 212.

[6] L'Estoile, *op. cit.*, p. 217.

[7] *CSP Spanish, 1587-1603*, p. 36, no. 35.

[8] Read, *Walsingham*, III, 193 ff.

[9] Blackwood, *Martyre de la Royne d'Escosse* ("Edinburgh," 1587), sig. ã iiiiʳ. See Chap. VII below.

[10] *CSP Spanish, 1587-1603*, pp. 54-55, nos. 54, 55.

[11] Cf. Blackwood, *Martyre* ("Edinburgh," 1587), p. "421" (i.e., 431).

[12] Blackwood, *Opera Omnia* (Paris, 1644), p. 506.

[13] Cf. *DNB*, "Crichton, William," and Michaud, *Biographie Universelle*, "Critton, George." On the poem in question, *De Lupae Anglicae Subactoribus Epigramma*, cf. note 43, below.

[14] Blackwood, *La Mort de la Royne d'Escosse* (1588), p. 101: "De la est aduenu que les Catholiques, & ceux qui luy portoient bonne volonté, tant des Angloys que des Francois, voulant escrire de ses deportemens, tant durant ce dernier acte, qu'au parauant, ne scachant pas ce qui passoit, l'ont mis en lumiere ainsi qu'ils l'ont estimé & imaginé estres: ce pendant les Angloys ne se sont pas oubliez de semer des bruits, & escrire à leur aduantage." Cf. Chap. VII, below.

[15] The text of the letter is reprinted from the autograph MS in the Bibliothèque Nationale by Alexandre Teulet in *Relations Politiques de la France et de l'Espagne avec l'Écosse*, IV (Paris, 1862), 169. It also appears in A. Labanoff, *Lettres Inédites de Marie Stuart* (Paris, 1839). p. 213. The arrival of the letter in Paris was noted by the Spanish ambassador Mendoza in a report to Philip II dated March 7, 1587 (*CSP Spanish, 1587-1603*, p. 34, no. 33).

[16] Teulet, *Relations Politiques*, IV, 170 n., cites a document preserved in the Bibliothèque Nationale entitled *Advis sur l'execution de la Royne d'Escosse, par M. de Chastre*. The author was apparently Claude de la Châtre, an ardent supporter of the Guise-League faction and personal emissary of Henri III to the court of Queen Elizabeth in 1574 (Hoefer, *Nouvelle Biographie Générale*). The document preserved in the Bibliothèque Nationale (25869 Colb. 35 V°) closely parallels Chateauneuf's account in substance and in language.

[17] "Le bruict est, que ladicte dame, mourant a persisté de dire que elle estoyt innocente; que elle n'avoyt jamais pensé a fere tuer la Royne; que elle pria Dieu pour la Royne d'Angleterre; et que elle chargea Melvin de dire au Roy d'Escosse, son fils, que elle le prioyt de honorer la Royne d'Angleterre comme sa mère, et ne se départir jamais de son amytié." (Labanoff, *Lettres Inédites*, p. 218.)

[18] [Paris?, 1587?] Scott 160 briefly describes the numerous editions and reprintings of the *Discours,* and notes that "it is evident that its publication must have taken place with the sanction, if not the en-

couragement of the Queen Mother and her son." Scott does not note a manuscript translation of the *Discours* in Italian, *Morte della Reina di Scotia* (ca. 1587?), which also transcribes Blackwood's *De Iezabelis . . . ad pios . . . carmen* (see note 38, below), preserved in the Morgan Library, New York (De Ricci, MA-292). The *Discours* is translated in W. E. Wilson, "The Earliest Printed Account of the Execution of Mary Queen of Scots," *Transactions of the Hawick Archaeological Society*, 1928, pp. 18-19.

19 *Registre-Journal*, p. 222. L'Estoile's own account of the execution of Mary is sympathetic to her in tone but follows the official English account in outline and in details. Cf. note 3, above.

20 Beaton's manuscript account, undated, is printed by W. R. Humphries in "The Execution of Mary Queen of Scots," *Aberdeen University Review*, XXX (1943), 20-25; Mendoza's version, dated March 7, 1587, is printed in *CSP Spanish, 1587-1603*, p. 34, no. 35; Dolfin's account, dated March 13, 1587, is printed in *CSP Venetian, 1581-1591*, p. 256, no. 484.

21 *CSP Venetian, 1581-1591*, p. 256, no. 484.

22 Cf. especially the dispatches reprinted in Teulet, *Relations Politiques*, IV, 61 ff. ("Discours de M. de Chasteauneuf, ambassadeur en Angleterre") and 137 ff. ("Advis pour M. de Villeroy," containing a detailed account of Mary's reception of the news of her sentence in December, 1586). Cf. note 28, below, for a striking example of the kind of detail apparently incorporated into the execution account from dispatches such as these. On Blackwood, cf. the "Elogium" prefacing his *Opera Omnia* (1644), p. 506, and Chap. VII, below.

23 I have not been able to identify positively this Sieur de Gondy. He was possibly either Pierre de Gondi (1533-1616), Cardinal Archbishop of Paris, noted equally for his religious zeal and his diplomatic missions for Henri III; or his brother, Albert de Gondi, duc de Retz (1522-1602), Marechal of France and frequently active on diplomatic missions for the king. In view of the appellation "Sieur," however, it is more likely that he was Jerome de Gondi, described simply as a diplomat who died in 1604 (Hoefer, *Nouvelle Biographie Générale*).

24 *Oraison Funebre . . . de . . . Marie Royne d'Escosse Morte pour la Foy* (Paris, 1588: Scott 169). Reprinted in Samuel Jebb, *De Vita et Rebus Gestis Mariae* (London, 1725), II, 671-686. Cf. Radouant, *Guillaume du Vair*, p. 105, for convincing evidence that du Vair and not de Beaune was the author of the published *Oraison;* Ch. Labitte, *De la democratie, chez les predicateurs de la Ligue* (Paris, 1841), pp. 31-

32, notes an account by the contemporary historian de Thou that, in its original form, the *Oraison* so violently expressed the extreme feelings of the Guise-League Catholic party that Henri III, whose private feelings in the matter were somewhat more restrained, forbade de Beaune to publish it. The published text of 1588 was also reprinted in the two editions of Blackwood's *Martyre de la Royne d'Escosse* published in that year (see Chap. VII below).

[25] *Harangve Fvnebre Sur La Mort de la Royne d'Escosse. Traduite d'Escossois en Francoys par N. L. R. P.* (s.l., n.d.). Scott 170 assigns the work to Paris, 1588. The translator, according to Scott, was Nicholas Loiseul; the head title ascribes the original Scots *Harangue* to "Reuerent Pere en Dieu M. I. L."

[26] Cf., for example, *Vera Relatione del Successo della Sereniss. Regina di Scotia, Condannata a morte dalla Regina d'Inghilterra sua sorella. In Milano. Et ristampata in Cremona. Appresso Christoforo Draconi 1587. Con licenza de' Superiori,* sig. [A4ʳ]. Scott 150 confuses this with a totally independent acccount by Dini da Colle (note 35, below). A few minor details in the versions of the French account preserved by the ambassadors are omitted in this Italian version, but only one element appearing in the *Vera Relatione*—the imprisonment and immediate release of Davison for carrying the execution warrant to Fotheringay—cannot be found in other versions of the Gondy account. However, since this same bit of news had been contained in Chateauneuf's original letter, the dependence of the Italian account on official French sources remains clear. Cf. also the following note.

[27] *Lettera di Sartorio Loscho Su la morte della Reina di Scotia . . . Bergamo, per Comino Ventura, 1587* (Scott, 146); *Il Compassionevole et memorabili caso della morte della Reina di Scotia* (Parma, 1587; Vicenza, 1587: Scott 151, 152). The two accounts are identical except for short paragraphs of personal greetings to friends in Italy that open and close Loscho's *Lettera,* omitted in *Il Compassionevole.*

[28] The only earlier appearance of this curious piece of misinformation is in a dispatch sent to France by Chateauneuf in the latter part of 1586 and printed by Teulet, *Relations Politiques,* IV, 61 ff. As Teulet observes (p. 81 n.), the appearance of such misinformation in Chateauneuf is difficult to explain, in view of the general accuracy of his reports. The slip, and Loscho's use of it, suggests, however, the probable source of much of the information added by Catholic propagandists to the basic Chateauneuf-Gondy account of the execution. Many of the details reported as occurring at the time of the execution had actually

been reported earlier as occurring at the time of Mary's trial and sentence in dispatches sent to France before the English placed an embargo on all information about Mary.

[29] John Bridgewater, *Concertatio Ecclesiae Catholicae in Anglia* (1594), fol. 207[v]. Cf. Chap. V, note 41, above; and Chap. VII, note 26, below.

[30] *Kurtzer unnd grundtlicher bericht wie die edel unnd from Königin auss Schotlandt Maria Stuarda, ir Mutter halb, auch von Königlichen Geblütin Franckreich dem Hauss Guisa geborn den 18 Februarii Anno 87 in Engellandt gericht worden und was sie für ein Gottseliges end genommen.* Scott 158; cf. p. 134, above. There is some slight evidence that the German version, where it follows the report of the execution itself, was translated from one of the several Latin versions of the official English account. Occasionally the German translator does not give a word in his own language but leaves it in the original Latin.

[31] *Waerachtich Verhael hoe ende in wat manieren de Coninginne van Schotlandt haer heeft ghewillichlijck begeuen ter doot ach-ter volghende de sententie byde Coningehinne van Engelant ende haren Raet den 16 Februarii [sic] 1587. gegeuen steruen-de int Catholicq Roomsche Ghel-one.* Scott 136; cf. p. 134, above.

[32] The appearance of this legend suggests a link between Mary's propagandists in Antwerp and Loscho's French sources who had access to Chateauneuf's earlier report. Cf. note 28, above.

[33] Scott 159; cf. p. 134, above. The Latin title reads: *Mariae Stuartae Scotorum Reginae, Principis Catholicae, nuper ab Elizabetha Regina, et ordinibus Angliae, post nouendecim annorum captiuitatem in arce Fodringhaye interfectae. Supplicium & Mors pro fide Catholica constantissima. In Anglia Vernacula Lingua primum conscripta: ideoque multis aspersa ex hostiū eius Reginae sententia; quae nec ipsa unquam confessa est, nec hactenus debite probata sunt. Nunc in gratiam Catholicorum fideliter, nullis plane omissis translata & edita: vt sanctissimae Principis martyrij feruor, animique inuicta constantia, ipsorum aduersariorum testimonio comprobata, toti mundo elucescat. Additis succinctis quibusdam animaduersionibus & notis: breuiq; totius Reginae eiusdem vitae Chronologia, ex optimis quibusque auctorebus collecta. Colonniae, Apud Godefridum Kempensem. Anno M.D. LXXXVII.*

[34] *Summarium Rationum, Quibus Cancellarius Angliae Et Prolocutor Puckeringius Elizabethae Angliae Reginae persuaserunt occidendam esse serenissimam Principem Mariam Stuartam Scotiae Reginam &*

Iacobi sexti Scotorum Regis matrem: Una cum Responsionibus Reginae Angliae et Sententia mortis: Quae Omnia Anglice primum edita sunt, et Londini a Typographo Regio impressa, ac deinde varias in linguas translata: His Additum Est Supplicium et Mors Reginae Scotiae, una cum succinctis quibusdam animaduersionibus, & confutationibus eorum, quae ei obiecta sunt. Opera Romoaldi Scoti. Ingoldstadii, Ex officina Wolffgangi Ederi. Anno M.D.LXXXVIII (Scott, 171). I have not been able to identify Romoaldus Scotus, and can only ask, as Thomas Dempster did in 1627, "Romualdus quis fuerit? aut vbi? quane vitae conditione vinxerit? mihi inexploratum" (*Historia Ecclesiastica Scotorum*, p. 573). For an account of *The Copie of a Letter*, see Chap. V, note 5, above.

[35] *Vera, e Compita Relazione del Successo della Morte della Christianissima Regina di Scotia.* The editions are described in Scott 147, 148, 149. Scott omits the edition "Stampata in Fiorenza, Dalle Scalee di Badia," found in the Huntington Library, and he surely errs in calling the *Vera Relatione del Successo* (150) a reprint of Dini da Colle's work (cf. note 26, above). I have not been able to identify Dini da Colle.

[36] Cf. A. F. Steuart, *The Trial of Mary Queen of Scots* (Edinburgh and London, 1923), pp. 22-42.

[37] *Registre-Journal*, p. 218.

[38] The principal publications of the *De Jezabelis* poems, as they may be called for convenience, are as follows: (1) *De Iezabelis Angliae Parricidiis ad pios Mariae Scotiae Reginae Manes Carmen*, apparently a single-sheet broadside printed in Paris in 1587, known through a statement by L'Estoile, *op. cit.*, p. 218, that it "fust affiché aux portes de l'église de Nostre Dame de Paris, le jour de la solemnité du service ...," and a copy transcribed in the Morgan Library MS *Morte della Reina di Scotia* (cf. note 18, above) with the prefatory note, "Questri Versi, stampati, furono attaccati alla porta della Chiesa maggiore di Parigi: ove S. M^te Christianiss. con la sua Nobilità alle Exequie fatte per la sereniss. Regina di Scotia" (p. 8). The poem was frequently reprinted, with additions and alterations, in later collections under the title *Aliud eiusdem argumenti auctum & emendatum post primam editionem*. (2) *De Iezabelis Anglae [sic] Parricidio varii generis Poemata Latina et Gallica* ("A Rovan" [1587?]); copies in Morgan Library and British Museum (Press Mark 11408.e.62[2]). (3) "Mariae Stvartae Scotorum Reginae Parentatis Authore [name erased] 1587": a MS title written on the first of two blank leaves at the beginning of

a pamphlet lacking title page or imprint in the British Museum (Press Mark 11408.e.62[1]) and entered in the British Museum *Catalogue of Printed Books* as *Latin Inscription, together with some Latin and French Poetry, in praise of Mary Queen of Scots* with the suggestion that it was printed at Douay. The pamphlet contains four leaves. Scott 161 cites it as "[A Tract, s.l. et a. Printed in Capitals]." (4) *Ode sur la Mort de la Tres-Chrestienne Tres-Illvstre Tres Constante, Marie Royne d'Escosse, morte pour la Foy, le 18. Februier, 1587. par la cruauté des Anglois heretiques, ennemys de Dieu. Auec l'oraison Funebre prononcee en Mars à nostre Dame de Paris, au iour de ses obseques & seruice. A Paris, Chez Guillaume Bichon, rue S. Iacques, a l'enseigne du Bichot.M.D.LXXXVIII. Avec Permission;* copies in the Signet Library, Edinburgh (Scott 168) and the Morgan Library. The latter, despite the identical title, lacks the *Oraison Funebre* and several poems found in the Signet copy. (5) *De Jezabelis Anglae [sic] Parricidio Varii Generis Poemata Latina et Gallica* (s.l., n.d.): Folger Library copy. This is the largest of the collections I have found. It lacks title page, imprint, and colophon; the title appears on sig. A[1^r] at the head of the first poem. A penciled note in modern hand at the bottom of this page reads "1587," but because of the fullness and context of this collection I am inclined to assign it to 1588. Scott 153 is apparently a copy of a similar edition he found in the British Museum; he observes that "a contemporary MS note in the BM copy says Brussells, 1587." A similar edition is also described in Brunet, *Manuel*, III, 530, which assigns the publication to Paris in 1587 or 1588. In the Folger copy, additions and corrections affecting many of the items in the collection have been made in what appears to be a sixteenth-century hand. (6) Most of the poems published in the foregoing collections were also appearing at the same time in the various editions of Adam Blackwood's *Martyre de la Royne d'Escosse;* cf. Chap. VII, notes 6, 10, below.

[39] *Registre-Journal*, p. 218.

[40] Mendoza to Philip II, October 24, 1587, *CSP Spanish, 1587-1603*, p. 159, no. 159. The particular collection of poems cannot be identified from the reference in the *Calendar*, as the editor concluded that "none of them appear to be worthy of reproduction."

[41] "Aliud eiusdem argumenti," in *De Jezabelis . . . Poemata Latina et Gallica* (Folger copy), sig. Bi^v.

[42] *De Jezabelis* (Folger), sig. Fiii^r; reprinted in G. Ascoli, *La Grand-Bretagne, devant l'Opinion Française* (Paris, 1927), p. 294, who attributes it to Perron. Jacques Davy, Cardinal du Perron, was *lecteur* to

Henri III, a celebrated French translator of the *Aeneid,* a spokesman for Catholicism against the French Protestant Duplessis-Mornay. Ironically, he later engaged in a pamphlet controversy with James I of England, Mary's son, on the rights of kings (Michaud, *Biographie Universelle*). According to Michaud, "Il prononça l'oraison funèbre de Marie Stuart, reine d'Ecosse," but where or when, I have not been able to determine. Cf. also "Bastarde incesteuse et vilaine publique," *De Jezabelis* (Folger), sig. Gii^{r-v}; Ascoli, *op. cit.,* p. 296.

^{43} In the Folger *De Jezabelis* collection see, for example, "De Jezabelis," sig. *A*ii^r; "Paraphrase du Poeme Latin," sig. Ai (reprinted in Ascoli, *op. cit.,* p. 280); and "Epicedion Mariae Stvartae . . . A. A. R.," sig. E[i]^r; cf. also "De Morte Reginae Scotiae Elegia ad Reges," in Blackwood, *Martyre* (Antwerp, 1588), p. "593" (i.e., 603); and the particularly obscene "De Lupae Anglicae Subactoribus Epigramma . . . G. C. S.," in *De Jezabelis* (Folger), sig. Dii^v:

> Clara subactorum si nomina forte requiris,
>> Qui subigunt Anglam perforiuntque lupam:
> Picquerinus primas partes sibi vindicat, eius
>> Qui raptae spolium virginitatis habet.
> Dudlius insequitur, quo non obscoenior alter,
>> Promptior in venerem nequitiane prior.
> Tertius e satyris Wormontius ortus hibernis,
>> Et Pacquintoni cauda asinina senis.
> Post hos Hattonus quo non membrosior alter,
>> Obscaenam hanc quamvis non satiarit anum.
> His modo successit Raulaei cauda salacis,
>> Assueti sacris, magne Priape, tuis.
> Istis luce palam meretrix coit anglica verum,
>> Innumeris moechis nocte silente coit.
> Ergo subactores satis est numerasse diurnos,
>> Nocturnos nemo dinumerare potest.

On the identity of "G. C. S.," see p. 146, above.

^{44}
> Anglois, vous dictes qu'entre vous
>> Un seul Loup vivant on ne trouve:
> Non, mais vous avez une Louve
> Pire qu'un milion de Loups.

De Jezabelis (Folger), sig. Biv^v; reprinted in Ascoli, *op. cit.,* p. 280.

^{45} Cf. for example, "Paraphrase du Poeme Latin" in *De Jezabelis* (Folger), sig. Ai^r; Ascoli, *op. cit.,* p. 288; and "Sonet: Les Vertues de Jesabel Angloise," in Blackwood, *Martyre de la Royne d'Escosse* ("Edinburgh," 1587), sig. [ã vii^r], reprinted in Ascoli, *op. cit.,* p. 307.

[46] "Piangi Inghilterra misera e infelice," in *De Jezabelis* (Folger), sig. Iiiij[v]. I have not found this curious item in any other collection. Cf. also the anagram by Malherbe:

Marie Stuvarte:

Sa vertu m'attire.

Tu as eu martire.

Tu es au martire.

Va tu es martire.

De Jezabelis (Folger), sig. Gii[v]; Ascoli, *op. cit.,* p. 297.

[47] Cf., for example, "Sur le Tombeau de Marie Stuart . . . Elegie en laquelle entreparlent le passant et la Muse," in *De Jezabelis* (Folger), sig. Iiii[r]; Ascoli, *op. cit.,* p. 305.

[48] *Ode Sur La Mort . . . Auec l'oraison Funebre* (Paris, 1588: Morgan Library copy), sig. [Aii[r]]; Ascoli, *op. cit.,* p. 308.

[49]

J'ay, nuit et jour, par ton vouloir, ô Sire,

Tracé ce pas qui me tire au martyre:

Martyre est-il, qui pour ton nom sacré

Me fait monter à toy par ce degré,

Et pour te suyvre, ô Dieu, par ceste voye?

Blackwood, *Martyre* (Antwerp, 1588), p. 631; Ascoli, *op. cit.,* p. 317. Cf. also the "Distique Latin" (*Martyre,* Antwerp, 1588), p. 644, in which Mary is made to ask, "Quid me tot Crucibus crucifixam Martyra Christi / Defles? num Christi crux mihi sola sat est?" I have not found these verses last quoted in any other collection.

[50] *Martyre* (Antwerp, 1588), p. 644; Ascoli, *op. cit.,* p. 326.

[51] *De Jezabelis* (Folger copy), sig. Ai[r]; Ascoli, *op. cit.,* p. 283.

[52] "De Morte Reginae Scotiae Elegia ad Reges," in Blackwood, *Martyre* (Antwerp, 1588), p. "591" (i.e., 601). I have not found this poem in any other collection.

[53] The *Monumentum Regale,* beginning "Maria Scotorum Regina, Regis filia, Regis Gallorum vidua, Reginae Angliae agnata," is found, among other places, in *Ode sur la Mort* (Signet Library copy; cf. note 38, above), and in the editions of Blackwood's *Martyre,* "Edinburgh" 1587, 1588, 1589 (cf. Chap. VII, note 6, below). John Nichols, *History and Antiquities of Fotheringay* (London, 1787), p. 58, writes that shortly after the interment of Mary at Peterborough "there was a table hanged up against the wall, which contained this inscription. This table continued not long, but was taken away, and cast aside, by whose hand or order I know not. . . ." J. Freebairn, *The Life of Mary Stewart* (Edinburgh, 1725), pp. 326-327, adds: "Great Search was made for the Author of this Epitaph, but he could not be discovered; but it was

afterwards found to be compos'd by the famous *Adam Blackwood."*

[54] "It Imaginen Mariae Scotorum ad Viatorum," signed G. C. S., in *De Jezabelis* (Folger), sig. Giii^r. These are probably the same verses as those signed "G. Cr. Scotus" and published at Antwerp in 1587 below a single-sheet engraving, probably by Richard Verstegan, of Mary's execution; cf. A. G. Petti, "Richard Verstegan and Catholic Martyrologies of the Later Elizabethan Period" in *Recusant History,* V (1959-1960), 80, and Chap. VII, below. The same verses may also have been published separately in Italy, for on December 23 / January 2, 1587-8, Stephen Powle wrote to Walsingham from Venice: "There have been sundry pictures of the Scottish Queen to be sold in divers places, with verses made by G. Cr. Scotus (for he putteth down no more letters) and I take it, printed at Rome, wherein, after many commendations of her virtues and especially of her miraculous patience at her death, he inveigheth in most opprobrious terms against her Majesty, and endeith with an exhortation to all princes of the earth to endeavor a revenge against her royal person and and estate" *(CSP Foreign, 1586-1588* [Vol. XXI, Pt. I], p. 455). The editor of the state papers identifies "G. Cr. Scotus" as "probably Guillaume Crichton, the Scottish Jesuit." The poet would more likely appear to have been George Crichton, or Critton (see p. 146, above). Cf. also "Piangi Inghilterra," in *De Jezabelis* (Folger), sig. Iiiii^v; and "De Morte Reginae Scotiae Elegia ad Reges," in Blackwood, *Martyre* (Antwerp, 1588), p. "591" (i.e., 601).

[55] Blackwood, *Martyre* (Antwerp, 1588), p. "591" [i.e., 601]; reprinted in Ascoli, *op. cit.,* p. 316.

[56] Cf. "Ode: Quelle Muse epandra mes vers," in *Ode Sur La Mort ... Auec l'oraison Funebre* (Paris, 1588: Morgan Library copy), sig. B[i]^v; Ascoli, *op. cit.,* p. 312.

[57] "A la Royne d'Angleterre sur ce parricide," in *De Jezabelis* (Folger), sig. Biv^v; Ascoli, *op. cit.,* p. 279.

[58] The appeal to James appears in the Latin epitaph by Blackwood, "Epitaphium Mariae Scotiae" *(De Jezabelis* [Folger], sig. Biii^r); "Epicedion Mariae" *(ibid.,* sig. E[i]^r); "Mariae Stuartae ... Parentatis" *(ibid.,* sig. Hiiii^v); and "De Morte Reginae" *(Martyre* [Antwerp, 1588], p. "591" [i.e., 601]).

[59] "Exhortation au peuple de France sur le trespas de la Royne d'Escosse," in *De Jezabelis* (Folger), sig. Giii^v; the poem was reprinted in *OEuvres poetiques du Sieur de la Bergerie* [i.e., Gilles Durant] (Paris, 1594), fol. 203^v, and in Ascoli, *op. cit.,* p. 297. Cf. also "Les Dernieres Parolles de la Royne d'Escosse," in Blackwood, *Martyre* (Antwerp, 1588), p. 631; Ascoli, *op. cit.,* p. 316.

[60] Blackwood's original *De Jezabelis,* which was available to those who attended the funeral observance for Mary at Notre Dame, made the threat also found in other poems that, if Henri failed to act, "strangers"—probably meaning Spain—would avenge Mary's death, and thus add further dishonor to the name of France. ("Aliud eiusdem," in *De Jezabelis* [Folger], sig. *B*ii; paraphrased as "Stances sur le mesme paricide" [*ibid.,* sig. *B*iiii^v; and Ascoli, *op. cit.,* p. 291]. The warning to act before Spain acts is also given in the "Exhortation" of Gilles Durant [cf. note 59, above]). A similar appeal to French national pride is expressed by Robert Garnier in his "Ode sur la Mort," frequently reprinted in these collections, when he asks, in effect, "Will we let a foreign people avenge our own injuries with a greater courage than ours, and as an infamous reproach to our posterity?" (*Ode Sur La Mort . . .* [Paris, 1588], sig. B.[i]^v; Ascoli, *op. cit.,* p. 311). And in a "Sonnet," "N. R. P.," who has been identified as Nicholas Rapin, Parisian, warned against danger from another quarter to both the politics and the pride of France if Henri does not avenge the death of Mary by force of arms:

> Si vous ne conioignez vos forces et voz cueurs,
> Vous serez le butin des Allemans vaincueurs,
> Et le suiect honteux de maintes tragedies.

(*De Jezabelis* [Folger], sig. Gii^r; Ascoli, *op. cit.,* p. 296, where the identification of authorship is suggested. Garnier in his "Ode" also warns against the Germans.)

[61] R. S. Rait and Annie I. Cameron, *King James's Secret* (London, 1927). See Chap. VIII, below.

[62] Read, *Walsingham,* III, Chap. XIV, especially pp. 198 ff.

[63] Gabriel de Guttery, *L'Histoire et Vie de Marie Stuart* (Paris, 1589), sig. ã viii^v (cf. p. 188, above).

[64] Read, *Walsingham,* II, 216.

NOTES TO CHAPTER VII

[1] Mendoza to Philip II, October 24, 1587, *CSP Spanish, 1587-1603,* p. 152, no. 157.

[2] Mrs. Maxwell Scott, *The Tragedy of Fotheringay* (London, 1905), p. 197.

[3] *Journal de Dominique Bourgoin Medecin de Marie Stuart,* published from the manuscript for the first time, in M. R. Chantelauze, *Marie Stuart son Procès et son execution* (Paris, 1876). Cf. also *Le Testament et Derniers Propos de la Royne d'Escosse, avant son supplice.*

Ensemble les legs qu'elle a laissé aux Officiers de sa maison (Paris, 1589, "avec permission"), a publication of the will and final bequests of Mary as they were apparently brought back from England by her servants.

[4] Mendoza refers to Gorion's account in his letter to Philip of October 24 (note 1, above).

[5] See note 13, below.

[6] The principal editions of Blackwood's work are: (1) *Martyre De La Royne D'Escosse, Dovairiere De France. Contenant le vray discours des traisons à elle faictes à la suscitation d'Elizabet Angloise, par lequel les mensonges, calomnies & faulses accusations dressees contre ceste tresuertueuse, trescatholique & tresillustre princesse sont esclarcies & son innocence auerée. Pretiosa in conspectu Domini mors sanctorum eius. A Edimbovrg. Chez Iean Nafeild. 1587.* Scott 144 indicates that the work was actually published in Paris. (2) *Martyre . . . averée. Auec son oraison funebre prononcée en l'Eglise nostre dame de Paris. Pretiosa . . . eius. A Edimbourg. Chez Iean Nafeild. 1588.* Scott 175 designates this the second edition. A number of the *De Jezabelis* poems appended here seem to have been drawn from the *Ode sur la Mort* (Signet Library copy; cf. Chap. VI, note 38, above). (3) *Martyre . . . aueree. Sont adioustees deux Oraisons funebres, l'vne Latine, & l'autre Francoise: & un liure de Poëmes Latins & François. Le tout sur le mesme subiect. Pretiosa . . . eius. En Anvers. Chez Gaspar Fleysben. M.D.LXXXVIII.* Scott 174 describes this as the first edition with a true imprint. The "liure de Poëmes," some thirty-five in all, are mainly those found in the *De Jezabelis* collections, the Folger *De Jezabelis* in particular (see Chap. VI, note 38, above). (4) *Martyre . . . averée. Auec deux Oraisons funebres: l'une Francoise, prononcee en l'Eglise Nostre-Dame de Paris: & l'autre, Latine. Et plusieurs Poemes Latins & Francois, sur le mesme subiect. Pretiosa . . . eius. A Edimbourg Chez Iean Nafield. 1589.* Scott 176 indicates Paris as the place of publication. Despite the title, the Latin funeral oration does not appear here. The contents are identical with (2), above. (5) *Histoire et Martyre de la Royne d'Escosse, douairiere de France, proche heretiere de la Royne d'Angleterre. Contenant les trahisons à elle faictes par Elizabet Angloise, par où on cognoist les mensonges calomnies & faulses accusations enuers ceste bonne Princesse innocente. Auec un petit liure de sa mort . . . Pretiosa in conspectu Domini mors Sanctorum eius. A Paris, Pour Guillaume Bichon, rue Sainct Iaques, au Bichot. M.D.LXXXIX.* Scott 180 notes

that, despite this title page, the British Museum copy contains only the *Martyre* as a bibliographically separate item, and that although Lowndes (*Manual,* III, 150) states that *La Mort,* though paged separately, is really a part of this book, the variety of separate editions of *La Mort* indicates that it was added as a supplement by the printer Bichon to some of the copies of this edition of the *Martyre.* On *La Mort,* see note 10, below.

⁷ References to this work appear in *CSP Domestic, 1581-1590,* p. 622, no. 91; *1591-1594,* p. 161, no. 142; and *1595-1597,* p. 339, no. 94. I have not been able to identify any published work that fits the description given in these accounts. For the circumstances of James's attitude, see Chap. VIII, below.

⁸ Blackwood, *Martyre* ("Edinburgh" [i.e., Paris], 1587), sig. aiiiiʳ.

⁹ Blackwood, *History of Mary Queen of Scots: a fragment,* ed. Alexander Macdonald (Edinburgh, Maitland Club, no. 31, 1834), p. ii.

¹⁰ The principal editions are: (1) *La Mort de la Royne d'Escosse, Douairiere de France. Où est contenu le vray discours de la procedure des Angloys à l'Execution d'icelle, la Constante & Royalle resolutiõ de sa maiesté defunte: ses vertueux deportements & derniers propos, ses Funerailles & enterremẽt, d'ou on peut cognoistre la traistre cruauté de l'Heretique Angloys à l'encontre d'vne Royne souueraine, Treschrestienne & Catholique, Innocente . . . 1588* [s.l.]. Scott 173 cites exemplars in the Signet (Edinburgh) and Scott (private) libraries. Scott 172 describes a 12ᵐᵒ edition of the identical text (in the Advocates Library, Edinburgh) from which the title page has been removed, and concludes that "in one or other form it was certainly issued separately in 1588, prior to the publication of *Histoire et Martyre*" (cf. 3, below). (2) *La Mort de la Royne d'Escosse . . . Innocente . . . M.D.LXXXIX.* Scott 179 suggests that this edition may be the first issue of the book, noting the statement on sig. o6ʳ, following the text, "Acheve d'imprime ce dernier jour de Decembre Mil cinq cens quatre vingtz & huit," and adding that it appears to be the production of a different printer from that of the other editions of *La Mort.* Apparently, according to Scott, copies of this edition were on occasion subsequently issued with the *Martyre* under the inclusive title, *Histoire et Martyre* (cf. 3, following). The British Museum copy of the present *La Mort* contains four folding woodcuts depicting the execution with descriptive verses appearing below each of the cuts. (3) *Histoire et Martyre de la Royne d'Escosse . . . Auec un petit liure de sa mort, consernant les figures de son arrest, procedure & malice des Anglois, l'execution d'icelle, leur grande*

tyrannie, sa constance & gaye resolution de sa maiesté, ses vertus, deportemens & derniers propos: son enterrement faict cognoistre la trahitre cruauté des heretiques Anglois enuers ceste Royne Chrestienne. Pretiosa . . . eius. A Paris . . . M.D.LXXXIX (cf. note 6, above). In the British Museum this copy of *La Mort* is separately bound, with separate signatures and pagination.

[11] *CSP Foreign* (Vol. XXII, July-December, 1588), p. 153.

[12] *La Mort de la Royne* (1588; Scott 173), p. 101; see Chap. VI, note 14, above.

[13] *Ibid.*, p. 110.

[14] *Ibid.*, p. 160.

[15] *Ibid.*, "Au Lecteur," where he says he has omitted nothing that could be discovered in Scotland, England, or France, including "les memoires des rapports verbalement faict par les seruiteurs de sa defuncte maieste au Roy de France."

[16] *Ibid.*, p. 70.

[17] *Ibid.*, p. 75.

[18] On the relation of *La Mort* to Bourgoin's account see Chantelauze, *Marie Stuart son Procès et son execution,* passim.

[19] *La Mort de la Royne* (1588), p. 80.

[20] *Ibid.*, p. 160.

[21] *La Harangue faicte à la Royne d'Angleterre pour la desmouvoir de n'entreprendre aucune Jurisdiction sur la Royne d'Escosse* (s.l., 1588). Scott 167. The *Harangue* is reprinted in Alexandre Teulet, *Relations Politiques de la France et de l'Espagne avec l'Ecosse* (Paris, 1862), IV, 115 ff. Cf. also Jacques de La Guesle, *Remonstrances faites . . . au nom du roi à Elizabeth, reine d'Angleterre, pour Marie, reine d'Ecosse,* in *Les Remonstrances de Messire Jacques de la Guesle,* ed. Du Jour (Paris, 1611).

[22] *Theatrum Crudelitatum Haereticorum Nostri Temporis* (Antwerp, 1587), Scott 155; a French translation, not listed in Scott, is entitled *Theatre des Cruautez des Heretiques de nostre Temps* (Antwerp, 1588). The British Museum *Catalogue of Printed Books* lists editions of the Latin version in 1587, 1588, 1592, and 1607; and of the French in 1588 and 1607. An edition of the Latin preserved in the Morgan Library is dated 1604. In both the Latin and French editions the imprimis of the censor is dated "Antwerp 14 Kal. Sept. 1587." For a complete account of Verstegan and the *Theatrum* see A. G. Petti, "Richard Verstegan and Catholic Martyrologies of the Later Elizabethan Period," *Recusant History,* V (1959-1960), 64-90. On Verstegan's earlier martyrology, see Chap. IV, above.

[23] British Museum Harleian MS 290, fol. 215, cited in Petti, *op. cit.*, p. 80.

[24] *Theatre des Cruautez* (Antwerp, 1588), p. 84.

[25] *Ibid.*, pp. 89-90: "On resuscitera / Un nouuel Hercules, qui remply de victoire, / De ses felons Tyrans ottera la memoire, / Et vengera la Royne occise mechamment / Par l'hostesse pariure, amenant hardiment / Ses vaisseaux sur la mer, pour purger la contree / De son sang allié cruellement souillee. / Qui ne craindra iamais le sceptre de Boullain, / Linage incestueux yure de sang human: /...." The links with Beaton and Blackwood suggest that Verstegan prepared his work in close coöperation with the exiled supporters of Mary who spearheaded the campaign in her behalf. The suggestion is strengthened by the appearance, on p. 87 of the *Theatre,* of the same motto that appeared on the title page of Blackwood's *Martyre*—"Precieuse est en la presence du Seigneur la mort de ses saincts" (Psalm 115). Cf. note 64, below.

[26] *Concertatio Ecclesiae Catholicae In Anglia Adversus Calvinopapistas Et Pvritanos Sub Elizabetha Regina quorundam hominum doctrina & sanctitate illustrium renouata & recognita. Quae Nunc De Novo Centum Et Eo Amplivs Martyrum . . . Cum gratia & Privilegio.* First published at Trèves in 1583, and subsequently at the same place, in expanded form, in 1588, 1589, and 1594. I have used the 1594 edition. See Chap. IV, above, and cf. *Cheltham Society,* XLVIII, 47-50, for an account of the work.

[27] *Concertatio* (1594), fols. 207[r-v]; cf. Chap. V, note 41, above. Bridgewater may have used the Latin version of the English account incorporated in Romoaldus Scotus's *Summarium Rationum* (1588), as, like Scotus, Bridgewater also sets forth replies to the Parliamentary arguments for the execution published by the English in *The Copie of a Letter* (cf. pp. 119, 159, above).

[28] *Concertatio,* fol. 211[r]: "ne quid reliquum Catholicorum pietati seruiret"; cf. *Summarium Rationum* (1588), p. 93: "ne vlli seruirent superstitioni." Other martyrologies might be noted here as probably containing notice of Mary, although I have not been able to consult them: Pedro de Ribodeneyra, S. J., *Hystoria Ecclesiastica del scisma del Reyno de Inglaterra . . . desde que comenco hasta la muerte de la Reyna de Escocia* (Lisboa, 1588: Scott 165); Girolamo Pollini, *L'Historia Ecclesiastica della Rivoluzion d'Inghilterra . . . ne quali si tratta di quello ch'e avvenuto in quell'isola da che Arrigo Ottava comincio a pensare di ripudiar Caterina . . . infino a quest' ultimi anni di Lisabetta . . .* (Roma, G. Facciotti, 1594); Diego de Yepes, Bishop of Taraçon,

Historia particular de la persecucion de Inglaterra, y de los Martiros ... desde el ano ... 1570 (Madrid, 1599). Although not strictly a martyrology, Robert Parsons' *Elizabethae Angliae Reginae Haeresim Calvinianam Propugnantis, saevissimum in Catholicos sui Regni edictum ... cum Responsione* (Augsburg, 1592; cf. Scott 184) might be added here. Designed as an answer to the severe edict against Catholic activities in England issued by Elizabeth in 1591, the work gives accounts of English Catholic martyrs, Mary foremost among them, to show that Protestants and not Catholics are the cause of all the troubles in England and Scotland.

[29] "Horribil piu che mai porse Megera," *Rime del Sig. Giulio Cortese* (Naples, 1588), reprinted in E. B. Reed, *Athenaeum* (May 30, 1908), p. 670.

[30] "De Nece Reginae Scotiae," *Maphei Cardinalis Barberini Poemata* (Oxford, 1726), p. 130. According to Thomas Dempster *(Historia Ecclesiastica Gentis Scotorum* [1627], p. 463), Barberini wrote the poem when he was an adolescent, probably at the time of Mary's death.

[31] "Decease, Release. Dum Morior, Orior," in *The Complete Poems of Robert Southwell, S. J.,* ed. A. B. Grosart (Fuller Worthies' Library: London, 1872), pp. 171-172. Cf. also "Elegia IX. Umbra Reginae Nobiles Viros Docet, Quid Sit de Rebus Hisce Fluxis Sentiendum" *(ibid.,* pp. 210-211). Grosart believed that the poem "I Dye without Desert" *(ibid.,* pp. 173-174) also presents Mary Stuart as "the supposed speaker," but the context does not make this conclusion clear. None of Southwell's poems on the Queen of Scots was published before 1603. According to Louise I. Guiney, *Recusant Poets* (London and New York, 1938), p. 247, the Lambeth Palace MS version of "Decease, Release" is endorsed, "Des vers de Mr. Southwell de la Royne d'Escosse: l'an 1596, reçeus au moi de feuvrier. Sa vertu m'attire." This concluding anagram on Mary's name also appeared in an anagrammatic poem by Malherbe in the *De Jezabelis* collections (see Chap. VI, note 46, above).

[32] *DNB,* "Adamson, Patrick." Cf. Chap. II, above. Adamson's elegaic poems on Mary, published in his *Reverendissimi ... Patricii Adamsoni ... Poemata Sacra* (London, 1619; Scott 209, *STC* 148), include "Illustrissimae ac Ornatissimae Heroniae Mariae D. O. M. Gratia Scotorum Regina Epitaphium" and "Eiusdem Pientissimi ac Doctissimi Praesulis moribundi, Apostrophe ad suam Animam."

[33] (Paris, 1868), pp. 101-155. Originally published as *Recueil des Dames* (1665). Cf. Scott 287. Translations in the following account are my own.

[34] Brantôme, *op. cit.,* pp. 105-119.

[35] These parallels are indicated by the editor of Brantôme, *Œuvres Complètes* (Paris, 1873), VII, 403-453. That Brantôme was also familiar with the official English account is suggested by the following passage: "Il y en a qui ont dit et escrit, mesmes des Anglois qui ont fait un livre de ceste mort et de ses causes: que la despouille de la reyne morte fut ostee au bourreau en luy payant la valeur en argent de ses habits et ornemens royaux" *(Vies des Dames Illustres* [Paris, 1868], p. 139).

[36] *Maria Stuarta, Regina Scotiae, Dotaria Franciae, Haeres Angliae et Hyberniae, Martyr Ecclesie, Innocens a caede Darleana: Vindice Oberto Barnestapolio. Continet haec epistola historiam pene totam vitae, quam Regina Scotiae egit misere, sed exegit gloriose. rationem tituli praefert frons sequentis pagellae . . . Ingoldstadii . . . M.D.-LXXXVIII.* The dedication to William Allen (sig. A2ʳ) is dated Venice, February, 1588 (Scott 164). Reprinted in Samuel Jebb, *De Vita et Rebus Gestis Mariae* (London, 1725), Vol. I.

[37] *DNB,* "Turner, Robert." Turner, professor at Douay, Rome, Eichstadt, and Ingoldstadt, became rector of the university in Ingoldstadt and died in 1599.

[38] *Maria Stuarta . . . Innocens* (1588), sig. A1ᵛ.

[39] *Ibid.,* pp. 41-44.

[40] *Ibid.,* p. 48.

[41] *Ibid.,* pp. 49-50.

[42] *Ibid.,* sig. A4ᵛ-A5ʳ. Cf. Chap. III, note 33, above.

[43] Note to Sir Francis Walsingham, December 16, 1588, *CSP Domestic, 1581-1590,* p. 565, no. 30. The informant is not indicated.

[44] *. . . Composee en Latin par Obert Barnestapolius, & faicte Françoise, par Gabriel de Gutterry Clunisois . . . A Paris, chez Guillaume Iulien* [1589]. Scott 178.

[45] Michaud, *Biographie Universelle:* "Gabriel de Guttery."

[46] *L'Histoire et Vie* (1589), sig. ãiiijʳ. Cf. Chap. V, note 41, above.

[47] *Ibid.,* p. 193. Similar to the Turner-Guttery biographical account in content and theme is a lengthy manuscript entitled *Maria Stuartae Reginae Scotiae historia tragica,* by Michael Eytzinger, an Austrian diplomat and historian who died in or shortly after 1595. (British Museum Harleian MS 582.) The manuscript of 49 leaves is possibly an English copy, for the Latin epitaph on the title page, beginning "Regibus orta, auxi reges, reginaq; vixi," is translated into English by the same hand at the bottom of the title page, and has been attributed to Andrew Melville (Chap. VIII, below). The manuscript is written

throughout in a clear, neat English hand. On Eytzinger, see *Allgemeine Deutsche Biographie* (Leipzig, 1877), "Eitzing."

[48] There may be a fifth. Hugh G. Dick calls my attention to the article "Chambres de Rhétorique," in *Bibliotheca belgica* (ser. 2, vol. 2 [1891-1923], p. 3), which records a performance in 1600 by the Chamber of Rhetoric at Aire in the Low Countries of *La mort et trahison faicte par la royne d'Angleterre en la personne de la royne d'Ecosse,* but I have not been able to learn anything of the nature or circumstances of this production.

[49] The manuscript of 79 leaves, preserved in the Morgan Library, New York, bears the title: *Maria Stvarta Tragoedia M. R^{di} D. Ioannis Bordesij societatis Iesu in Collegio Braidensi Mediolani latino sermone recitata; praemissis tamen quibuscunque actibus singulis argumentis, lingua Italica explicatis; Anno M.D.LXXXIX. die [sic]*. Bordes may have had hopes of publishing his work. In 1590, the year after its production, he sent the manuscript to his old friend and teacher in Rome, Francisco Benci, author of *Ergastus,* the first published Jesuit drama, asking him to polish and refine the *Maria Stuarta*. See James E. Phillips, "Jean de Bordes's *Maria Stuarta Tragoedia:* The Earliest Known Drama on the Queen of Scots," in *Essays Critical and Historical Dedicated to Lily B. Campbell* (Berkeley and Los Angeles, 1950), pp. 45-62, where the author, the play, and the sources are discussed at length. The following account is based on this article.

[50] Le Père Jouvancy, *Ratio docendi et discendi* (1685), quoted in Ernest Boysse, *Le Théâtre des Jesuites* (Paris, 1880), p. 27.

[51] Morgan MS, fol. 1^v and 2^v.

[52] "Minister sacrorum Elizabethę Haeretica," Morgan MS fol. 1^v.

[53] Cf. *La Mort de la Royne* (1588), p. 47, and Morgan MS, Act. V, sc. ii. Note that just as Blackwood in *La Mort* cites and quotes Mary's physician, Bourgoin, as his main authority for this information, so Bordes in his play assigns the speech containing the same material to the character of the Doctor.

[54] As examples of the parallels, cf. Bellièvre's appeal to Elizabeth in the name of the King, Queen, and the Queen Mother of France (Teulet, *Relations Politiques,* IV, 128), and Bordes' ambassador's identical plea (Morgan MS, fol. 26^v); also Dini da Colle, *Vera, e compita* (cf. Chap. VI, above), sig. [A3^r], and Morgan MS, fol. 63^v.

[55] Morgan MS, fol. 51 ^{r-v}. The garden episode may have been suggested by the historical fact that a rumor, widely circulated in January, 1587, asserted that Mary had attempted to escape. Paulet branded the

rumor as a seditious libel in a letter to Davison dated January 30, 1587 (reprinted in Scott, *The Tragedy of Fotheringay*, p. 156), but it was apparently still circulating after the execution (Walsingham to Stafford, March 9, 1587, *CSP Foreign, 1586-1588*, p. 241).

[56] *Adriani Roulerii Insulani Stuarta Tragoedia. Sive Caedes Mariae Serenissimae Scot. Reginae in Angl. Perpetrata, Exhibita ludis Remigialibus a Iuuentute Gymnasij Marcianensis. Duaci, 1593*, ed. Roman Woerner (Berlin, 1906). Cf. also Woerner's "Die Älteste Maria Stuart-Tragödie," in Herman Paul, *Germanistische Abhandlung* (Strassburg, 1902), pp. 259-302.

[57] *Stuarta Tragoedia*, ed. Woerner, p. v.

[58] *Ibid.*, p. 8, "Synopsis": ". . . captivorum chorus iuuvenum et puellarum mala Scotiae religionibus neglectis comparet veteris Iudaeae malis."

[59] *Ibid.*, p. 65: ". . . Moravius, Agaris Ismael satu, / Amplexus urbes et Caledoniam draco / Caput leonis pressit imposito pede: / Mox cessit odiis anima privati nocens, / Et Iezabeli praeiit ad furvam Styga." Roulers apparently interpreted the assassination of Murray in 1570 as a portent of Elizabeth's fate.

[60] See Chap. IV, note 92, above, on Comes and Genebrardi, and Chap. V, above, for the official English account.

[61] *Stuarta Tragoedia*, ed. Woerner, p. xi.

[62] Cf. Luigi Firpo, *Bibliografia degli Scritto di Tommaso Campanella* (Torino, 1940), pp. 182-183 (no. 70). See also Carl Kipka, *Maria Stuart im Drama der Weltliteratur* (Leipzig, 1907), p. 103.

[63] Quoted from *CSP Spanish, 1587-1603*, pp. 294-295, no. 293 (May 1588).

[64] Cf. Naudé, "Elogium" (Blackwood, *Opera Omnia* [1644], sig. ī), who describes "Herae suae colendissimae mortis historia, tum etiam apologia, qua rectae fidie, ut ipse interpretabatur odio interfectae innocentiam, aduersus editum ab Angliae proceribus libellum, ac demum versibus in Elisabetham aculcatissimis, & boni subditi, & literatissimi viri partes sustineret . . ." Cf. also "L'Imprimeur au Lecteur" (*ibid.*, p. 508), on Blackwood's close contact with James Beaton, Archbishop of Glasgow, who was a key figure in the dissemination of the Chateauneuf-Gondy account (cf. Chap. VI; and note 25, above).

[65] Blackwood's influence is also revealed in Roger Baynes, *The Baynes of Aquisgrane, The I. Part, & I Volume. Intituled Variety. Contayning Three Bookes, in the forme of Dialogues, under the Titles following, Viz. Profit, Pleasure, Honour . . . Printed at Augusta in Germany.*

M.DC.XVII. (*STC* 1650.) See A. C. Southern, *Elizabethan Recusant Prose, 1559-1582* (London, 1950), p. 388; and in William Rainolds, *Calvino-Turcismus, i.e., Calvinisticae Perfidiae cum Mahumetana Collatio, et utriusque sectae Confutatio* (Antwerp, 1597). Rainolds died in 1594; his *Calvino-Turcismus* was completed and published by his friend William Gifford (cf. Southern, *op. cit.,* p. 52). In connection with the works of Baynes and Rainolds, Sir Walter Lindsay's *Relacion del estado del Reyno de Escocia, en lo tocante a nuestra Religion Catolica* might be mentioned as carrying on the fight for Catholicism in the name of the Queen of Scots. It was published in Spain, where the author was residing at the time, in 1594 (Scott, 185). Probably in the same vein are two works recorded by Scott which I have not consulted: Antonio de Herrera, *Historia de lo Svcedido en Esocia, è Inglaterra en quarenta y quatro anos que binio Maria Estuarda, Reyna de Esocia* (Madrid, 1589), Scott 181, reprinted in Jebb, *De Vita et Rebus Gestis Mariae,* II, 329-440; Scott 182 records another edition published in Lisbon in 1590; cf. also A. E. Meterano Belga, *Historia Belgica Nostri Potissimum temporis Belgii sub quatvor Burgundis et totidem Austriacis Principibus coniunctionem & gubernationem breuiter . . . inscripto . . . Cum gratia et priuilegio* (1598), Scott 186, who also notes editions in Flemish, French, and German.

NOTES TO CHAPTER VIII

[1] Conyers Read, *Mr. Secretary Walsingham* (Cambridge, Mass., 1925), III, 339. Cf. also J. E. Neale, *Queen Elizabeth* (New York, 1934), p. 387. Burghley himself prepared in English and French a "new discourse" in 1593 designed "to make the King of Scots appear wholly devoted to this [i.e., English] crown and religion" (*CSP Domestic, 1591-1594,* p. 342).

[2] On the Act of Association, see pp. 75, 112, above. James expressly requested formal recognition of himself as "lawful and nearest successor to the Crown, failing [Elizabeth's] bodily succession." (*Hatfield Papers,* III, 267-268, dated July, 1587, quoted in R. S. Rait and Annie I. Cameron, *King James's Secret* [London, 1927], p. 202.)

[3] *Letters of Queen Elizabeth and King James VI of Scotland,* ed. John Bruce for the Camden Society (London, 1849), p. 46. The letter is probably from March, 1587.

[4] *King James's Secret,* p. 207.

[5] The tract, headed *1589. Est natura hominum nouitatis auida* (Scott

177), has been reprinted by A. F. Pollard in *Tudor Tracts, 1532-1588* (Westminster, 1903), pp. 475-484.

⁶ Pollard, *Tudor Tracts,* p. 482.

⁷ The case of William Leonard is documented in *CSP Domestic, 1595-1597,* pp. 86-87, no. 66; p. 94, no. 83. Cf. T. M. Cranfill, "Barnaby Rich and King James," *ELH,* XVI (1949), 70. For further examples of Elizabeth's conciliatory attitude, cf. *CSP Scotland,* II, 748, and E. M. Albright, *Dramatic Publication in England* (New York, 1927), p. 152.

⁸ See Kerby Neill, "The *Faerie Queene* and the Mary Stuart Controversy," *ELH,* II (1935), 192-214. Cf. also A. C. Judson, *The Life of Edmund Spenser* (Baltimore,1945), p. 180.

⁹ F. I. Carpenter, *A Reference Guide to Edmund Spenser* (New York, 1950), p. 42.

¹⁰ On the distinction between "license" and "privilege" see W. W. Greg, *Some Aspects and Problems of London Publishing* (Oxford, 1956), pp. 89-102.

¹¹ Quin, who was born in Dublin about 1575, was apparently studying at the University of Edinburgh when he was presented to James in 1595; he subsequently was appointed tutor to James's sons, Henry and Charles, and migrated with the King to England, where he died about 1634 *(DNB).* Cf. also notes 12 and 16, below, for additional evidence of Quin's activities in behalf of James's claims to succession.

¹² Something of the nature of such a rejoinder may be revealed in the series of anagrams, epigrams, and sonnets in various languages that Quin had written in 1595 in defense of James's claims, and which were subsequently published in 1600 under the title *Sertum Poeticum In Honorem Iacobi Sexti . . . A Gualtero Quinno Dubliniensi contextum. Edinburgi Excudebat Robertus Waldgraue Typographus Regius 1600. Cum Priuilegio Regio. STC* 20567. One sonnet, beginning "A peerless pearle, and prince Claims Arthurs Seat" (sig. B3ʳ), is particularly interesting in this connection because it uses the Arthurian theme similar to that of Spenser's epic, and a form soon to be made celebrated by Spenser: the sonnet with interlocking rhymes. The sonnet was apparently one of those presented to King James by Quin in December, 1595, in the manuscript volume of verses recorded in *CSP Scotland,* II, 700-701, no. 79.

¹³ Harington, *A Tract on the Succession to the Crown* (MS 1602), Roxburghe Club (London, 1880), p. 46. Cf. p. 208, above.

¹⁴ Neale, *Queen Elizabeth,* p. 387. Harington provides contemporary confirmation of this explanation when he observes, "A strong impres-

sion remained in [Elizabeth's] mynde, that if she should allowe and permitt men to examine, discusse, and publishe whose was the best title after hirs, some would be ready to affirme that title to be good afore her" (*A Tract on the Succession* [1880], p. 39).

[15] Robert Bowes to Burghley, September 8, 1594, *Cal. Scot. Papers*, XI (1593-1595), p. 430. Melville's poem, *Principis Scoti-Britannorum natalia*, was printed at Edinburgh by Robert Waldegrave (*STC* 17807).

[16] George Nicolson to Robert Cecil, February 25, 1597/8, transcribed from Public Records Office document in Carpenter, *A Reference Guide to Edmund Spenser*, p. 42. Cf. *CSP Scotland*, II, 747.

[17] *A Tract on the Succession*, pp. 39, 118.

[18] Leslie's work is reported by Bernardino de Mendoza to Philip of Spain as "a little book in Spanish, written by the bishop of Ross, giving the English genealogies. He has had it published also in Latin, French, and English, and it shows that your Majesty is the legitimate heir to the Crown . . .," April 9, 1587, *CSP Spanish, 1587-1603*, p. 65, no. 65. On Cardinal Allen's book, and on the Catholic dilemma in England generally, see M. A. S. Hume, *The Great Lord Burghley* (New York, 1906), pp. 457-458; and Helen D. Stafford, *James VI of Scotland and the Throne of England* (New York, 1940), pp. 146-156. A further example of the dissension among English Catholics is found in the work, possibly translated by William Watson, written by Etienne Pasquier, *The Iesuites Catechisme. Or Examination of Their Doctrine* (London?, 1602; *STC* 19449), fol. 171, where a Catholic writer argues "that the Iesuits were the cause of the death of Mary Queen of Scots, together with a briefe discourse, what mischiefe they have wrought in England." Pasquier had earlier published a similar attack entitled *The Jesuits Displayed* (London, 1594; *STC* 19448). Cf. also "Summary of Letters from Count de Oliverares," June 27, 1588, *CSP Spanish, 1587-1603*, p. 324, no. 327; and *ibid.*, p. 122, no. 125, where the Jesuits Allen and Parsons are arrayed against the Jesuit William Crichton.

[19] "Imprinted at N. [Antwerp?], 1594" (*STC*, 19398). Father J. H. Pollen (*The Month*, CI, 1903, pp. 523-526) argues that Richard Verstegan wrote the *Conference*, and that Parsons had a share in the work and was largely responsible for its publication.

[20] *Elizabethae . . . edictum . . . cum Responsione* (1592). See Chap. VII, note 28, above.

[21] *Elizabethae . . . Responsione*, p. 31.

[22] *A Conference*, p. 117.

[23] *Elizabethae . . . Responsione*, p. 94.

[24] *A Conference,* p. 117.

[25] [Edinburgh, R. Waldegrave], 1598 (*STC* 25245). The *Exhortation* proper was composed in 1587 and caused Wentworth to be sent to prison for raising the succession question (Neale, *Queen Elizabeth,* p. 315); the *Discourse* is indicated as having been written two years before Wentworth's death in 1597. Wentworth was a brother-in-law of Sir Francis Walsingham, so that his views on the succession may represent those of one of Elizabeth's chief councilors, if not of the Queen herself.

[26] *A Pithie Exhortation* (1598), p. 31.

[27] Neale, *Queen Elizabeth,* p. 315. See note 25, above.

[28] George Nicolson to Robert Cecil, December 15, 1599, *CSP Scotland,* II, 799.

[29] (MS 1602) Roxburghe Club, London, 1880.

[30] *Ibid.,* p. 106.

[31] *Ibid.,* p. 118; cf. Chap. VII, note 65, above.

[32] *Ibid.,* p. 119. I quote the text given in *The Letters and Epigrams of Sir John Harington,* ed. N. E. McClure (Philadelphia, 1930), pp. 280-281.

[33] *Ibid.,* p. 118.

[34] In one case, at least, not even the manuscript seems to have survived. In February 1597/8 George Nicolson, an English agent in Edinburgh, reported to Sir Robert Cecil that "Dixon, that taught the Art of Memory in England, is answering Doleman." (*CSP Scotland,* II, 747. A transcript of the letter is printed in Carpenter, *A Reference Guide to Edmund Spenser,* p. 42.) This was apparently Alexander Dickson, who had published a Latin treatise on memory in London in 1593, but nothing that he may have written on the subject of the succession seems to have survived.

[35] *The Right of Succession* (London, 1703), p. 345.

[36] *Ibid.*

[37] *Ibid.,* p. 84.

[38] *STC* 23334. Cf. Chap. III, above. On the complex relationships among Stow's numerous historical publications see Conyers Read, *Bibliography of British History: Tudor Period* (Oxford, 1933), no. 292. I have by no means consulted all of Stow's known publications, but have taken the versions described here as representative of his shifting policies.

[39] The fate of a single sentence in Stow's account of Mary serves to illustrate his sensitivity to the changing situation. In his 1570 edition of *A Summarie of the Chronicles* (fol. 410) Stow concluded his account

of Darnley's death with the cautiously vague observation that the Scottish consort "was shamefully murthered, the reuenge whereof remayneth in the mighty hande of god." In his 1579 edition of *The Summarie* (p. 386) he deleted the concluding reference to vengeance, which could have been interpreted as a veiled hint at what Mary deserved. But in *The Annales* of 1592 (p. 1126), when ambiguity about Mary's affairs and conduct was again in order, he restored the original statement.

⁴⁰ *Annales* ... (1592), p. 1260.

⁴¹ *Ibid.*

⁴² *Albions England: A Continued Historie of the same Kingdome* ... *now reuised and newly inlarged by the same author* (London, 1597: *STC* 25082ᵃ), p. 244. The 1597 text used here is simply a reissue of the 1596 edition (*STC* 25082). The earlier editions, in which no reference to Mary was made, appeared in 1586 (*STC* 25079), 1589 (*STC* 25080), and 1592 (*STC* 25081). The Mary Stuart material was reprinted without change in the editions of 1602 and 1612.

⁴³ *Ibid.*

⁴⁴ *Ibid.*

⁴⁵ *Ibid.* In addition to Buchanan, Warner draws heavily but without acknowledgment on *The Copie of a Letter to ... Leycester* for his account of why Mary deserved to be executed. See Chap. V, above, especially pp. 121-122, where Holinshed's reprint of the *Letter* is described.

⁴⁶ Cf. L. B. Campbell, *Shakespeare's Tragic Heroes* (Cambridge University Press, 1930), especially Section I; Willard Farnham, *The Medieval Heritage of Elizabethan Tragedy* (Berkeley, Calif., 1936).

⁴⁷ The fate of Babington and his fellow conspirators was presented as such a "tragedy" in "The Complaynte of Anthonye Babington" in Richard Williams, *A Poor Man's Pittance,* a manuscript collection of poems dedicated to King James (ed. F. J. Furnivall, *Ballads from Manuscripts* [London, Ballad Society, 1873], II, 5). In view of the dedication, it is not surprising to find no reference to Mary Stuart in Babington's account of his treason.

⁴⁸ British Museum Additional MS 29,401, fols. 28ᵛ-29ʳ. Cf. also the five-part song, "In Angells weede," about 1613, British Museum Additional MS 29,401, fols. 30ᵛ-31ʳ.

⁴⁹ *Prose and Verse by John Dickenson,* ed. A. B. Grosart (London, 1878), p. xiii, and *STC* 6817 through 6820, identify the Latinist with the euphuistic romancer, although *DNB* disagrees. See Leicester Bradner, *Musae Anglicanae* (New York, 1940), pp. 42-43. The editions after

the first in 1601 appeared in 1602, 1603, and 1605, each with additions and corrections that did not alter the Mary Stuart material.

⁵⁰ *Speculum Tragicum. Regum, Principum, & Magnatum superioris sœculi celebriorum ruinas exitusque calamitosos breviter complectens: In quo & iudicia divina & imbecillitas humana insignibus exemplis declarantur ... Auctore I. D.* (Delft, 1601). Cf. Scott 197.

⁵¹ *Speculum Tragicum* (Leyden, 1605), p. 6: "Magnates quidem aliquot non admodum celebres inservisse me fateor, at obiter, & propter quandam vel fortunae, vel culpae, vel aliam denique similitudinem, cui temporis etiam ratiōe interdum post posui. . . ."

⁵² *Ibid.*, p. 93.

⁵³ *Ibid.*, pp. 95-96: "quod immoderata apud Reginam gratia non minus immoderate abuteretur."

⁵⁴ *Ibid.*, p. 93: "qui Scoticae Reginae causa in Anglia periunt."

⁵⁵ *Ibid.*, p. 98.

⁵⁶ *Ibid.*: "misere rerum humanarum inconstantiae iudicijque divini documentum singulare."

⁵⁷ *Inscriptiones Historicae Regum Scotorum, continuata annorum serie a Fergusio primo Regni Conditore ad nostra tempora ... Amsteldami ... 1602.* Scott 191; translated as *A Trewe Description of the nobill Race of the Stewards ...* (Amsterdam, 1603); Scott 196; *STC* 12886.

⁵⁸ *Inscriptiones* (1602), p. 59; the complete "Inscription" on Mary is as follows: "Tot soboles regum, & genitrix, & regia Conjux, / Cui triplices titulos Regia sceptra dabant. / Fors plures merui. Frustra haec tamen omnia. Nemo / Magna putet, Sortis quae penes arbitrium."

⁵⁹ *Ibid.*, sig. K2ʳ: "Fortunae imperio major quae stare videbar, / Flebile mox fio ludibrium dominae" (complete).

⁶⁰ *Ibid.*, p. 59: "Regibus orta, auxi Reges, Reginaeq; vixi: / Ter nupta & tribus orba viris, tria Regna reliqui. / Gallus opes, Scotus cunas, habet Anglia sepulchrum." Reprinted as *Epigrammata: Mariae Reginae Scotorum Epitaphium,* in *Delitiae Poetarum Scotorum,* ed. A. Johnston (Amsterdam, 1637), II, 112. The English translation is from *The New Monthly Magazine and Literary Journal* (London, 1832), Pt. I, pp. 593-594. Both Latin and English also appear on the title leaf of Eytzinger's manuscript *Historia Tragica* (cf. Chap. VII, note 47, above).

⁶¹ *Ibid.*, pp. 58-59: "Regum adii fortunam omnem, rerumq́; labores; / ... Tibi debita Nate / Sceptra dedi ... regnum / Spe tenui in-

concussum animo, sperare licebat / Dum licuit spirare. Et nunc cervice securim / Accipio secura." Reprinted in *Delitiae Poetarum Scotorum,* II, 112.

[62] Ed. John Fry (London, 1810), who argues for Wenman's authorship. The same poem is contained in British Museum Egerton MS 2401 fol. 1^v, under the title "The Sad Complaint of Mary Queen of Scots." Hanna Lohmann, in her edition of the poem which she entitles *The Life and Tragedy of the Royal Lady Mary Late Queen of Scots* (Berlin, 1912), attributes the work to John Woodward and assigns it (not very convincingly) to the years 1587-1589.

[63] *Legend of Mary Queen of Scots,* ed. Fry, pp. 6-7.

[64] *Ibid.,* p. 11.

[65] *The Essayes of Michael, Lord of Montaigne, translated into English by John Florio* (London, 1928), I, 71. The definitive edition of the original *Essais* was first published in 1595; Florio's translation, in 1603.

[66] On the circumstances under which the play was composed and published, see *Les Tragédies de Montchrestien,* ed. L. Petit de Julleville (Paris, 1891). To this should be added the important material presented in Frances Yates, "Some New Light on 'L'Écossaise' of Antoine de Montchrétien," *Modern Language Review,* XXII (1927), 285-297. The play was first published in *Les Tragédies d'Ant. de Montchrestien* (Rouen, [1601]). Cf. Scott 190, which dates this first edition 1600. In subsequent editions of *Les Tragédies* (Rouen, 1604; Myort, 1606), the play is entitled *Tragedie de la Reine d'Escosse.* In the following discussion, I have used the separate edition of the play published at Rouen in 1603, entitled *Escossoise ou le Desastre Tragedie. Seconde edition.*

[67] *Tragédies,* ed. Petit de Julleville, Intro., pp. xxviii-xxix. Michaud *(Biographie Universelle)* and Funck-Brentano *(Revue bleue,* September 14, 1889, p. 343) argue that Montchrestien's Protestantism was a late, even last-minute, development (cf. *Tragédies,* ed. Petit de Julleville p. xxix, n. 1).

[68] *Escossoise, ou le Desastre Tragedie* (Rouen, 1603), sig. Aij^v. The theory of tragedy in terms of which Montchrestien worked is summed up by H. C. Lancaster when he says: "It is essentially a play that shows us an eminent person lamenting over a terrible misfortune that has befallen or will befall him through fate or human cruelty . . . The psychology of the characters and the causes that bring about the tragic event are neglected. . . . For physical and psychological actions are sub-

stituted rhetorical developments on religious, philosophical, and political themes, expressed in lengthy tirades. . . . It is exemplified by Montchrestien, who gives it its most poetic expression if not its most dramatic" (*A History of French Dramatic Literature in the 17th Century* [Baltimore, 1929], I, i, 19).

[69] Quoted in Yates, *op. cit.*, p. 292, where the dramatist's indebtedness to Matthieu is established. Matthieu's work was published in 1597.

[70] *Escossoise* (1603), pp. 52-53.

[71] *Ibid.*, pp. 24-26.

[72] Sir Ralph Winwood, *Memorials of Affairs of State in the Reigns of Queen Elizabeth and King James I* (London, 1725), I, 398, quoted in Yates, *op. cit.*, p. 286.

[73] Thomas Parry to Cecil, February 13, 1604, Public Record Office State Papers, Foreign, France, 51, quoted in Yates, *op. cit.*, p. 287.

[74] The account is that given in *Le Mercure François*, printed in *Documents concernant la Normandie*, ed. A. Héron (1883), p. 188. Cf. *Tragédies*, ed. Petit de Julleville, p. xxiii, and Yates, *op. cit.*, pp. 288-289, who questions the reliability of the account.

NOTES TO EPILOGUE

[1] F. R. Johnson, *A Critical Bibliography of the Works of Edmund Spenser* (Baltimore, 1933), pp. 21, 33. Cf. Chap. VIII, above.

[2] *STC* 25084, and Chap. VIII, above.

[3] Cf., for example, Julius Caesar Capaccio, *Illustrium Mulierum . . . Elogia* (Naples, 1608; Scott 201), pp. 131, 133, in which Elizabeth is reviled in familiar terms—"Ob Fidei Contemptum Execranda"—and Mary is praised as a holy martyr victimized by heretic rebels.

[4] *Sanctarum Precationum Prooemia . . . Augustoriti Pictonum* (1608; Scott 202). *DNB*, "Blackwood, Adam," records an edition in 1598 which I have not seen. On p. 39 appears the Latin poem, "Pro Scotiae Regina quo tempore . . . profugit in Angliam," written by Blackwood on the occasion of the Queen's flight into England (cf. Chap. IV, note 79, above). The second collection is Blackwood's *Varii Generis Poemata* (Poitiers, 1609; Scott 203), where several of his contributions to the *De Jezabelis* collections are reprinted (cf. Chap. VI, above). The new poem is entitled "Iacobi Primi, Magnae Britanniae seu Scotangliae & Hiberniae regis, inauguratio," in Blackwood, *Opera Omnia* (1644), pp. 489-504. Prefixed to the poem is a Latin prose address to the King, dated

1606, which indicates that the poem was written two years earlier (pp. 482-489).

[5] *An excellent new ballad shewing the petigree of ... King James* (London, [1603]), reprinted in *The Shirburn Ballads, 1585-1616,* ed. Andrew Clark (Oxford, 1907), p. 319. Given his background, Sir Thomas Craig's *Ad Iacobum sextum e sua Scotia decedentum paraeneticon* ([Edinburgh], 1603; *STC* 5968) and his *Serenissimi principis Iacobi Britanniarum regis στεφανοφορια* ([Edinburgh], 1603; *STC* 5971) should perhaps also be mentioned in this connection, although I have not seen these works.

[6] The letter is reprinted in Mrs. Maxwell Scott, *The Tragedy of Fotheringay* (London, 1905), p. 231.

[7] Cf. *DNB,* "Howard, Henry, Earl of Northampton."

[8] Transcriptions of the epitaph as it now appears on Mary's tomb in Westminster Abbey are published in *Cal. Scot. Papers,* IX (1586-1588), 314; William Combe, *The History of the Abbey Church of St. Peters, Westminster* (London, 1812), II, 160-162; and J. Crull, *Antiquities of St. Peters, or the Abbey Church at Westminster* (London, 1742), I, 103-107.

[9] British Museum MSS, Cotton Titus C, VI, fols. 207 through 211 (three versions); Sloane MS 3199, fols. 336 through 339 (two versions).

[10] Sloane MS 3199, fol. 336^v; cf. also British Museum MSS, Cotton Caligula C, IX, fol. 630.

[11] *Annales rerum Anglicarum et Hibernicarum regnante Elizabetha* (London, 1615; Scott 208, *STC* 4496). An English translation, *Annales. The true and royal history of Elizabeth* ... appeared in London in 1625 (Scott 217; *STC* 4497).

[12] E. Fueter, *Histoire de l'Historiographie Moderne* (translated from the German by Emile Jeanmaire, Paris, 1914), p. 203.

[13] Camden apparently did not go so far, as is sometimes asserted, as to send an anti-Marian account based on Buchanan to the French historian de Thou and then print an adaptation of Blackwood's version of affairs as his own. But Camden was clearly encouraged to take a cautious attitude with regard to Mary and her history. See J. W. Thompson, *History of Historical Writing* (New York, 1942), I, 607-609, especially note 63, p. 608. Cf. also E. M. Thompson in *DNB,* "Camden, William." The correspondence between Camden and de Thou is summarized in Pierre Bayle, *Dictionnaire Historique et Critique,* Nouvelle Édition (Paris, 1820), IV, 370-371.

[14] De Thou letter, April 13, 1608, in Bayle, *op. cit.,* IV, 371.

[15] Bayle, *op. cit.,* IV, 374.

[16] *Ibid.,* IV, 370. The list is printed in *Camdeni . . . Epistolae,* ed. Thomas Smith (London 1691).

[17] William Camden, *Britannia,* tr. Richard Gough (London, 1806), I, xvi-xvii: "The Life of Mr. Camden."

[18] Thomas Smith, *G. Camdeni vita* (London, 1691), p. 54, quoted in Bayle, *op. cit.,* IV, 369.

[19] Camden, *Annales* (1625), pp. 137-138.

[20] *Ibid.,* pp. 144 ff. [Bk. III].

[21] *Ibid.,* p. 180 [Bk. III].

[22] *Ibid.,* pp. 200 ff. [Bk. III].

[23] *Ibid.,* pp. 112-113 [1630 ed., Bk. III].

[24] *Ibid.,* p. 115 [1630 ed., Bk. III].

Index

INDEX

Works dealing with Mary Queen of Scots that were published or written within the years covered by this survey are entered under the author's name by short title, or by short title only when the work is anonymous. Page and note numbers referring to the principal descriptive and bibliographical accounts of these works are indicated by an asterisk. Collections, later editions and translations, and later commentaries are indicated by name of author or editor only.